Living & Working in BRITAIN

• A Survival Handbook •

David Hampshire

Survival Books • Bath • England

First published in 1991
Ninth edition published 2017

Cover photograph: Castle Combe, Wiltshire
Illustrations, cartoons and maps © Jim Watson

Survival Books Limited
Office 169, 3 Edgar Buildings, George St, Bath, BA1 2FJ, United Kingdom
+44 (0)1305-246283, info@survivalbooks.net
www.survivalbooks.net and www.londons-secrets.com

British Library Cataloguing in Publication Data
A CIP record for this book is available
from the British Library.
ISBN: 978-1-909282-87-2

Printed in China by D'Print Pte Ltd.

Acknowledgements

My sincere thanks to all those who contributed to the successful publication of this ninth edition of Living and Working in Britain and the previous editions of this book. They include Robbi Forrester Atilgan for updating and research, Peter Read (further research), David Woodworth (proof-reading) and John Marshall (desktop publishing and photo selection), plus Graeme Chesters, Kitty Strawbridge, Joanna Styles, Julia Thorpe, Peter Turner and Catherine Wakelin. Also many thanks to Jim Watson for the illustrations and maps.

Finally, a special thank you to the many photographers – the unsung heroes – whose beautiful images add colour and bring Britain to life.

Southwold Pier, Suffolk

What Readers and Reviewers Have Said About Survival Books:

"If I were to move to France, I would like David Hampshire to be with me, holding my hand every step of the way. This being impractical, I would have to settle for second best and take his books with me instead!"

Living France

"We would like to congratulate you on this work: it is really super! We hand it out to our expatriates and they read it with great interest and pleasure."

ICI (Switzerland) AG

"I found this a wonderful book crammed with facts and figures, with a straightforward approach to the problems and pitfalls you are likely to encounter. The whole laced with humour and a thorough understanding of what's involved. Gets my vote!"

Reader (Amazon)

"Get hold of David Hampshire's book for its sheer knowledge, straightforwardness and insights to the Spanish character and do yourself a favour!"

Living Spain

"Rarely has a 'survival guide' contained such useful advice – This book dispels doubts for first time travellers, yet is also useful for seasoned globetrotters – In a word, if you're planning to move to the US or go there for a long term stay, then buy this book both for general reading and as a ready reference."

American Citizens Abroad

"It's everything you always wanted to ask but didn't for fear of the contemptuous put down – The best English language guide – Its pages are stuffed with practical information on everyday subjects and are designed to complement the traditional guidebook."

Swiss News

"A must for all future expats. I invested in several books but this is the only one you need. Every issue and concern is covered, every daft question you have but are frightened to ask is answered honestly without pulling any punches. Highly recommended."

Reader (Amazon)

"Let's say it at once. David Hampshire's Living and Working in France is the best handbook ever produced for visitors and foreign residents in this country; indeed, my discussion with locals showed that it has much to teach even those born and bred in l'Hexagone. It is Hampshire's meticulous detail which lifts his work way beyond the range of other books with similar titles. This book is absolutely indispensable."

The Riviera Reporter

"Covers every conceivable question that might be asked concerning everyday life – I know of no other book that could take the place of this one."

France in Print

"It was definitely money well spent."

Reader (Amazon)

"The ultimate reference book – Every conceivable subject imaginable is exhaustively explained in simple terms – An excellent introduction to fully enjoy all that this fine country has to offer and save time and money in the process."

American Club of Zurich

Important Note

Britain is a diverse country with many faces, a variety of ethnic groups, religions and customs, and continuously changing rules, regulations – particularly with respect to immigration, social security, the National Health Service, education and taxes – interest rates and prices. Note that a change of government in Britain can also have far-reaching effects on many important aspects of life. However, the biggest change in a generation (or two) is the historic vote by the British people in 2016 to leave the European Union (see page 18).

I cannot recommend too strongly that you check with an official and reliable source (not always the same) before making any major decisions or taking an irreversible course of action. Don't, however, believe everything you're told or read, even – dare I say it – herein!

To help you obtain further information and verify data with official sources, useful websites and references to other sources of information have been included in all chapters and in **Appendix A**. Important points have been emphasised throughout the book, some of which it would be expensive or foolish to disregard.

Contents

16. SPORTS 241

17. SHOPPING 261

Author's Notes

- 'Britain' – as used in this book – comprises Great Britain (the island which includes England, Wales and Scotland) and Northern Ireland, the full name of which is the 'United Kingdom of Great Britain and Northern Ireland', usually shortened to 'UK'; Britain and the UK are therefore (again, as used in this book) to all intents and purposes, synonymous. The British Isles is the geographical term for the group of islands, which includes Great Britain, Ireland and many smaller islands surrounding Britain. I have attempted to be specific regarding information that applies to Britain or the UK as a whole and those that apply only to England, Wales, Scotland or Northern Ireland.
- Frequent references are made in this book to the European Union (EU), which comprises Austria, Belgium, Bulgaria, Croatia, Cyprus, the Czech Republic, Denmark, Estonia, Finland, France, Germany, Greece, Hungary, Ireland, Italy, Latvia, Lithuania, Luxembourg, Malta, the Netherlands, Poland, Portugal, Romania, Slovakia, Slovenia, Spain, Sweden and the UK. The European Economic Area (EEA) comprises the EU countries plus the European Free Trade Association (EFTA) countries of Iceland, Liechtenstein and Norway, plus Switzerland (which is an EFTA member but not a member of the EEA). In this book, references to the EU generally also apply to EEA countries and Switzerland.
- All times are shown using the 12-hour clock; times before noon are indicated by the suffix 'am' and times after noon by 'pm'.
- Unless otherwise stated, all prices quoted are in pounds sterling (GB£) and include VAT at 20 per cent. They should be taken as estimates only, particularly property prices – which change frequently – although they were correct at the time of publication.
- His/he/him also means her/she/her (please forgive me ladies). This is done to make life easier for both the reader and the author, and isn't intended to be sexist.
- British English and spelling is used throughout the book.
- A list of **Useful Websites** is contained in **Appendix A.**
- A physical map of the UK is shown inside the front cover and a map of the counties inside the back cover.

Introduction

Whether you're already living or working in Britain or just thinking about it – this is **THE book** for you. Forget about those glossy guide books, excellent though they are for tourists; this book was written especially with you in mind and is worth its weight in black pudding. Furthermore, this fully revised and updated 9th edition is printed in colour. *Living and Working in Britain* has been written to meet the needs of anyone wishing to know the essentials of British life – however long your intended stay, you'll find the information contained in this book invaluable.

General information isn't difficult to find in Britain; however, reliable and current information specifically intended for foreigners living and working in Britain isn't so easy to find, least of all in one volume. Our aim in publishing this book is to help fill this void and provide the comprehensive, practical information necessary for a relatively trouble-free life. You may have visited Britain as a tourist, but living and working there is a different matter altogether. Adjusting to a different environment and culture and making a home in any foreign country can be a traumatic and stressful experience, and Britain is no exception.

Living and Working in Britain is a comprehensive handbook on a wide range of everyday subjects and represents the most up to date source of general information available to foreigners in Britain. It isn't, however, simply a monologue of dry facts and figures, but a practical and entertaining look at life.

Adjusting to life in a new country is a continuous process, and although this book will help reduce your novice phase and minimise the frustrations, it doesn't contain all the answers (most of us don't even know the right questions to ask!). What it *will* do, is help you make informed decisions and calculated judgements, instead of uneducated guesses and costly mistakes. Most importantly, it will save you time, trouble and money, and repay your investment many times over.

Although you may find some of the information a bit daunting, don't be discouraged. Most problems occur only once and fade into insignificance after a short time (as you face the next half a dozen ...). Most foreigners in Britain would agree that, all things considered, they love living there. A period spent in Britain is a wonderful way to enrich your life, broaden your horizons, and, with any luck (and some hard work) you may even make your fortune. I trust this book will help you avoid the pitfalls of life in Britain and smooth your way to a happy and rewarding future in your new home.

Good Luck!

David Hampshire

January 2017

1.

FINDING A JOB

Finding a job in the UK isn't always straightforward, even for qualified and experienced citizens of European Union (EU) countries seeking work in the UK's major cities. Nevertheless, many foreigners – and particularly Europeans – find that the number and variety of opportunities in the UK far outweigh those in their home countries. If you don't automatically qualify to live or work in the UK, for example by birthright or as an EU national, you'll usually find it more difficult to obtain a work permit (see page 51) than to find a job. And do be aware that the position of EU nationals in the UK is likely to change with the UK's decision to leave the EU, expected to take effect no later than March 2019 (see Brexit below for more information).

The UK is a small country with a relatively large population (and high population density), high youth unemployment, an expensive social security (welfare) and state health system, and an acute lack of housing, all of which make immigration something of a sensitive issue. The government has talked about taking steps to substantially reduce the number of foreigners permitted to settle in the UK in recent years, without actually doing anything. However, the large huge influx of workers from EU (mostly Eastern European) countries in the last decade or so has resulted in high net migration, which was a key factor in the Brexit vote.

The size of the foreign-born population in the UK increased from around 3.8 million in 1993 to over 8.3 million in 2014, during which period the number of foreign citizens increased from around 2 million to o §1ver 5 million. The total workforce in the UK is around 32 million, including almost 8.5 million part-time workers.

BRITAIN & THE EUROPEAN UNION

While Britain remains a member of the EU, nationals of all EU countries (except Croatia, until 2018) have the right to freely enter, live and work in the UK – or any other member state – without a work permit provided they have a valid passport or national identity card and comply with that member state's laws and regulations on employment. EU nationals are entitled to the same treatment as British citizens in matters of pay, working conditions, access to housing, vocational training, social security and trade union rights. Their immediate dependants are also entitled to join them and enjoy the same rights.

The UK has long been a somewhat reluctant member of the EU, which culminated in a referendum (the second such referendum since 1975) on UK membership in June 2016 when the UK voted to leave the EU. When the UK joined the EU many believed they were joining a trading block (albeit a protectionist one designed to keep non-EU goods and people out), but the EU has developed into a political union with all the ramifications that involves, not least a considerable loss of sovereignty.

Brexit

The most important consideration for anyone planning to live or work in Britain, either in the short or long term, is Britain's historic decision to leave the European Union (EU) – termed Brexit (British Exit) – in a referendum held on 23rd June 2016. The actual mechanism to leave the EU will begin with the invoking of Article 50 – due to happen before the end of March 2017 (after this book goes to press) – after which the UK will have two years to 'negotiate' its exit from the EU.

One of the key points of the negotiations will be the rights of EU nationals to live and work in the UK (and UK nationals to live and work in the EU), given that the UK's stated intention is to leave the EU single market and the customs union (EU free trade area) – a so-called 'hard' Brexit (a 'soft' Brexit would mean somehow remaining within the single market).

The British government plans to restrict freedom of movement of people from the EU, but also wishes to retain as much access to the single market as possible: some sort of compromise over both is likely as it's in both parties' interests.

Leaving the EU won't only affect the UK's relationship and trade with the EU and the 27 other member countries, but it will also influence the relationship between England and the other countries that make up the United Kingdom (not least Scotland, which voted to remain in the EU, and Northern Ireland, which has a land border with the Republic of Ireland, an EU member). It will also have a huge influence on Britain's future European and world trade relations, exchange rates, cost of living and laws.

The consequences of leaving the EU will probably take many years to become clear, but a certain amount of turmoil is expected in the short to medium term. However, the immediate Armageddon forecast by the remain campaign didn't materialise (although the pound has predictably fallen in value) – and probably never will – and although the uncertainly regarding future trading arrangements is causing anxiety among exporting businesses, many experts and analysts believe that the UK will eventually be better off as an independent nation.

EMPLOYMENT PROSPECTS

You shouldn't count on obtaining employment in the UK unless you've a firm job offer, special qualifications and/or experience for which there's a strong demand – unless, of course, you're looking for a part-time or low-paying job, for which there are usually plenty of vacancies, particularly in London. If you want a good job, you must usually be well qualified and speak fluent English. If you plan to arrive in the UK without a job – always assuming you've the right to legally work in the UK – you should have a detailed plan for finding employment on arrival and try to make some contacts before you arrive (the internet is invaluable in this respect). It's difficult to find permanent work in rural areas, and it isn't plain sailing in cities and large towns unless you've skills or experience that are in demand.

☑ SURVIVAL TIP

Many people turn to self-employment or starting a business in order to make a living, although this path is strewn with pitfalls for newcomers.

Before moving to the UK to work, you should dispassionately examine your motives and credentials and ask yourself the following questions: Do you need a firm job offer in order to obtain a work visa? What kind of work can you realistically expect to do? What are your qualifications and experience? Are they recognised in the UK? How good is your English? Are you prepared to take a low-paid job in order to improve your English and gain experience? Are there any jobs in your profession or trade in the region where you wish to live? Could you become self-employed or start your own business? The answers to these and many other questions can be quite disheartening, but it's better to ask them before moving to the UK rather than afterwards.

UNEMPLOYMENT

Unemployment rose sharply after the financial crisis and recession during the late 2000s but has been falling since 2013 and the UK's official unemployment rate stood at 4.9 per cent or just over 1.6 million people in mid-2016. Some analysts claim that the real unemployment figure is much higher when the 'economically inactive' – those formerly seeking work, who've simply given up because they cannot find any – are included in the statistics.

Unemployment varies from region to region. In large parts of northern England, the Midlands, Scotland, Wales and Northern Ireland, it's far higher than the national average, particularly in regions where the emphasis has been on traditional manufacturing, employing semi-skilled or unskilled workers. The inner cities suffer from a similar problem, and are characterised by long-term unemployment among the middle-aged, and even some London boroughs have above-average levels of unemployment. Another worrying trend in recent years has been the rise in youth unemployment, which hit a peak of 22 per cent in 2012, although in mid-2016 the unemployment rate among 16- to 24-year-olds had fallen to 13.6 per cent (620,000).

The UK suffers from low investment, mediocre skill levels, low productivity, high labour costs and the lack of a clear strategy for the future. The manufacturing sector has long been in decline, although there has been a recovery in certain industries (e.g. car manufacturing) in recent years. Even once bullet-proof industries are fading away or feeling the pinch and reports about the loss of manufacturing jobs are a perennial feature of news bulletins, although theses have been compensated for by the increase in jobs in the service sector. However, low interest rates in recent years and the reduced value of the pound in 2016 (after the Brexit vote) has given exports a boost.

Unemployment is no respecter of age or experience. Just as many school leavers struggle to get work, so redundant managers in their 40s and 50s have found it increasingly difficult to find jobs. Many secure professions such as banking, insurance and the civil service no longer offer 'jobs for life'. The lesson is that nobody is immune from unemployment: accountants, bankers and IT experts have all felt its chilly blast over the last few decades. For today's manager, job security comes from having saleable skills (constantly updated with further education and training) and a portable pension to go with them.

WORKING HOURS

Although the British don't have a reputation for hard work, many Britons are workaholics, particularly among the managerial and professional classes, and most Britons see themselves as hard-working. British employees work among the longest average hours in the European Union and 12-hour days and work-filled evenings aren't uncommon. Redundancies and cost-cutting have increased the pressure on employees, particularly white-collar workers, many of whom now do the work of two or more people. Stress, anxiety and depression due to overwork are increasingly common complaints, and account for the loss of over 11 million working days a year, according to a recent Health and Safety Executive report. See also **Working Hours** on page 34.

INDUSTRIAL RELATIONS

A huge reduction in strikes in the '80s and '90s has essentially continued, particularly in the private sector, although government budget cuts since 2011 have pushed many public sector workers to threaten and even carry out coordinated industrial action, a situation that looks likely to continue. Anti-union legislation by the Conservative government in the '80s muzzled the trade union movement and unions must now ballot members before undertaking industrial action. However, there was a worrying trend in 2016 when some union bosses seemed keener for their members to strike than negotiate with management, which culminated in a series of strikes, e.g. by junior doctors and railway workers.

QUALIFICATIONS

The most important qualification for working in the UK is the ability to speak English fluently (see pages 28 and 135). Once you've overcome this hurdle, you should establish whether your trade or professional qualifications and experience are recognised. If you aren't experienced, British employers expect your studies to be in a relevant discipline and to have included work experience, i.e. on-the-job training. Professional or trade qualifications are required to work in many fields in the UK, although these aren't as stringent as in some other EU countries.

Theoretically, qualifications recognised by professional and trade bodies in one EU country should be recognised in the UK. In practice, recognition varies from country to country, and in some cases foreign qualifications aren't recognised by British employers or professional and trade associations. All academic qualifications should also be recognised, although they may be given less 'value' than equivalent British qualifications, depending on the country and the educational establishment concerned. A ruling by the European Court declared that when examinations are of a similar standard and differences aren't extensive, then individuals ought to be required to take additional examinations only in the particular subject areas which don't overlap, in order for their qualification to be acceptable.

For a comparison of academic qualifications or to find out whether a foreign vocational qualification is recognised in the UK and what its British equivalent is, contact UK NARIC (Oriel House, Oriel Road, Cheltenham, Glos. GL50 1XP, 0871-330 7033, www.naric.org.uk). You can find out whether your profession is regulated in the UK via the UK National Contact Point (NCP) website (www.ecctis.co.uk/UK%20 ncp/default.aspx). If your profession isn't listed, it probably isn't regulated and you'll need to contact UK NARIC to find out the equivalent British qualification.

GOVERNMENT EMPLOYMENT SERVICE

Jobcentre Plus is the name of the government employment service; until 2011 is was an executive agency of the Department of Work and Pensions, although now it's just a brand. Its task is to provide help for the unemployed, but particularly those who've been jobless for over six months or who are disabled or disadvantaged. It's responsible for paying unemployment benefits – Jobseeker's Allowance (JSA) and Employment and Support Allowance (ESA) – through its network of offices, helping with other relevant benefits, and otherwise assisting in two ways: by placing people directly in jobs and by offering guidance and counselling so that jobseekers can find the best way to return to employment, e.g. through education or training.

Jobcentre Plus offices advertise jobs and training courses, operate a number of programmes and training initiatives, and provide a wide range of publications about the help available. Jobs are advertised online via Universal Jobmatch (www.gov.uk/jobsearch), part of the UK government's all-encompassing public sector information website Gov.uk (www.gov.uk), which also provides information on benefits, voluntary positions and much more.

Although most towns have at least one Jobcentre Plus office, there's increasing pressure on jobseekers and benefit claimants to search and apply online, so rather than filling out forms applicants are now encouraged to phone a call centre and speak to an agent – or fill out an online form – and staff will arrange an interview, if necessary, at a local Jobcentre. You can still drop into a Jobcentre but you may be nudged in the direction of the computers or required to make an appointment to see an advisor.

A wide range of jobs is advertised on the Universal Jobmatch website, which is managed by the employment website Monster (www.monster.co.uk). Jobs can be searched via job title, skills or location, e.g. chef, accounting or Leeds, but you need to log in to save search results and apply for jobs. Increasingly jobseekers are being encouraged to go online to look for work and Jobcentres have terminals where you can search for jobs if you don't have internet access at home.

Check the Universal Jobmatch website regularly; employers post new job leads daily and the good ones don't remain vacant for long. Some job-hunters claim the better positions disappear before they even make it onto the website! When you hit the 'Apply' button you may be redirected to the employer's website where you can apply for the job directly. For more help call Jobcentre Plus (0345-606 0234) or contact your local Jobcentre via the central number (0345-604 3719).

European Employment Service

Jobcentre Plus is also responsible for European Employment Service (EURES) operations in the UK, which is the European system for exchanging job applications and vacancies between member states. Details are available in all Employment Service offices in each member country, plus advice on how to apply for jobs.

Local offices also have access to overseas vacancies held on the National Vacancy Computer System (NATVACS). The main source of information is the EURES Job Mobility Portal (http://ec.europa.eu/eures/home.

jsp?lang=en), which contains details of national employment agencies, EURES advisors and a lengthy (if sometimes out of date) listing of jobs in each country.

RECRUITMENT CONSULTANTS

Private recruitment consultants and employment agencies proliferate in all major cities and towns in the UK (in London they even outnumber pubs), and are big business. Most large companies are happy to engage consultants to recruit staff, particularly when they're seeking executives, managers and professional employees. Head-hunters, as they're also known, account for around two-thirds of all top level executive appointments in the UK, while others specialise in certain fields only, such as nursing and medical staff; computer and IT specialists; accounting, sales, secretarial and office staff; engineering and technical specialists; and catering, industrial and construction workers.

Many more deal exclusively with 'temps', i.e. temporary office staff, baby-sitters, home carers, nannies and au pairs, housekeepers, cooks, gardeners, drivers, hairdressers, security guards, cleaners, labourers and factory hands. Specialist nursing agencies, which are fairly common, also cover related occupations such as physiotherapy, occupational and speech therapy, and dentistry, plus domiciliary and residential care workers.

Agencies, which must be licensed by local councils, don't usually charge employees a fee, but are paid by employers. Hourly rates paid should include an additional amount in lieu of holiday pay after a qualifying period, if employees don't take a paid annual holiday. Agencies must deduct PAYE income tax (see **Chapter 14**) and National Insurance contributions (see **Chapter 13**) if employees don't operate their own limited company.

> If you're using agencies to look for work, you'll find an outline of your legal rights at www.gov.uk/agency-workers-your-rights/overview.

A list of agencies specialising in particular trades or professions is available from the Recruitment and Employment Confederation (020-7009 2100, www.rec.uk.com). To find local agencies google 'employment agencies in xxxx' (insert the name of the town or area) or look in the Yellow Pages under 'Employment Agencies' (visit www.yell.com) and in local newspapers. Agency jobs are also advertised via the internet and many recruiters post jobs on the Universal Jobmatch website (www.gov.uk/jobsearch).

CONTRACT JOBS

Contract, or freelance, jobs for specialists in fields such as accountancy, engineering, IT and nursing are available through many employment agencies. Rates vary considerably, but rise to £100 an hour or more for, say, a highly-qualified computer specialist.

Contract work may be sub-contracted or obtained directly from a particular company. Contractors may work at home or on a client's or contract company's premises. Sub-contractors in the building industry (and some others) require a special permit in order to be classed as self-employed. The potential for home-based work in the UK is huge, particularly within the computer industry, which is keen to exploit the number of IT professionals (particularly women) wishing to work part-time from home. There are many websites, such as www.contractoruk.co.uk, www.contractjobs.com and www.itcontractjobs.co.uk, targeted at those looking to hire staff or obtain contract work.

Workers for most British consultancy companies are permanent company employees, although they often work full time for another organisation on a contractual basis (it can become quite complicated). Contract workers who wish to be classed as self-employed must set up a limited company (the most common choice for long-term contractors) or register as a sole trader (www.gov.uk/set-up-sole-trader/overview); otherwise PAYE income tax and National Insurance contributions must be deducted from payments by their employer, e.g. an employment agency.

Non-EEA employees of foreign companies who are living and working in the UK temporarily require a work permit, which must be obtained by their British employer (unless employment is for a brief period only). Many British companies avoid the need for work permits (and save money) by out-sourcing tasks to overseas companies (e.g. in Eastern Europe and Asia) where labour is much cheaper.

MINIMUM WAGE

The UK has a minimum wage – actually two different minimum wage rates, the National Minimum Wage and the National Living Wage, introduced in April 2016 (see www.gov.uk/national-minimum-wage-rates).

The National Minimum Wage is the minimum hourly rate that most workers are entitled to by law, which depends on a worker's age and whether they're an apprentice. In October 2016 it was £6.95 per hour for those aged 21-24, £5.55 for those aged 18-20, £4 for under 18s and £3.40 for first-year apprentices. The National Living Wage was introduced in April 2016 and is in effect a national minimum wage for all working people aged 25 and over; it's set at a minimum rate of £7.20 per hour (October 2016).

In 2015, the government decreed that the minimum wage premium for employees aged over 25 should be 60 per cent of average earnings by 2020, by which time it's expected to rise to around £9 per hour. However, this may be reviewed, as many employers have expressed opposition to the increased minimum wage, which has resulted in sharply increased labour costs. National Minimum Wage rates change in October, while the National Living Wage rate changes in April.

Nobody should receive less than the minimum wage. You can use the confidential Pay and Work Rights helpline (0800-917 2368) to obtain information or to make a complaint if you're being underpaid.

The minimum wage should not be confused with the **voluntary living wage**, which is an alternative hourly rate based on the amount people need to cover the basic costs of living and was £8.25 in 2016 (£9.40 in London). It's set by the Living Wage Foundation (livingwage.org.uk) and is a voluntary rate, but nearly 3,000 UK employers choose to pay it and the figure is rising.

PART-TIME JOBS

Some 8.5 million people (three-quarters of them women) work part-time in the UK in offices, pubs, shops, factories, cafés and restaurants, and many young foreigners combine part-time work with study and improving their English. Most part-time workers are poorly paid, although the introduction of the minimum wage (see above) in 1999 improved matters.

Part-time employees formerly enjoyed little protection from exploitation by employers, but the Part-time Workers (Prevention of Less Favourable Treatment) Regulations 2000 and two subsequent amendments changed that. Part-time workers must now receive the same hourly pay and overtime rate as comparable full-time workers, equal rights to sickness and maternity pay, paid holiday entitlement in proportion to that of comparable full-time staff, and similar access to pension schemes. There should be no difference in the length of service required to qualify for these benefits.

The definition of a part-time worker under new legislation is one who works fewer than the normal hours for the business in question. These regulations apply to all businesses, but not all employers are aware of them. An increasing number of companies operate a job-share scheme, where two or more employees share one job and divide the hours between them.

In March 2016 over 800,000 workers were employed on zero-hours contracts, under which employer aren't obliged to provide workers with any minimum working hours, and workers aren't obliged to accept any of the hours offered. These contracts have grown in popularity with employers (but not employees) since the 2008 global financial crisis and are especially prevalent in the health, domiciliary care, hospitality and warehousing sectors.

Many jobs listed below under Temporary & Casual Jobs are also available on a permanent part-time basis.

TEMPORARY & CASUAL JOBS

Temporary and casual jobs differ from part-time jobs in that these jobs are usually for a fixed period only, e.g. from a few hours to a few months, or work may be intermittent. People employed in temporary, seasonal and casual jobs comprise around 6 per cent of all employees. Around two-thirds of large companies use temporary staff at some time, mostly in the summer when permanent staff are on holiday, and usually in clerical positions. Employers usually require your national insurance number and sometimes a P45 tax form (see **Chapter 14**).

Some employers, illegally, pay temporary staff in cash without making any deductions for tax or national insurance (see **Working Illegally** on page 27).

Casual workers are often employed on a daily, first-come, first-served basis. Pay for casual work is usually low and is sometimes paid cash in hand.

Temporary jobs are also advertised in on the Universal Jobmatch website (www.gov.uk/jobsearch) and on community websites such as Gumtree (www.gumtree.com).

For information about your legal obligations regarding tax and National Insurance, contact HM Revenue and Customs (www.gov.uk/government/organisations/hm-revenue-customs).

WORKING WOMEN

Women make up around 47 per cent (over 15 million) of the total British workforce of some 32 million, of which over 8 million are part-time employees. A woman doing the same, or broadly similar, work as a man and employed by the same employer is legally entitled to the

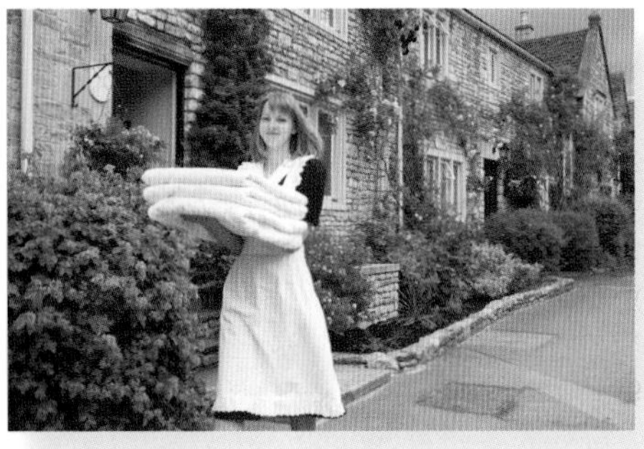

same salary and other terms of employment. As in most western countries, although there's no official discrimination, in practice this often isn't the case. On average, women earn around 25 per cent less than men, although the pay gap between the sexes is narrowing, particularly in senior positions. In recent years, employers have been trying harder to retain their female staff and many have established crèches and even 'granny' crèches (for elderly parents) to discourage employees from leaving.

Although women are breaking into the professions and the boardroom in ever-increasing numbers, they often find it difficult to reach the very top of their profession, where males continue to dominate. The main discrimination among women executives and professionals isn't in salary or title, but in promotion opportunities, as many companies and organisations are reluctant to elevate women to important positions (partly due to fears that they may leave and start a family). This invisible barrier is known as the 'glass ceiling'.

> Although 'the best man for the job is often a woman', this isn't always acknowledged by employers, many of whom still prefer the standard male candidate aged between 25 and 40.

Self-employment among women in the UK has increased steadily since the '90s, particularly among women from ethnic minorities, despite the fact that banks and other financial institutions are reluctant to provide finance. Women now make up almost one-third of the self-employed and over 30 per cent of new businesses are started by women. Prowess (www.prowess.org.uk) is an association supporting women to start and grow their business, while a useful website for following current developments is www.everywoman.com.

SALARIES

It can be difficult to determine the salary you should command in the UK, and getting the right pay for the job is something of a lottery. Salaries can also vary considerably for the same work in different parts of the UK. Those working in London and the southeast are the highest paid, mainly due to the higher cost of living, particularly accommodation (although the disparity between the north and south of England contracts and expands in response to economic developments).

Usually, salaries are negotiable and it's up to each individual to ensure that he receives pay and benefits commensurate with his qualifications and experience (or as much as you can get!). Minimum salaries exist in some trades and professions, but generally it's every man for himself. In some companies, trades and professions, along with the public sector, wages are decided by national pay agreements with the unions.

Your working hours in the UK may differ from those elsewhere and depend on your profession and where you work. For most executives, professionals and 'white-collar' or office workers, between 35 and 38 hours a week is the official norm, particularly in London and other major cities. 'Blue-collar' (manual) workers theoretically work from 37.5 to 40 hours a week, although for many it's much longer when overtime is included.

There's now officially a maximum (optional) 48-hour week under EU regulations, although actual working hours in the UK are longer than in many other EU countries.

The huge disparity between the salaries of the lowest and highest paid employees in the UK is far wider than in most other western European countries. At the bottom end of the scale, some 15 per cent of employees earned less than £3.50 an hour before the statutory minimum wage set at that figure was introduced in April 1999. At the other extreme, executive and managerial salaries have been increasing in leaps and bounds and are now far higher than in other European countries.

In 2016, the average salary for a chief executive officer (CEO) of one of the UK's top 100 companies was over £4 million, taking into account performance-related bonuses, share options and 'fringe benefits' (known as perks – short for perquisites) such as chauffeured company cars. Corporate 'fat-cat' abuse of salaries and perks is more prevalent in the UK than in any other industrialised country. Surprisingly, even failure to produce a profit rarely impacts on 'performance' bonuses enjoyed by CEOs.

Salaries for some professionals have also soared in recent years, e.g. top commercial lawyers can earn well over £1 million a year! Meanwhile, back in the real world, the Annual Survey of Hours and Earnings compiled by the Office for National Statistics, stated that the average UK worker earned £27,600 in the 2014-15 tax year.

Many employees, particularly company directors and senior managers, enjoy perks (benefits) the value of which may even exceed their monthly salary. Most companies offer benefits for executives and managers which may even continue after retirement, and may include a free company car (possibly with a chauffeur); free health insurance and health screening; paid holidays; private school fees; cheap or free home loans; rent-free homes; free rail season tickets; free company restaurants; non-contributory company pensions; share options; interest-free loans; free tickets for sports events and shows; free subscriptions to clubs; and 'business' conferences in exotic places.

The perks of board members in many companies make up almost 50 per cent of their total remuneration (to keep it out of the hands of the tax man). In addition, executives often receive a huge 'golden hello' when they start a job, and a similar payment (which can sometimes run into millions of pounds) should they be made redundant or be forced to resign.

SELF-EMPLOYMENT

Anyone who's a British citizen, an EU national or a permanent UK resident (see **Chapter 3**) may work as a self-employed person in the UK. This includes participating in partnerships and co-operatives, operating a franchise and doing commission-only jobs, as well running a private business. Unlike most other EU countries, there are few restrictions and little red tape for anyone wanting to start a business or enter self-employment in the UK. One of the government's main initiatives for reducing unemployment has been to encourage people to start their own businesses.

The number of self-employed has risen dramatically over the past 20 years, and is now over 15 per cent of the labour force (over 4.5 million people), which is among the highest in the European Union and rising. Redundancy (and the difficulty in finding full-time employment) is often the spur for the over 45s to start their own business. Those aged 45

 **Caution**

For many people, starting a business is one of the quickest routes to bankruptcy known to mankind. In fact, many people who open businesses would be better off investing in lottery tickets – at least they would then have a chance of getting a return on their investment! Most experts reckon that if you're going to work for yourself you must be prepared to fail.

to 55 account for a disproportionate number of new business start-ups (although many are hollow 'consultancies', where professionals eke out a living on commission), while the number of over 65s who are self-employed more than doubled to half a million between 2009 and 2014.

Information & Professional Advice

A wealth of free advice and information for budding entrepreneurs is available from government agencies, local councils and the private sector. Many books are published on self-employment and starting your own business including *The Financial Times Guide to Business Start Up* (annual) and *The FT Essential Guide to Developing a Business Strategy: How to Use Strategic Planning to Start Up or Grow Your Business* (both FT Publishing). Libraries are also another excellent source of information.

A large number of local authority agencies and government departments provide free professional advice and assistance about starting and running a business, including finance and borrowing; marketing and selling; setting up and naming a company; bookkeeping and tax; premises and employment; advertising and promotion; patents and copyright; and equipment and computing. These include the government-run Business Support Helpline (0300-456 3565; see www.gov.uk/business-support-helpline for numbers in Scotland, Wales and Northern Ireland) and enterprise or business advice centres, some of which are financed by local councils. To find your local enterprise or advice centre, search online or consult your local telephone directory or Yellow Pages.

Local support is available through the National Enterprise Network which directs you to enterprise support services across England (www.nationalenterprisenetwork.org); there are similar online 'hubs' for Scotland, Wales and Northern Ireland. The best place to start is the Gov.uk website (www.gov.uk/starting-up-a-business). Another useful website is Start Up Britain (www.startupbritain.org), which is packed with advice from entrepreneurs.

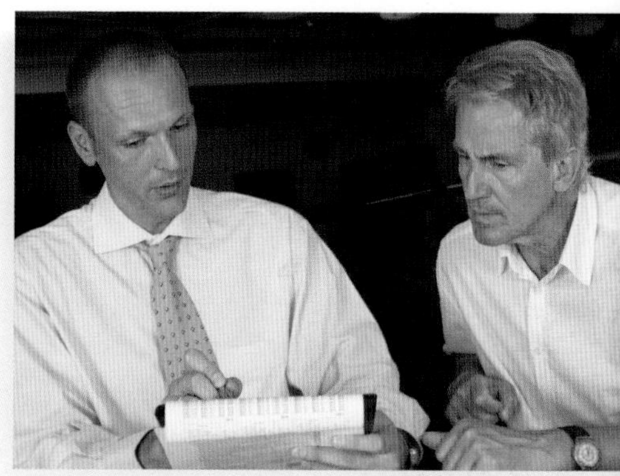

If you wish to start a business in the London area, a number of organisations exists to help, including Greater London Enterprise (10-12 Queen Elizabeth Street, London SE1 2JN, 020-7403 0300, www.gle.co.uk), set up by the London boroughs.

WORKING ILLEGALLY

There are millions of people working illegally in the UK (including many children), although only a relatively small percentage are foreigners. The vast majority of illegal workers are British or foreign nationals who've the right to work in the UK, but who fail to declare their income (or total income) to HM Revenue and Customs. The illegal labour market (usually called the black or shadow economy) thrives in the UK, and is estimated to be worth some £150 billion a year (around 10 per cent of national income), which although high is estimated to be only half that of Greece, Italy or Spain.

If you're tempted to work illegally, you should be aware of the consequences, as the black economy is a risky business for both employers and employees. A foreigner found working illegally is usually fined and may be deported and may be refused future entry into the UK. Non-payment of income tax or national Insurance is a criminal offence in the UK and offenders are liable to large fines and even imprisonment. Employees without permits have no entitlement to government or company pensions, unemployment benefits, accident insurance at work or legal job protection.

LANGUAGE

English is the most important and most widely used language in the world, and is spoken by some 1.5 billion people as their first or second language. It's the world's *lingua franca* and is the language of the United Nations, international peacekeeping, world banking and commerce, air traffic control, academic research, computers (particularly the internet), space travel, scientific discovery, news gathering and popular entertainment.

If you're planning to live or work in the UK you'll need to speak, read and write English well enough to find your way around, e.g. dealing with government officials, public transport and shops, and to understand and hold conversations with the people you meet. Your English proficiency is important if you've a job requiring a lot of contact with others or which involves speaking on the telephone or dealing with other foreigners, who may all speak their own 'dialect' of English.

It's particularly important for students to have a high standard of English, as they must be able to follow lectures and take part in discussions in the course of their studies. This may also require a much wider and more technical or specialised vocabulary. For this reason, most universities and colleges won't accept students who aren't fluent in English and many require a formal qualification, e.g. a pass at GCSE or the Cambridge proficiency examination. Prospective students can assess their English fluency by taking the International English Language Testing Service (IELTS) test at British Council offices in over 100 countries.

> If you wish to improve your English before starting work or a course of study in the UK, there are language schools throughout the country where you can enrol in a part-time or full-time course lasting from a few weeks to a year (see **Chapter 9**).

Non-EU nationals wishing to settle permanently in the UK must pass the 'knowledge of life and language in the UK' test (better known as the Life in the UK test) as a condition of their application. This applies to spouses and partners as well as to highly skilled migrant workers. Since 2010, spouses and partners, including fiancé(e)s and same-sex partners, must prove their English language ability before being granted an entry visa. For more information on language requirements and approved courses, see the UK Visas and Immigration section of the Gov.uk website (www.gov.uk/government/organisations/uk-visas-and-immigration).

Whether you speak British or American English (or some other form) is usually irrelevant, although some foreigners have a problem understanding the British (who often don't understand each other's accents), and even Americans initially have some problems understanding the natives. The main difference between standard British English and standard American English is in the spelling (English spelling is a minefield) and pronunciation, plus a 'few' colloquialisms thrown in to confuse the issue. There are many regional accents in the UK, which is the way people pronounce their words, but few dialects, where a unique vocabulary, grammar and idiom are employed. The English spoken by television and radio newsreaders is usually referred to as 'Standard English'.

If you're working or living in Wales and have children of school age, they may be obliged to learn Welsh – something that has proved unpopular with non-Welsh parents. In the north-western Highlands and Islands of Scotland, some 60,000 people speak Gaelic, which is taught (but isn't compulsorily) in schools in the region. Similarly, Irish is an optional subject in schools in Northern Ireland.

2. EMPLOYMENT CONDITIONS

Employment conditions in the UK depend largely on an employee's individual contract of employment and an employer's general employment conditions. Some aspects of your working conditions described in this chapter are prescribed by law and, although many employers' pay and conditions are more generous than the statutory minimum, some still offer pay and conditions that are actually illegal. The UK belatedly signed up to the European Union (EU) social chapter, giving its workers the same rights as those in other EU countries. Fears that this, and the introduction of the minimum wage, would lose 'millions of jobs', to quote one Conservative politician, have proved unfounded. However, there are fears that workers could be worse off after Brexit (see page 18) when EU legislation will no longer apply to the UK.

There's often a huge disparity between the working conditions of hourly-paid workers and salaried employees (i.e. monthly-paid), even between those employed by the same company. As in most countries, managerial and executive staff generally enjoy a much higher level of benefits than lower-paid employees (as do public sector employees). Employees hired to work in the UK by a foreign (non-British) company may receive a higher salary (including fringe benefits and allowances) than those offered by British employers.

Pre-Brexit, citizens of EU member states working in the UK have the same rights as British nationals, for example with regard to pay, working conditions, vocational training and trade union membership. The employment conditions of non-EU nationals are generally the same as British nationals, although their employment is usually subject to the granting of a work permit.

The Department for Business, Innovation and Skills (BIS) is responsible for government policy on employment, business law and other work matters. They can be contacted by phone (020-7215 5000) but most information is available via the Gov.uk website (www.gov.uk/browse/working). The rights of employees are explained in detail in a series of publications by the Advisory, Conciliation and Arbitration Service (ACAS, 0300-123 1100, www.acas.org.uk).

CONTRACT OF EMPLOYMENT

Under British law, a contract of employment exists as soon as an employee proves his acceptance of an employer's terms and conditions of employment, e.g. by starting work, after which the employer and employee are bound by the terms offered and agreed. The contract isn't always in writing, although under the Employment Protection (Consolidation) Act

1978 (as amended), and the Part-time Workers (Prevention of Unfavourable Treatment) Act 2000, an employer must provide employees with a written statement containing certain important terms of employment, and additional notes, e.g. regarding discipline and grievance procedures. This must be done within two months of starting work.

A written contract of employment should usually contain all the terms and conditions agreed between the employer and employee. There's no distinction between full-time and part-time workers with regard to their rights in the workplace.

You usually receive two copies of your contract of employment (which may be called a 'statement of terms and conditions' or an 'offer letter'), both of which you should sign and date. One copy must be returned to your employer or prospective employer and the other (usually the original) is for your personal records. There are generally no hidden surprises or traps for the unwary in a British contract of employment although, as with any contract, you should know exactly what it contains before signing it. If your knowledge of English is imperfect, you should ask someone to explain anything you don't understand (British companies rarely provide foreigners with contracts in a language other than English).

Any special arrangements or conditions you've agreed with an employer should also be contained in the contract. If all or any of the above particulars are contained in a collective agreement, an employer may refer employees to a copy of this or other documents, such as work rules or handbooks, wage regulation orders, sick pay and pension scheme conditions, and the rules relating to flexible working hours and company holidays. Before signing a contract of employment, you should obtain a copy of any general employment conditions (see below) or documents referred to in the contract, and ensure that you understand them.

Employment is usually subject to satisfactory references being received from your previous employer(s) and/or character references. In the case of a school leaver or student, a reference may be required from the principal of your last school, college or university. For certain jobs, a pre-employment medical examination is required, and periodical examinations may be a condition of employment, e.g. where good health is vital to the safe performance of your duties. If you require a work permit to work in the UK, your contract may contain a clause stating that 'the contract is subject to a work permit being granted by the authorities'.

Employees must be notified in writing of any changes to their terms and conditions of employment, at the very latest one month before their proposed introduction. This must be done explicitly and, as noted previously, only in agreement with the workforce. Employers cannot just change contractually agreed terms to suit themselves. Failure to provide a contract or the unilateral change of contractual terms are grounds for an appeal to an Employment Tribunal.

Information on employment contracts is available on the Gov.uk website (www.gov.uk/browse/working/contract-working-hours). The Advisory, Conciliation and Arbitration Service (www.acas.org.uk) also publishes guidance on the subject.

GENERAL EMPLOYMENT CONDITIONS

In addition to a contract of employment, you should receive a copy of an employer's general employment terms and conditions (including benefits, rules and regulations) that apply to all employees, unless otherwise stated in individual contracts of employment. General employment conditions are usually referred to in employment contracts, and employees usually receive a copy on starting employment (or in some cases beforehand).

General conditions normally include the following.

Validity & Applicability

There's usually a paragraph stating the date from which they take effect and to whom they apply.

Place of Work

Unless there's a clause in your contract stating otherwise, your employer cannot change your place of work without your agreement. The place of work refers to a town or area of a large city, rather than a different office or a new building across the street. Some contracts state that you may occasionally be required to work at other company locations.

Salary & Benefits

Your salary is stated in your contract of employment, where salary reviews, overtime rates, piece and bonus rates, planned increases and cost of living rises may also be included. Only general points, such as the payment of your salary into a bank account and the date of salary payments, are usually included in general conditions. You should generally receive an itemised pay statement (or wage slip) with your salary if it's paid weekly in cash (rare nowadays), or separately when your salary is paid monthly into a bank account.

Salaries in the UK are generally reviewed once a year, although the salary of a new employee may be reviewed after six months. Annual increases may be negotiated by individual employees, an independent pay review board or by a union (or unions), when the majority of a company's employees are members (called collective bargaining).

Generally, if the employer needs you badly and you're dealing from a position of strength, you're better off negotiating your own salary increases. Otherwise, joining a union and letting them do it for you is more effective. A percentage of your annual salary increase is usually to compensate for a rise in the cost of living (usually applicable in the UK), although some employees (particularly in the public sector) may receive pay rises below the annual rate of inflation.

Commission & Bonuses

Your salary may include commission or bonus payments, calculated on your individual performance (e.g. based on sales) or the company's performance as a whole, which may be paid regularly (e.g. monthly or annually) or irregularly. Some employers pay all employees an annual bonus (usually in December), although this isn't normal practice. When a bonus is paid, it may be stated in your contract of employment, in which case it's obligatory. In your first and last year of employment, an annual bonus is usually paid pro rata if you don't work a full calendar year.

Some employers operate an annual voluntary bonus scheme, based on each employee's individual performance or the company's profits (a profit-sharing scheme),

although this may apply only to senior management and professionals. If you're employed on a contract basis for a fixed period, you may be paid an end-of-contract bonus.

When discussing salary with a prospective employer, you should take into account the total salary package, including commission, bonuses and benefits such as a company car or a low-interest home loan. In industry, particularly in small firms, production workers are often paid at bonus or 'piece-work' rates based on their productivity.

Working Hours

Working hours in the UK are amongst the longest in Europe. A study by EurWORK (the European Observatory on Working Life) showed that the British work an average 40.8 hour week, compared with the French (37.9 hrs) and Italians (38 hrs). Only people in Luxembourg and Romania work a longer week (over 41 hours on average).

Under the EU Working Time Directive, which came into force in 1998 in the UK, the maximum working week is officially 48 hours (averaged over 17 weeks), although employees can choose to opt out of the 48-hour maximum.

Hours vary depending on your employer, your position and the type of industry in which you're employed. For example, the official working week in most manufacturing industries is around 37.5 to 40 hours, while many office employees work 35 to 38 hours a week (a 35-hour week is usually referred to as 9 to 5 or 9am to 5pm). At the other end of the scale, some employees in hospitals, security, construction, transportation, catering and hotels may work up to 100 hours a week, although the average in these fields is usually between 50 and 60.

For reasons of safety, employees must have rest breaks during the day, and a daily rest period of 11 consecutive hours and a weekly rest period of 24 hours. Night-shift working is limited to eight hours a night, averaged over 17 weeks. Before formal restrictions on working hours were introduced, an estimated 2.7 million UK workers spent longer than 48 hours on the job each week. However, following their introduction (in 2007), an estimated 3.2 million people (13 per cent of the workforce) were working over 48 hours, which illustrates how little impact they've had. Some professional staff also average almost ten hours a week of extra unpaid work.

Shop floor (blue-collar or manual) workers in many companies are required to clock in and out of work, while white-collar (e.g. office) workers may not, even when working in the same building. Employees caught cheating the clock are liable to instant dismissal.

If a company closes for the period between Christmas and New Year or on unofficial holidays, you may be required to compensate for this by working extra hours each week. If applicable, this is stated in your general conditions. Your working hours may not be increased above the hours stated in your general conditions without compensation or overtime being paid. Similarly, if you've a guaranteed working week, your hours cannot be reduced (i.e. short-time working) without your agreement.

Your hours also cannot be changed without your agreement unless there's a clause (sometimes referred to as a 'mobility clause') in your contract. In reality, an employer is unlikely to change or reduce your hours without agreement if he wants to retain your goodwill and services. If you refuse short-time working and are subsequently dismissed, you can usually regard yourself as being made

redundant (see **Redundancy** on page 41), in which case you should receive compensation.

Paid overtime among blue-collar workers is often considered a perk, and not something to be avoided at all costs, as in some other countries. Often, one of the first questions a worker asks about a job is, "how much paid overtime is available?". Overtime is a lucrative bonus in some jobs, while in others it's a matter of economic necessity, without which many workers would find it difficult to survive. It's the only way for low-paid workers, in expensive areas such as London, to earn anything remotely like a living wage. In between these two extremes, many salaried employees are required to work long hours for no extra pay, including many managers and executives. In general, working hours are a matter of agreement between employers and employees and their representatives, e.g. unions.

Employers cannot normally require people to work excessive hours or unsuitable shift patterns which are likely to lead to ill health or accidents caused by fatigue, e.g. the working hours of most goods or passenger-vehicle drivers are strictly controlled by law. Many employers are instituting more flexible working hours and often permit employees to take part in job-sharing (where two people share a job), an annual hours scheme (where employees work an agreed number of hours a year), voluntary reduced time, and working part of the time at home.

Overtime & Compensation

Working hours for employees who work a flexi-time system are usually calculated on a monthly basis. Companies usually allow employees to carry forward extra hours worked and take time off at a later date, or carry forward a deficit and make it up later. Payment may be made for overtime, depending on company policy or your general conditions. Most companies pay overtime for work that's urgent and officially approved, and many prefer salaried (i.e. monthly-paid) employees to take time off in lieu of overtime worked or expect them to work unpaid overtime. Middle and senior management employees aren't generally paid or compensated for overtime.

When paid, overtime rates are usually the normal rate plus 25 per cent on weekdays and Saturdays, and plus 50 per cent on Sundays, although this isn't universal; in retail, for example, workers may only receive their usual hourly rate for working overtime, even at weekends. The overtime rates you can expect should be spelt out in your contract of employment. Employees who work on public holidays may be paid double time (a 100 per cent supplement). In some industries and jobs, overtime terms and rates are agreed with a trade union.

Travel & Relocation Expenses

Your travel and relocation expenses to the UK (or to a new job in another region of the UK) depend on your agreement with your employer, and are usually detailed in your contract of employment or general conditions. If you're hired from outside the UK, your air or other travel costs to the UK are usually paid by your employer or his agent. You can also claim any additional travel costs, for example the cost of transport to and from airports. If you travel by car to the UK, you can normally claim a mileage rate plus the cost of the ferry or the equivalent air fare.

Most British employers pay your relocation expenses to the UK up to a specified amount, which may be a percentage of your salary, a block allowance or specific expenses such as removal, legal and estate agency fees only. The allowance should be sufficient to move the contents of an average house and you must normally pay any excess costs yourself. A company may ask you to obtain two or three removal estimates when they're liable for the total cost of removal. If you don't want to bring your furniture to the UK or have only a few belongings to ship, it may be possible to use your allowance to purchase furniture locally.

National Insurance

State social security consists of National Insurance (NI) contributions that entitle you to a pension, unemployment and other benefits. NI contributions are compulsory for most residents of the UK and are usually deducted at source from your gross salary by your employer. For details, see **National Insurance** on page 192.

Medical Examination

Many British companies require prospective employees to have a pre-employment medical examination performed by a doctor nominated by them. An offer of employment is usually subject to an applicant being given a clean bill of health. This may be required for employees over a certain age only (e.g. 50) or for employees in particular jobs, e.g. where good health is of paramount importance for reasons of safety. Thereafter, a medical examination may be necessary periodically (e.g. every one or two years) or may be requested at any time by your employer.

Medical examinations may be required as a condition of membership of a company health, pension or life insurance scheme. Most companies also insist on employees having regular health screening, particularly senior managers and executives.

Cars & Driving Licence

Many British employers provide senior employees such as directors, senior managers and professionals with a company car, although few jobs paying below around £30,000 a year offer a company car as a benefit unless it's necessary to do your job. If you're provided with a company car, you usually receive full details about its use and your obligations on starting employment. If you lose your licence (e.g. through drunken driving) and are unable to fulfil the requirements of your job, your employment is usually terminated (i.e. you're fired), and you may not be entitled to any compensation. If a company car is provided, check what sort of car it is, whether you're permitted to use it privately and, if so, who pays for the petrol for private mileage. Some companies require employees to make a contribution towards the cost of providing a non-essential company car.

Using a company car for private purposes affects your tax position. Many companies offer employees a car allowance rather than provide a company car, which prevents employees having to pay onerous taxes. Company cars are usually replaced every two or three years or after 70,000mi (112,000km). Most companies allow employees to buy secondhand company cars at advantageous prices.

Company Pension Fund

Pensions have undergone an overhaul in the last few years, as the government tries to ensure all workers make some provision for their retirement years. One aspect of this is the introduction of mandatory workplace pensions: these have been phased in over a period of years, starting in 2012 and ending in April 2017, when all employers must be enrolled in a pension scheme.

Many company pensions used to be based on your final salary, but these proved to be too expensive for employers and most have now been closed to new employees.

Workplace pensions apply to anyone aged over 22 and earning more than £10,000 a year; contributions are based on 8 per cent of earnings of which employees contribute half. Those earning less can still opt in, although employers aren't required to contribute if you earned less than £112 a week in 2016 (or its monthly equivalent). See www.gov.uk/workplace-pensions for more information.

Company pension funds have been traditionally regarded as a good deal, although in recent years they haven't done so well due to the fluctuation in the value of stocks and shares. Many funds face severe shortages and are in crisis and could even go bankrupt; private pension funds aren't protected in the UK and companies can usually dip into them at will. That said, most company pension funds offer much better terms than you can obtain privately, for example, from a private pension plan.

See **Private Pension** on page 194 for more information.

Accident Insurance

All employers, including even the smallest trader, are required to have occupational accident insurance for employees working on their premises, whether in a factory, office, shop, warehouse or residential accommodation. An employer is required to notify the appropriate authority immediately in the case of a death or serious injury as the result of an accident, or when anybody is off work for more than three days as a consequence.

Although the primary responsibility for safety rests with the employer, employees are required by law to ensure that they co-operate with their employers and that they don't endanger themselves or anyone else by their acts or omissions. There are usually specific regulations for activities involving high risks, e.g. when operating electrical equipment and certain classes of machinery, and the use of chemicals or dangerous materials. The number of people injured at work each year in the UK totals over 600,000 and there are also more than 125 fatalities, although incidents are decreasing due to more stringent health and safety regulations.

For more information, contact your local Health & Safety Executive (www.hse.gov.uk) office.

Income Protection

Income protection in the event of sickness or an accident depends on your employer, your personal contract of employment, your length of employment and whether you're paid weekly or monthly. Most salaried employees (i.e. monthly-paid) automatically receive sick pay when sick for a short period. Usually, you must have been employed for a minimum period before you're entitled to sick pay, e.g. 13 weeks, which may coincide with your probationary period. Employees paid an hourly rate may not be paid at all for any illness lasting less than four days, after which time they receive Statutory Sick Pay (SSP). SSP is not over-generous: in 2016 the weekly rate was just £88.45 a week.

Your employer may have an occupational sick pay (OSP) scheme, under which you receive your full salary for a number of weeks in the event of sickness or after an accident. OSP is often provided by employers as part of a company pension scheme, although less than 50 per cent of private sector companies have an OSP scheme.

Miscellaneous Insurance

Other insurance provided by your employer is usually detailed in your general working conditions. This may include free life and health insurance, which also covers travel abroad on company business. Free life insurance is typically four times annual salary for top managers and directors. Some companies provide free membership of a private health insurance scheme, although this may apply only to executives, managers and key personnel. Check that health insurance includes your family. Companies may also operate a contributory group health insurance scheme, offering discounted subscriptions for individual private membership.

Sickness Notification

You're usually required to notify your employer as soon as possible of sickness (or an accident) that prevents you from working, i.e. within a few hours of your normal starting time. Failure to do so may result in you not being paid for that day's absence. You're required to keep your boss or manager informed about your illness and when you expect to return to work. For periods of under seven days, you must usually provide a self-certificate of why you were absent, on your return to work. If you're off work for longer than seven days you're required to obtain a doctor's certificate, known as a 'fit note' as in fit (or not) to work. NHS doctors don't usually provide 'fit notes' for absence from work through sickness for periods of less than seven days.

Annual Holidays

Your annual holiday entitlement usually depends on your profession, position and employer, and your individual contract of employment. Holiday pay and entitlements are decided by individual or collective bargaining, e.g. by unions. Under EU rules, employees are entitled to a minimum 5.6 weeks of annual leave which works out at 28 days, including any public holidays. Some employers give employees over a certain age, e.g. 50, an extra week's holiday, and may grant additional holidays for length of service and for senior positions (but no time to take them!).

> Part-time workers have the same statutory rights as full-time workers, i.e. if they work half the hours of a full-time worker, they receive half the paid holiday entitlement. Equal treatment is now mandatory.

A company's holiday year may not correspond to a calendar year, but may run from 6th April to 5th April (the following year) to coincide with the government's financial year in the UK. Holiday entitlement is calculated on a pro rata basis (per completed calendar month of service) if you don't work a full 'holiday' year. Usually, all holidays must be taken within the holiday year in which they're earned, although some companies allow employees to carry them over to the next year.

Before starting a new job, check that any planned holidays will be approved by your new employer. This is particularly important if they fall within your probationary period (usually the first three months), when holidays aren't generally permitted. Holidays may normally be taken only with the prior permission of your manager or boss, and in many companies must be booked up to one year in advance. Most companies allow unpaid leave only in exceptional circumstances, such as when all your holiday entitlement has been exhausted.

If you fall ill while on holiday, your holiday entitlement may be credited to you, provided you obtain a doctor's certificate. If you resign your position or are given notice, most employers will pay you in lieu of any outstanding holidays, although this isn't an entitlement and you may be obliged to take the holiday at your employer's discretion.

Public Holidays

Compared with many other European countries, the UK has relatively few public or national holidays (although Americans will be delighted!), normally referred to as bank holidays, as they're days on which banks are officially closed. Schools, businesses and many shops are also closed on public holidays. The British celebrate no national, independence or revolution day(s), and the only national religious holidays are Christmas and Easter. The box (below) shows official public holidays in the UK.

If a public holiday falls on a weekend, there's usually a substitute holiday on the following Monday. An increasing number of British companies close during Christmas and New Year, e.g. from around noon or 5pm on 24th December to 1st January (inclusive) or 2nd January in Scotland. To compensate for this shutdown and, perhaps, other extra holidays during the year, employees may be required to work extra hours throughout the year, or may

Public Holidays

Date	Holiday
1st January	New Year's Day
2nd January	New Year's Bank Holiday (Scotland only)
17th March	St Patrick's Day (N. Ireland only)
March/April: Variable date	Good Friday
March/April: Monday after Good Friday	Easter Monday (not Scotland)
First Monday in May	May Bank Holiday
Last Monday in May	Spring Bank Holiday (not Scotland)
12th July	Orangeman's Day (N. Ireland only)
First Monday in August	Summer Bank Holiday (Scotland only)
Last Monday in August	Summer Bank Holiday (not Scotland)
30th November	St Andrew's Day (Scotland only)
25th December	Christmas Day
26th December	Boxing Day

be required to take part of their annual holiday entitlement. Part-time staff now have equal rights in this area.

You aren't usually required to work on Sundays and public holidays unless otherwise stated in your contract of employment. There are no statutory rights regarding what you should be paid for working on Sundays or public holidays, which depends on whether Sundays are included in your regular work pattern.

Some companies pay 1.5 times the usual rate on bank holidays, while others pay the standard rate. You may also be given time off in lieu. When employment involves working at weekends and on public holidays (e.g. shift working), you may be compensated in your basic salary or paid a shift allowance.

Compassionate & Special Leave

Whether or not you're paid for time off work, or time lost through unavoidable circumstances (e.g. public transport strikes or car breakdowns), depends on your employer, if you're paid monthly or weekly (e.g. with an hourly rate of pay) and, not least, whether you're required to punch a clock. The attitude in the UK to paid time off depends on your status and position. Executives and managers (who admittedly often work much longer hours than officially required) have much more leeway regarding time off than a factory worker.

All employees are allowed by law to take time off work for the following reasons:

- A pregnant woman is entitled to 'reasonable' paid time off for ante-natal care.
- A trade union official is entitled to paid time off for trade union duties and training for such duties, and employees may also be paid to attend union meetings during working hours (some make it a full-time occupation). Similarly, a safety representative is allowed paid time off in connection with his safety duties.
- Time off for public duties such as service as a Justice of the Peace, juror or court witness, councillor or school governor, or as a member of a statutory tribunal or authority, although your employer isn't required by law to pay you.
- If you're made redundant, you're entitled to 'reasonable' paid time off to look for a new job or to arrange training in connection with a new job.

Many British companies also provide paid compassionate or special leave on certain occasions, which may include your own or a family marriage, birth of a child, or the death of a close relative. The grounds for compassionate leave may be listed in your general conditions.

Pregnancy & Confinement

All women, irrespective of their length of service, are entitled to 52 weeks' maternity leave (26 weeks' 'ordinary' leave plus 26 weeks' 'additional' leave – although only the Department for Work & Pensions knows the reason for these designations).

Pregnant women are entitled to maternity leave and pay (known as statutory maternity pay or SMP), depending on the length of their employment (at least 26 weeks) and income (at least equal to the lower earnings limit for national insurance contributions). Part-time employees have equal rights. In 2016, SMP was 90 per cent of a woman's average weekly earnings (AWE) for the first six weeks and £139.58 (or 90 per cent of your pay if your AWE is lower) for the next 33 weeks. If you aren't eligible for SMP, you may be entitled to a maternity allowance from Jobcentre Plus or, failing that, Employment and Support Allowance (ESA). Visit www.gov.uk/maternity-allowance/how-to-claim or call Jobcentre Plus on 0345 608 8610 for more information.

Fathers-to-be or partners of pregnant women are entitled to two weeks' paid leave and may also qualify for up to 26 weeks' 'additional' leave.

Employment-related benefits such as private medical insurance, use of a company car and pension contributions must continue during the leave period. Some employers provide enhanced benefits, including the payment of full salary for some or all of the maternity-leave period. At the end of the 52-week period, you've the right to return to the same job. (Compulsory maternity leave is two weeks after the birth or four weeks if you work in a factory, during which time you aren't legally permitted to work.) Most companies count periods of absence for maternity leave as continuous employment for the purpose of calculating an employee's number of years' service, but not when calculating annual holiday.

Time off work for sickness in connection with a pregnancy is usually given without question, but it may be unpaid unless authorised by a doctor. You're guaranteed the right to 'reasonable' time off work for antenatal care without loss of pay, irrespective of how long you've been employed (usually a clinic or hospital appointment card must be produced).

A pregnant or nursing woman cannot be required to work overtime, and a woman cannot be dismissed because she's pregnant or for any reason connected with her pregnancy. If she's dismissed, she has an automatic claim for unfair dismissal, irrespective of her length of service. It's also illegal to refuse a woman a job because she's pregnant, provided this doesn't prevent her from doing the job.

Information about maternity rights and pay is available on the Gov.uk website (www.gov.uk/maternity-pay-leave). Other useful sources of information include ACAS (www.acas.org.uk) and Maternity Action (www.maternityaction.org.uk).

Retirement

The default retirement age was abolished in 2011, meaning that workers can no longer be forced to retire. However, the age at which the state pension is paid is being increased so working longer is becoming a necessity rather than a choice. Since April 2010, the state pension age has been 65 for both men and women, but is set to rise to 66 in the near future and to 67 a few years later. For more information, contact the Pension Service (0800-731 7898, www.gov.uk/contact-pension-service). The Future Pension Centre can advise on what age you can retire at and how much state pension you may be entitled to (0345-3000 168, www.gov.uk/future-pension-centre).

Redundancy

The Redundancy Payments Scheme covers most workers who are employed under a contract of employment, provided employees have at least two years' continuous service and meet the conditions outlined below. The main exceptions are those who've reached

> You qualify for redundancy pay if you're dismissed wholly or mainly due to your job being phased out, or when your employer wishes to reduce his workforce.

retirement age and continue to work, Crown servants, and apprentices, whose service ends at the end of their apprenticeship contract.

If you're made redundant, you're entitled to your normal notice period, or pay in lieu of notice, and are additionally entitled to redundancy pay. You're also usually entitled to reasonable time off work with pay to look for another job or arrange training. The amount of redundancy pay you receive depends on whether your employer pays the minimum amount required by law or more, either voluntarily or, for example, under pressure from trade unions. It may also be possible to take voluntary redundancy or early retirement and receive an early pension, e.g. in the case of ill health.

The Employment Protection (Consolidation) Act 1978 (as amended) states that an employee aged 18 to 65 who has worked continuously for 16 hours or more a week over a period of two years (or eight or more hours a week) continuously for five years is entitled to a statutory redundancy lump sum payment. The amount payable is based on a sliding scale depending on your age, length of service and salary. The older you are, the more redundancy pay you receive (pro rata). The basic payment is half a week's pay for each complete year of service after the age of 18 until age 22, one week for each year after the age of 22 until age 41, and one and a half weeks' pay for each year after the age of 41.

After the age of 64, the total amount you receive is reduced by one 12th for each complete month of your age above 64. The amount of redundancy payments payable reduces for those above retirement age; consult the Redundancy Payments Helpline (see below) for details.

There's a limit to the amount of a week's pay that may be taken into account, which in 2015 was £464. It changes annually, in line with the retail price index. The maximum amount payable in 2016 was £14,370 (30 weeks at £479 per week) after 20 years' service – the maximum period of employment taken into account. You can expect to receive your statutory redundancy payment at about the same time as you leave your job, and it's tax-free. However, any additional redundancy payments you receive from your employer may be taxable, although you should confirm the details with a tax office.

For further information about redundancy payments, contact the Redundancy Payments Helpline on 0345-145 0004 (www.gov.uk/redundancy-payments-helpline).

References

In the UK, an employer isn't legally obliged to provide an employee with a written reference. If you leave an employer on good terms, he'll normally provide a written reference on request. If your employer refuses to give you a written reference or gives you a 'bad' reference, it's advisable to ask your immediate boss or a colleague for a written reference. In the UK, prospective employers usually contact your previous employer (or employers) directly for a reference, orally or written. This can be bad news for employees, as they have no idea what has been said about them, and whether it was true or false.

Trade Union Membership

Trade unions went through a bad time in the '80s under the Conservatives, and were largely legislated into toothless tigers. Membership fell sharply by around 30 per cent, and this process was exacerbated when entire industries disappeared, and with them, their old-established trade union traditions. There were some 6.5 million employees trade union members in 2015, well below the figures at the peak of membership in 1979.

There are around 60 trade unions in the UK, ranging from major players such as Unison, the public sector workers' union with over 1.3 million members, to smaller organisations representing specialised trades. Since the Fairness at Work Act 2000, independent trade unions in organisations employing over 20 workers have had the right to claim recognition for collective bargaining if they can show that they enjoy majority support among the workforce through a ballot. Once recognised, they have rights to information and consultation and officials can take time off to carry out their duties.

By continental standards, this sounds utterly tame and yet seems an achievement when contrasted with the recent past. As a consequence of the Thatcher era, many companies are now non-union. Surprisingly, the majority of union members are now professionals, managers and service providers rather than manual workers, who often lack any protection at all. Industrial action taken by the lowest-paid workers, who often do the hardest and most unpleasant jobs, is rare and it's usually higher paid workers (who can cause the maximum disruption) who go on strike.

Whether you're better off as a member of a trade union depends on the industry in which you're employed. In those in which they're recognised, employees' pay and conditions are decided by a process of collective bargaining between trade unions and employers.

Employers aren't allowed to discriminate against an employee in selection, promotion, transfer or training, and neither can he be dismissed because he belongs or wishes to belong to a trade union, even if many companies are non-union and still don't officially recognise any trade unions. However, individual employees may be members. Legally, employees have the straightforward right to join or not join a union.

More information is available from the government's Gov.uk website and from ACAS. Another good source is the Trade Unions Congress (020-7636 4030, www.tuc.org.uk). The TUC's WorkSMART website (www.worksmart.org.uk) contains a wealth of information about workers' rights and other work-related issues.

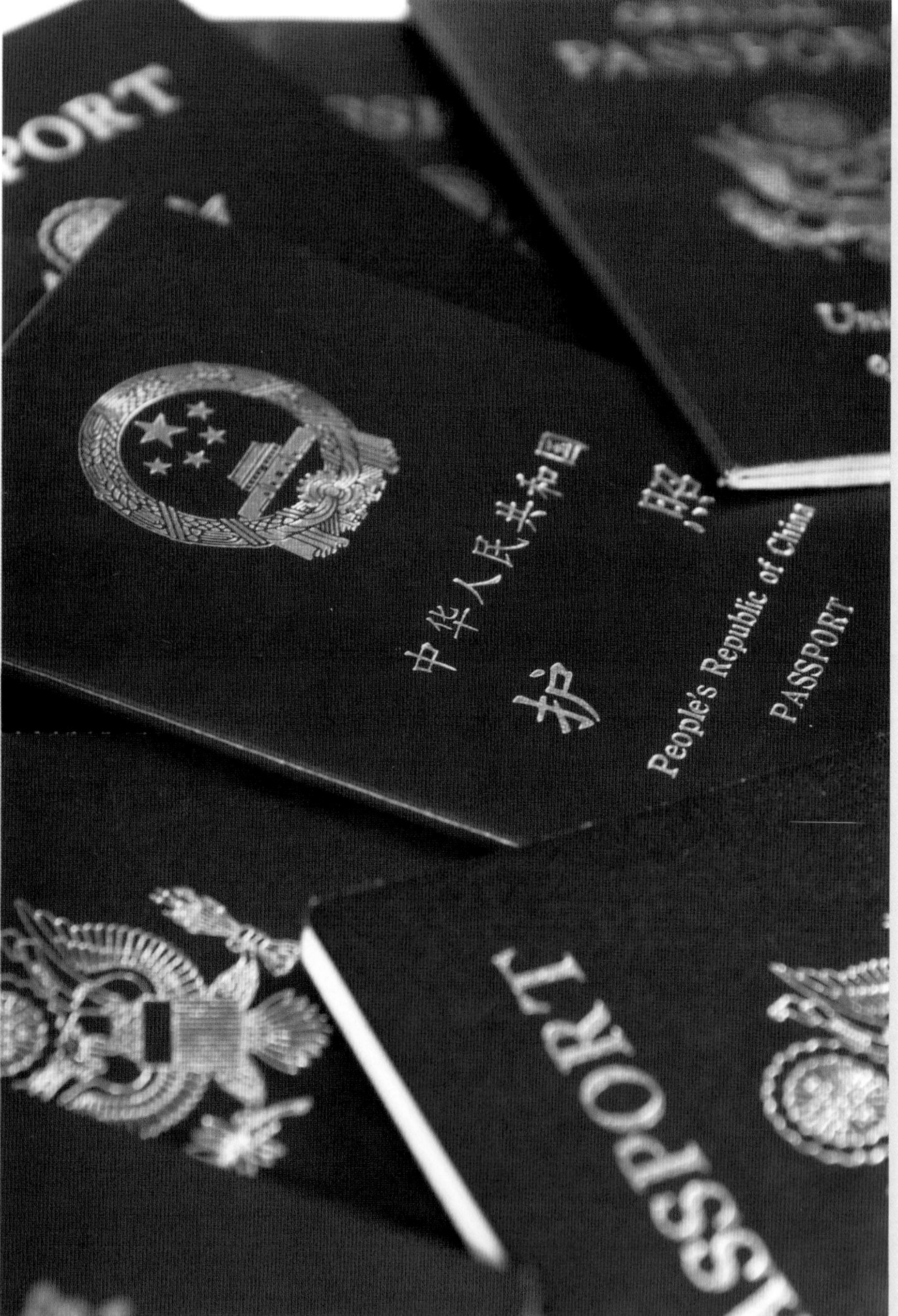
中华人民共和国
护照
People's Republic of China
PASSPORT

3.

PERMITS & VISAS

Before making any plans to live or work in the UK you must ensure that you've the appropriate entry documentation (e.g. a visa), as without it you won't be allowed into the country. If you aren't a national of an EU country or Switzerland you may need to obtain entry clearance (but see Brexit below). This applies to those intending to stay permanently, coming to the UK to work, and nationals of countries whose citizens require a visa to visit the UK. If you're in any doubt whether you require clearance to enter the UK you should enquire at a British Embassy, High Commission or other British Diplomatic Mission (collectively known as British Diplomatic Posts) overseas before making plans to travel to the UK.

The UK has strict laws restricting the entry of foreigners seeking political asylum and those who may be intending to look for work illegally. With the exception of those who aren't subject to immigration controls (e.g. EU citizens and Commonwealth citizens with a parent born in the UK), the onus is on anyone coming to the UK to prove that they won't violate the immigration laws.

You must 'satisfy the immigration officer' that you qualify under the immigration rules and officials aren't required to prove that you may break the laws and can refuse entry on the grounds of suspicion only. If you're refused entry, you'll be 'removed' and sent back to your home country at your own expense (this isn't the same as deportation and doesn't automatically prevent you returning at a later date). You're given the reason in writing and may appeal, but only after your departure if you don't have prior entry clearance (see **Entry Certificate** on page 51).

Nationals of some non-Commonwealth and non-EU countries who've been given permission to remain in the UK for over six months, or who've been allowed to work for over three months, are required to register with the police. When applicable, this may be stamped in your passport on entry or by UK Visas and Immigration, a division of the Home Office, when granting an extension of stay. The Home Office (called the Interior Ministry in many countries) has the final decision on all matters relating to immigration.

▲ Caution

Immigration is a complex subject and is undergoing sweeping changes as the government becomes increasingly selective about who it will allow into the country. As such, the information in this chapter is intended only as a general guide. You shouldn't base any decisions or actions on the information contained herein without confirming it with an official and reliable source. The latest information about immigration and permits can be obtained from UK Visa and Immigration (www.gov.uk/government/organisations/uk-visas-and-immigration).

BREXIT

The decision of the UK to leave the European Union (termed 'Brexit' – see page 18), due to take effect no later than the end of March 2019 – depending on the date the UK officially gives notice to leave and the process taking two years to complete – will end the automatic right of EU citizens to live and work in the UK. This doesn't mean that there will no longer be immigration from the EU, but prospective workers or residents will need to qualify and probably obtain a permit before doing so, and it's expected that it will be more difficult for unskilled/unqualified EU migrants to work in the UK.

This isn't expected to have any impact on immigration from non-EU countries, and could actually result in higher immigration from these countries. One of the key reasons that many Britons voted to leave the EU was the high and uncontrolled immigration from EU countries. Total net migration (people arriving minus those leaving) to the UK in the year ending June 2016 was 335,000, with EU net migration 189,000 and non-EU net migration 196,000.

ILLEGAL IMMIGRATION

Permit infringements are taken seriously by the authorities and there are penalties for breaches of regulations, including fines and even deportation for flagrant abuses. The police and immigration authorities can arrest anyone 'reasonably suspected' of being an illegal alien and can obtain search warrants to enter homes and places of employment. The penalties for harbouring illegal aliens are severe, with prison sentences and heavy fines imposed on offenders.

Carriers (i.e. airlines and shipping lines) are fined £2,000 plus costs for each passenger they land without valid documentation (especially visas). All vehicles, including private cars, may be searched on entering the UK if the authorities suspect there are stowaways on board. Owners, hirers or drivers of vehicles in which illegal immigrants have hidden may, similarly, be liable to a penalty of up to £2,000 for each illegal immigrant discovered, irrespective of whether they were aware of their presence.

UK VISAS & IMMIGRATION

UK Visas and Immigration (UKVI) is the Home Office department responsible for the UK visa system, and was formed from the section of the UK Border Agency (UKBA) which was disbanded in 2013. UKVI handles general enquiries about immigration rules and procedures and queries about specific cases. Like many government agencies, it encourages people to make contact online, although there are designated phone numbers depending on which country you're calling from.

The UKVI website (www.gov.uk/government/organisations/uk-visas-and-immigration) provides comprehensive information and enables you to download application forms and other printed material. The old public enquiry offices in Belfast, Birmingham (Solihull), Cardiff, Croydon, Glasgow, Liverpool and Sheffield have been rebranded as 'premium service centres' and you pay a hefty £500 surcharge to make your visa application in person (for addresses see www.gov.uk/ukvi-premium-service-centres/find-a-premium-service-centre).

> The FCO doesn't accept visa enquiries, nor can you phone UKVI direct about visa enquiries. Contact options are email, live webchat or phone, and the latter two options are subject to (quite high) charges.

UKVI is also responsible for issuing visas and providing information about who needs one, and is represented at British missions and embassies abroad – a complete list can be found on the Foreign & Commonwealth Office (FCO) website (www.gov.uk/government/organisations/foreign-commonwealth-office). Applicants can check whether they need a visa on the UKVI website and then apply for one via the Visa4UK website (www.visa4uk.fco.gov.uk) or www.gov.uk/apply-uk-visa. There are visa application centres in most countries (see www.gov.uk/find-a-visa-application-centre), some of which are operated in partnership with VFS Global (www.vfsglobal.com).

Points-based System

A points-based system (PBS) for work visa applicants was introduced in 2008 and was the largest shake up of the immigration system for 45 years. It was designed to help British businesses recruit the skills they need from abroad and assure the British public that only skilled migrants the country needs come to the UK. It replaced over 80 existing immigration routes with the following four tiers (each with different points' requirements), which were intended to make the system clearer and easier to understand. Tier 3 was aimed at lower-skilled workers and was never officially implemented, and has been discontinued.

- **Tier 1: High-value migrants** – entrepreners, investors, highly skilled people and those with 'exceptional talent', for example scientists and academics (no sponsor required);
- **Tier 2: Skilled Workers** with a job offer, for example doctors, engineers, professional sportspeople, ministers of religion (sponsor required);
- **Tier 4: Students** (sponsor required);
- **Tier 5: Youth Mobility and Temporary Workers**, for example charity workers and sportspeople taking part in competitions (sponsor usually required).

The points-based system only covers migrants from outside the EU and Switzerland, although there are some restrictions on nationals of countries that have recently joined the EU, i.e. Croatians. Migrants must pass a points-based assessment before they're given permission to enter or remain in the UK.

Because immigration rules change so quickly, the system was revised almost as soon as it was introduced:

- **Tier 1:** This tier has been subject to increasing restrictions and since 2011 the General category has only been available to people who already have permission to stay (leave to remain) in the UK. People with 'exceptional talent' are required to obtain an 'endorsement' of their abilities – judged by such UK worthies as the Arts Council and Royal Society – before making an application; entrepreneurs and investors need to show sufficient funds, i.e. £50-200,000 to start a business, while investors need a minimum of £1 million.
- **Tier 2:** Applications on this level must have sponsorship (from their employer) and, in most cases, a proposed salary of at least £20,800 a year (2016 figure). Periodically, a cap is set on the number of applicants, which varies with fluctuations in the jobs market.
- **Tier 4:** Students need a place on an approved course and funds to support themselves.
- **Tier 5:** Most applicants require a sponsor.

The number of points a migrant needs and the way that points are awarded depend on the tier under which the migrant is applying. Points are awarded to reflect a migrant's ability (e.g. a worker's skills), experience, age, English language skills and maintenance funds. It's a fair, transparent and objective system that enables potential migrants to assess their likelihood of making a successful application and should help reduce the number of failed applications.

Migrants applying under all tiers except tier 1 and tier 5 (Youth Mobility) require a sponsor. If a UK organisation wishes to recruit or sponsor a migrant under tiers 2, 4 or 5, they must first apply for a sponsor's licence. Under tiers 2 and 5, the sponsor must be a UK-based employer and under tier 4, a UK-based educational institution that meets 'highly trusted' status – the latter condition is to prevent poor quality or bogus colleges from sponsoring students. Migrants wishing to come to the UK under tier 5 (Youth Mobility) don't require a sponsor, but only certain nationalities can apply.

The emphasis on sponsorship effectively shifts much of the responsibility for migrants onto sponsors – employers and colleges – which must pass stringent checks in order to qualify. The sponsor obtains a certificate of sponsorship on the employee or student's behalf, without which they cannot apply for entry clearance. However, applicants must still satisfy the points criteria.

Entry Clearance

With the exception of EEA and Swiss nationals (while Britain is still a member of the EU at least), all foreigners entering the UK may need entry clearance – which confirms that a person qualifies under the Immigration Rules for entry to the UK – from the Home Office or a British Diplomatic Post in their country of residence, before their arrival in the UK.

Entry clearance in the form of a visa or entry certificate also applies to returning (non-British) residents who've been abroad for over two years.

Entry clearance is usually issued for a single entry, but may also allow multiple entries for a number of years, e.g. two (a fee is payable depending on the type of entry clearance issued). Clearance is necessary to come to the UK for the following reasons:

- Settlement as the dependant of a UK resident – 'settled' and 'settlement' are terms used to describe the situation of permanently resident foreigners living lawfully in the UK, with no time limit on their stay;
- Residence as a person of independent means;
- To undertake employment;
- For business purposes;
- To accompany or rejoin anyone in the above categories as a dependant;
- To be reunited with a spouse;
- To enter as a fiancé(e) planning marriage and settlement;
- To exercise rights of access to a child resident in the UK;
- To visit for longer than six months;
- For any purpose in the case of nationals of a visa country (see **Visas** below).

Unless there are special circumstances, you should always apply for entry clearance before arriving in the UK. What type of clearance you need depends on whether you're a visa national (see **Visas** below). Those entering the UK for employment must usually have a work permit (see **Work & Other Permits** below) issued by UKVI and denoted by their visa. When applying for entry clearance you must produce documentary evidence that you meet the requirements of the immigration rules covering the category under which you're applying. These may include any of the following:

- A certificate of sponsorship obtained by your sponsor;
- A letter from a bona fide university, polytechnic, college or school, stating that you've been accepted on a full-time course of study and that you've paid your fees in full (or have been awarded a grant or scholarship);
- Evidence that your qualifications for a job or a course of study are genuine and satisfactory, e.g. certificates, diplomas and references;
- Evidence that you've sufficient knowledge of the English language, if necessary;
- Evidence that you aren't a carrier of tuberculosis (TB) if you come from certain countries (see www.gov.uk/tb-test-visa/overview);
- Evidence that you're able to support yourself and any dependants during your stay in the UK without recourse to public funds (social security), e.g. a bank statement, letter from a bank or other evidence of financial support or, in the case of a student, a letter from a sponsor or scholarship agency.

If your stay is for a short period only, you may be required to give an assurance that you'll leave the UK at the end of that period.

Entry clearance is also required for any dependants you're bringing with you or who will join you in the UK. If applicable, you must prove that you're married and that you can support your dependants as well as yourself. Failure of your dependants to obtain entry clearance may mean that they're refused entry. When applying for entry clearance, you must complete forms requiring your first names (Christian or forenames), family name (surname) and date of birth. If these are written in a different order in your own culture, you need to establish how they will be written in English and always complete all forms in the same way. This is particularly important for those whose language isn't written in Roman script, e.g. Arabic, Chinese or Russian.

If you're refused entry clearance, you're given the reason in writing and told whether or not you've the right of appeal and the time limit within which you must do this. Always double check the time limits, as they're observed rigorously. If you're unsuccessful in this, don't travel to the UK, as you'll be refused entry. Entry clearance doesn't, however, guarantee you entry into the UK.

Reasons for refusing entry to someone with entry clearance include deceiving the authorities to obtain entry clearance (e.g. an undisclosed criminal record); a change of circumstances since the entry clearance was granted; a decision by the authorities that your presence in the UK isn't conducive to the public good (someone likely to ferment trouble); or when medical reasons make it undesirable to admit you. However, the e-Borders system which requires passengers to provide carriers with passport information prior to starting their journey, which is then passed to the Home Office, should reduce the chances of this happening.

Anyone who arrives in the UK with entry clearance and is refused entry has the right of appeal and cannot usually be sent back until the appeal has been heard.

Anyone entering the UK may be referred to a medical inspector for an examination at their port of entry. In practice, this is only carried out if travellers come from places where contagious diseases are particularly prevalent or where outbreaks have recently occurred. Those who give medical treatment as the purpose of their visit or who appear to be in bad health are also more likely to be examined. Admission can be refused on medical grounds, but this doesn't apply in the case of returning residents.

In all cases of correspondence or contact with British consular officials or Home Office departments, you must ensure that you fully understand everything and seek help if you aren't absolutely certain.

VISAS

Nationals of certain countries, officially called 'visa nationals', require a visa to enter the UK, irrespective of the purpose of their visit, e.g. holiday, residence or employment. If you need a visa and arrive without one, you'll be sent back to your home country at your own expense. Visitors' visas are issued for a maximum stay of six months and are never extended beyond this period. If you want to stay longer you must leave and apply for a new visa. Visa nationals aren't permitted to change their status. For the latest information about which nationalities require a visa, see Gov.uk's interactive tool (www.gov.uk/check-uk-visa).

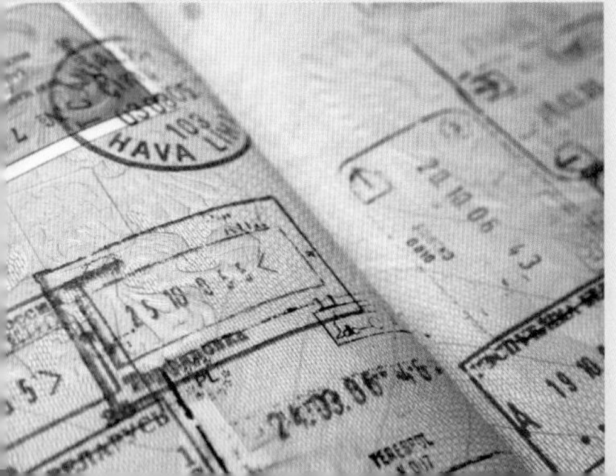

If your 'leave to remain' expires while you're in the UK and you haven't applied for an extension, you're committing a criminal offence and could be fined, imprisoned and/or recommended for deportation (see page 61). If you're deported, it's extremely difficult, if not impossible, to return to the UK.

If you're a visa national and planning a trip abroad while in the UK, you should ensure that you've a multiple-entry visa; otherwise you'll require a new visa from a British Diplomatic Post or visa application centre. Always check the latest rules before travelling. You're liable to examination at the port of entry to confirm that you qualify for re-admission, and reports of people having difficulties at this point aren't unknown. Before leaving the UK, ensure that your passport doesn't need renewing and that your leave to remain won't expire within the next few months. If your leave to remain is due to expire within around two months of your planned return, you should renew it before leaving the UK. You should make your application in person, as a postal application usually takes some time to be processed.

If you don't have time to obtain a visa before leaving the UK, or your multiple-entry visa expires while you're abroad, you must apply for a new visa from a British Diplomatic Post abroad before returning to the UK. For this you'll require the same documentation that was necessary to obtain your original entry clearance. On your return to the UK, you may be required to show evidence of your reason for coming to the UK and that you've sufficient funds to support yourself and any dependants (this also applies to non-visa nationals with limited leave to remain in the UK).

You may also need a visa to visit other countries if you're travelling from the UK; up-to-date information about this and other travel

> ☑ **SURVIVAL TIP**
>
> Since December 2007, all UK Visa applicants, including those wishing to study, have been required to provide biometric data – 10-digit finger scans and a digital photograph – as part of the application process.

requirements is available from travel agencies or your home country's embassy or consulate in the UK. Applications must be made in advance. Visas are usually valid for one to three months only and are often expensive. Note that it can take weeks or even months to obtain a visa for some countries, particularly some African and Middle Eastern countries, during which time the embassy may retain your passport. There are companies in major UK cities (e.g. London) that obtain visas for a fee.

Entry Certificate

Non-visa nationals, such as Commonwealth citizens coming to the UK for a stay of over six months, require an entry certificate. This requirement is applied to all nationalities who were previously exempt. If you're coming for six months or less, it isn't compulsory to apply for entry clearance before travelling to the UK. However, it may be in your best interest as there are only limited circumstances in which those without entry clearance are allowed to extend their permission to remain in the UK. Moreover, if you're refused entry to the UK for any reason, an entry certificate entitles you to an immediate right of appeal in the same way as a visa.

An entry certificate is issued by a British Diplomatic Post and is required by nationals of the following countries: Anguilla, Antigua, Ascension, Australia, Bahamas, Barbados, Belize, Bermuda, Botswana, Brunei, Canada, Cayman Islands, Dominica, Falklands, Gilbert & Ellice Islands, Grenada, Grenadines, Kiribati, Leeward Islands, Malaysia, Mauritius, Montserrat, Namibia, Nauru, New Hebrides, New Zealand, Papua New Guinea, St Helena, St Lucia, St Vincent, St Kitts & Nevis, Samoa, Seychelles, Sikkim, Singapore, Solomon Islands, Tonga, Trinidad & Tobago, Tristan da Cunha, Tuvalu, Vanuatu, Virgin Islands and Western Samoa.

WORK & OTHER PERMITS

It's difficult to obtain entry clearance to work in the UK if you don't qualify under a permit-free category (see below). Unless you're an entrepreneur or investor with a large amount of money to invest, permission to work in the UK must be obtained by an employer for a named worker. The permission takes the form of a certificate of sponsorship – a virtual document identified by its reference number – which is issued for a specific job and for a specified period.

Most permits are issued to skilled workers under tier 2, although temporary workers (tier 5) also require permission to work in the UK, as do volunteers. Rising unemployment in the last few years means that employers must meet rigorous conditions before they can employ non-EEA nationals, and the list of requirements and regulations is subject to frequent change.

The government publishes a shortage occupation list (regularly revised) that lists the types of jobs for which visa nationals may be required. In 2016, scientists, engineers and medical practitioners featured prominently, along with social workers, chefs and ballet dancers. For any position that isn't listed, the employer must ensure that the application passes the resident labour market test. This requires him to advertise the job extensively to ensure that no one already settled in the UK is available and qualified to do it. The salary and conditions of employment offered must be equal to those prevailing for similar jobs; the qualifications and experience must be exactly what's required and they must usually have been acquired outside the UK. Employees are expected to have an adequate knowledge of English.

In order to employ a non-EEA national, the employer must first obtain a sponsor licence and you should be sure that any organisation offering you a job is licensed to do so. Licences can only be obtained by legitimate organisations, companies and educational establishments, and they aren't issued to recruitment agencies intending to hire out the services of the worker in question to other parties.

Important

Spouses and children under 18 wishing to accompany or join a work permit holder in the UK must obtain entry clearance before travelling. Failure to do so may mean that they're refused entry.

If a prospective employee fits all the criteria the sponsor/employer must apply for permission to work on his behalf. Supporting documentation includes evidence of the applicant's qualifications and experience (including original references), the job description and evidence of advertising (plus full details of any replies received).

Another route open to tier 2 applicants is via an intra-company transfer. This allows staff and graduate trainees to be transferred to the UK by an overseas employer for the purposes of work, training or gaining specialist skills.

Applications for sponsorships and to sponsor employees are handled by UKVI, which has a sponsorship, employer and education helpline (0300-123 4699). Help is also available by email from the Business Helpdesk (businesshelpdesk@homeoffice.gsi.gov.uk) or see the Gov.uk website (www.gov.uk/uk-visa-sponsorship-employers). Applications can be made online and by post.

Most tier 2 general work permits are issued initially for up to three years, although they can be extended provided the certificate of sponsorship remains valid and the job qualifications and salary remain at or above the correct rate for the position.

If the overseas worker is already living in the UK the application must be made before their current permission to work expires, otherwise they must stop working while the application is being considered. In this case, passports and police registration certificates must also be submitted with the application, where applicable.

When an application has been approved, the sponsorship certificate number is forwarded to the prospective employee abroad.

Just having a sponsor and valid job offer isn't the end of the story. A work permit holder must also satisfy the points system by proving that they have sufficient knowledge of the English language and that they can provide accommodation and support any dependants without recourse to public funds such as benefits.

Permit holders aren't permanently restricted to the particular job for which their permit was issued, but are expected to remain in the same profession at an equivalent level and salary, e.g. you cannot switch from being a doctor to working in a shop. One of the reasons behind the closure of the tier 1 General category to applicants from outside the UK was that many 'highly skilled' migrants were discovered to be working in lower skilled jobs, such as driving taxis or working in supermarkets. The consent of the authorities is required in order to change jobs.

A work permit is valid for entry into the UK within six months of its date of issue and is usually issued for a period of one year, unless issued for a shorter period, or up to three years for tier 2 General applicants. Permits valid for one year can usually be extended on application to UKVI. It's difficult to obtain permission to employ someone who's already in the UK, who came here for a reason other than employment, e.g. as a visitor or a student.

Once a work permit holder has completed five years of employment in the UK, they may be able to apply for the removal of the time limit on their stay, which is termed 'settlement'. When the time limit is removed you may take any employment without reference to the authorities.

Certain categories of people can work full or part-time without a work permit, e.g. the wife of a work-permit holder, or, with certain restrictions, a student (see page 57), although permission is necessary in other cases.

Up to date information about sponsorship and work permits is provided on UK Visa and Immigration's website (www.gov.uk/government/organisations/uk-visas-and-immigration).

It's strictly forbidden for any non-EU national to work in the UK without permission. If you're discovered working without a permit or permission, you're liable to deportation or prosecution, which could lead to a heavy fine or even imprisonment. Your employer is also liable to a fine of around £10,000 per illegal employee.

EEA/Swiss Nationals

If you're an EEA/Swiss national you can enter the UK in order to take up or seek employment, establish a business or become self-employed without a work permit (but this may change in the future - see **Brexit** of page 18). You can remain in the UK for as long as you wish without obtaining a residence permit or registering with the police.

If any members of your household aren't EEA nationals, they should apply for a residence card. These cards aren't compulsory but provide proof that the holder is legally resident. For further information, contact the EEA residency enquiries – European enquiries contact centre (0300-123 2253).

Other British Nationals

In addition to British citizens with the right of abode in the UK, there are a number of British nationals who don't automatically have this right, termed 'other British nationals'. These are citizens of British colonies (or former colonies) who were granted British citizenship in the days when it was the ambition of the British Empire to paint the whole atlas pink, and bestow British citizenship on everyone (see page 281). There are a number of categories:

- **British Overseas Territories Citizen (BOTC):** Citizens of British colonies (e.g. Gibraltar) who only have the right to citizenship of that country, and who've been subject to British immigration law since 1962.
- **British National (Overseas):** This is a category created so that Hong Kong residents, who aren't regarded as Chinese citizens under Chinese nationality law, wouldn't become stateless when their BDTC status (see above) ended on 1st July 1997.

- **British Overseas Citizens:** People in former British colonies who were unable to gain citizenship of that country when independence was gained. These are mainly people of Indian and Chinese descent from East African countries, Malaysia and Singapore.
- **British Subjects:** Mainly people born in a princely state in India who weren't in India at the time of the passage of Indian independence and citizenship laws, and therefore didn't gain Indian citizenship.
- **British Protected People:** People from former colonies or territories previously under the protection of the UK, who were unable to gain citizenship on independence.

Any British national (except a BOTC) who enters the UK legally but for a temporary period, e.g. as a visitor, cannot, in practice, be deported, as he's effectively stateless and no other country would be under any obligation to receive him. A British national (as defined above) who's granted permission to settle in the UK must obtain entry clearance issued by a British Diplomatic Post before travelling. If he has dependants in the UK, he must show that he's able to support them without recourse to public funds.

Youth Mobility Scheme

The Youth Mobility Scheme replaced the working holidaymaker scheme in 2008, albeit with much greater restrictions. It allows (primarily) single people aged from 18 to 30 to come to the UK on an extended working holiday for a maximum period of two years. To qualify you must be a national of Australia, Canada, Japan, Monaco or New Zealand, or a British Overseas Territories, British Overseas or British Nationals (Overseas) citizen (see above).

Nationals of Hong Kong, South Korea and Taiwan may also apply, but need a certificate of sponsorship. Married couples can also apply to the scheme if both qualify, but applicants mustn't have dependent children aged under 18. You cannot apply again if you've already been to the UK under the working holidaymaker or youth mobility scheme.

> **☑ SURVIVAL TIP**
>
> The Youth Mobility Scheme also replaced a number of other programmes including those for au pairs, exchange students, e.g. the BUNAC scheme and the Japan youth exchange scheme.

Applicants need a tier 5 permit and must also meet the points requirement (see above). These include proving that you've sufficient funds (£1,890 in 2016) at the time of the application to cover your return journey and at least the first month after arrival. You must register with the police on arrival and be able to support yourself without recourse to public funds.

There are no restrictions on the type of employment you can do over the two years, which can be almost any sort of work, full- or part-time. You can also study, work as an au pair or pursue a career (professional sport and entertaining are excluded), although there are limits on self-employment. Any time spent outside the UK during the two-year period counts towards the maximum two years allowed in the country (from the date you were first given permission to enter the UK).

Note that it isn't possible to arrive as a visitor and apply for the Youth Mobility Scheme, as all applications must be made from outside the UK.

Entrepreneurs

If you wish to enter the UK to establish a business or work as self-employed and aren't an EU national, you must obtain entry clearance (see page 51) before arrival in the form of a tier 1 permit (entrepreneur). The government is keen to attract wealthy entrepreneurs and has provided a fast track to settlement (see page 61) for those who establish successful businesses offering employment to settled workers.

To set up in business you must show that you're investing a minimum of £50,000 and can support yourself (and any dependents) without any help from the state. The £50,000 limit is mainly aimed at graduate and post-graduate students wishing to remain in the UK, and the rules are slightly more relaxed if you can put up a £200,000 investment. The visa allows you to start up or take over one business or more, but you must remain self-employed and cannot boost your income by working for someone else. A business can take one of the following forms: sole trader, a partnership, or a UK registered company.

Incentives to set up in business are available to people from overseas on the same basis as they are to British nationals, including grants, training assistance and business premises for rent or lease. Financial assistance is available for manufacturing investment that's judged to be particularly beneficial to the British economy. British government and EU financial incentives may be available for businesses established in areas where there's high unemployment or other economic problems (designated 'assisted areas').

A business person with the appropriate entry clearance may be accompanied by his spouse and any children under 18, who are initially admitted for one year provided they also have entry clearance. Annual extensions are granted, provided the immigration rules continue to be met, and settlement is normally granted after five years' residence or, in certain cases, three years (see page 61).

If you don't qualify as a business person, a self-employed person with special talents or skills (e.g. an entertainer, artist, sportsman or sportswoman), or aren't covered by the points-based tier 1 Entrepreneur category, it's difficult to obtain permission to enter the UK and work as a self-employed person.

Investors

A non-EEA national who has at least £2 million at his disposal can apply for a tier 1 Investor permit. An investor must deposit a minimum of £2 million in sterling in a regulated financial institution based in the UK. The initial entry clearance is for three years but can be extended and it's possible to apply for settlement after three years of continuous residency, or sooner if your assets amount to over £5 million.

Spouses & Partners

The spouse of a non-EEA national with permission to live or work in the UK is granted entry clearance provided the marriage is genuine, the couple have been together for at least two years and have actually met (the marriage cannot be arranged blind, as many are in Asian countries), and that they have somewhere to live and can support themselves without recourse to public funds. This means being able to prove that you or your partner have an income of at least £18,600 a year, plus £3,800 for one dependent child and £2,400 for each additional child.

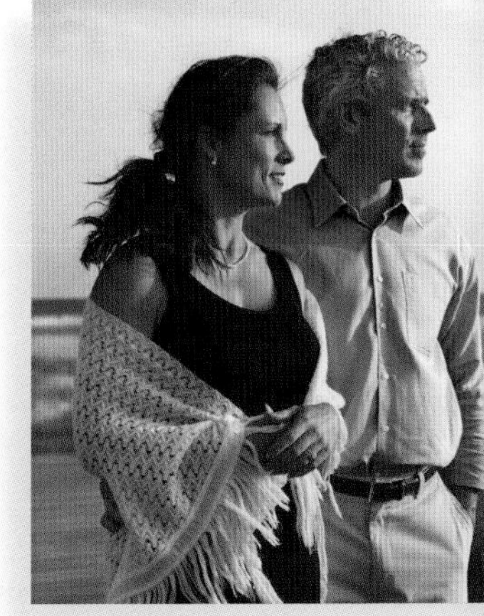

Both parties must be aged 21 or over and since November 2010 there's been a requirement to prove that you can speak English, evidenced by passing an approved language test in your home country unless you come from an English-speaking country or have a degree which was taught in English. An application for entry clearance must be made to a British Diplomatic Post or via a visa application centre before travelling to the UK.

On arrival, a spouse is given permission to stay and work for 33 months. Towards the end of the period provided the couple are still married and intend to carry on living together the spouse may apply to remain in the UK longer or even permanently – this is known as indefinite leave to remain (ILR) and since 2012 it has only been available if you've lived with your partner in the UK for five years. If you marry while in the UK on another type of visa, e.g. student, it may be possible to switch to a spouse visa provided you meet all the requirements and have leave to remain of more than six months – but you cannot arrive on a visitor visa and marry in an attempt to prolong your stay.

All the above conditions also apply to civil partnerships and to unmarried/same-sex partnerships, although in the latter instance the partners must have been together for two years prior to making their application.

Fiancé(e)s & Proposed Civil Partners

The fiancé(e) or proposed civil partner of a non-EEA national settled in the UK who wishes to enter for marriage and settlement must obtain entry clearance before travelling to the UK. Applicants must satisfy officials that a marriage or registration ceremony will take place within six months and that the 'primary purpose of marriage isn't to obtain entry or remain in the UK'. Both partners must be aged 21 or over and intend to live together permanently, and they must have actually met.

'Marriages of convenience' to foreigners aren't illegal unless performed for money and, in any case, don't give foreigners the right to enter or remain in the UK. You must also show that you won't call on public funds and that you've access to funds and accommodation in the UK without having to work. The English language requirement for spouses and partners also applies (see above).

If you're permitted entry to the UK as a fiancé(e), you're initially granted entry for six months in order to get married, during which time you're forbidden to work. If you enter the UK for a purpose other than marriage, e.g. as a tourist or student, and subsequently get married to someone who has permanent resident status in the UK, you must return home and apply to come back as a spouse.

After marriage, you're initially permitted to stay for two years and six months with no restrictions on working, after which you need to apply to extend your visa. After five years you may be eligible to apply for settlement (see page 61). Foreigners with limited leave to remain in the UK who get married to a British or EEA national or a British resident, thus acquiring the right to remain in the UK, often find themselves subject to intense scrutiny by the immigration authorities.

> It's unofficially estimated that thousands of foreigners enter into marriages of convenience each year in order to remain in the UK, with 'professional' brides and grooms charging up to £5,000 a time!

Children

Children under 18 (including natural children, step-children and adopted children) are granted permission to remain in the UK when both their parents are temporarily resident in the UK or have been granted permission to settle. An application for entry clearance for

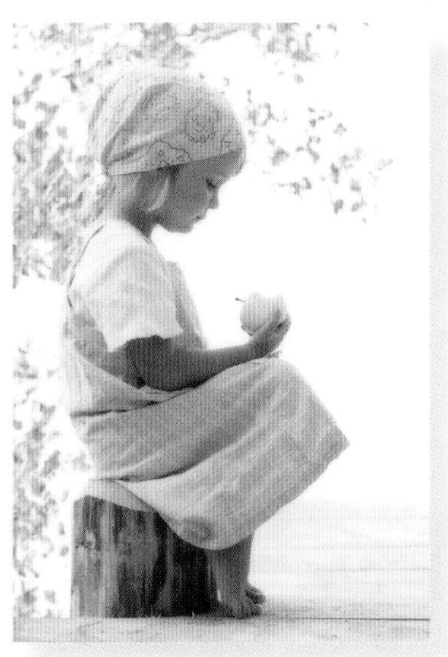

children must be made to a British Diplomatic Post before travelling to the UK. If only one parent is resident in the UK, he must show that he has sole responsibility for a child's upbringing or that serious or compelling family or other circumstances render their exclusion undesirable.

In practice, it's usual for a child under 12 to be allowed to join a single parent, particularly the mother, in the UK. Children over 18 must usually qualify for entry clearance in their own right, although some consideration is given to unmarried daughters under 21 with no close relatives in their home country. Children must be maintained without recourse to public funds and in 2016, a couple applying to bring in a spouse and one child must show they have an annual income of at least £22,400.

Relatives

Apart from EU nationals, foreigners permanently resident in the UK may invite relatives who are abroad, other than a spouse or children under 18, to live with them under restricted circumstances. The widowed mother, grandmother, father or grandfather of a British resident may be granted such permission, provided they're aged over 65, or both parents may be if one is over 65. A parent or grandparent aged over 65 who has remarried may be admitted if he or she cannot look to the spouse or children of that second marriage for support. Other relatives aged under 65 and over 18 are admitted only if the authorities deem that 'exceptional compassionate circumstances' exist.

In all cases, a British resident must be able to support and provide accommodation for his dependants without recourse to public funds. They must have been financially dependent on him for some time prior to coming to the UK, and must usually have no close relatives in their home country.

Students

Since 2008 all non-EEA and Swiss students have been subject to the points-based system for students (tier 4). Any student applying to study in Britain or wishing to extend their stay must be sponsored by a UK-based educational institution which has been registered with UK Visas and Immigration as a licensed sponsor. They must fulfil the points requirement, which is based on a number of factors including confirmation of acceptance for studies (CAS) on a course with an approved education provider, their English language skills and maintenance funds. The only students who can study without a visa are student visitors on a course of study of six months or less who are non-visa nationals, and even then they will find it easier if they first obtain an entry certificate.

The student category has been tightened up due to the large number of applicants – students account for around two-thirds of non-EU migrants entering the UK each year – and abuse of the system, whereby many students studying at private colleges have disappeared off the radar and, often, into the jobs market. The government sees restricting the number of foreign students in the UK as one way of reducing immigration numbers and it's possible that in future foreign students may only be admitted to attend leading universities. As always, check for the latest situation with a UK diplomatic post in your own country before making any plans.

Under the current rules, students are permitted to enter the UK only for the duration of a course, and must convince the authorities that they intend to leave Britain at the end of their course of study. The course must be full or mostly full-time and must occupy a minimum of 15 hours a week during the daytime (9am to 5pm). You cannot combine a variety of part-time courses in order to make up the required 15 hours of study per week, and evening courses don't qualify as full-time study. For details of the types of courses that have approval, see www.gov.uk/tier-4-general-visa/overview.

You must have sufficient funds to pay your course fees and to support yourself. In the case of married students, you may be able to bring your spouse and children under 18 (if accompanied by them), although this depends on the level of course you're taking and, of course, you must be able to support your dependents without recourse to public funds. You must prove that you're married by producing a marriage certificate. If your country of residence has strict foreign exchange controls, it's important to make arrangements for banking facilities in the UK or for money to be sent to you.

The spouse of a student and children under 18 aren't permitted to work unless they've been given leave to enter or remain in the UK for 12 months or more or if the course is below degree level. On arrival, you must have a letter from the college or school where you've been accepted as a student stating your study hours, the length of your course and that you've paid (or can pay) your fees. The authorities may check that you're attending classes. If you're permitted to enter the UK to study, you're usually granted permission to remain for the period of your course or at least one year, unless you're enrolled in a short course. You may be required to register with the police.

Students who've been granted leave to stay for over six months and don't have a stamp in their passports prohibiting employment may take part-time work (evenings and weekends up to a maximum of 20 hours per week, depending on the type of course you're taking) or full-time holiday employment. However, you shouldn't rely on finding part-time work in order to help pay for your course or living expenses, as this may be impossible in many parts of the UK.

There's no need to obtain permission before earning some money, although restrictions still exist. As the consequences of breaking the law can be extreme, and regulations change at regular intervals, always check with your college welfare officer about the prevailing situation before taking a job. You can download guidance notes from the UK Council for International Student Affairs (UKCISA, www.ukcisa.org.uk).

If you're formally prohibited from working in the UK, you must first

apply to UKVI to have the prohibition lifted before your college can apply for permission to organise practical work experience.

Overseas students aren't permitted to work in the UK after completing their studies unless there are exceptional circumstances, e.g. a student is highly qualified in a field of work where there's an acute shortage of skills. This is the case at the moment in electronics, engineering, technology and some health-related areas. If you wish to stay in the UK and work, you must find an employer who's licensed to sponsor you under the tier 2 skilled workers scheme.

Prospective students and those planning to study for less than six months (and their dependants) have no right of appeal against refusal of entry clearance and refusal of leave to enter, although they will receive a detailed explanation why their application was refused and can then make a second application.

Au Pairs

Under the points-based system, au pairs come under tier 5 (Youth Mobility Scheme), which allows young people to come and experience life in the UK for up to two years, but this is limited to the nationals of certain countries (see **Youth Mobility Scheme** on page 54).

Medical Treatment

A foreign national who wishes to enter the UK for medical treatment must satisfy the immigration officer that he has been accepted for consultation or treatment as a private patient, and that the latter is of finite duration. Evidence must be available that he can pay for it and support himself while undergoing treatment. He may also be medically examined on arrival before being permitted entry, and anyone suffering from a communicable (contagious) disease may be refused entry.

Visas are issued for either six or 11 months and extensions are possible only if the visitor provides evidence that it's necessary from someone of NHS consultant rank or who appears in the Specialist Register of the General Medical Council. Visitors aren't permitted to enter or remain in the UK in order to receive treatment on the National Health Service.

Visitors

EU and Swiss nationals are free of restrictions. Non-EU nationals can visit the UK for a period of up to six months as tourists, to visit family and friends or undertake business activities, but entry clearance is still necessary (see page 51). If in doubt about what you must do, contact a British Diplomatic Post before arranging travel. Although there's nothing to stop anyone leaving the UK for a few days after remaining for six months, and then returning for another six months, if the authorities think that someone is spending more time in the UK than in their country of origin (or residence), or are really living in the UK, entry will be refused.

> ☑ **SURVIVAL TIP**
>
> Visitors have no right of appeal against refusal of entry clearance and refusal of leave to enter, although they can make a second application after receiving an explanation why their original application was refused.

The passports of visitors, who of course aren't entitled to work in the UK, may be stamped with 'no work or recourse to public funds', and this is strictly enforced. Visitors may be required to convince immigration officers that they're staying for a short period only and won't attempt to find work in the UK. You may be asked to prove that you can support yourself financially during your stay or that you've relatives or friends who can support you, and to show a return ticket or the funds to buy one.

Visitors are usually given permission to stay for six months, even when planning a short visit only. If you're given permission to stay for less than six months on entry, you can apply to extend your stay up to a maximum of six months. If you want to establish temporary residence for longer than six months and believe that you're eligible under the immigration rules, you should apply at a British Diplomatic Post before coming to the UK. This may apply if you're an academic or are visiting a child in school.

Frequent visitors (e.g. business people) can apply for a multiple-entry visitor's visa, valid for one, two, five or ten years. Non-EEA nationals may transact business during a visit, but unpaid employment and self-employment are forbidden in addition to paid employment and professional activity. Business visitors may attend trade fairs, conferences, short classroom training courses and meetings, provided such activities are essential for fact-finding purposes as recipients of services or briefings by British businesses. Prospective entrepreneurs can apply for a special six-month visit via to arrange their funding, prior to applying for a tier 1 work permit.

Refugees

The only people who don't need to apply for refugee status on arrival in the UK are those whose refugee status has already been decided abroad under the terms of the United Nations Refugee Convention. Otherwise, to be granted refugee status in the UK, you must prove that you've 'a well-founded fear of persecution in your own country for reasons of race, religion, nationality, or membership of a particular social group or political opinion'.

Since 2000, the provisions of the Human Rights Act have also come into play. This forbids the authorities from breaching a person's fundamental human rights, which means that if someone can show that return to the country from which they fled would do this, they must be offered protection. People whom the Home Office believes would be in danger if they returned home, even if they don't fall into the above categories, may also be permitted to stay.

If you arrive in the UK seeking asylum, you should apply for it immediately on arrival. If you're already in the UK and political events in your home country make it impossible or dangerous for you to return there, you can apply to the screening unit in Croydon (020-8196 4524 for appointments). Asylum seekers may be fingerprinted and in certain circumstances may be detained while their application is being decided.

The Home Office endeavours to decide on applications within six months, but there's usually a huge backlog of cases and it can take much longer. Asylum seekers aren't allowed to work in the UK while their case is being considered although if it still isn't decided after 12 months, you can apply for permission to work. While an application for asylum is pending, you're unable to travel abroad, although, if you're granted asylum you can apply for a United Nations Travel Document.

If your application is refused, you've the right of appeal. Appeals are heard by the Tribunal Service for Immigration and Asylum, which is independent of UKVI. If the Home Office believe that you could have claimed asylum in a safe third country, which you passed through on your way to the UK, it may try to remove you there to pursue your claim further. Some legal options remain to you, but taking professional advice is vital.

If you need help with claiming asylum or supporting yourself while waiting for a decision, or you've been refused asylum, there are a number of agencies which can help. The government runs the Asylum Support Application UK helpline on 0808-8000 631 or you can turn to the independent charity Asylum Help (0808-8000 630, http://asylumhelpuk.org). Another good source of advice is the Refugee Council (PO Box 68614, London E15 9DQ, 020-7346 6700, www.refugeecouncil.org.uk).

For more information, visit UK Visas and Immigration's website (www.gov.uk/browse/visas-immigration/asylum).

SETTLEMENT

Settlement is the name given to the status of permanent residence in the UK, which means you can stay in the UK indefinitely without any restrictions on working or the need for a work permit. A foreigner married to a British citizen can apply for settlement (also known as indefinite leave to remain or ILR) after five or, in some cases, 10 years of residency. Foreign nationals who've held a residence permit for five years and who've been in continuous employment, self-employment or business in the UK, can also apply for settlement. Settlement may also be granted to the spouse of anyone who qualifies for settlement, provided both partners have been resident in the UK on the same temporary status for the same period.

The Life in the UK test is a computerised test consisting of 24 multiple-choice questions based on a government handbook. It was originally conceived as a citizenship test and still applies to EEA nationals who wish to become UK citizens. The test is taken at an approved test centre and the pass mark is around 75 per cent. It isn't easy – many UK nationals would have trouble passing it first time – but you can take the test as many times as necessary until you pass.

Since 2007, any non-EEA nationals applying for settlement must first prove that they have sufficient knowledge of language and life in the UK (KOL), unless they're in an exempted category, e.g. aged over 65. To do this they either take the Life in the UK test (see box above) or take and pass an approved course on English language and citizenship. For more information, see the UKVI website (www.gov.uk/english-language).

New rules introduced in 2011 have made settlement harder. Applicants must have no criminal convictions while work permit holders must meet the same income criteria as they did when they last renewed their visa. The government is keen to halt the natural progression to settlement by temporary residents successively renewing their permits and it's likely that obtaining settlement will become more difficult in future.

DEPORTATION

Any infringements concerning work permits, entry clearance, overstaying leave to remain and police registration are taken seriously by the authorities. If you break the immigration laws, the Home Secretary can issue a deportation order sending you back to your own country (at your own expense). The grounds for deportation include:

- Illegal entry into the UK;
- Failure to comply with your conditions of entry, e.g. working without a permit or official permission;
- Overstaying your leave to remain without obtaining an extension;
- Conviction of a criminal offence for a person aged over 17 (when deportation is recommended by a court);
- Your presence isn't considered to be in the public interest;
- Being the dependant of a deportee.

Anyone breaking the immigration laws also faces a fine and/or imprisonment. If, in the opinion of the immigration authorities, someone entered the UK illegally or by deception, then he can be ejected from the country under a process called removal without a court or appeal process. Police and immigration officers have the right to apprehend (without a warrant) anyone whom they 'reasonably suspect' is in breach of the immigration law.

Orford Craft Shop

4.
ARRIVAL

On arrival in the UK to take up employment or residence, your first task is to negotiate immigration and customs, which are overseen by the Border Force (the section of the Home Office that controls British borders). Non-EU nationals must complete a landing card on arrival in the UK. These are distributed on all international flights to the UK and are available from the information or purser's office on ships and ferries.

The UK isn't a signatory to the Schengen (www.schengenvisainfo.com/schengen-visa-countries-list) security agreement (named after a Luxembourg village on the Moselle River where the agreement was signed), which came into effect on 1st January 1995 and introduced an open-borders policy between 26 European countries. The UK and Ireland aren't members but take part in some aspects of Schengen, such as police and judicial co-operation in criminal matters, the fight against drugs and the Schengen Information System (SIS). Therefore anyone arriving in the UK from a 'Schengen' country must go through the normal passport and immigration controls.

In addition to information about immigration and customs, this chapter contains checklists of tasks to be completed before, or soon after, arrival and when moving house, plus suggestions for finding local help and information.

IMMIGRATION

When you arrive in the UK, the first thing you must do is go through Passport Control, which is usually divided into two areas: 'European Union (EU)/EEA & Swiss Nationals' and 'All Other Passports'. Make sure you join the right queue. Passport control is staffed by immigration officers who have the task of deciding whether you're subject to immigration control, and if so, whether or not you're entitled to enter the UK. You must satisfy the immigration officer that you're entitled to enter the UK under whatever category of the immigration rules you're applying to do so. Present your passport to the immigration officer with the following, as requested:

- Entry clearance (visa or entry certificate);
- A completed landing card (all non-EEA nationals);
- A letter from a bona fide educational establishment stating that you've been accepted on a full-time course of study;
- Evidence that your qualifications for a job or a course of study are adequate, e.g. certificates or diplomas;
- Evidence that you're able to support yourself and any dependants during your stay without recourse to public funds, e.g. a bank statement or letter from a bank, or evidence of financial support such as cash, travellers cheques and credit cards;
- Evidence that any children travelling with you are related to you or that you've permission to bring them into the UK (birth or adoption certificate, letter of permission);
- If your stay in the UK is for a short period only, you may need to give an assurance that you'll leave at the end of that period.

There are automatic ePassport gates at some airports that you can use if you've a recent EU biometric passport, i.e. one with a 'chip' in it. These gates use facial recognition technology to check your identity against the photo in your passport.

If you leave the UK for any reason after your initial entry, e.g. for a holiday, you'll be required to produce the same documents for re-admission. If you're entering the UK from a country other than an EU member state you may also be required to have immunisation certificates. Check the requirement in advance at a British Diplomatic Post abroad before arriving in the UK.

Since 2009 the Home Office has been progressively introducing fingerprint checks for holders of biometric visas and biometric residence permits, which contain the applicant's fingerprint information; this is a quick process using an electronic scanner.

The UK immigration authorities aren't required to establish that you'll violate the immigration laws and can refuse your entry on the grounds of suspicion only.

ENTRY REFUSAL

If you're refused entry into the UK, your legal position depends on whether or not you obtained entry clearance (see page 51) before arrival, as described below:

With Entry Clearance

If you're refused entry and have entry clearance (i.e. a visa, entry certificate or work permit), you cannot, in most cases, immediately be sent back to your home country, but are permitted to make an appeal (in the first instance to an independent adjudicator) and are allowed to remain in the UK until it's been heard. However, there's no right of appeal in the case of people with visitor's visas, unless they're coming as 'family visitors' within the terms of the immigration rules, or as prospective or short-term students on a course of six months or less.

You're given the reason for refusal in writing and told how to make an appeal against the decision. There's a strict time limit within which an appeal must be made and in the hands of the authorities. The address to which it must be sent is on the Notice of Appeal itself (if you're returning it by post, use the special delivery service).

You should immediately seek legal advice by contacting a regulated immigration advisor (see www.gov.uk/find-an-immigration-adviser) or the nearest Citizens Advice Bureau (www.citizensadvice.org.uk). If you're a student, you can contact the United Kingdom Council for International Student Affairs (UKCISA, 9-17 St Albans Place, London N1 0NX, 020-7788 9214, open weekdays 1-4pm, www.ukcisa.org.uk).

If you entered the UK to work or study, you should continue with your plans, but it would be unwise to make any long-term commitments (such as paying for a long course of study or signing a long lease on a property), in case you lose your appeal and must leave the UK. Your action pending an appeal may depend on the advice you receive, regarding the strength of your case and the likely outcome of your appeal.

Without Entry Clearance

If you've no entry clearance, you're usually required to return to your home country (or the country from where you arrived) immediately, although you may be given a short period of temporary admission until a final decision is made. If you aren't granted temporary admission you may be held in a detention centre, e.g. at Heathrow airport. If this happens you need to obtain legal advice immediately by contacting a regulated immigration advisor (www.gov.uk/find-an-immigration-adviser).

If you cannot convince immigration to allow you to stay, you should leave the UK voluntarily. If you refuse to leave voluntarily (or if you go into hiding), you'll be detained and forcibly removed, which could make it impossible for you to return to the UK in the future. If you leave voluntarily, there's no bar on re-entry, provided you can satisfy the immigration officials on your return. Contact anyone necessary before leaving.

You can appeal against the refusal, but only after you've returned to your home country.

CUSTOMS

When you enter the UK to take up temporary or permanent residence, you can usually import your personal belongings duty and tax free. Any duty or tax due depends on where you came from, where you purchased the goods, how long you've owned them, and whether duty and tax has already been paid in another country. There are no restrictions on the importation of goods purchased tax and duty paid in another EU country, although there are limits for certain goods, e.g. tobacco, beer and wine (see page 277).

All ports and airports in the UK use a system of red, green and blue channels. Red means you've something to declare and green that you've nothing to declare, i.e. no more than the customs allowances, no goods to sell, and no prohibited or restricted goods. Blue channels may only be used by passengers arriving from another EU country. If you're certain that you've nothing to declare, go through the green channel (or blue if arriving from within the EU); otherwise you should go through the red channel. Customs officers make random checks on people going through the green and blue channels, and there are stiff penalties for smuggling.

If you're arriving by ferry with a motor vehicle, random checks can be rigorous – even to the point of dismantling the vehicle in search of undeclared or prohibited items!

A list of all items that you're bringing in is useful, although the customs officer may still want to examine your belongings. If you need to pay duty or tax, it must be paid at the time the goods are brought into the country. Customs accept cash (sterling or euro notes only) and major debit and credit (MasterCard and Visa) cards. If you're unable to pay on the spot, customs will keep your belongings until you pay the sum due, which must be paid within the period noted on the back of your receipt. Postage or freight charges must be paid if you want the goods sent on to you.

Your belongings may be imported up to six months before, but no more than one year after your arrival, after transferring your residence. They mustn't be sold, lent, hired out, or otherwise disposed of in the UK (or elsewhere in the EU) within one year of their importation, without first obtaining customs authorisation.

If you're shipping your personal belongings (which includes anything for your family's personal use – such as clothing, cameras, television and stereo, furniture and other household goods) – unaccompanied to the UK, you must complete (and sign) customs form C3, obtainable from your shipping agent and HM Revenue & Customs (www.gov.uk/government/organisations/hm-revenue-customs), and attach a detailed packing list. If you employ an international removal company, they will handle the customs clearance and associated paperwork for you. Any items originally obtained in the UK or within the EU can be imported into the UK free of customs and excise duty or VAT, provided:

- Any customs duty, excise duty or VAT was paid and not refunded when they were exported from the UK (or the EU in the case of customs duty).
- They were in your private possession and use in the UK before they were exported.
- They haven't been altered abroad, other than necessary repairs.
- They're brought back within three years.

The personal belongings you're allowed to bring into the UK duty and tax free depend on your status.

PROHIBITED & RESTRICTED ITEMS

The following items are prohibited:

- Controlled drugs (e.g. opium, heroin, ecstasy, morphine, cocaine, cannabis, amphetamines, and LSD),
- Offensive weapons (e.g. flick knives and any knives designed as a weapon or disguised to look like everyday objects, swordsticks, knuckledusters, truncheons and some martial arts weapons).
- Pornographic material, in particular material featuring children or acts of extreme violence, i.e. porn which isn't freely available in the UK.

The following goods are restricted, although some may be imported with a special licence:

- Firearms, including gas pistols, electric shock batons and self-defence sprays, ammunition and explosives (including fireworks). See www.gov.uk/guidance/import-controls-on-offensive-weapons for the regulations concerning the importation of firearms. Note that it's illegal to own a handgun in the UK and the ownership of other guns is strictly controlled (except among criminals!).
- Live animals. Illegally imported animals are either exported immediately or destroyed and the owners are always prosecuted. They face (and invariably receive) a heavy fine and/or imprisonment. The introduction of the PETS Travel Scheme (see page 294) has made it both easier and cheaper to bring in certain pets legally, although this doesn't cover farm animals such as pigs or chickens, and there are further restrictions on birds. Any animal not covered by PETS must go into quarantine for six months. For more information, contact the Pet Travel Scheme Helpline (0370-241 1710, pettravel@ahvla.gsi.gov.uk, www.gov.uk/take-pet-abroad).

> **▲ Caution**
>
> It's a criminal offence to attempt to smuggle an animal into the UK – and it's usually discovered.

- Endangered animals or plants or products made from them. This includes animals and all birds, whether alive or dead (e.g. stuffed) and certain articles derived from protected species, including ivory, reptile leather, fur, skins and goods made from them. These can only be imported if you've a valid CITES permit (www.cites.org).
- Meat, poultry and most of their products (whether cooked or not), including ham, bacon, sausage, paté, eggs and milk. Certain fish or fish eggs are also prohibited. You can check which items are banned or

restricted from your country of origin via the DEFRA personal import rules database (www.gov.uk/personal-food-plant-and-animal-product-imports).

- Certain plants, seeds, vegetables, bulbs and fruits – although it's a complicated subject. For information, contact the Food and Environment Research Agency (FERA, 0300-1000 313).
- Non-approved radio transmitters and cordless telephones.
- Rough (uncut or unpolished) diamonds from outside the EU.

Counterfeit or fake goods, such as DVDs, clothes and handbags, from non-EU countries may be confiscated on arrival in the UK.

For further information concerning anything other than animals, contact DEFRA's Customer Contact Unit (Nobel House, 17 Smith Square, London SW1P 3JR, 03459-335577 or +44-20-7238 6951 from outside the UK, defra.helpline@defra.gsi.gov.uk, www.gov.uk/government/organisations/department-for-environment-food-rural-affairs).

If you're caught trying to smuggle any goods that aren't duty and tax free customs may confiscate the goods, and if you hide them in your car, they can confiscate that as well! If you attempt to import prohibited items you may also be liable to criminal charges or deportation.

POLICE REGISTRATION

Nationals from certain countries are required to register with the police within seven days of their arrival in the UK, even when staying in temporary accommodation. This depends on the type of entry clearance granted and the length of stay. When applicable, the requirement to register with the police is stamped in your passport, either on entry or by UK Visas and Immigration (UKVI) when granting your entry clearance or an extension of stay. In the case of an extension, you'll have seven days to comply.

Police registration applies to visa nationals aged 16 or over who've been given limited permission to enter or stay in the UK (confusingly called 'leave to enter' or 'leave to remain') for longer than six months. If your stay is of less than six months' duration, it doesn't apply – travellers on short-duration visit visas aren't required to register with the police. In particular, it applies to:

- Employees and most temporary workers
- Students
- Businessmen and investors
- Entrepreneurs and the self-employed
- People of independent means
- Those awaiting decisions on their refugee status

The spouse or partner and dependants aged 16 or over of someone required to register with the police must also register. Exceptions include children aged 16 and under, seasonal workers at agricultural work camps, the private servants of diplomatic households, clergymen, spouses, civil and unmarried partners of people settled in the UK, family members of EEA and Swiss nationals, a person exercising access rights to a child resident in the UK,

☑ SURVIVAL TIP

You're required to carry your Police Registration Certificate with you at all times, but not your passport.

the parents of a child at school in the UK who have 'leave to remain' to visit their child, or those formally granted asylum. If you've been granted settlement or residency in the UK (usually stamped as 'indefinite leave to remain' or 'indefinite leave to enter'), then police registration isn't required.

If you're required to register it will be stamped in your passport and you'll be told which police station to report to. In the Metropolitan Police area (Greater London), you must register at the Overseas Visitors Record Office (OVRO, 323 Borough High Street, London SE1 1JL, 020-7230 1208). Business hours are 9am to 4pm, Mondays to Fridays, and you should expect to wait a long time (unless you're first in the queue). Bear in mind that the office may close early (e.g. 2.30pm) during busy periods. In other towns and cities, enquire at your local police station.

You'll require your passport, visa or entry clearance, any letters from the UKVI, two passport-size photographs and the fee. It's also wise to take a copy of your marriage certificate (if applicable) and birth certificate with you; students require a letter from the educational institution where they're studying which confirms that they're enrolled there.

Details, such as your name, address, occupation, nationality, marital status and the date your permission expires, are entered in a green booklet called a Police Registration Certificate (PRC). If the PRC isn't given to you on the spot, you may need to surrender your passport, which will be returned to you later with your certificate. Make a photocopy or a note of the certificate's number, date, and place of issue in case you lose it (in which case the fee must be paid again).

It's recommended that you take your PRC with you when travelling abroad, as this will make re-entry into the UK easier, although it should be surrendered to an immigration officer if you're travelling abroad for longer than two months. Re-registration is required within seven days of changing your address and within eight days of changing any other details, including the issue of a new visa.

COUNCIL TAX REGISTRATION

All residents or temporary residents of the UK are required to register with their local authority or council for council tax soon after moving into a new home, either in the same council area or a new area, except when you're renting accommodation and council tax is included in the rent (which will be stated in the contract with your landlord). For information about council tax, see page 211.

EMBASSY REGISTRATION

Nationals of some countries are required or requested to register with their local embassy or consulate in the UK as soon as possible after their arrival. Even if registration isn't mandatory, most embassies like to keep a record of their nationals resident in the UK and it may help to expedite passport renewal or replacement.

FINDING HELP

One of the difficulties facing new arrivals is how and where to obtain help with day-to-day problems. This book was written in response to that need. However, in addition to the comprehensive general information you'll find here, you'll also require detailed local information. How successful you are at finding help will depend on your employer, the city or area where you live, your nationality and your English proficiency.

Obtaining information isn't a problem, as there's a plethora of data available in the UK on every conceivable subject, but much of it isn't intended for foreigners and their particular needs. Your local council offices, library, tourist information centre and Citizens Advice Bureau are excellent sources of reliable information on almost any subject, and of course information is also available online, in particular through the government's www.gov.uk website. Some large employers may have a department or staff whose job is to assist new arrivals, or they may contract this job out to a relocation consultant.

There are expatriate clubs and organisations for nationals of many countries in most areas, many of which provide detailed local information regarding all aspects of living in the UK, including housing costs, schooling, names of doctors and dentists, shopping information and much more. Clubs may produce data sheets, booklets and websites, and organise a variety of social events, which may include day and evening classes ranging from local cooking to English-language classes. One of the best ways to get to know local people is to join a social club, of which there are hundreds in all areas of the UK (search for 'Clubs and Associations' online or via www.yell.com).

Embassies and consulates usually provide information bulletin boards (jobs, accommodation, travel) and maintain lists of social clubs for their nationals. Many businesses produce books and leaflets containing valuable information for newcomers and local libraries and bookshops usually have books about their areas. You may find that friends, colleagues and acquaintances proffer advice based on their own experiences and mistakes. However, although they invariably mean well, bear in mind that their advice may be invalid for your particular area or situation or simply out of date.

Salisbury Cathedral

11
11

5. ACCOMMODATION

In most regions, accommodation to buy or rent isn't difficult to find, depending, of course, on what you're looking for and how much you can afford to pay. There are, however, exceptions, e.g. London, where property at an affordable price is virtually impossible to find unless you're a millionaire, and rents (in relation to average salaries) are astronomical. Accommodation usually accounts for around a quarter to a third of the average family's budget, but can rise to 40 or 50 per cent in high cost areas such as London.

Successive governments have failed to ensure that the housing supply matches demand, which has led to a crippling shortage of housing. There are signs that the government is (at last) beginning to address the problem, but it will be many years before there's sufficient housing for all (if ever). The UK is facing a critical shortage of rental accommodation and it has been estimated by the Royal Institute of Chartered Surveyors that at least 1.8 million more households will be looking to rent rather than buy a home by 2025.

Home ownership increased steadily from the '80s onwards, thanks to easier access to mortgages, a relatively restricted rental market (and high rents), and the fact that property is an excellent investment and buying is generally no more expensive than renting. The British have an obsession with property ownership (principal, second and investment homes) that's unparalleled in most other European countries. However, it took some hard knocks when the 2007 financial crisis sparked a sudden drop in property values (leaving many people with negative equity) and made it harder for prospective buyers to obtain a mortgage. In 2016, the rate of ownership among under-44s had fallen by 17 per cent in a decade.

As a consequence, the average age of first-time buyers has soared and today many people have zero prospects of ever owning a home. It's increasingly difficult to obtain a mortgage, despite the government's 'help to buy' scheme (www.helptobuy.gov.uk), as the deposit and salary necessary are prohibitively high for most people. Meanwhile, the value of property continues to soar and already unaffordable prices and rents are becoming more unaffordable by the day.

BRITISH HOMES

British homes are usually built to high standards and, whether you buy a new or an old home, it will usually be sturdy. There are stringent regulations in most towns regarding the style and design of new homes and the restoration of old (listed) buildings. The UK offers a vast choice of properties (few countries have such a variety of housing), including some of the most luxurious and expensive homes in the world. At the bottom end of the market, properties are likely to be terraced or semi-detached houses, whereas more expensive homes are detached and may be built on a half- or one-acre (2,000-4,000m²) plot.

In recent years, Britons have taken to apartment living in London and other cities (although often more out of necessity than choice), many of them more or less tasteful conversions of rambling old detached homes and even hospitals, schools, churches, mills, warehouses, offices and factories. 'Loft' conversions (e.g. of former warehouses) are popular, due to their high ceilings and general spaciousness. Barn conversions are also popular (and expensive), but rare due to the lack of barns (although you can cheat and have a barn-style home built from new).

The British usually prefer older homes with 'charm and character' to modern homes, although a common compromise is a new home with pseudo-period features such as wooden beams and open fireplaces. Although new properties may be lacking in character, they're usually well equipped with modern conveniences and services, which cannot be taken for granted in older properties. Standard fixtures and fittings in modern houses are more comprehensive, and generally of better quality than those found in old houses. For example, central heating, double or triple glazing and efficient insulation are standard in new houses. Central heating may be gas-fired (the most common) or oil-fired, or a home may have electric night-storage heaters or under-floor heating.

The down side to buying a modern home is that the average new British home is barely half the size of what they were in the '20s; average homes 90 years ago measured 1,647ft^2 and had four bedrooms, while today's equivalent has only three bedrooms and is a mere 925ft2. Modern homes are also darker and artificially lit, with little natural light. Overall the UK now has the smallest homes on average in Europe and the government has proposed that developers be made to construct homes to a specific size or above.

Garages & Parking

A lockable garage or private parking space is desirable in cities, where there's limited on-street parking (which may be some way from your home) and a high incidence of car theft and thefts from cars.

A garage or private parking space isn't usually included in the price when you buy a flat (particularly in cities), although private off-road parking may be available at an additional cost, possibly in an underground garage. Modern townhouses, semi-detached and detached homes usually have a small drive and garage or car port. Smaller homes may have a single garage, while larger homes often have integral double garages. Parking isn't usually a problem when buying an old home in a city suburb or the country, although a property may not have a purpose-built garage.

In a modern apartment or townhouse development, a garage or parking space may be provided although in areas where space is at a premium it may be charged as an extra, and the price can be high, e.g. £10,000 to £20,000 for a parking space (or up to £100,000 in central London!). The cost of a garage or parking space isn't always recouped when selling, although it makes a property more attractive to buyers and may clinch a sale. You can rent a garage or parking space in most cities, although the cost can be high.

☑ SURVIVAL TIP

Bear in mind that in a large development, the nearest parking area may be some distance from your home. This may be an important factor, particularly if you aren't up to carrying heavy shopping hundreds of metres to your home and possibly up several flights of stairs.

Without a private garage or parking space, parking can be a nightmare, particularly in London. In most cities it's necessary to obtain a resident's parking permit from the local council to park on public streets, although this doesn't guarantee that you'll be able to find a parking space. Free on-street parking is difficult or impossible to find in city centres, although on-street parking permits are usually available for residents.

THE HOUSING MARKET

Since the '80s, the UK housing market has undergone a cycle of boom and bust. Until mid-2007, property prices rose dramatically throughout the UK due to high demand and a shortage of homes for sale. Low interest rates also gave rise to rampant speculation, encouraged by the widespread availability of buy-to-let mortgages, introduced in 1997 and responsible for much of the housing inflation. However, over-heating of the property market and the 'sub-prime crisis' in the USA in 2007 (where US lenders sold billions of dollars of bad home loan debts – so called 'sub-prime' – to banks around the world) precipitated a meltdown of world financial markets and a severe credit squeeze.

This triggered a property slowdown in 2007, which quickly became a full-blown crash – prices fell by around 15 per cent between March 2008 and March 2009. Recovery was slow and erratic but such is the British passion for bricks and mortar that by May 2014 prices were almost back at their pre-crash peak (between 2013 and 2016 average house prices increased by around 20 per cent). Prices fell slightly in 2016 in some areas after the imposition of a swingeing stamp duty surcharge for second homes and the Brexit vote, but in the long term are expected to rise inexorably.

BUYING PROPERTY

Buying a house or apartment in the UK is usually a good long-term investment, and despite periodic recessions, most people still find buying preferable to renting. For a newcomer, whether you buy or rent depends on how long you're planning to stay and where you're planning to live. If you're planning to stay for just a few years, you'll probably be better off renting. For those staying longer buying may be the better option, particularly as this is generally no more expensive than renting, but you shouldn't expect to make a huge profit, especially in the short term.

Property has always been a good long-term investment. Between 1997 and 2007 it out-performed the stock market and all forms of savings, and many homeowners have dramatically increased the value of their family homes by 'trading up' – that is, buying a larger and more expensive home every five years or so. One of the reasons for the huge rise in property values in most regions in the last few decades has been the realisation that owning property isn't just about having a roof over your head, but can be an excellent long-term investment. For many families, investing in property has become an alternative to a private pension.

The last financial crisis notwithstanding, property values in the UK tend to double roughly every seven years. Although that level of growth may be hard to sustain in the near future, property remains one of the best long-term investments, particularly as the demand for homes far outstrips the supply, a situation that's expected to continue indefinitely. Much of southeast England, where demand is strongest, is heavily built up, and those who live there are opposed to further development (now that they have their homes!), which will delay or restrict widespread development. However, in the long term, it has been estimated that one-fifth of England will be built on by the year 2050.

For those who can afford it, home ownership has many benefits, not least the fact that you can make a tax-free profit (or a tax-free loss!) in a relatively short period, as no capital gains tax (see page 216) is payable on the profits from the sale of your principal home.

Prices

In July 2016, the average price of a home in England and Wales – according to the government Land Registry (www.landregistry.gov.uk) – was £216,750 (a rise of 8.3 per cent compared to the previous year), although values vary widely depending on the region or city, as well as by property type. The average London home, for example, was almost £484,716 and the average for property in the southeast of England nearly £313,315, whereas in the northeast of England it was just over £129,750. Overall, detached houses averaged just over £325,943, semi-detached houses £203,734, flats (apartments) £195,178 and terraced (row) houses £176,013. Average prices were £143,711 in Scotland, £144,828 in Wales and £123,241 in Northern Ireland.

If you've cash available or a secure route to finance, and especially if you're willing to undertake some renovation work, there are some bargains to be had when buying property. Since the late 2000s, when repossessions began to rise again, auctions have become becoming increasingly popular, although it's essential to carry out legal checks and a survey before you bid. Even with a straightforward purchase, you may be able to negotiate a reduction of around 5 per cent or even more (particularly if someone is looking for a quick sale in a buyer's market).

On the other hand, most sellers and estate agents price properties higher than the market price or the price they expect to receive, knowing that prospective buyers will try to drive the price down. So always haggle over the price, even if you think it's a bargain. This is, in fact, one of the few occasions in the UK when you're expected to haggle over the price, although you should try to avoid insulting the owner by offering a derisory amount.

Stamp Duty

Purchase Price	Stamp Duty	2nd Home Surcharge
Up to £125,000	0%	3%
£125,001-£250,000	2%	5%
£250,001-£925,000	5%	8%
£925,001 to £1.5m	10%	13%
over £1.5m	12%	15%

Stamp Duty

Stamp Duty (or 'stamp duty land tax') is the tax you pay when you buy property. It's levied at progressive rates (2-12 per cent) on each portion of the price – as shown in the table

below – so increases incrementally with the value of the property. The lower threshold is £125,000, below which no stamp duty is charged. Since April 2016 there has been a stamp duty surcharge on second homes (see table opposite) that has dampened demand for second homes.

If you buy a property for £275,000, you'll pay £3,750 in stamp duty, which is made up of zero on the first £125,000, £2,500 on the next £125,000 and £1,250 on the remaining £25,000. It's complicated and rates differ for commercial properties so the government provides a stamp duty calculator (www.hmrc.gov.uk/tools/sdlt/land-and-property.htm). In Scotland the tax is known as 'land and buildings transaction tax' (LBTT) and the thresholds differ slightly (see www.scotland.gov.uk/topics/government/finance/scottishapproach/lbtt).

Contracts

When buying property in England, Wales or Northern Ireland, prospective buyers make an offer subject to survey and contract. Either side can amend or withdraw from a sale at any time before the exchange of contracts (when a sale is legally binding). (The authorities have resisted introducing a deposit scheme when an offer is accepted, as is common in most other countries.) In a seller's market, gazumping – where a seller agrees to an offer from one prospective buyer and then sells to another for a higher amount – is rampant, and isn't illegal. On the other hand, in a buyer's market, a buyer may threaten to pull out at the last minute unless the seller reduces the price (called 'gazundering').

There's no gazumping in Scotland, as neither side can pull out once an offer has been made and accepted.

RENTED ACCOMMODATION

Rented accommodation is the answer for those who don't want the trouble, expense and restrictions involved in buying a house, or who are staying in the UK for just a few years (when buying isn't usually worthwhile). Traditionally, there was never a strong rental market in the UK – unlike in most other European countries – as most people prefer to buy. However, the situation has changed considerably in the last decade, due to the explosion of buy-to-let mortgages which created an army of private landlords and, post-2007, to the growing number of people unable to get on to the housing ladder and forced to rent instead.

There are now so many potential tenants that good quality rental properties are quickly snapped up. Those with three or more bedrooms (particularly detached houses) located in good areas are in short supply everywhere. Rental accommodation can also be prohibitively expensive and the quality of properties often leaves much to be desired, particularly at the lower end of the market. You should be aware that the UK rental market is a jungle; Britain has one of the least regulated letting markets in Western Europe, with little legal protection against unscrupulous agents and landlords.

One of the reasons for the growth of the UK rental market is the dearth of mortgage funding. A decade ago, it was relatively easy to obtain a 95 or even a 100 per cent mortgage with repayments over 25 or 30 years, which made it cheaper or no more expensive to buy a home than to rent one. By 2015, however, you have to put up a 5 per cent deposit to stand any chance of obtaining a mortgage – any mortgage – while the best deals are available only to those who can put down 20 per cent or more.

Properties are let both furnished and unfurnished (or possibly part-furnished). The furniture and furnishings in rental properties vary considerably from poor to excellent – not surprisingly, luxury properties are much better furnished and equipped than inexpensive studios and one-bedroom flats.

Rental property can usually be found in two to six weeks in most areas, with the exception of large houses (four or more bedrooms), which are rare and expensive. Family accommodation in particular is in short supply in London, with the possible exception of luxury homes with enormous rents. Most people settle for something in the suburbs or country and commute to work. If you must travel into a city centre (particularly London) each day, you should be prepared to spend at least an hour or more travelling each way. (Note that rents in central London are usually quoted per week and not per month!).

Most rented property is let through letting agencies or estate agents, who act on behalf of landlords and charge an 'administration fee' for taking up references, drawing up tenancy agreements and preparing an inventory. You must also pay one month's rent in advance, depending on the type of property and the rental agreement, plus a deposit against damages equal to one or two months' rent (see **Deposits** below). Agents usually have a number of properties available for immediate occupancy and lists are normally updated weekly.

You should have no problem finding something suitable in most areas if you start looking at least four weeks before the date you wish to take occupancy. Most letting agents require a reference from your employer (or previous employer if you've been less than one year with your current one) and bank and credit references, or in the case of a company let, copies of audited accounts and status.

Rental Costs & Standards

Rental costs vary considerably depending on the size (number of bedrooms) and quality of a property, its age and the facilities provided. There isn't a lot of difference in rents for furnished and unfurnished properties, although luxury furnished properties are considerably more expensive than unfurnished properties. The most important factor of all is the neighbourhood and region; rents are generally lowest in Scotland, Northern Ireland, Wales and the North of England, and highest in London and the southeast.

No. Bedrooms	Monthly Rent
Bedsit/Studio	£500-750
1	£500-1,000
2	£750-1,500
3	£1,000–2,500
4 or more	£2,000-3,000++

Rents are also – not surprisingly – lower in rural than urban areas. As a general rule, the further a property is from a large city or town, public transport and other facilities, the cheaper the rent.

In recent years rents have been rising inexorably due to increased demand and the general shortage of housing. In August 2016 (source: https://homelet.co.uk) the average UK rent was £913, ranging from a high of £1,497 in Greater London to £535 in the northeast. However, averages don't tell the full story and rents in desirable areas, cities and towns – particularly central London – are much higher than the average and prohibitively expensive for anyone on an average salary. A **rough** guide to average monthly rents for apartments and houses in the southeast of England (outside Greater London and the M25 motorway) is shown in the table above.

The rents shown are for good quality modern or renovated properties and don't include properties located in the central area of large towns, in major cities or in exclusive residential areas, for which the sky's the limit. In central London, rents are double or treble the minimum shown above, while in some remote country areas they may be lower. On the other hand, monthly rents for desirable houses with four or more bedrooms are £3,000 to £5,000 per month in many areas.

Rental Contracts

The 1988 Housing Act caused something of a revolution in the rental market by deregulating new lettings in the private sector. Prior to this the law (the Rent Acts) had kept a stranglehold on rent levels and the general freedom of landlords, and was heavily weighted in favour of tenants. However, the new act was much more landlord friendly – it made it much easier for landlords to evict unwanted tenants – although it also encouraged greater choice and competition in the rental market and ignited the buy-to-let movement.

The law was amended again under the Housing Act (1996) and since 1997 all new lettings have automatically been assured shorthold tenancies unless otherwise agreed. Exceptions include when the rent is over £100,000 per annum or for other arrangements such as company lets, which are generally known as 'common law' or 'contractual' tenancies. You must be over 18 to hold a tenancy agreement.

There are a number of useful websites detailing the legal rights and duties of both landlords and tenants, including Shelter (www.shelter.org.uk) and Gov.uk (www.gov.uk/private-renting/your-rights-and-responsibilities). A Citizens Advice Bureau (www.adviceguide.org.uk) can offer advice regarding the legal aspects of renting and your rights.

Assured Shorthold Tenancy

All new tenancies since 1997 have automatically been assured shorthold tenancies (AST), which provide a landlord with a guaranteed right to repossess his property at the end of the term, but don't provide long-term security for tenants and aren't regulated by any rent controls.

A new AST is usually a 'fixed-term tenancy' lasting for a set period: usually six months or a year, although some landlords are reluctant to agree an initial period longer than six months (they want to make sure that you're a good tenant before committing to a longer term and may also wish to increase the rent). Even if the period is shorter than six months, tenants have the right to stay in the property for six months unless the landlord has good grounds for repossession (see below). An AST can also be set up on a week to week or month to month roll-over basis, known as a 'periodic tenancy'. At the end of a fixed term, the landlord and tenant may agree a new fixed term or the agreement may continue as a periodic tenancy.

The landlord is legally entitled to repossess the property at the end of the fixed period, provided he gives you notice in writing two months before the expiry of the fixed term. If the agreement then becomes a periodic tenancy, the tenant must give a months' notice in writing (landlord must give two months' notice) to terminate it.

If you've any questions regarding your rental agreement or problems with your landlord, you can ask a Citizens Advice Bureau (www.adviceguide.org.uk) for advice. They'll also check your rental agreement and advise you of your rights under the law.

Deposits

After signing an assured shorthold tenancy you must usually pay one month's rent in advance, depending on the type of property and the rental agreement, plus a deposit against damages equal to one or two months' rent. Your deposit should be repaid when you leave, provided there are no outstanding claims for rent, unpaid bills, damages or cleaning.

It isn't unknown for a landlord to make a claim for 'professional' cleaning running into hundreds of pounds, even when you leave a property spotless.

Since 2007 all deposits taken by landlords and agents for assured shorthold tenancies (ASTs) in England and Wales must be protected by an authorised Tenancy Deposit Scheme (TDS). These schemes were designed to implement a speedy and efficient settlement of deposit disputes and remove much of the mutual suspicion that used to build up towards the end of a tenancy, which frequently led to the last month's rent being withheld for fear of the landlord refusing to return a deposit. They guarantee the return of tenants' deposits, less any legitimate expenses owed to the landlord, and remove the burden from letting agents of having to resolve irreconcilable differences of opinion between landlords and tenants.

The three deposit providers are Deposit Protection Service, MyDeposits and the Tenancy Deposit Scheme, and different service providers are available in Scotland and Northern Ireland. For further information, see www.gov.uk/deposit-protection-schemes-and-landlords.

UTILITIES

Utilities is the collective name given to electricity, gas and water companies (and usually also includes telephone companies). All the UK's utility companies have been privatised in the last few decades, quickly followed by increased prices and worse service. In more recent years, most people have been able to choose their electricity and gas supplier, and the increased competition initially led to lower prices.

The UK's energy bills are around the average in Europe. According to Ofgem – the energy regulator – in August 2016 the average annual variable (dual-fuel) tariff was £1,066 and the cheapest available tariff £770, although many people pay much more than this (up to double). With a few brief exceptions, the price of energy (as gas and electricity is increasingly known) has been rising steadily since the mid-2000s, and in recent years people have been urged to shop around for the best rates.

The UK's energy suppliers are regulated by the Office of Gas and Electricity Markets (OFGEM, www.ofgem.gov.uk). Complaints about services should be directed first to the supplier and then, if you still aren't satisfied, to the Energy Ombudsman (www.ombudsman-services.org/energy.html).

Comparing Rates

It's possible to make savings by choosing your gas or electricity supplier prudently, although some two-thirds of households are stuck on the most expensive variable tariffs, rather than a fixed-rate tariff. Many companies provide both electricity and gas and offer contracts for the supply of both fuels, called a dual-fuel deal. This may result in a discount, although you usually need to pay your energy bill monthly by direct debit to get the best rate. Most companies guarantee prices for a period (called fixed-rate tariffs) when you buy gas and electricity from them or when you switch companies.

There are numerous price comparison sites, which claim to be able to save you £300 or more on your annual energy bill (and most other household bills). However, what they don't tell you is how they make their mega-millions, which is by promoting the energy companies that pay them the highest fees! Some companies cover the whole country, while others cover certain regions only.

> If your current provider has a lower rate for new customers he usually won't transfer you to this rate. You may need first to switch to another supplier and then switch back 24 hours later to take advantage of it.

The best rates are often offered by the smaller companies such as www.avroenergy.co.uk, www.extraenergy.com, www.first-utility.com, www.gbenergysupply.co.uk, www.ovoenergy.com and www.soenergy.com, and green energy companies such as www.ecotricity.co.uk and www.goodenergy.co.uk, although they aren't as financially secure as the big six and some have gone bust. Whatever company you're with, you should regularly shop around to check whether you can get a better deal from another supplier.

Energy companies are installing free smart meters that show the amount of energy you use as you use it and how much it's costing you (like watching a taxi meter!).

Electricity

The electricity supply in the UK is 240 volts (V) AC, with a frequency of 50 hertz (cycles). This is suitable for all electrical equipment with a rated power consumption of up to 3,000 watts. For equipment with a higher power consumption, a single 240V or 3-phase, 380 volts AC, 20 amp supply must be used (this is usually only installed in large houses with six to eight bedrooms or industrial premises). Power cuts are rare in most parts of the UK. However, if a power cut lasts for over 12 hours and is the energy supplier's fault, then you should qualify for compensation: see www.citizensadvice.org.uk/consumer/energy/energy-supply).

To have the electricity connected or reconnected, you must choose an electricity company and complete a form; you can usually make your application online. There's sometimes a small charge for connection and you should allow at least two days for it to be done. If you're in the UK for a short period only, you may be asked for a security deposit or to obtain a guarantor, e.g. your employer. You should contact your electricity company and give them the meter reading when you move in and again when you vacate a property.

If at all possible you should avoid paying for your energy via a pre-payment meter – usually offered to households that find it difficult to budget for huge bills – which is the most expensive way to pay for electricity and gas.

Plugs

Irrespective of the country you've come from, all your plugs will require changing, or a lot of expensive adapters will be required. Modern British plugs have three rectangular pins (which are, of course, unique to the UK) and are fitted with fuses as follows:

Fuses

Fuse Rating (Amps)	Colour	Use/Watts
1 (or 2)	Green	Shaver adapters (2-pin) only
2	White	Standard lamp
3	Red	Maximum 750W
5	Grey	750 to 1,250W
13	Brown	1,250 to 3,000W

If you aren't sure what sort of fuse to use, consult the instructions provided with the apparatus. The fuse rating (amps) is calculated by dividing the wattage by the voltage (240). For maximum safety, electrical appliances should be turned off at the main wall point when not in use (the DOWN position is ON and the UP position is OFF).

Bulbs

Electric light bulbs were traditionally of the Edison type with a bayonet fitting, which is unique to the UK (the British pride themselves on being different). To insert a bulb you push it in and turn it clockwise around 5mm. However, nowadays bulbs (and lamps) with a screw fitting are also widely available. Bulbs manufactured for use in the US mustn't be used in the UK, as they will explode.

Low-energy light bulbs – both compact fluorescent lamp (CFL) and, increasingly, LED bulbs – have virtually taken over from the old-style tungsten bulbs which are now difficult to buy, although some people prefer them and they still change hands at car boot sales and market stalls (and retailers are permitted to sell existing stock). Low-energy bulbs are more expensive than ordinary bulbs, but they (allegedly) save money through their longer life and reduced energy consumption.

Bulbs for non-standard electrical appliances (i.e. appliances not made for the British market) such as refrigerators, freezers and sewing machines, may not be available in the UK (so bring extras with you). Plug adapters for imported lamps and other electrical items may be difficult to find, so it's advisable to bring a number of adapters and extension leads with you which can be fitted with British plugs.

Gas

Mains gas is available in all but the remotest areas of the UK. However, you may find that some modern houses aren't connected to the mains gas supply. If you're looking for a rental property and want to cook by gas, make sure it already has a gas supply. You must have a meter installed in order to be connected to mains gas (there may be a charge for this depending on the gas company). In some remote areas without piped gas, homes may have a 'bottled gas' (e.g. Calor Gas) cooker. If you buy a house without a gas supply, you can usually arrange to have a gas pipeline installed from a nearby gas main. Note, however, that the cost can be prohibitive and depends on the distance involved.

Gas is the cheapest fuel for central heating and water heating, particularly if you've a high-efficiency condensing boiler. However, to reduce bills and obtain the maximum benefit from your heating system, your home must be well insulated (see **Heating** below). Cooking with gas also costs the average family less than with electricity.

Gas Companies

Prior to market liberalisation in 1998, gas was supplied throughout the UK by British Gas, which was the monopoly supplier to some 20 million homes. Nowadays, gas is supplied by the 'big six' energy providers (British Gas, EDF Energy, E.ON UK, Npower, Scottish & Southern Energy and Scottish Power) and numerous smaller companies (see **Comparing Rates** above).

If your new home already has a gas supply, simply contact the company of your choice to have the gas supply reconnected or transferred to your name (there may be a connection fee) and the meter read. You must contact your gas company to get a final meter reading when you vacate a property.

Servicing & Safety

Gas appliances must be fitted by independent gas fitters (who offer the fastest service) or your gas company. If you use an independent gas fitter, choose one who's registered with the Gas Safe Register (0800-408 5500, www.gassaferegister.co.uk), who can provide the names of members in your area.

Gas central heating boilers, water heaters and fires should be checked annually, particularly open-flued water heaters, which are illegal in bathrooms (faulty gas appliances kill people every year). Free gas safety checks are carried out for those aged over 60, the disabled and those living alone in receipt of a state disability benefit.

Gas installations and appliances can leak and cause explosions or kill you while you sleep. If you suspect a gas leak, first check to see whether a gas tap has been left on or a pilot light has gone out. If not, then there's probably a leak, in your home or in a nearby gas pipeline. Ring your local gas emergency service (0800-111 999 in England, Scotland and Wales and 0800-002 001 in Northern Ireland) immediately and vacate the house as quickly as possible.

Landlords are legally obliged to carry out an annual safety inspection of all gas appliances, including central heating boilers and cookers, and must provide tenants with a copy.

Water

The water industry in England and Wales was privatised in 1989, when ten regional water companies were created to provide water and sewerage services (there are also a number of local water-only companies). You're unable to choose your water company (unlike electricity and gas companies) as they have a monopoly in their region. Around half of households in England and Wales (including new homes) have water meters. Which means you're billed for the actual water used (plus a standing charge), rather than fixed charge. Whether having a meter will save you money depends on your water usage and the size of your home (smaller households may find it cheaper not to have a meter). Water meters are voluntary and must be paid for by homeowners.

For all other households, water and sewerage rates are based on the rateable value of a property (although rates were abolished in April 1990 and replaced by the council tax). In Scotland, fresh water is charged as an addition to the council tax (which includes sewerage) and in Northern Ireland, water and sewerage are paid as part of the domestic rates (there's no council tax). Water services are regulated 'independently of the government' by Ofwat (www.ofwat.gov.uk).

Heating

Most UK homes have central heating (including all new homes) or storage heater systems, many of which also provide hot water. Central heating systems may be powered by oil, gas (the most common), electricity or solid fuel, e.g. coal or wood. Whatever form of heating you use, you should ensure that you have good insulation, including double glazing, cavity-wall insulation, external-wall insulation, floor insulation, draught-proofing, pipe lagging, and loft and hot water tank insulation, without which up to 60 per cent of heat goes straight through the walls and roof.

Many companies advise and carry out home insulation, including gas and electricity companies, who produce a range of leaflets designed to help you reduce your heating and other energy bills. There are also government-run energy efficiency schemes, which provide grants and loans towards insulation and other energy-saving measures.

> According to the Office of National Statistics, cold weather kills some 25,000 a year in the UK and many elderly people are forced to choose between heating and food in winter.

The cheapest method of central heating is gas, which is cheaper than other forms of central heating and hot water systems, particularly if you've a high-efficiency condensing boiler. Some homes have storage heaters that store heat from electricity supplied at the cheaper off-peak rate overnight, and release it to heat your home during the day. In an apartment block heated by a central system, radiators are usually individually metered, so you pay only for the heating used.

Renewable energy, i.e. energy gained from natural resources rather than fossil fuels, is attracting increasing interest, with government grants available to offset the high cost of installing the necessary equipment. Solar panels that provide hot water and/or electricity, wind turbines and ground source heat pumps (which harness the heat of the earth) are increasingly being incorporated into new house designs, although having them installed into an existing property can be disruptive and it can take many years to recoup the cost. It's now generally agreed by the experts that solar panels won't save you anything like as much as manufacturers' claim and for most people they're unlikely ever to recoup their initial cost.

For more information, contact your gas or electricity company or the Energy Saving Trust (0300-123 1234 in England, see www.energysavingtrust.org.uk for other contacts).

Angel of the North, Gateshead, Tyne & Wear

POST
OFFICE

6. POSTAL SERVICES

There's a post office in most towns and many villages in the UK and the organisation offers over 100 services, many of which are described in this chapter. The term 'post office' is used in the UK as a general term for three separate businesses: the Royal Mail, Post Office Limited and Parcelforce. For the sake of simplicity the term 'post office' has been used throughout this chapter to refer to all these services.

Inland post refers to mail to addresses in Great Britain, Northern Ireland, the Channel Islands and the Isle of Man, although the Channel Islands are considered an international destination by Parcelforce. Of some 11,500 post office branches, only around 300 are now operated directly by the post office. The remainder are franchise offices or sub-post offices run on an agency basis by sub-postmasters, which don't offer all the services provided by a main post office. Sub-post offices are often located in supermarkets, stationers and newsagents. The post office also has *bureaux de change* kiosks in selected WH Smith stores that are open seven days a week.

In addition to providing postal services, the post office acts as an agent for a number of government departments and local authorities (councils), including passport and driving licence applications, and pension and benefits' payments. The post office is also the largest chain of outlets for national lottery tickets, and provides bureau de change facilities in main branches (where it buys and sells foreign currency free of commission), an international money transfer service in conjunction with MoneyGram, plus a range of financial services such as credit cards, mortgages and insurance.

The courier industry, particularly in London and other major cities, is growing rapidly and the UK is a major centre for international air courier traffic. Major companies include Federal Express, DHL, DPD, UPS, TNT, Hermes, Yodel, plus the post office Parcelforce service.

The post office produces a wealth of free brochures about postal rates and special services, most of which are available from any post office; their helpline (03457-740740) and website (www.royalmail.com) are a good source of information about the numerous specialised services available to businesses. Post Office Ltd, a subsidiary responsible for counter services, has its own phone number and website (0345-611 2970, www.postoffice.co.uk) detailing its services.

BUSINESS HOURS

Post office business hours are usually from 9am to 5.30pm, Mondays to Fridays, and from 9am to 12.30pm on Saturdays. In small towns and villages, there are sub-post offices (usually part of a general store) that provide most of the services offered by a main post office. Sub-post offices usually close for an hour at lunchtime, e.g. 1pm to 2pm, Mondays to Fridays, and may also close on one afternoon a week, usually Wednesday. Main post offices in major towns don't close at lunchtime. There are post offices at major international airports, some of which are open on Sundays and public holidays.

The post office website (www.postoffice.co.uk) contains a branch finder feature that lists opening hours.

LETTER POST

This section contains information about postcards, letters, small packets and printed papers, although it isn't always easy to know when a 'packet' becomes a 'parcel' (for parcels, see **Parcel Post** below). The post office usually offers a choice of first and second class domestic mail delivery.

Letters are priced on a combination of size and weight, reflecting the cost of sorting large letters which must be done manually instead of by machine. A letter should be no larger than 240mm x 165mm x 5mm and weigh no more than 100g. If it exceeds these dimensions and weight it's classed as a large letter up to a maximum size of 353mm x 250mm x 25mm thick and a weight of 750g. The largest 'letter' size is a package which can measure up to 610mm x 460mm x 460mm; there's no weight limit for first class packets but second class packets are limited to 1kg.

Domestic postcards and 'standard' letters up to 100g in weight cost 64p first class (55p second), while a large letter, e.g. the size of a magazine, with a maximum thickness of 25mm and weighing up to 100g costs 96p (75p second class). Prices increase with weight: up to 250g £1.27 (£1.20); up to 500g £1.71 (£1.54); and up to 750g £2.46 (£2.09).

Anything larger than a large letter or weighing more than 750g is classified as a parcel. These can be small (450mm x 350mm x 160mm and up to 2kg) or medium (610mm x 460mm x 460mm, up to 20kg). Postage costs from £3.35 (£2.85 second class) up to 1kg and £33.40 (£28.55) for a parcel weighing between 10kg and 20kg. Larger and heavier parcels must be sent by courier, i.e. Parcelforce. The current rates are shown on the Post Office website (www.postoffice.co.uk/mail) and prices normally increase annually.

Domestic delivery targets are the next working day after collection for first class mail and the third working day after collection for second class. Some 90 per cent of first class post is delivered the next day. It's unnecessary to mark post as first or second class, as any item which is posted with less than first class postage is automatically sent second class.

Airmail has been rebranded as International Standard and has a similar complex set of charges as for domestic mail, with destinations categorised as Europe (which includes a big slice of Asia) and world zones 1 and 2. The cost of sending letters abroad starts at £1.05 for the first 10g (which is also the cost for postcards), £1.52 up to 100g to Europe and £2.25 to world zones 1 and 2. There's also a small parcels and printed papers rate costing from £3.55 to £4.55 (depending on destination) for 100g, £4.05 for 250g (to Europe) up 2kg (£21.50 to Australasia). International economy (the old surface mail) starts at 90p for a letter (10g) up to £13.25 for a 2kg parcel. Larger and heavier parcels can be sent via Parcelforce Worldwide.

All domestic and international postal charges are listed in leaflets available from post offices and from the Royal Mail website which includes a handy price finder (www.royalmail.com/price-finder).

General Information

- Post boxes are red and are usually free-standing, but may be set into (or attached to) a wall. Main and sub-post offices have post boxes outside, but branches in shops may not. Collection times are shown on all post boxes. Post is collected several times a day from main post offices, Mondays to Saturdays; there's no Sunday collection, and the final collection on a Saturday may be as early as 12.30 even from a post office. Times are indicated on the collection plate.
- There's one delivery of post a day from Mondays to Saturdays in all areas – there are no longer morning AND afternoon deliveries, and post can turn up quite late in the day. If you want a first class letter to reach its destination on the next working day, you must ensure you post early in the day.
- You can receive post free of charge via selected post offices through the international *Poste Restante* service (where post is addressed to main post offices) for a maximum of three months. Post sent to a *Poste Restante* address is returned to the sender if it's unclaimed after 14 days. Identification, e.g. a passport or driving licence, is necessary for collection.
- Most mail is sorted by machine, which is facilitated by the use of full and correct postal addresses (omitting all punctuation) with town, city or country names in capitals. Postcodes (zip codes) which allow addresses to be identified down to part of a street or even to an individual house, should never be omitted. You can find the postcode of most UK addresses via the Post Office website (http://postcodefinder.postoffice.co.uk/), which also displays a map showing the location.
- Stamps can be purchased from post offices and from over 40,000 shops (e.g. stationers, newsagents and general stores) throughout the UK that sell books of six or 12 first or 12 second class stamps, and books of four large letter stamps (first and second class). Stamps marked 1st or 2nd, but without a value, are valid indefinitely (even when prices change) for inland post up to 100g in weight or in part payment for heavier items.

> ☑ **SURVIVAL TIP**
>
> Rather than have your mail held by the post office, it may be better to have it redirected to a friend (see **Change of Address** on page 92). This way they can check your mail while you're away and let you know by email when something important arrives or a company is threatening to send a bailiff round when you haven't paid a bill!

- It's possible to pay for postage online and print a label or envelope. An online tool helps you calculate the postage and you can pay using a debit or credit card or by setting up a prepay account.
- If you're going to be away from your home for up to two months, you can have your mail held by the post office and delivered on a day of your choice. The Keepsafe scheme can operate over a number of days (your choice), with the cost based on the actual period chosen. Five days' notice is required. Keepsafe can be requested by phone (0345-7777 888) or in person at a post office. You can download an application form from www.royalmail.com/personal/receiving-mail/keepsafe.

Important, Valuable or Urgent Mail

The post office provides a number of services for the secure and fast delivery of important and urgent post to domestic and foreign addresses.

- A certificate of posting is available free on request at any post office counter. A number of items can be listed on one leaflet. A maximum of £20 is payable in compensation for the loss or damage of ordinary letters or parcels for which a certificate of posting has been obtained. Without this certificate the post office isn't liable to pay compensation. There's no compensation for valuables sent by ordinary post.
- Recorded delivery, now known as 'Signed For', requires a signature to confirm delivery. It costs from £1.74 to send a 100g letter first class (£1.65 second class) and you can claim up to £50 in compensation if Royal Mail fails to deliver. This service is also available for parcels up to 20kg.
- If you're sending money, jewellery, valuable documents or anything needing secure and speedy delivery within the UK, you should use one of the Special Delivery services. Special Delivery 'Guaranteed by 1pm' costs from £6.45 for a item weighing up to 100g up to £44.20 for a 20kg package, and guarantees delivery by 1pm the next day (Monday to Friday or Saturday for an extra fee) to addresses in England, Wales, Northern Ireland or urban areas of Scotland.

A return address must be written on the back of all post sent by Signed For or Special Delivery – and is advisable for all important mail.

- For really urgent post, there's also a service called Special Delivery Guaranteed by 9am. Prices start from £21.36 for a 100g package and go up to £35.64 (2kg). A form must be completed and a receipt is provided. A signature is collected on delivery and the time is noted. You can track mail and obtain an electronic proof of delivery online.
- If your item arrives later than the guaranteed delivery time, you can contact Customer Service (0345-774 0740) and reclaim your fee. The maximum standard compensation for loss or damage is £50 (£500 for Special Delivery 1pm), which can be increased to £2,500 for a small additional fee or £10,000 with consequential loss insurance.

PARCEL POST

The standard inland parcel service is operated by Royal Mail and handles over one million parcels and packages daily, which are delivered within one to three working days in the UK. There are restrictions on the size of parcels, depending on the service. Royal Mail parcel post includes the services detailed below.

Standard Parcel Post

This service is for non-urgent parcels to any address in the UK (including Saturday deliveries). The cost of sending domestic parcels is from £3.35 first class for 1kg (£2.85 second class) up to £33.40 (£28.55) for 20kg. Some post offices don't accept parcels weighing over 10kg.

Compensation for loss or damage is limited to £20 per parcel, provided you complete a certificate of posting when sending a parcel. Higher compensation is possible if you use one of the Special Delivery services (see above). Domestic parcels can measure 610mm x 460mcm x 460mcm and weigh up to 20kg. Anything larger or heavier must be sent by Parcelforce, which provides inland express parcel delivery services and services to foreign destinations.

Urgent and Next-day Services

Parcelforce usually delivers within 48 hours, but a number of next-day services are also available. These include Express9, Express10, ExpressAM and Express24, which guarantee delivery by 9am, 10am, noon or the end of the day to most UK destinations. Compensation for loss or damage of up to £200 is included in the fee up to a maximum of £2,500. Parcels must be signed for on arrival. See www.parcelforce.com/sending-parcel/parcel-delivery/expressam for rates.

Parcelforce International delivers to 240 countries and territories worldwide, offering four levels of service, ranging from 'express' (next day delivery to Europe and North America) and 'priority' (delivery within three or four working days) to 'value' (from four working days) and 'economy' (a month or more). There are also express parcel services to Europe and Ireland. The maximum international parcel weight varies depending on the destination, but is usually 30kg. Parcels weighing over 10kg are accepted only at main post offices.

Further information about Parcelforce services is available from Parcelforce (0344-800 4466, www.parcelforce.com).

Customs Declaration

Parcels and small packets sent to international addresses outside the European Union must be accompanied by a customs declaration label CN22 for items valued at up to £270 and label CN23 for goods valued above £270. Note that the post office classes the Channel Islands, Andorra, Canary Islands, Gibraltar, San Marino and the Vatican City as being outside the EU. If an item being sent is of 'no commercial value' (NCV), you should write this on the customs form under 'value'. Forms are available from post offices.

COLLECTING POST

If the postman calls with post requiring a signature or payment when you aren't at home, he'll leave a collection form. These items of post include recorded letters, registered letters, surcharged items, special delivery/express, insured items, perishable goods, a parcel which is too bulky to be left for underpaid items. If you receive post from abroad on which customs duty or VAT is payable, this is collected by the post office (sums over £50 are collected only at main post offices). You can choose to collect an item which couldn't be delivered or you can

complete the bottom part of the collection form and instruct the post office to:

- Allow someone else to collect it on your behalf (identity must be shown);
- Have it redelivered on a date of your choosing;
- Have it delivered to another address, e.g. a business or a neighbour.

To collect an item you need to present the collection form at your local Letter Delivery Office, the address of which is printed on the form. Check the opening hours in advance as some are open for collections only in the mornings, e.g. 8am to noon, Mondays to Fridays and 8am to 11am on Saturdays. Identification is usually required and the address on your ID must be the same as that on the item to be collected. Post is retained for three weeks.

You can rent a private PO Box at most main post offices for £252 a year (£144 for six months). Collection must usually be made during normal opening hours. You can also hire a private box for parcels at a Parcelforce delivery depot, offices of Mail Boxes Etc. and others.

A private courier company must usually obtain a signature for deliveries and if you aren't at home, they will leave a form asking you to contact them about re-delivery.

CHANGE OF ADDRESS

Your post can be redirected to a new or temporary address in the UK for a charge of £31.99 for three months, £41.99 for six months and £59.99 for a year, or between three and four times these charges to an address abroad. Charges are per surname, not per household. All letters are redirected to inland addresses by first class post (whether or not they were originally sent first class). Information about post redirection is available on 0345-774 0740. Parcelforce also operates a redirection service for parcels (0344- 800 4466).

A redirection application form is available from post offices or can be downloaded from the Post Office website. It's best to arrange the redirection at a post office as you need to show proof of your name and address and this must be with original documents such as a passport, driving licence or a recent utility bill. It must be completed at least five working days before you wish redirection to begin (it can be completed up to three weeks in advance). You can renew your redirection up to a maximum of two years and renewals can be done online (www.royalmail.com/personal/receiving-mail/redirection).

7. COMMUNICATIONS

Most UK homes have a fixed-line telephone line (although many people now manage without one), while mobile phone use is among the highest in the world. Most telephone exchanges are digital and you can make direct calls to anywhere in the UK and to most countries in the world. The cost of calls has fallen sharply in the last decade (even ET could afford to phone home now!) due to increased competition, and the UK now has one of the world's most competitive telecommunications' markets.

The telephone network in the UK is dominated by British Telecom (abbreviated to and universally known as BT), which was created in 1984 when the state-owned monopoly was privatised. When the telecommunications market was opened to national and international competition in 1991, the UK stood at the forefront of technology in this sector. Well over 100 companies are licensed to operate telecommunications services, and competition, although less intense than a few years ago, is still keen, so it's worth shopping around.

The general emergency telephone number throughout the UK is 999 or 112 (see also **Emergency Numbers** on page 102).

Many users can choose between BT, cable and satellite companies such as Virgin and Sky, and a large number of indirect operators. It can be difficult to decide which company to choose, with the increasing number and complexity of schemes and 'bundles' on offer (even from the same company), which seem designed to confuse customers and prevent comparisons being made.

Increasingly, telephone and internet services are offered together in a 'bundle' – sometimes with the added temptation of cable/satellite television as well. Initial prices can appear low, e.g. £5 a month for internet and weekend calls – but costs may be reduced for a limited initial period and increase sharply once the honeymoon period is over. Add in the cost of line rental (£15-19 per month) and it's easy to end up paying between £30 and £40 a month. In October 2016, regulations regarding the advertising of telephone, broadband and line rental packages were changed to make it easier for customers to compare like with like in order to assess the value of different packages.

The best option will depend on how much you use your phone, when you make most calls, what sort of calls you make (e.g. local, national or international), and how frequently you call mobiles.

The websites www.broadbandchoices.co.uk, www.simplifydigital.co.uk and www.uswitch.com provide tariff comparisons from various providers to help you decide which company offers the best deal. Bear in mind, however, when using comparison sites that they're paid to promote certain companies and deals, and therefore aren't always impartial.

We have based much of our information in the chapter on BT, not because we recommend them but because they're the biggest phone provider in the UK. There are many more service providers to choose from – some considerably cheaper – but to include all their services and prices here would require a tome the size of the telephone directory!

Among the best phone deals are those offered by Plusnet (www.plus.net), Direct Save (www.directsavetelecom.co.uk), Fuel (www.fuelbroadband.co.uk), Sky (www.sky.com), TalkTalk (www.talktalk.co.uk), Tentel (www.tentel.co.uk), Virgin Media (www.virginmedia.com) and Vonage (www.vonage.co.uk), most of which offer lower call rates than BT; companies also normally offer packages that offer unlimited "free" phone calls, but whether they're worth the extra cost depends on how much you expect to be using your landline. Note that you can now pay your line rental to any telephone provider and don't have to stick with BT.

TELEPHONE INSTALLATION & REGISTRATION

Before moving into a new home, check whether there's a telephone line and that the number of lines or telephone points is adequate (new homes usually have phone lines and points in most rooms). If a property has a cable connection, you could decide not to have a standard phone line installed (see www.cable.co.uk to check). If you move into an old house or apartment, a telephone line will probably already be installed, although there won't be a phone and there may be only a few connection points.

If you're moving into accommodation without a phone line, you must ask BT or another provider to install one. Residential line installation takes from 4 to 16 working days (depending on the area) and the cost is around £130 (£65 when ordered online), although charges are usually waived if you take out a contract that includes broadband or a TV deal. Activating an existing line costs up to £50. Fees also apply when having a second or additional line installed.

Once you've a BT linebox or master socket, you can install as many additional sockets as you like, but you shouldn't connect more than four telephones to one telephone line. You can buy landline cordless phones with up to four handsets.

If you're moving to a new address in the same code area, it's usually possible to retain your existing number. For information, call 0800-800 150 (or 0330-1234 150 from a mobile).

USING THE TELEPHONE

Using the telephone in the UK is much the same as in any other country – with a few British eccentricities thrown in for good measure. It's important to know what kind of telephone you're calling and what it's costing. A number's prefix tells you what type of number it is; for example 00 (international dialling), 01/02 (national area codes), 03 (UK-wide numbers), 07 (mobiles and personal numbers), 08 (freephone and special rate services) and 09 (premium rate services).

Free numbers (freephone) have an 0800 prefix. They're usually provided by businesses that are trying to sell you something or, having sold you something, provide a free telephone support service. However, many companies are introducing or switching to 03 numbers instead of providing a freephone number.

Numbers with the prefix 0844 and 0845 are, in theory, charged at the local rate, irrespective of where you're calling from, while those with the prefix 0870/0871/0872 are charged at premium rate, even when you're calling locally (see www.saynoto0870.com). Both can be considerably more expensive than calling a geographical (01/02) number or UK-wide (03) – as much as 10p a minute with some providers. With more people using mobile phones, and having inclusive minutes for calling 01/02/03 numbers, many businesses and organisations are moving over to 03 prefixes.

☑ SURVIVAL TIP

Be wary of using premium rate numbers and don't allow your children access to them (they can be barred or blocked). Some people (or their children) have unwittingly run up bills of thousands of pounds using these numbers!

Premium rate numbers – usually providing specialist information and entertainment – begin with 09 and can cost as much as £3 per minute. These are beloved by TV and scratch card 'competition' operators, where everyone's a winner, and the 'prizes' are paid for by call charges – the 'message' can last five minutes or more.

For a full breakdown of prefixes and what they cost to call, the Office of Communications (Ofcom) provides a guide (www.ofcom.org.uk/phones-telecoms-and-internet/advice-for-consumers/costs-and-billing/how-much-does-a-phone-call-really-cost).

When dialling a UK number from overseas, you must dial the international access code used in the country from which you're calling (e.g. 011 from the US or 00 from most other countries), followed by the UK's international code (44), the area code without the first 0 (i.e. 20 for London) and the subscriber's number. For the central London number 7123 4567, you dial the access code followed by 44-20-7123 4567.

Telephone numbers are usually dictated one digit at a time on the phone, except for repeated numbers, e.g. 11 or 222, which are given as double one or treble two. Zero is usually read as the letter 'O' (oh).

Calling Features

Caling Features are additional services available from BT and other phone companies for subscribers connected to a digital exchange. They usually incur a fee, either monthly or per use and include call diversion, call waiting, ring back, 1471, BT answer 1571, call barring, anonymous call rejection, choose to refuse, caller display, call sign, caller redirect, three-way calling, reminder call, BT test and text alert.

Many services can be combined for a flat monthly fee, e.g. BT rates are £4.25 per month for one service, £8.50 per month for two to four services, and £11.50 per month for five or more services. There are also a number of per use calling features, where you pay a set fee each time you use the service. Calling features are offered by most service providers, not just BT, and fees may vary.

For an explanation and fees for calling features, see the BT Calling Features User Guide (http://bt.custhelp.com/app/answers/detail/a_id/9061/~/user-guides-for-phones-and-calling-features).

CALL RATES

Call rates vary considerably in the UK depending on the time of day, day of the week, the area and – not least – the telephone company.

Local & National Call Rates

BT remains by far the largest telephone company in the UK and therefore its rates are shown here simply as an example of call charges. This isn't meant as an endorsement of the company, which charges some of the country's highest rates, and you can usually save money by using another company (see above).

BT charges a monthly line rental fee of £18.99 (including VAT) for a residential line although its Line Rental Saver option offers a 10 per cent discount provided you pay a year in advance (£205.08). Like most other providers, BT doesn't price different types of call so that you can see at a glance how much you're being charged, but includes its call charges in what it calls 'plans', as follows:

- **Unlimited Weekend:** calls made between midnight Friday and midnight Sunday, which are included free with your line rental.
- **Unlimited Evening & Weekend:** calls made between 7pm and 7am Monday to Friday, plus weekends (see above). The plan costs £3.50 a month.
- **Unlimited Anytime:** calls to any UK landline number at any time. The plan costs £8.50 a month and also includes free calls to 0845 and 0870 numbers, and half price calls to mobiles. However, 'free' only applies to calls lasting up to an hour so you must ring off and dial again or you'll be charged the normal rate.

The cost of all BT plans and services can be downloaded in a PDF file: www.productsandservices.bt.com/products/lib/pdf/BT_phonetariff_residential.pdf. VAT at 20 per cent is levied on line rental and call charges.

International Call Rates

All private telephones in the UK are on international direct dialling (IDD), allowing calls to be dialled direct to some 200 countries and reverse charge (collect) calls to be made to some 140 countries. To make an international call, dial 00, the country code, the area code without the first zero (with a few exceptions, such as Italy) and the subscriber's number. Dial 155 for the international operator to make non-IDD calls, credit card calls, person-to-person and reverse charge calls (which aren't accepted by all countries), and 118 505 for international directory enquiries.

The codes for the major cities of many countries are listed in telephone directories under International Information, including the time difference. (One sure way to upset someone is to wake them at 3am!) To find out more about international direct dialling, country codes, BT international services and related topics, see www.bt.com or ring the international operator on 155.

> ☑ **SURVIVAL TIP**
>
> You can buy a UK & International Phone Card (£5, £10 or £20) from the Post Office (0330-001 0111, www.postoffice.co.uk/international-phonecards), which allows you to make cheap UK and international calls, e.g. 2-4p per minute from landlines.

BT offers call packages that offer discounts on these prices, such as Friends & Family International, which costs £1.35 a month and reduces the cost of calling many popular destinations to around 3p per minute. If you make a lot of international calls, the

International Freedom package includes up to 600 minutes of free calls to selected countries for just £7.50 a month. International charges and plans are listed on the BT website (www.bt.com). In 2016, BT's standard daytime rates were around 75p per minute to Australia, France, Germany and New Zealand, and 45p to Canada, Ireland, Japan and USA, PLUS a 19p setup fee per call.

Note that many other companies charge a standard flat rate for calls to, for example, Australia and the USA, which may be as low as 2p per minute.

BILLS

BT bills you for your line rental, phone rental and calls either quarterly (every three months) or monthly if you pay by direct debit; other providers may have different billing arrangements. If applicable, the telephone connection fee is included in your first bill. BT provides all customers with itemised bills stating the date and time, duration and cost of each call. Customers can choose to have only certain calls itemised.

BT phone bills can be paid by in full by direct debit or via a monthly payment plan (to spread costs evenly throughout the year). Other payment methods include by phone or online using your debit or credit card, by bank transfer, at a bank or post office, by post (cheques) or using a BT payment card at participating outlets – but opting for one of these adds another £2 to your BT line rental costs. With a direct debit, your account is debited around ten days after the billing date.

If you don't pay your phone bill within a few days of receiving it, you'll receive a reminder or a phone call and will have a further ten days in which to pay it (or a week if you pay by direct debit), after which you may be charged extra for late payment. If your bill remains unpaid for longer than 28 days (or 21 in the case of direct debit payments), your phone is disconnected, usually without any further notification.

If you've a query and cannot obtain satisfaction from BT customer services (0800-800 150) – or another service provider – you can contact the Ombudsman Services (www.ombudsman-services.org). Complaints about telephone bills are also dealt with by the Office of Communications (Ofcom, 020-7981 3040, www.ofcom.org.uk).

MOBILE PHONES

The UK is one of the world's most prolific users of mobile phones, which are now an everyday 'necessity' for the vast majority of the population. Mobile phone network providers include 3, O2, EE and Vodafone, plus many smaller companies (such as Family Mobile, Giffgaff, Tesco and Virgin) who buy time from the major operators and offer their own services.

There's little discernible difference in coverage between the major companies. All offer 2G and 3G coverage across 99 per cent of the UK, while the 4G network (see www.4g.co.uk) – which provides higher mobile broadband speeds – is much less widespread. In a survey conducted by the National

Infrastructure Commission (NIC) in 2016, the UK's 4G coverage was rated a lowly 54th in the world – behind countries such as Albania, Lithuania and Romania – at just 57.9 per cent. The quality of any mobile phone reception is terrible in many parts of the country and customer service even worse. Details about areas of coverage are available on websites such as http://ukmobilecoverage.co.uk and www.uswitch.com/mobiles/guides/mobile_phone_coverage.

In 2016, roaming call charges within the EU (plus Norway, Iceland and Liechtenstein) were reduced from around 16.5p to 4p per minute and will be abolished completely in 2017. In other countries (outside the EU) you can now avoid the hugely inflated 'roaming' charges by simply purchasing a foreign or global SIM card (see www.globalsimcard.co.uk). In some cases you may need a separate local SIM for each country, although UK2Abroad (www.uk2abroad.com) has a global SIM card that can be used in many countries.

Phones are sold by retail outlets, including the main mobile operators' stores, e.g. EE, O2, etc., specialist dealers (e.g. Carphone Warehouse), department and chain stores (e.g. Dixons) and supermarkets, all of whom have arrangements with service providers or networks to sell airtime contracts alongside phones. You should deal with an independent company that sells a wide range of phones and can connect you to any network, but you shouldn't rely on getting good or impartial advice from retail staff, some of whom know little or nothing about phones and networks.

Retailers advertise almost daily in magazines and newspapers, with constant offers. Phones are even available free if you're willing to sign a contract, which ensures that retailers and network providers can make a huge profit through line rental and call charges. If you make few calls from a mobile phone, the best phone may be a cheap pay-as-you-go model, without a contract. The cheapest type of contract is a SIM only deal (you provide the phone). Phones can also be purchased secondhand, e.g. on Ebay.

Before buying a phone, compare the battery life, memory capacity, weight, size and features (including a camera, internet access and texting), which may include automatic call back, unanswered call store, mailbox, call timer, minute minder, lock facility and call barring (etc.). In fact, it's impossible to buy a phone that will simply allow you to make and receive phone calls!

Before buying a mobile phone, check the reviews and comparison tests in surveys conducted by *Which?* (www.which.co.uk/reviews/mobile-phones/article/how-to-choose-the-best-mobile-phone) and *What Mobile* magazine (www.whatmobile.net), and check comparison websites such as www.billmonitor.com, www.broadbandchoices.co.uk/mobile and www.mobilechoiceuk.com. Ofcom (http://consumers.ofcom.org.uk/phone/mobile-phones) also provides independent advice on choosing a mobile phone provider.

DIRECTORIES & DIRECTORY ENQUIRIES

British telephone subscribers, both business and private, are listed in *The Phone Book*, a set of directories each covering a local area, with businesses and private subscribers listed in separate sections. If you don't have the latest local edition when you move into a new home, you can get one free from BT. Those

 **Caution**

When it comes to making calls to directory enquiries, the short answer is DON'T.

for adjacent areas can be obtained for a fee (0800-833400, www.shop.bt.com/products/phone-book-finder.html).

However, the easiest way to look up a phone number is to use an online directory such as the Phone Book (www.thephonebook.bt.com), Yellow Pages (www.yell.com), 118 118 (www.118118.com) or 192 (www.192.com). Other free directories include Thompson Local directories (www.thomsonlocal.com).

These are probably the most expensive calls you can make to anyone – even more expensive than calling your aunt in New Zealand! A 45-second phone call to 118 118 will cost you over £6, while calls to the BT directory enquiries number 118 500 cost a similar amount, although you can use their online service (www.bt118500.com/index.publisha) free of charge.

INTERNET

Broadband internet is now standard in the UK, where very few users depend on dial up and even ADSL is old technology. The UK government (and businesses) is keen for people to do everything online, from claiming benefits to paying taxes, and broadband speeds are accelerating to cater to this need.

According to the government website (www.gov.uk/gosuperfast), in 2016 some 90 per cent of UK homes and business had access to 'superfast' broadband – the best in the European Union – which it defines as download speeds in excess of 24Mbps, although fibre optic cables (that deliver real superfast broadband) allegedly deliver speeds of up to 300Mbps. The main providers of superfast broadband are BT Infinity (also used by EE, Sky and Talk Talk) and Virgin Media.

You can check whether superfast broadband is available in your area by visiting the Gov.uk website (http://gosuperfastchecker.culture.gov.uk), www.broadband.co.uk/checker or www.broadbandchecker.co.uk (and many others). Note that you need to take all claimed speeds – which are usually 'up to', meaning the quoted maximum may only be available at 6am on a Sunday – with a large pinch of salt. You can check your actual broadband speed with www.broadbandspeedchecker.co.uk.

The broadband market is fiercely competitive and you can connect for as little as £5 per month or even free for 12 months, although many cheap deals are introductory offers and may not include all the costs. You also need check what the monthly fee is after the 'honeymoon' period and how long you're

tied into a contract. 'Bundles' which include phone calls and even subscription TV are commonplace, and should save you money. Costs have fallen dramatically in recent years and many providers now offer deals which include home phone line rental, free UK calls, inexpensive international calls and fast (but not superfast) broadband for a little as £25 per month. Many broadband providers include free connection and a router if you subscribe to their service, although they can impose quite heavy charges if you exceed your monthly download limit. It's best to have an 'unlimited' service, particularly if you're a heavy user.

You can compare broadband packages from numerous providers via a comparison website such as Broadband Finder (www.broadband-finder.co.uk), Broadband Genie (www.broadbandgenie.co.uk) and Cable.co.uk (www.cable.co.uk/broadband/packages).

You can access broadband through your mobile phone, saving the expense of a landline. Coverage is improving all the time and you can almost dispense with a home phone and router if you've a smartphone, e.g. an iPhone, Blackberry or Samsung Galaxy, or a tablet such as the must-have iPad. Mobile packages usually include some data usage, and cost from £5 a month. Deals vary considerably and costs soon mount up if you exceed your monthly allowance, therefore it's wise to overestimate your data requirements.

One way to save on your data 'spend' is to hook up to a wifi hotspot, which can be found throughout the UK in cafés, fast-food restaurants, many supermarkets and libraries, although services aren't necessarily provided free. Many websites list wifi hotspots such as My Hotspots (www.myhotspots.co.uk). There are also a number of 'free' wireless internet providers in the UK – such as BT's OpenZone (www.btwifi.co.uk) – although you usually need to subscribe in order to receive a reliable service (BT charge from £4 per hour to £15 per month with a 12-month contract).

There are a number of internet magazines published in the UK, including *Net* and *WebUser*.

MOVING HOUSE OR LEAVING BRITAIN

When moving house or leaving the UK, you must notify your telephone (and internet) companies at least 14 days in advance if you're moving to another provider or 30 days if you're cancelling a contract (for BT dial 0800-345 7310 or 0330-123 4150). When moving house and remaining within the same code area, you should be able to retain your existing number. Don't forget to have the telephone line disconnected when moving house, otherwise the new owners or tenants will be able to make calls at your expense.

When taking over a phone in a new property, you must ensure that you're connected to the company of your choice, i.e. preferably one with low rates and high-speed broadband.

EMERGENCY NUMBERS

The national emergency numbers in the UK are 999/112, which are for police, fire and ambulance emergencies, plus coastguard, cave and mountain rescue services. The emergency code 112 was introduced throughout the EU in 1992 to aid foreign visitors, and is used in addition to the original 999 number.

Emergency calls are free from all telephones, including payphones. When you dial 999/112, the operator asks you which

For less urgent medical enquiries you can dial 111 (free), while the non-emergency number for the police is 101 (15p per call from landlines and mobiles).

emergency service you require ("Emergency, which service please?") and you're immediately switched through to that service. You must state clearly your name, location and give a brief description of the emergency. Some payphones are reserved for emergency 999 calls, shown by a flashing message.

In addition to providing an emergency transport service for those in urgent need of medical attention, the ambulance service also deals with the victims of accidents such as drowning, asphyxiation (lack of oxygen), choking, electrocution, serious burns and hanging. In addition to attending fires, the fire service attends traffic accidents, natural and man-made disasters, and extricates people who are trapped, e.g. in a building. The fire brigade may charge for special services, such as supporting a house that's in danger of collapse as a result of subsidence (or rescuing a cat from a tree!).

The Samaritans provide a confidential counselling service in times of personal crisis. Local numbers are available in telephone directories, along with numbers for other organisations offering free help and advice such as Alcoholics Anonymous. Local hospitals are also listed here. See also **Emergencies** on page 173.

8. TELEVISION & RADIO

Television in Britain has come a long way in the last couple of decades. Twenty years ago there were a handful of conventional analogue television stations, with cable and satellite TV available for those who were prepared to pay more (which people did mainly for their sports and movie channels). Nowadays digital broadcasting has brought around 100 free-to-air TV channels to everyone and streamed online television has made the choice wider still, offering further channels (some needing a subscription), the ability to catch up with programmes on conventional stations, and the potential to stream recent film releases on a pay-to-view basis. In 2016 it was estimated that watching live or recorded 'conventional' TV still accounts for over three times as much as streamed TV, but the gap is closing fast.

TELEVISION

British television (TV) was once widely reckoned to be the best in the world – not that this is saying a great deal when you consider the standard of most conventional TV worldwide. Although British broadcasters generate the usual surfeit of nonsense (e.g. inane game shows and 'reality' TV – people' or celebrities doing daft things, sometimes labelled 'tabloid' TV), and show a good deal of imported (mostly American) soaps and films to cater for couch potatoes, they also produce many excellent programmes.

These include nature, culture and travel documentaries, motoring programmes, serialised adaptations of novels, bespoke TV films, situation comedies and variety shows; as well as music programmes, chat shows, sports events, and news and current affairs programmes. But British drama is by and large overshadowed by the glossy productions emerging from the US these days, the products of budgets a British TV producer could only dream of…

The presentation of many programmes has become increasingly 'showbiz', and presenters and newscasters have become 'celebrities' in their own right (often more so that those they're interviewing!).

Explicit sex and extreme violence are becoming commonplace, even before the so-called watershed time of 9pm, before which programmes with 'adult' content shouldn't be aired. If you find anything offensive you can make a complaint to the Office of Communications (OFCOM, www.ofcom.org.uk).

Broadcasting Standards

The television broadcasting standard isn't the same in the UK as in most other countries; and TVs and DVD players manufactured for use in the US (NTSC standard) won't function in the UK. Most European countries also have a different TV broadcasting system from the UK, and use the PAL B/G standard, except for France, which has its own standard called SECAM. The British standard is a modified PAL-I system.

> **☑ SURVIVAL TIP**
>
> If you bring a TV to the UK from the US or the continent, you'll get either a picture or sound, but not both. A TV can be converted to work in the UK, but it usually isn't worth the trouble and expense.

Stations

BBC television (www.bbc.co.uk) has been broadcasting regularly since 1936 and introduced a second station (BBC2) in 1964. There are now several other BBC channels, including BBC4 (www.bbc.co.uk/bbcfour) for arts, science, history and business programmes; BBC News 24 (www.bbc.co.uk/bbcnews24); BBC Parliament; plus a couple of children's channels. BBC HD, which broadcasts selected programmes on Freeview (terrestrial digital television) in high definition, was launched in 2010. (BBC3 ceased broadcasting in March 2016.)

The first regular commercial programmes began in London in 1955, broadcast by a company originally called Independent Television (ITV, www.itv.com), on a station now known as ITV1. ITV1 broadcasts regional programmes (there are 15 regions) and national programmes, such as news and soaps. ITV2, 3, 4 and ITVBe show a mixture of repeats, reality shows, sport, and programmes aimed at the youth market. There's also a children's channel, CITV. Two more terrestrial national commercial TV stations, Channel 4 (www.channel4.com) and Five (www.channel5.com), were launched in 1982 and 1997 respectively and have spawned their own spin-offs, including E4, More4, Film4, 5* and 5 USA.

All five terrestrial/free-to-air TV stations (see below) – BBC1, BBC2, ITV1, Channel 4 and Five – can be received throughout the UK. The BBC channels carry no advertising, and are publicly funded through an annual TV licence (see below) and the trading activities of BBC Enterprises. The other stations have regular 'commercial breaks' (approximately every 10 to 15 mins), which are becoming longer and more frequent and make watching programmes a chore (better to record them or watch them on one of the online 'catch up' services such as BBC iPlayer).

Since the introduction of terrestrial digital broadcasting the big five have been joined by a host of smaller commercial channels, as outlined below. Most TV stations broadcast 24 hours a day, and programmes usually start on the hour or half hour.

TV Licence

An annual TV licence (£145.50 for colour, or £49 for the three people who still have black and white sets) is required by anyone with a TV. Licences are free if you're aged 75 or over and registered blind people are generously offered a reduction of 50 per cent on production of a local authority certificate for the blind.

If you only watch DVDs, non-BBC online playback services or clips on You Tube, the licence fee isn't payable (although it's difficult to prove you don't watch BBC if you've a TV in your home). The licence fee covers any number of TVs in a home. Note that since September 2016, you've required a licence even if you only watch BBC TV online via BBC's iPlayer 'catchup' service. The fine for not having a licence is up to £1,000.

TV licences can be purchased from TV Licensing (0300-790 6165, www.tvlicensing.co.uk) and must be renewed annually. The fee can be paid by direct debit, credit or debit card, at PayPoint outlets or via a TV licensing savings or payment card that allows you to spread the cost. If you're leaving the UK, you can obtain a refund on any unexpired three-month period of a TV licence by applying in writing to Customer Services at the address above. The old-style paper licences are still available, but you can also opt to have the licence emailed to you.

Transmission

All British television is digital and has been since 2012 when the last analogue transmitters were turned off. Digital television provides a superior picture, DVD-quality sound, widescreen cinema format and access to many more stations, as well as interactive services. As Britain has gone digital, so people have been getting their television fix in ever-more varied ways: from cinema-type curved widescreen TVs, via laptops and desktops to tablets and mobile phones. 3D television was trialled at the 2012 Olympics but never took off, due partly to the high cost.

Many homes still have rooftop aerials and a lot of channels are free-to-air (see below) – new televisions come with an integrated Freeview service that includes 70 TV channels – but increasingly TV is also available by satellite, cable and via the internet. This means you no longer have to watch a show when it's broadcast but can see it later (at a time and place that suits you) on catch-up TV such as BBC iPlayer (www.bbc.co.uk/iplayer) or ITV Hub (www.itv.com/hub/shows) and even gorge yourself on entire boxed sets (series) of popular dramas such as *Breaking Bad* and *Downton Abbey*.

You can also watch TV online via a web browser using a service such as TV Catchup (www.tvcatchup.com), where you simply select a channel to watch or download one of the apps available.

Terrestrial (free-to-air) TV & Freeview

Terrestrial TV – or free-to-air TV as it's often described – is available across the UK and broadcasts 70 national channels, 12 HD (high-definition) channels and 30 radio stations from the Freeview platform. Channels include the four main broadcasters (BBC, ITV, C4 and Five) and their spin-offs, plus a number of general channels (e.g. Pick, Dave, Quest and Yesterday), local, news, sport, children's and even adult entertainment channels. Freeview also provides access to 'catch-up' channels such as ITV+1 and C4+1 and to text-based services such as BBC Red Button.

There are no monthly fees, and all you need to watch is an aerial and either a Freeview-enabled TV or set-top box – boxes cost from around £20. A Freeview+ box allows you to record programmes and watch catchup TV via Freeview Play, costing from around £90. In areas with poor reception you may require an aerial upgrade. For further information, contact Freeview (0345- 650 5050, www.freeview.co.uk). All new digital TVs include Freeview as standard.

Satellite TV

Satellite TV offers the widest choice of channels and service providers – the bigger your dish, the more channels you can watch,

and it's the only choice for those who want to watch foreign-language TV. The UK's largest satellite TV provider is Sky (0808-160 1465, www.sky.com), which provides a wealth of programmes including general entertainment, children's programmes, news, sports (some major sports' events are shown exclusively on Sky) and movie channels, plus pay-per-view movies. You can also receive numerous radio stations via Sky, including most popular stations.

Sky's latest receiver is called Sky Q, which allows for reception in Ultra HD (e.g. for sports and films) and allows you to record as many as four channels while watching a fifth, so you never need to miss a programme again (you can store over 1,000 hours of programmes in SD with the 2tb box). You can also watch everything from your main box on tablets around the home and even save recording to a tablet or laptop PC and watch programmes on the go. **However, bear in mind that you need a special Sky Q satellite dish, and communal dishes usually need to be upgraded to this standard.**

In late 2016 Sky were offering TV bundles from £20 per month, although the price can escalate fast when you start adding extras such as multiscreen (£12 per month), cinema (£18) and sports (£27.50). You can also receive your phone line and broadband from Sky (various packages). Contracts run for a minimum of 12 months. Once the equipment is installed, it's your property, and you don't have to return it to Sky at the end of your contract.

If you don't want to be tied to a monthly subscription, Freesat (0345-313 0051, www.freesat.co.uk) gives you access to over 200 free TV and radio channels, with the same pause-rewind-and-record and HD options. The catch is that you have to pay for a receiver (from £20-90) and provide your own dish.

Satellite programmes are listed in most national daily newspapers and general TV magazines, and Sky boxes include an interactive TV guide.

Cable TV

Cable television in the UK was originally confined to areas of poor reception (e.g. due to geographical features or high-rise buildings) or where external aerials weren't permitted. However, there has been an explosion in cable TV over the last few decades; millions of homes can now receive cable and there are over 3.7 million subscribers (although the UK still has a long way to go to match European countries such as Belgium, the Netherlands and Switzerland, where 90 per cent of the populations have access to cable TV).

☑ SURVIVAL TIP

If you take out a TV subscription, you usually get a better deal if you opt for a bundle including phone and broadband. Providers often waive installation or equipment charges and may offer other incentives. However, check for long contract tie-ins and low prices that soar after a 12 months.

The main provider is Virgin Media (0345-454 1111/2222, www.virginmedia.com), which is available to some 55 per cent of UK households and offers over 160 channels. Its selling point is the TiVo box which lets you record and store entire TV series, as well as accessing many channels' catch up services. Virgin Media's offers start at around £12 per month for their basic TV, broadband and phone deal (£26 per month after 12 months) plus a £14.99 activation fee. If you want BT and Sky Sports, the monthly fee soars to £55 per month (£87.50 per month after 12 months). You also have to budget for the rental of a Virgin landline t £19 a month.

Streaming Services

Twenty years ago most people depended on unreliable-dial up connections for access to the internet, but in 2005 dial up was overtaken by broadband as a way of getting online. The faster speeds provided by broadband have enabled truly high definition television that these days can be streamed not only to computer monitors, but also via wifi to smart televisions, phones and tablets around the home.

So popular has streaming become that Sky, the principal satellite broadcaster, has launched its own streaming services under the brand of Now TV (www.nowtv.com). Customers can subscribe to one or all packages, which include Movies (£9.99 for a monthly pass), Entertainment (£6.99) and Sport (£33.99). The Entertainment pass provides access to some of the major Sky channels – including Sky 1, Sky 2, Sky Atlantic and Sky Arts – and the monthly pass scheme means that you could subscribe for the next season of, say *Game of Thrones,* then not renew your subscription until the subsequent season begins the following year.

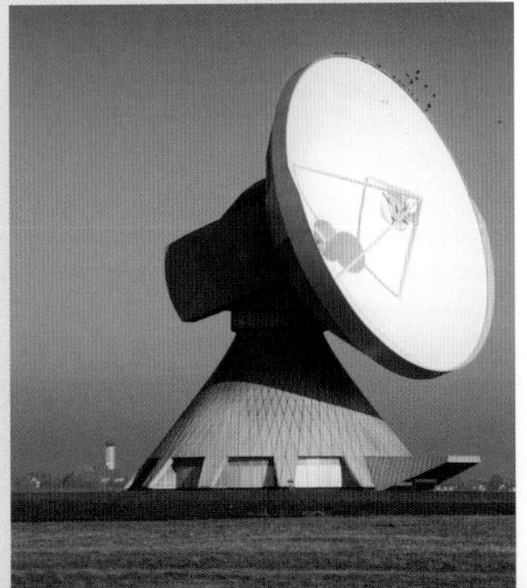

In a similar fashion, football fans could choose to subscribe to Sky Sports for just the winter months.

Netflix is one of the success stories of the digital age – it doesn't just stream other people's films and TV shows, but also commissions its own, such as the hugely popular political drama *House of Cards*. You can hook up to Netflix from £5.99 a month (0800-096 6379, www.netflix.com/gb/).

Amazon Prime Instant Video (www.amazon.co.uk/primevideo) operates in a similar way to Netflix, in that it offers customers their pick of a wide range of video on demand (feature films, video box sets and TV programmes) rather than TV channels. Amazon has also recently begun producing its own programmes and series, including *The Man in the High Castle* and *The Grand Tour* motoring extravaganza (presented by the former BBC *Top Gear* trio). Amazon Prime Video is free to subscribers to the annual Amazon Prime service (which offers other advantages for regular customers of their shopping website) or is available on packages starting from £5.99 per month.

DVDs

At one point over three-quarters of UK homes owned a DVD or blu-ray player and the British rental market was one of the largest in the world. However, the way we rent films has been steadily changing since the late 2000s with the advent of streaming – where you can have a film sent direct to your TV or laptop via the internet – and rentals (and sales) of DVDs have been falling for years. There are no longer DVD rental shops on every high street, although it's still possible to hire DVDs by post. The widest range is probably offered by Lovefilm by Post (www.amazon.co.uk/lovefilm). You can compare rental deals via DVD Rental (www.dvdrental.co.uk).

Alternatively you can buy or rent videos individually to watch online from companies including Amazon Video and Wuaki (www.wuaki.com). The cost is usually around £3.50 for a film in normal definition or £4.50 in high definition. There are also many high street stores (such as supermarkets and Argos) selling physical DVDs or you can buy them online from numerous companies (just Google 'DVD films') such as Amazon, Play (www.play.com) and Zavvi (www.zavvi.com). The best place to buy secondhand DVDs is at car boot sales, where they're sold for just a few pounds.

DVDs may be encoded with a region code, restricting the area of the world in which they can be played. The code for Western Europe is 2, while discs without any region coding are called all-region or region 0 discs. However, you can buy all-region DVD players and DVD players can be modified to be region-free, allowing the playback of all discs (see www.regionfreedvd.net or www.moneysavingexpert.com/shopping/dvd-unlock).

RADIO

Radio reception in the UK is generally excellent, including stereo reception, although FM reception isn't always good in cars. The radio audience in the UK is almost equally split between the British Broadcasting Corporation (BBC) and commercial radio stations, although the BBC has been losing listeners to commercial stations at an increasing rate in recent years. Community and ethnic radio is also popular in many areas, and a number of universities and colleges operate their own radio stations. You can also listen to most major radio stations via the Internet or via a TV with freeview, satellite or cable reception.

> There's no advertising on BBC radio stations, which are financed by the government and the revenue from TV licence fees, as no radio licence is necessary in the UK.

BBC

The BBC operates five national radio stations (and other digital stations – see below) with easy to remember (if unimaginative) names: BBC Radio 1 (FM 97-99) for contemporary music; BBC Radio 2 (FM 88-91) for 'easy-listening' music; BBC Radio 3 (FM 90-93) for classical music, jazz and occasionally drama and poetry; BBC Radio 4 (FM 92-95, FM 103-105, LW 198) for conversation, comedy, drama, documentaries, magazine programmes and news; BBC Radio 5 Live (MW 693, 909) for news, current affairs and sport; and BBC Radio 6 music (DAB 12B). There are also over 50 BBC local radio stations (see http://news.bbc.co.uk/local/hi/default.stm) with around 8 million listeners.

BBC radio programmes are published in the *Radio Times*, in national newspapers and listed on the BBC website (www.bbc.co.uk/radio).

Commercial Radio

Radio is still a popular entertainment medium in the UK, where some 50 million people or 90 per cent of adults listen to the radio every week for, on average, 21 hours a week. Yet there are only some 300 commercial radio stations in the whole of the UK, compared with around 1,000 in France and Italy and over 9,000 in the US.

Stations vary from large national stations with vast budgets and millions of listeners, to tiny local stations run by volunteers with just a few thousand listeners. They provide national or local news and information, music and other entertainment, education, consumer advice and traffic information, and provide listeners with the chance to air their views through phone-in programmes, emails and text messages. Advertising on commercial radio is limited to around ten minutes per hour but is usually less.

In the past there weren't enough radio frequencies available to accommodate a large number of national commercial radio stations, but the arrival of digital radio has opened the door to many more. The main commercial stations are, in descending order of listenership, Heart, Capital, Smooth, Classic FM, Kiss and Magic: all of these bar one play popular music, the exception being Classic FM which broadcasts a slightly homogenised form of classical music.

Digital Radio

Digital radio offers better sound quality and less interference than analogue radio. It's available in around 90 per cent of the UK which has the largest digital radio network in the world, offering some 300 stations with more being added all the time. It's estimated that some 40 per cent of all radio listeners use a digital platform and the government is considering switching off analogue radio signals in the not too distant future when the figure exceeds 50 per cent and national DAB coverage is comparable to FM.

You need a digital radio (costing from around £25) to receive it the traditional way, but programmes are also broadcast via television, e.g. Freeview (25 stations) and cable services such as Virgin (60 plus stations), and the internet – the latter option allows you to tune in to not just UK digital radio, but radio from all around the world.

All national BBC radio stations are broadcast digitally and there are digital-only stations, including BBC Radio 1 Xtra, Radio 4 Extra, Radio 5 Live Sports Extra and Radio 6 Music. Commercial radio has also gone digital, and many national and semi-national stations, including Absolute Radio, Classic FM, Jazz FM, Smooth Radio and Talksport, are available digitally.

TV & Internet Radio

If you've satellite TV, you can also receive radio stations via your satellite link. For example, BBC Radio 1, 2, 3, 4 and 5, BBC World Service, Sky News Radio, Absolute, Classic FM, Talksport and many foreign (i.e. non-English) stations can be received by subscribers to Sky satellite TV services. Satellite radio stations are listed in the service providers' electronic programme guides. As mentioned above, some 30 radio stations – including most of the major ones – are also available via Freeview digital television.

If you've an internet connection you can listen to hundreds of radio stations via websites such as www.internetradiouk.com (for UK radio stations) – including all the main BBC stations – www.live-radio.net/us.shtml (US radio stations) and www.internet-radio.com, which has links to hundreds of music stations from around the world that you can choose by genre.

9. EDUCATION

British schools have a mixed reputation: while the quality of state education varies widely from superb to failing, the UK is famous for its excellent public schools and universities, which educate hundreds of thousands of foreign students a year from all corners of the globe.

Full-time education is compulsory in the UK for all children between the ages of five (four in Northern Ireland) and 16, including the children of foreign nationals permanently or temporarily resident in the UK for a year or longer. Note, however, that in England children who entered secondary education after September 2007 are required to remain in full-time education until the age of 18, either in an apprenticeship or training; spending 20 hours or more a week working or volunteering; or in part-time education (full-time paid employment is against the law for under-18s). No fees are payable in state schools, which are attended by over 90 per cent of pupils.

Most state schools (primary and secondary) are co-educational (mixed) day schools, with the exception of a few secondary schools that accept boarders. Private fee-paying schools – of which there are over 2,500 in the UK, including American, international and foreign schools – include day and boarding schools and are mostly single-sex, although an increasing number of junior and some senior schools are co-educational. Admission to a state school for foreign children is dependent on the type and duration of the residence permit (see **Chapter 3**) granted to their parents.

One of the most important decisions facing parents in the UK is whether to send their children to a state or private school. In some areas, state schools are the equal of the best private schools, while in others (particularly in neglected inner city areas) they lack resources and achieve poor results. Your choice of state and private schools will vary considerably depending on where you live.

The UK's education system has had a bad press in recent years and, according to many surveys, is falling behind the leading countries, particularly in mathematics (math) and science. There's a dearth of vocational education and training in the UK, and general educational standards are inferior to those in some other countries, particularly when it comes to maths and science; in 2014 the UK was rated number six in a ranking of the world's top educational systems (source: www.edudemic.com/learning-curve-report-education), behind South Korea, Japan, Singapore, Hong Kong and Finland.

Many parents prefer to send their children to a private school, often making financial sacrifices to do so. Although private education is no longer the preserve of the nobility and the wealthy, fees have soared in recent years (as schools have attracted an ever-increasing number of affluent foreign children), and middle class British families are being priced out.

In addition to a detailed look at state and private education, this chapter also contains information about higher and further education and language schools.

There's no legal obligation for parents in the UK to educate their children at school and they may educate them themselves or employ private tutors. Parents educating their children at home don't require a teaching qualification, although they must satisfy the local education authority (LEA) that a child is receiving full-time education appropriate for his or her age, abilities and aptitudes (they will check and may test your child).

Information

There has never been as much information available about schools, both state and private, as there is today. To help you choose an appropriate school, all state primary and secondary schools must publish a prospectus giving details of their educational, religious and social policies. A list of schools in a given area can be obtained from county or borough education offices in England and Wales (listed in telephone directories). Secondary schools are also required to publish full details of their GCSE and GCE A-level results (see **Examinations** on page 124). The government also publishes school performance tables (www.gov.uk/school-performance-tables) and has a feature that allows you to compare school and college performance (www.compare-school-performance.service.gov.uk).

One of the best sources of information about UK schools is Schoolsnet (www.schoolsnet.com), the first website to give parents the chance to write their own reviews of any school in the country. Since its creation in 1999 it has earned a reputation as the leading online guide to schools in the UK, with over 250,000 registered users and detailed profiles, exam results and inspection reports of some 36,000 schools.

Other education-related websites include Education UK (www.educationuk.org), the BBC (www.bbc.co.uk/learning), the Department for Education (www.education.gov.uk) and Edubase (www.education.gov.uk/edubase/home.xhtml), a government portal that allows you to search for schools in your area. ACE Education Advice and Training (www.ace-ed.org.uk), provides information on all matters relating to state education and operates a telephone advice line (0300-0115 142, 10am-1pm, Mondays to Wednesdays).

There are a number of publications for parents faced with choosing a suitable state or private school, including the *Good Schools Guide* by Ralph Lucas (www.goodschoolsguide.co.uk). *The Sunday Times* provides an online guide (www.thesundaytimes.co.uk/sto/public/goodschools/article444384.ece) to the best primary and secondary schools in the UK, ranked by exam results (there's a subscription fee of £2 per week). You can also consult an independent adviser such as Gabbitas Educational Consultants Ltd. (020-7734 0161, www.gabbitas.co.uk), who can provide advice and information on all aspects of education in the UK.

An invaluable organisation for overseas students is the UK Council for International Student Affairs (UKCISA, 020-7788 9214, www.ukcisa.org.uk). It's a registered charity established in 1968 to promote the interests and needs of overseas students in the UK and those working with them as teachers, advisors or in other capacities.

The British Council (which has offices in around 80 countries) is the national office responsible for providing information and advice about educational visits and exchanges, and provides foreign students with information regarding all aspects of education in the UK. You can contact the UK customer service team in Manchester (0161-957 7755, www.britishcouncil.org/education).

STATE SCHOOLS

The term 'state' is used here in preference to 'public' and refers to non-fee-paying schools controlled by Local Education Authorities (LEAs) and funded from state taxes and local council tax revenue (officially called maintained schools). This is to prevent confusion with the term 'public school', used in the US (and Scotland) to refer to a state school, but which in England and Wales usually means a private fee-paying school. Private schools are formally referred to as independent schools in England and Wales.

The role of LEAs is held by the 152 local authorities (councils) in England, 32 Scottish councils and five education and library boards in Northern Ireland, while in Wales the councils of the counties and county boroughs are responsible for education. All state schools have a governing body, usually comprised of a number of parent representatives and governors (appointed by the LEA), the head teacher and other serving teachers. In Scotland, education authorities must establish school boards (consisting of elected parents and staff members) to participate in the management and administration of schools. Most state schools also have a Parents and Teachers Association (PTA).

Once you've made the decision to send your child to a state school, most experts advise that you stick to it for at least a year to give it a fair trial. It may take your child this long to adapt to the change of environment and the different curriculum, particularly if English isn't a child's mother tongue.

Types of School

There are various kinds of state school in the UK, including community schools, foundation and trust schools, voluntary-aided and voluntary controlled schools, free schools and academies, and city technology colleges (all described below). LEAs also provide schools for children with special educational needs (see **Special Education** on page 124).

State schools in England and Wales are usually classified as follows:

In some parts of England and Wales, the transfer age from First to Middle school and from Middle to Secondary school is one year later than shown above (i.e. 8 and 12 respectively instead of 7 and 11). In Scotland the transfer to secondary schools is made at the age of 12.

Type of School	Age Group
Nursery	Up to 5
Infant or First School	5 to 7 or 5 to 8
Junior /Middle	7 to 11 or 8 to 12
Primary	5 to 11
Secondary	11 to 16
Upper/High School	12/13 to 18
Secondary Plus	11 to 18
Sixth Form College	16 to 18/19

Community Schools

Community schools are run entirely by the local authority which owns the building and employs the staff. The local community is able to use the facilities.

Foundation & Trust Schools

In Foundation Schools, the governing body employs the school's staff and has primary responsibility for admission arrangements. The school's land and buildings are owned by the governing body or a charitable foundation. Some form a trust with an outside partner, such as a business or charity.

Voluntary-aided & Voluntary Controlled Schools

Voluntary-aided and voluntary controlled schools provide primary and secondary education, and are financially maintained by LEAs. The difference is that voluntary-aided school buildings are, in many cases, the responsibility of voluntary bodies, e.g. a church or a foundation (some are referred to as 'faith' schools – see below). Schools with C of E (Church of England) or Catholic in their name may be aided schools. County schools are owned by LEAs and wholly funded by them. They're non-denominational (not church aided or supported) and provide primary and secondary education.

Free Schools

A free school in England is a type of academy (see below), a non-profit-making, independent, state-funded school that's free to attend but which isn't controlled by a local authority. These are usually new schools established by teachers, independent schools, charities, community and faith groups, universities, businesses and groups of parents. Free schools are funded directly by central government and share with academies a greater control over their finances, curriculum, and teachers' pay and conditions. They're subject to the same school admissions code as all other state-funded schools.

Academies

Introduced in the late 2000s, academies are established by sponsors in partnership with the local authority and Department for Education, but are managed independently (by an academy trust) from the local authority and funded directly by central government. Academies aren't required to follow the national curriculum and can set their own term times. However, they must follow the same rules on admissions, special education needs and exclusions as other state schools.

Some academies have sponsors such as businesses, universities, other schools, faith groups or voluntary groups, who are responsible for improving the performance of the school. Converting to an academy is often seen as a way for successful schools to operate outside the control of their local education authority (LEA). Around two-thirds of comprehensive schools are academies and some 15 per cent of primary schools.

City Technology Colleges

City Technology Colleges are urban-based, independently managed secondary schools with a curriculum geared towards science, technology and the world of work. They're owned and funded by companies as well as central government, but not by local authorities. They have a particular emphasis on practical skills and offer a range of vocational qualifications as well as GCSEs and A-levels.

Faith Schools

These can be any of the above, but are associated with a particular religion, e.g. Catholic or Muslim schools. They must follow the national curriculum except for religious studies, where they're free to teach about their own religion. The admissions criteria and staffing policies may be different too, although anyone can apply for a place.

Choosing a State School

The quality of state schools, their teaching staff and the education they provide, varies considerably from region to region, LEA to LEA, and from school to school. If you want your children to have the best possible education, it's essential to get them into a good secondary school, even if it means moving house and changing your job. You can express a preference for a particular state school and don't have to choose a school within your local LEA. However, priority is usually given to children with a family member already at a school, children with special family or medical circumstances, and to children living in a school's catchment area.

It's vital to research the best schools in a given area and to ensure that your child has a good chance of being accepted at your chosen school before buying or renting a home. Admission to most state schools is decided largely on the local catchment area; if you live outside a school's area your child may not be admitted. Homes near the best state schools are at a premium, and prices in many areas have risen due to high demand; it's said that the UK has a selective state education system, based not on ability or exams, but on wealth, i.e. being able to afford a home in the catchment area of a good school. The best schools are oversubscribed by parents desperate to a secure a place for their children, some of which receive over ten applicants for each place.

Many parents are dissatisfied with their child's school. You can appeal against a refusal, as thousands of parents do each year, although most are unsuccessful. An LEA is obliged to provide transport or pay travelling expenses only when the nearest state school is over 2mi (3km) from home for under-8s or over 3mi (5km) for over-8s.

> **☑ SURVIVAL TIP**
>
> Bear in mind that paying a premium to live near a popular state school may not be the best option, and you may be better off spending the money on private education.

Admission

You should address enquiries about admission (enrolment) to state schools to the Chief Education Officer of the LEA or contact school secretaries or head teachers directly. If possible enquiries should be made well in advance of taking up residence in a new area. The school year in England and Wales normally begins in September and runs until July of the following year, while in Scotland it generally runs from mid-August to the end of June and in Northern Ireland from September to June. Most local councils publish information about school

School Terms

Term	2016/2017
Autumn	5th Sep to 16th Dec
Half-term	24th to 28th Oct
Spring	5th Jan to 31st Mar
Half-term	13th to 17th Feb
Summer	18th Apr to 21st Jul
Half-term	29th to 2nd June

admissions, and information is also available from the local Education Department.

Terms & School Hours

The school year is usually divided into three terms (autumn, spring and summer, a throwback to when children helped with the harvest), which are separated by 14 weeks holiday. The mid-term (or half-term) is usually marked by a one-week break. The typical term dates are shown above, although the actual dates and the length of holidays vary depending on the school and area (the dates shown are for the City of Westminster in London). You can check the school terms for any area in England and Wales via the Gov.uk website (www.gov.uk/school-term-holiday-dates) by entering your postcode.

Terms are a flexible length to accommodate the main public holidays, although sometimes holidays such as Easter fall within term time. Schools publish holiday dates well in advance, thus allowing plenty of time to schedule family holidays during official school holidays. Holidays shouldn't be taken during term time in England, although many parents ignore this and risk a fine of £60 or worse. The situation in Wales, Scotland and Northern Ireland varies (see www.gov.uk/school-attendance-absence/overview).

It's unwise to take a child out of school, particularly when he should be taking examinations or during important course work assignments. The GCSE examinations (see page 124) are scheduled for late May and June, and if your child misses an exam you may have to pay the fee again for him to take it later.

The school day in state schools is usually from 9am to noon and 1pm to 3.30pm or 4pm, Mondays to Fridays. Some (usually secondary) schools keep what are termed 'continental hours', starting at 8.30am and finishing at 2.30pm (with a short lunch break). There are no state school lessons on Saturdays.

Provisions & Uniforms

Most primary and secondary schools provide lunches (cafeteria self-service or buffet-style) for around £1.50-2.50 per day and parents are permitted to join a child for lunch in some schools. It may be necessary for pupils to order meals in advance and to book meals for a whole week, i.e. no meals on odd days. A child whose mother doesn't go out to work, and who lives within walking or cycling distance of school, may go home for lunch.

Most schools allow children to take a snack for morning break, e.g. biscuit, apple or crisps (chips), and milk is on sale in some schools. The quality of school meals and child nutrition in general has been a matter of public debate in recent years, and as a consequence in September 2014 the government started providing free lunches for children in reception (the first year at primary school) and years 1 and 2 of primary school. Free lunches are also provided for pupils whose parents receive certain benefits, who may also be exempt from paying for travel and school outings.

All secondary schools provide covered cycle racks for pupils who cycle to school. Primary school children usually need a school bag or satchel and a small bag or box for a packed lunch; a pencil case with pencils, etc. (not obligatory); gym shoes (plimsolls), shorts, T-shirt and a towel for games and exercise periods; and a sports bag for above (if the satchel is too small).

Although most state schools have a school uniform, the rules about wearing them may vary. In some schools it's obligatory, in others it isn't (rules may be more relaxed in infant and junior schools). Less well-off parents, e.g. those claiming Income Support (see **Chapter 13**), may qualify for a uniform grant and some secondary schools may also help with the cost of uniforms. State schools went through a period in the '60s when school uniforms were unfashionable and were considered by educationalists to inhibit personality, in addition to being a burden on less well-off families (which is still the case).

However, in recent years many state schools, particularly comprehensive schools, have reintroduced school uniforms in an attempt to instil in students a sense of identity, discipline and pride in their school. Those in favour of uniforms also argue that they enhance a school's reputation and, contrary to earlier belief, the children whose parents cannot afford good clothes don't stand out, as everyone wears the same. Some schools rigorously enforce school dress regulations and will send home pupils that don't comply.

Nursery & Pre-school

Attendance at a nursery school or kindergarten for children aged under five isn't compulsory. All children must start compulsory schooling in the term following their fifth birthday. A government scheme introduced in 1998 makes provision for part-time, 'early years' education for three and four year olds until they reach school age. Children are guaranteed up to 15 hours' free nursery education over 38 weeks of the year at a nursery or a preschool, registered play scheme, Sure Start Children's Centre or with a child-minder. This is one of the lowest provisions of nursery education in Europe (in Belgium and France, 95 per cent of children attend a nursery school).

Children aged from three to five years may be catered for in local state nursery schools, in nursery schools attached to primary schools or through registered play schemes. However, the provision of state nursery schools by LEAs isn't mandatory, although LEAs must ensure that there are places at play schemes if there aren't sufficient state nursery schools. Admission to nursery education is usually on a first-come, first-served basis. Nursery schools have no catchment area and you can apply to any number of schools, although you must put your child down for entry as soon as possible. One advantage of putting your child down for entry at a state nursery school attached to a primary school is that it usually ensures that your child has a place at the primary school later when he comes of age.

The cost of private nursery school varies, and is usually from £80 to £120 per week for 25 hours a week and up to £200 per week full-time, although in London it can cost over

☑ SURVIVAL TIP

Nursery school is highly recommended, particularly if a child or its parents aren't of English mother tongue. After one or two years in nursery school, a child is integrated into the local community and is well prepared for primary school – particularly if English isn't spoken at home.

£150 per week for 25 hours and double this full-time. School hours vary, but may be from 9am to noon (morning session) and 12.15pm to 3.15pm (afternoon session). Children who attend nursery school all day usually require a packed lunch (a mid-morning snack and drink may be provided by the school). There are over 800 nursery schools in the UK using the Montessori method of teaching.

If you're unable to have your child accepted by a state-aided nursery school, you must pay for him to attend a private pre-school playgroup. Many playgroups accept children from the age of two, but stipulate that they must be toilet trained. Informal play facilities are provided by private nursery schools and playgroups, or may be organised by parents and voluntary bodies such as the Pre-School Learning Alliance (020-7697 2500, www.pre-school.org.uk), which provides places for some 800,000 under fives. To find out what nursery schools and playgroups there are in your area, contact your local authority or Family Information Service (www.familyinformationservices.org.uk).

Children attend between two and five weekly sessions of two and a half hours a day on average. Parents pay a fee each term and are encouraged to help in the running of the group. A playgroup doesn't generally provide education (just educational games) for under-fives, although research has shown that children who attend nursery school are generally brighter and usually progress at a faster rate than those who don't.

A number of books are available for parents who wish to help their young children to learn at home, which most educationalists agree gives children a flying start at school.

Primary School

Primary education in the UK begins at the age of five (four in Northern Ireland), and in state schools is usually co-educational (mixed boys and girls). Primary school consists mainly of first or infant schools for children aged five to seven (or eight), middle or junior schools for those aged 7 to 11 (or 8 to 12), and combined first and middle schools for both age groups. In addition, first schools in some parts of England cater for children aged from five to eight, nine or ten, and are the first stage of a three-tier school system (first, middle and secondary). Some primary schools also provide nursery classes for children aged five.

LEAs must provide a primary school place at the start of the term following a child's fifth birthday, although some admit children earlier. If a child attends a nursery class at a primary school, he usually moves up to the infants' class at the same school, although it isn't compulsory. Entry to a primary school isn't automatic and parents must apply to the head for a place. In England and Wales the transfer to secondary schools is generally made at age 11, while in Northern Ireland it can be 11 or 12. In Scotland primary school lasts for seven years and pupils transfer to secondary school at the age of 12. In a few areas children may take the 11-plus examination, which determines whether they go on to a grammar or high school, or to a comprehensive school (see **Examinations** on page 124).

Secondary School

Secondary schools are for children aged from 11 or 12 to 16 and for those who choose to stay on at school until age 18 (called 'sixth formers'). Those who don't must continue with some sort of education or training until they're 18 in England. Most state secondary schools are co-educational, although there are many single-sex schools in Northern Ireland. Students are streamed in some secondary schools for academic subjects. The main kinds of secondary schools are as follows:

Middle Schools: Although regarded as secondary schools, middle schools accept children aged eight or nine who move on to senior comprehensive schools at age 12 or 13.

Comprehensive Schools: Admission is made without reference to ability or aptitude. Comprehensive schools provide a full range of courses for all levels of ability, from first to sixth year (from ages 11 to 18, although some cater for 11 to 16-year-olds only) and usually take students from the local catchment area. In some counties, all secondary schools are comprehensive.

Grammar Schools: Have a selective intake and provide an academic course for pupils aged from 11 to 16 or 18 years. In areas where the 11-plus examination is retained (see **Examinations** below), entry to grammar school is for the 25 per cent or so who pass. In recent years grammar schools have fallen out of favour with some because they tend to favour the middle classes over the less privileged, and so an announcement in 2016 that their number may be increased proved highly controversial. However, there's no disputing that they are the UK's best performing schools by a long way.

High Schools: These are provided in some areas for those who pass their 11-plus exam, but aren't accepted at a grammar school.

Sixth Form Colleges: Schools where 16-year-olds study for two years for GCE A-levels. They also take students from comprehensive schools catering for 11 to 16-year-olds.

City Technology Colleges: Specialises in technological and scientific courses for children aged 11 to 18 (see below). City Technology Colleges are usually located in deprived parts of the UK.

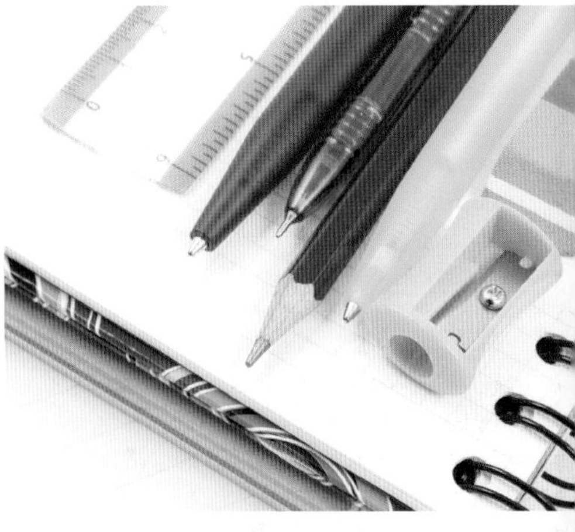

Some two-thirds of comprehensive schools are also termed academies, which are set up by sponsors in partnership with the local authority and Department for Education, but managed independently (run by an academy trust) from the local authority and funded directly by central government. Academies aren't required to follow the national curriculum and can set their own term times. A free school in England is a type of academy, a non-profit-making, independent state-funded school, that's free to attend but which isn't controlled by a local authority. Free schools are funded directly by central government and share with academies a greater control over their finances, curriculum, and teachers' pay and conditions.

Comprehensive schools are usually divided into five- or seven-year groups, with the first year having the youngest children, e.g. 11-year-olds. At the age of 16, students can take GCSE examinations (see **Examinations** below) or leave school without taking any exams, although in England they must stay in some form of education or training until their 18th birthday.

After taking their GCSEs, students can usually stay on at school for the sixth form (or transfer to a sixth form college) and spend a further two or three years studying for A-level examinations, usually in order to qualify for a place at a university. They can also retake or take extra GCSEs or study for vocational qualifications such as BTEC (Business and Technology Education Council), OCR Nationals and City & Guilds at a sixth form college.

Around 40 per cent of all students stay on at secondary school to take A-levels. The average pupil to teacher ratio in most state secondary schools is around 22, although class sizes are over 30 in some schools and tend to be larger in primary schools. Teaching time is from 22 to 26 hours in secondary schools, but may be increased to boost exam results.

City technology colleges are state-aided, independent of LEAs, and are a recent innovation in state education for 11 to 18-year-olds. Their aim is to widen the choice of secondary education in disadvantaged urban areas and to teach a broad curriculum with an emphasis on science, technology, business understanding and arts technologies. Although initially received with hostility and scepticism by the educational establishment, technology colleges have proved a success and many have converted to academies.

Curriculum

The Education Reform Act of 1988 established the progressive introduction of a national curriculum in primary and secondary schools, for the years of compulsory schooling from the age of 5 to 16. This means that children in all parts of England now receive the same basic education, which makes comparisons between how children are performing at different schools easier and facilitates transfers between schools. Before the national curriculum, head teachers (also called headmasters or headmistresses) in England and Wales were responsible for determining the curriculum in their schools in conjunction with LEAs and school governors.

Key Stages

Key Stage	Age	Year Groups (Classes)
1	5 to 7	1 & 2
2	7 to 11	3 to 6
3	12 to 14	7 to 9
4	14 to 16	10 & 11

The national curriculum was introduced in 1989 ostensibly to bring the UK into line with Europe. It underwent a major (and controversial) revision in recent years after it was decided that old curriculum wasn't sufficiently challenging (pupils in other countries have much more demanding curriculums) and pupils now study some subjects earlier and in more depth. The new curriculum sees a shift in focus for some subjects and overall is tougher than previously, particularly regarding numeracy and literacy. The new curriculum – introduced in 2015 – covers all ages and will be phased in over a number of years to eventually include GCSEs and A-levels. The changes only apply to schools in England and schools in Scotland, Wales, Northern Ireland and the Isle of Man are unaffected (they have their own equivalents).

The curriculum consists of 12 subjects that all children must study: English, mathematics, science, history, geography, information and communication technology (ICT), music, art and design, citizenship, physical education (PE), design and technology (D&T) and a modern foreign language (in secondary schools from the age of 11 years).

English, mathematics, science and physical education are termed 'core' subjects, because they help children to study other subjects, and are compulsory up to GCSE level. Other subjects are termed 'foundation' subjects. Religious education must be part of the curriculum but is decided locally; parents can, however, decide whether their child takes part.

Schooling is divided into four 'key stages', which help parents know what their children are learning at various ages. Parents receive a report at the end of each key stage (see table opposite) at ages 7, 11, 14 and 16, based on national attainment targets. Progress at key stages is based on teachers' assessments and testing, culminating in sitting GCSE examinations at the end of key stage 4.

Other subjects may be taught in addition to the national curriculum and religious education, and are decided by individual schools. All schools are required to publish information in their prospectus and in the governing body's annual report about what's taught at a school.

Children with special education needs also follow the national curriculum, where possible. Note that academies and state-funded schools in England that are outside local authority control have significant freedom in what they teach, and aren't required to follow the national curriculum. For further information see www.gov.uk/national-curriculum/overview and www.theschoolrun.com/overview-english-education-system.

In Wales, the curriculum is basically the same as in England. The main difference is that Welsh-speaking schools teach Welsh as a core subject and other schools in Wales teach Welsh as a foundation subject. For more information, see www.walesonline.co.uk/news/education and www.theschoolrun.com/overview-welsh-education-system.

In Scotland, there's no set national curriculum and education authorities and individual head teachers decide what's taught. However, a 'curriculum for excellence' is being implemented covering eight key areas: languages (including English and Gaelic in Gaelic-speaking areas, plus modern languages); mathematics; sciences; technology; expressive arts (including art, design, music and drama); social studies; health and well-being; and religious and moral education. These form the core area and are supplemented by other activities that make up the elective area. More information is available from Education Scotland (www.educationscotland.gov.uk/index.asp) and www.theschoolrun.com/overview-scottish-education-system.

In Northern Ireland, there's a common curriculum for all schools (revised in 2007-08), with several areas of study, including: English (and Irish); maths; science and technology; modern languages; arts (art, design, music and drama); environment and society (including history and geography); learning for life and work (including citizenship and personal development); physical education and religious education. All secondary school pupils study a European language, and the Irish language is available in Irish-speaking schools. Secondary schools are known as post-primary schools in Northern Ireland. There are also grammar schools, where admission is based on an academic selection test. For more information, see www.theschoolrun.com/northern-irish-education-system.

Examinations

Before the introduction of comprehensive schools, the 11-plus examination was sat by all pupils in England and Wales at the age of around 11, and was the major turning point in a child's schooling. The major objection to the 11-plus was that it decided a child's future education at too young an age and left little room for late developers (very few children who failed the 11-plus made it into higher education). However, the 11-plus hasn't quite passed into history and it's still taken by primary school pupils in a few areas, where those who pass go on to a grammar or high school. Those that fail attend a comprehensive school. Places at advanced secondary schools are limited, therefore in addition to achieving the required 11-plus pass mark, pupils also require a recommendation from their head teacher.

> Concessions are made for dyslexic children taking GCSE and A-level exams, which allow them to use an amanuensis or word processor to write answers and to have exam questions read out to them or recorded on tape.

In England, Wales and Northern Ireland, the main examination usually taken at age 16 after five years of secondary education is the General Certificate of Secondary Education (GCSE). The General Certificate of Education Advanced (A) level may be taken after a further two years of study (years 12 or 13). Some schools also offer AS levels in certain subjects for gifted and talented students in Years 10 and 11 (ages 14 to 16), which are similar to the first year (or half) of an A-level course. There are around 80 AS and A-level subjects available and many students studying for A-levels take three or four AS levels in their first year, which means you can keep your options open about which subjects to study as a full A-level.

In Scotland, the main examination is the Scottish Qualifications Certificate (SQC). These are divided into four levels, with SQC standard (ordinary) grade courses taken after four years of secondary education and the SQC higher grades (highers and advanced highers) after a further two years.

Passes in the GCE A-level and SQC Higher grade exams are the basis for entry to higher education, and are recognised by all British and European universities and most American colleges. In recent years there has been a debate over whether GCSE and A-level standards are falling, although GCSE and A-level results remain the best guide to a school's teaching standards.

Special Education

Special education is provided for children with moderate or severe learning difficulties (e.g. a hearing, speech, or sight impediment, a physical disability or autism) or a behavioural problem that prevents or hinders them from attending a mainstream school for their age group. However, whenever possible, children with special education needs (SEN) are educated in mainstream schools in order to give them the same education as other children. Most LEAs provide an educational psychological service for children with behavioural problems and will inform you about special schools in your area.

ACE Education Advice and Training (0300-0115 142, www.ace-ed.org.uk) can answer questions and provide advice on special education, and information is also provided by Special Needs UK (www.specialneedsuk.org), who publish a handbook, and John Catt's *Which School? for Special Needs* guidebook (www.specialneedsguide.co.uk), now in its 25th year.

PRIVATE (INDEPENDENT) SCHOOLS

Private fee-paying schools are officially termed independent schools (although historically referred to as public schools) because they're independent of local or central government control. The UK is renowned for the quality and variety of its private schools, which include such world-famous schools as Charterhouse, Eton, Harrow, Roedean, Rugby, Sherborne, Westminster and Winchester. Many private schools, including many of the most famous names, are run as charitable foundations. Schools may be owned by an individual, an institution or a company, and, although traditionally the preserve of the wealthy, they also attract able pupils from less-privileged backgrounds through scholarships.

> Don't assume that all private schools are excellent or that they automatically offer a better education than state schools (particularly grammar schools.

There are over 2,500 private day and boarding schools in England and Wales, 150 in Scotland and around 15 in Northern Ireland, educating around 7 per cent of school age children (18 per cent of pupils over the age of 16). Schools take pupils from the ages of 2 to 19 and include boarding (from the age of five) and day schools (some are both), single-sex and co-educational schools. Some schools cater for special education needs and there are also private schools for gifted children in art, music, theatre or dance.

Although fee-paying, most private schools aren't run for profit and all surplus income is reinvested in the running of schools. Private schools receive no grants from public funds and are owned and managed by special trusts, usually with a board of governors who look after the school and its finances. The head teacher is responsible to the governors but usually has a free hand to hire staff and make day-to-day decisions.

Private education is very expensive in the UK and while it was once possible for middle class families to educate their children privately, it's now increasingly the preserve of the wealthy. Over the last ten years school fees have risen faster than the rate of UK inflation every year. Fees vary considerably depending on a variety of factors, including the age of pupils, the reputation and quality of the school, and its location (schools in the north of England are generally cheaper than those in the south). Day prep school fees can range from £5,000 to £15,000 per year or more in London, while day fees for senior schools range from £10,000 to £20,000. The average senior boarding fees

Type of School	Age	Notes
All-through	2 to 18	Caters for all ages from nursery to senior or sixth form.
Pre-preparatory	2 to 7	Equivalent to LEA nursery and infant schools. Usually attached to junior schools.
Junior/Preparatory	7 to 11/13	Leads to admission to senior schools at 11+ or 13+ when the CEE (see below) is taken.
Senior	11 to 13/18	Sometimes has a separate lower school for pupils aged 11 to 13.
Sixth Form	16+	Many senior schools admit students at 16+, usually to study for GCE A-levels.

Private Schools

are around £30,000 per year but some senior boarding schools exceed £40,000. If you want to board a child from the age of 5 until taking his A-levels, it can easily cost over £300,000!

Many senior and some junior schools provide scholarships and means-tested bursaries for bright or talented pupils – awarded as a result of competitive examinations – which vary in value from full fees to a small proportion of the total cost.

Type of Schools

Private schools range from nursery (kindergarten) to large day and boarding schools, and from experimental schools to traditional institutions. A number of independent schools are also available for religious and ethnic minorities, for example schools for Muslims, where there's a strict code regarding the segregation of boys and girls. Most private schools are single-sex, almost equally split between boys' and girls' schools, but there are a number of mixed schools (co-educational) and a number of boys' schools admit girls to their sixth forms (by which time sex education is part of the curriculum!). The different kinds of private school are shown in the table above.

Most private junior schools (also called preparatory or prep schools) cater for boys from the age of 7 to 13 years, but some are for girls only and an increasing number are co-educational. Junior schools usually prepare pupils for the Common Entrance Examination (CEE) to senior private schools, which is a qualifying exam to test whether prospective pupils will be able to cope with the standard of academic work required. The CEE is set by the CEE board and marked by the school which the pupil plans to attend. It's normally taken at 13 for boys and mixed schools and 11 for girls schools. Entrance to many private schools is by an exam (e.g. the CEE), a report or assessment, or an interview.

Most private schools provide a similar curriculum to state schools and set the English GCSE (see **Examinations** above) and GCE A-level examinations. Some Scottish schools set the Scottish Qualifications Certificate (SQC) standard (ordinary) and higher grade examinations. Private school pupils can also take the International Baccalaureate (IB) examination – set by a Swiss board and offered in some 200 private UK schools – which is recognised as a university entrance qualification in over 100 countries.

You should make applications to private schools as far in advance as possible (before conception for the best schools!). Obviously, if you're coming from abroad, you won't usually be able to apply one or two years in advance, which is usually considered to be the best time to book a place. It isn't usually simply a matter of selecting a school and telling the head when you'll be bringing little Cecil or Gertrude along. Although many nursery and junior schools accept pupils on a first-come, first-served basis, the best and most exclusive schools have waiting lists and a demanding selection procedure.

Most popular schools, particularly day schools in the greater London area and other cities, have long waiting lists. Don't rely on enrolling your child in a particular school and neglect other alternatives, particularly if the chosen school has a rigorous entrance examination. When applying, you're usually requested to send previous school reports, exam results and records. Before enrolling your child in a private school, ensure that you understand the withdrawal conditions in the school contract.

Further Information

There are a number of guides to private schools in the UK, including *The Independent Schools Guide* and *The Gabbitas Top 500 Independent Schools* (both Kogan Page) and *The Good Schools Guide* by Ralph Lucas (Lucas Publications). The online Guide to Independent Schools website (www.guidetoindependentschools.com) allows you to search a directory of over 550 Independent boarding and day schools, while www.bestschools.co.uk also offers advice on the best UK private school for your child. Good advice is also available from the Independent Schools Council (ISC, www.isc.co.uk), who 'publish' an annual census downloadable free from their website.

Another excellent guide is the annual *Independent Schools Yearbook* edited by Judy Mott (Bloomsbury), which contains details of governing bodies, staff, admission, entrance examinations, scholarships and fees for major private secondary schools for boys and some preparatory schools. In addition to private schools that follow a largely British curriculum, there are also American, international and foreign-language private schools in the UK.

HIGHER EDUCATION

Post-school education is generally divided into higher and further education. Higher education (tertiary) is usually defined as advanced courses of a standard higher than A-levels (see **Examinations** on page 124) or equivalent and usually refers only to first degree courses. Courses may be full-time, part-time or sandwich courses (courses that combine periods of full-time study with full-time training and paid work in industry and commerce). Degree level courses are offered by some 165 universities and higher education establishments, including the Open University. In addition, there are hundreds of Colleges of Higher Education (CHE), many of which provide teacher-training courses.

The UK is internationally renowned for the excellence of its leading universities and

King's College, Cambridge University

other higher education establishments, which include the world-famous Oxford (12th century) and Cambridge (13th century) universities, collectively referred to as 'Oxbridge'.

The age of admission to university is usually 18 (although they admit exceptional students at a younger age) and courses usually last three or four years. This is seen as a huge advantage for foreign students from countries where courses often last much longer, and results in British universities attracting over 100,000 overseas students annually. There are also many American colleges in the UK, mainly in the London area. For information, contact the Educational Advisory Service, The Fulbright Commission (020-7498 4010, www.fulbright.co.uk).

In the last decade, there has been a boom in higher education, and around 40 per cent of all school leavers now attend university or post-secondary education. Since the '80s, the number of undergraduates has risen sharply and in 2014-15 there were 2.25 million students studying at UK higher education institutions. Today's 18-year-olds have a 60 per cent chance of going to university at some time in their lives.

Fees

The major obstacle to students nowadays is a financial one. In 2010, the UK government removed the cap on tuition fees and universities can now charge full-time students as much as £9,000 a year (rising to £9,250 for 2017-18). English students were the hardest hit by the changes, although they also apply to students from the EU. In 2014, the standard tuition fee for an undergraduate degree course in Scotland was £1,820, although students from elsewhere in the UK were being charged the full £9,000. Fees for students in Wales and Northern Ireland were pegged at £3,810. The Complete University Guide (www.thecompleteuniversityguide.co.uk) lists current fees for UK universities.

No UK student is expected to pay the fees upfront; instead it's added to any maintenance loan they receive (see below) to be paid off over a number of years once they're working.

Student Loans

Loans are available to cover students' living costs while at university. For the 2016-17 academic year the maximum loan students could borrow was £6,904 per year if living at home and £8,200 per year if living away from home (£10,702 if living in London). Students begin to repay loans in April three years after starting a course, but only if your income is above the income threshold of £17,495 (plan 1) or £21,000 (plan 2). You pay 9 per cent of your income above the threshold; for example if your income is £25,000 a year, you would repay £56 per month on plan 1 and £30 per month on plan 2. Repayments are automatically deducted from your salary and interest is payable on the balance.

Applications for government loans (and grants, see below) should be made via the Gov.uk website (www.gov.uk/apply-for-student-finance/how), which includes a calculator to check how much you may be eligible for. The Student Finance Company (www.slc.co.uk) oversees the provision of loans and grants to UK students and has links to services for students in England, Scotland, Wales and Northern Ireland.

Details of funding are available from around 80 British Council offices worldwide and from a comprehensive website (www.educationuk.org/scholarships). However, with a scholarship you must be able to support yourself during your studies.

Grants

In addition to loans, students may be eligible for a maintenance grant of up to £3,387 (2015-16 academic year) a year if their family income falls under a threshold (£25,000 a year) – or a proportion of the grant amount if the income is higher (between £25,000 and £42,620 a year). Unlike loans, grants don't need to be repaid, but are available only to those studying full time. Other funding may be available direct from universities in the form of scholarships or bursaries – contact a college's administration department – and from charitable trusts. You can contact the Educational Grants Service (020-7254 6251, www.family-action.org.uk) to see whether you qualify. Extra help is also available to those with a disability or with dependants to support.

Banks also offer students interest-free overdrafts, although these should be treated with caution. An increasing number of companies and professional organisations (plus the military) sponsor higher education, in return for a number of years of service.

EU Students

Student finance is also available to EU nationals working in the UK and their children, and to officially recognised refugees and their children (those granted Humanitarian Protection). EU nationals who are normally resident within the EU are eligible for loans (covering university fees only) on the same basis as British residents, but must pay their own living expenses. Grants covering living expenses are only available to students who've been resident in the UK (or the Channel Islands or the Isle of Man) for the three years immediately prior to the first year of their course.

The factors determining eligibility for grants and loans and the amounts available are complex and depend on a number of factors, including nationality, residency, the course provider and the student's (and his parent's) financial resources. For more information see the Gov.uk website (www.gov.uk/student-finance/who-qualifies).

Non-EU Students

Most overseas students from outside the EU must pay the full cost of their courses and living expenses. Exceptions include non-EU nationals who are settled in the UK through work or family connections, and asylum seekers (although this depends on their status). Fees for overseas students may be much higher than the maximum 'home' student fee of £9,000 a year – some universities charge overseas students over double this amount. UK Universities (www.universitiesuk.ac.uk) publish an annual survey of fees paid by international students, while the UK Council for International Student Affairs (UKCISA, www.ukcisa.org.uk)

provides information on fees and who may qualify to pay 'home' fees.

There are public and private scholarships and award schemes available to overseas students, particularly at postgraduate level. These are provided by the British government, the British Council, universities and individual colleges, and by a number of private trusts and professional bodies.

Entrance Qualifications

The usual minimum qualification for entrance to a university is a mixture of GCE A-levels (see Examinations on page 124) or SQC highers (set in Scotland). Generally, the better the university and the more popular the course, the higher the entrance qualifications. Admissions are decided by a points-based system administered by the Universities and Colleges Admissions Services (UCAS). Each course has a minimum number of points and points are awarded for qualifications. A-levels score high, with 140 points awarded for an A* A-level down to 40 points for grade E, while Scottish qualifications achieve between 130 and 10 points. The full points 'tariff' is shown on the UCAS website (www.ucas.com/ucas/undergraduate/getting-started/entry-requirements/tariff/tariff-tables/1021).

In order to achieve sufficient points for a chosen course, applicants usually need a minimum of two or three A-level passes in relevant subjects and three GCSE passes (minimum grade C), including a foreign language and English and mathematics. The minimum entrance requirements are set by individual universities and colleges and vary considerably. The basic A-level entry requirement for most diploma courses is an A-level E grade and some colleges of higher education and universities may accept students with a couple of A-level D grades. However, faced with an increasing number of applications, universities have become more selective, and some in-demand courses require students to have at least two A-levels at A* grade. Even universities that previously dropped their entry requirements for courses for which there were insufficient qualified applicants, e.g. engineering, are raising the bar again.

A-levels aren't the only passport to university. Other qualifications such as BTECs and the International Baccalaureate (IB) are also accepted, and institutions may be more flexible in their entrance requirements with regard to 'mature' students (aged 21 or over). Some 20 per cent of university students are aged over 35.

> Foreign students require a thorough knowledge of English, which is usually examined unless a certificate is provided. Contact individual universities for detailed information or visit the UCAS website (www.ucas.com).

Generally, overseas students' qualifications which would admit them to a university in their own country are taken into consideration. However, passes in particular GCSE or A-level subjects (or equivalent) may still be required.

Courses

The university academic year runs from September or October to June or July (the following year) and is divided into three terms of eight to ten weeks. Students study a main subject plus one or two subsidiary subjects and specialise in their main subject for the first one or two years. The main subject is often subdivided into parts, each taught by a different professor or lecturer, e.g. mathematics may be subdivided into pure, applied, geometry and algebra. In some universities, it's possible for students to design their own degree courses.

Many students choose a sandwich course, which includes a year spent working in industry or commerce.

Degrees

The most common degrees awarded are a Bachelor of Arts (BA) and a Bachelor of Science (BSc). Bachelor's degrees are given a classification, the highest of which is an 'honours' degree, awarded when the course includes extra detail in the main subject. The highest pass is a first-class degree which is quite rare. Second-class degrees classified as 2.1 (very good) and 2.2 (average) are usual, while a third-class degree is poor. The lowest classification is a 'pass'. Second degrees are usually a Master of Arts (MA) or a Master of Science (MSc), which are awarded to Bachelors for a one-year course in a subject other than their undergraduate subjects.

Students who do post-graduate work in the same subject(s) as their undergraduate work, usually do a two-year Master of Philosophy (M-Phil) or a three-year Doctor of Philosophy (PhD) research programme. In some Scottish universities, a Master's degree is awarded as the first degree in arts subjects. Graduates who wish to qualify as teachers must do a four-year Bachelor of Education (BEd) degree course or a one-year post-graduate training course at a university or teacher training college (known as a Postgraduate Certificate of Education or PGCE).

Applications

To apply for a place at university, you should begin by writing to the Admissions Officer of selected universities, giving your personal details and asking for information. Alternatively, you can find information about courses and facilities on university websites. All formal applications for entry to full-time, first degree (undergraduate) courses at British universities must be made to the Universities and Colleges Admissions Services (0871-468 0468 or 0044-330 3330 230 from outside the UK, www.ucas.com). The website has a search facility listing all available courses and institutions across the UK, together with course and fee information, entry requirements and facts about the course provider (well over 100,000!).

Applicants can apply online for a maximum of five courses (which may be at five different universities), for which there's a fee of around £24 (or £13 if applying for just one course) in the 2016-17 academic year. The number of applicants per university place varies considerably from university to university. It's wise not to make all your applications at universities where competition for places is at its fiercest (unless you're a genius). The most popular universities have numerous applications for each place available, with the most popular courses including medicine, law, and arts courses such as English.

The university year usually begins in October, therefore you should make your application in autumn of the year before you plan to start your course, e.g. apply in the autumn of 2017 for entry in October 2018. UCAS accepts applications from mid-September of the previous year and the closing date for most courses is 15th January (15th October for medicine, dentistry, veterinary medicine and veterinary science courses and courses at Oxford or Cambridge universities, where applicants apply direct to colleges and may need to take an entrance exam). Those with a number of offers must choose two by May or June; otherwise they're deemed to have rejected all offers of a place.

Accommodation

The cost of accommodation is a major factor for many students when deciding which university to attend, and an increasing number of students live at home and study locally due to rising costs. Following acceptance by a college or university, students are advised to apply for a place in a hall of residence ('in hall') or other college accommodation, such as self-catering houses and apartments. Such accommodation is limited to around one-third of all students, although most universities accommodate all first year students. Students should write as soon as possible after acceptance to accommodation or welfare officers, whose job is to help students find suitable accommodation (college and private).

Some colleges guarantee accommodation to overseas students for the duration of their course. The cost of accommodation in halls of residence varies considerably, starting from around £65 a week and rising to over £100 a week at some London colleges. Many students rent privately-owned apartments or houses that are shared with other students, although in many areas this kind of accommodation is difficult to find and expensive (from around £75 a week in the provinces or from £125+ a week in London). A guide to the cost of living is available at www.thestudentroom.co.uk/wiki/the_cost_of_student_living_throughout_the_UK.

UKCISA provides comprehensive information about student accommodation on its website (www.ukcisa.org.uk/international-students/preparing--planning/planning-your-accommodation) and the British Council's customer service team (0161-957 7755, www.britishcouncil.org) also provides information and advice on studying in the UK for overseas students, while its sister website (www.educationuk.org) also contains comprehensive information about studying in the UK.

Open University

In addition to the traditional universities (where students attend all lectures at the university), the UK also has an Open University (OU). It has no central campus and most study work is done at home.

> The OU is one of the major success stories of British education and, since its establishment in 1969, it has enrolled well over a million people.

The Open University is, as the name suggests, open to all, irrespective of age, occupation, background or previous qualifications. There are no entry qualifications, no admission interview and no barriers of any kind, and courses are filled on a first-come, first-served basis. You must simply be aged 18 or over, resident in the UK and be willing to do a lot of hard work!

Open University students study at home in their spare time. The OU formerly had an extensive network of regional centres and study centres to provide face-to-face support to students, but nowadays the emphasis is more on online learning; however, you do have the opportunity to meet fellow students at residential summer schools. In addition to traditional degree courses, the OU offers short courses, self-contained study packs and post-graduate degrees.

For further information contact the Student Registration and Enquiry Service (0300-303 5303, www.open.ac.uk).

Further Information

There are many useful books for those planning to enter higher education, including *The Times Good University Guide* by John O'Leary (Times Books), the *UCAS Guide to Getting into University and College* (UCAS), *Choosing Your Degree Course and University* by Brian Heap (Trotman) and *The Virgin Guide to British Universities* by Piers Dudgeon (Virgin). UKCISA (www.ukcisa.org.uk) also provides a wealth of information for prospective foreign students in the UK. *The Sunday Times*, and other 'quality' newspapers, publishes a free 'University Guide', usually in September.

There are numerous online sources of information about university education including the Complete University Guide (www.thecompleteuniversityguide.co.uk), the Universities and Colleges Admissions Services (UCAS, www.ucas.com) and Unistats (http://unistats.direct.gov.uk), the official website for comparing UK higher education course data.

APPRENTICESHIPS

An apprenticeship gives you hands-on experience, a salary and the opportunity to gain qualifications while you work or even obtain a degree. It's a combination of on the job training with study (usually one day a week) meaning you can earn while you learn. It usually takes between one and four years to complete an apprenticeship, depending on which level you take. Apprenticeships are available across a wide range of industries and many high quality, prestigious companies offer them. For an advanced apprenticeship, most employers require five GCSE passes (or the equivalent) or an intermediate apprenticeship. For a higher apprenticeship most employers require A-levels (or equivalent) or an advanced apprenticeship.

If you lack the qualifications necessary for an apprenticeship or would like to get a taste of a particular job or industry, you may wish to consider work experience before committing to an apprenticeship. You'll learn from and work alongside experienced people as they go about their daily tasks, develop skills, make contacts and learn more about the kind of job you'd like to do.

In recent years many young people have been choosing an apprenticeship rather than studying for a third-rate degree. An apprenticeship provides a clear career path with a good salary and secure employment, whereby many graduates with poor degrees end up in low-paid, dead-end jobs requiring no qualifications at all – in addition to substantial student loan repayments!

Information about traineeships and apprenticeships is available from many sources, including Get In Go Far (www.getingofar.gov.uk/work-experience), Gov.uk (www.gov.uk/topic/further-education-skills/apprenticeships) and Skills for Care (www.skillsforcare.org.uk/learning-development/apprenticeships/apprenticeships.aspx).

FURTHER EDUCATION

Further education generally embraces everything except first degree courses taken at universities and colleges of higher education (although the distinction between further and higher education is often blurred). Further education courses may be full or part-time and are offered by universities, colleges of technology, technical colleges (often referred to as 'tecs'), colleges of further education (CFE), adult and community colleges, and by numerous 'open learning' institutions. Each year, half a million students attend further education courses at universities alone, which are often of short duration and job-related, although courses may be full or part-time and may include summer semesters.

Qualifications that can be earned through further education include GCSE, GCE A-level, International Baccalaureate, BTEC (e.g. higher national certificate and diploma), Scottish Vocational Qualifications (SVQs), City and Guilds, Bachelor's and Master's degrees, MBA degrees, and a range of other nationally and internationally recognised certificates and diplomas. Qualifications for school-leavers include BTECs, National Vocational Qualifications (NVQs), SVQs and OCR Nationals.

The Business and Technology Education Council (BTEC) organises over 250 courses, designed with the co-operation of major companies in various fields, available in colleges, training centres and companies. BTEC courses are a combination of academic and practical, and cover everything from computer studies to engineering, catering to travel and tourism. BTEC trains over 200,000 students annually and offers six course levels ranging from BTEC first, BTEC national and BTEC higher national certificates, plus diplomas up to BTEC advanced professional awards, which are the equivalent of a university degree.

NVQs are practical awards based on competence in a particular field, e.g. sales, marketing and distribution, and health and social care, and are awarded over five levels. They can be studied while in employment or as part of an apprenticeship. An NVQ 5 is the equivalent of higher national certificates and diplomas, i.e. just below a degree.

The sheer number of qualifications is confusing and it's difficult to compare their values. There are frameworks that attempt to do this, such as the Qualifications and Credit Framework, which awards credits to qualifications and units of learning. The Office of Qualifications and Examinations Regulation provides some useful downloads on its website (www.ofqual.gov.uk).

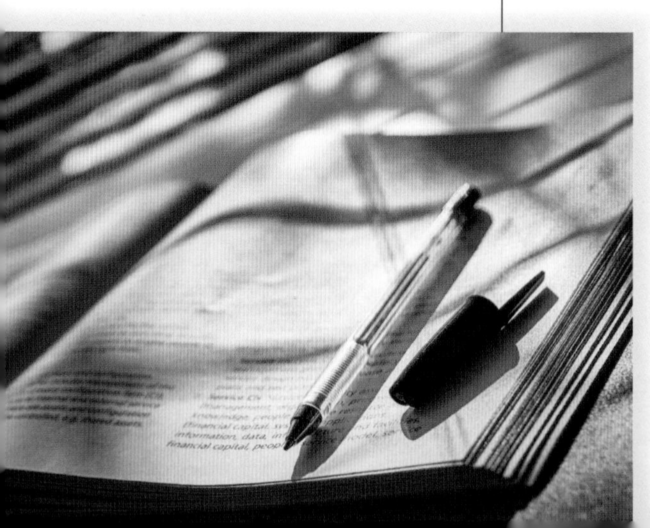

Most correspondence colleges are private commercial operations, although there are a few exceptions, including the National Extension College (NEC), which has no entry qualifications. NEC courses are generally acknowledged to be among the best in open learning and include GCSEs, A-levels, general education, business skills, and personal development courses. For information contact NEC (01223-400200, www.nec.ac.uk).

The UK Open College (www.ukopencollege.co.uk) offers over 600 courses and is one of the largest online suppliers of home study courses in the UK, while the Open College of the Arts is an educational trust that caters for those wishing to develop their artistic abilities, but who wish or need to work from home. Courses at the latter include art and design, creative writing, drawing, painting, textiles, sculpture, garden design, photography, singing, the history of art, music and calligraphy. For information contact the Open College of the Arts (0800-731 2116 or +44-1226 730495 from outside the UK, www.oca-uk.com).

Some institutions, such as the Open University and Warwick University Business School, offer distance learning Master of Business Administration (MBA) courses for those who cannot or don't wish to study on a full or part-time, locally taught basis. There are many institutions offering MBA courses, which together accept some 20,000 students (many from overseas). The Open University alone enrols over 10,000 managers each year, making it the largest business education institute in the UK. Many other business schools offer MBA courses, covering subjects such as banking, business administration, communications, economics, European languages, information systems, management, marketing, public relations, and social and political studies.

The National Institute of Adult Continuing Education (0116-204 4200, www.learningandwork.org.uk) was established in 1921 (as the British Institute for Adult Education) and is the national unit in England and Wales for literacy, numeracy and related communication skills. It also has a limited but important role in the development of English for speakers of other languages (ESOL) courses. The Institute, which merged with the Basic Skills Agency in 2007, publishes a wide range of information leaflets and booklets, including a comprehensive *Publications* catalogue downloadable from their website.

General information about adult education and training is available free in many towns and cities from educational guidance units (usually part of the public library service) and adult guidance agencies. The National Careers Service is the government initiative anyone wishing to plan or change their career and/or wanting to study for new qualifications (https://nationalcareersservice.direct.gov.uk). It provides careers' advisors (0800-100 900) and helps with learning and funding further education. Similar services are available in Scotland (www.myworldofwork.co.uk) and Wales (www.careerswales.com). The official guide to adult education courses is Floodlight (www.floodlight.co.uk), which provides a search facility by postcode or course type.

LANGUAGE SCHOOLS

If you don't speak English fluently (or you wish to learn another language) you can enrol in a language course at one of over 5,000 language schools in the UK. Obtaining a working knowledge of English while living in the UK is relatively easy, as you're constantly immersed in the English language and have the maximum

☑ SURVIVAL TIP

It's important to choose the right language course, particularly if you're studying English in order to continue with full-time education in the UK and must reach a minimum standard or gain a particular qualification.

opportunity to practise (the British aren't renowned for their proficiency in foreign languages). However, if you wish to speak or write English fluently, you must usually attend a language school or find a private tutor. Over 600,000 students come to the UK each year to learn English, 75 per cent from Western Europe, thus ensuring that English as a Foreign Language schools are big business.

If you want to study at a college of higher or further education, you must demonstrate a good standard of English and be able to prove this with a recognised qualification in English (or a degree taken in English) or by taking an approved course. Non-EU students coming to learn English must have an authorised sponsor.

There are English-language schools in all cities and large towns; however, the majority of schools, particularly those offering intensive courses, are to be found in the south. The largest concentration of schools is in London and the world-famous university towns of Oxford and Cambridge. There's also a large number of schools along the south coast of England, particularly in Brighton and Bournemouth, while Edinburgh is the most popular location in Scotland.

You may find it advantageous to choose a school that's a member of English UK (020-7608 7960, www.englishuk.com), the association of recognised English language-teaching establishments in the UK. English UK's website includes a searchable database of schools and courses. The British Council's Education UK website (www.educationuk.org) also has an 'institution search', enabling you to find a course that suits your requirements.

Most language schools offer a variety of classes depending on your current language ability, how many hours you wish to study a week, how much money you want to spend and how quickly you wish to learn. Full-time, part-time and evening courses are offered by many schools, and many also offer residential courses or accommodation with local families (highly recommended to accelerate learning). Courses that include accommodation (often half board, consisting of breakfast and an evening meal) usually offer excellent value for money. If you need to find your own accommodation, particularly in London, it can be difficult and expensive.

Don't commit yourself to a long course of study (particularly an expensive one) before ensuring that it's right for you. Most schools offer a free introductory lesson and free tests to help you find your appropriate level. Many language schools offer private and small group lessons.

Among the best value for money English courses are those run by state colleges under the control of Local Educational Authorities (LEAs), the Department for Education, or the Scottish Education Department. These are often called English for Speakers of Other Languages (ESOL) and may be subsidised for UK residents (including EU citizens and non-EU nationals with a residency permit). Some are designed to help foreigners pass the Life in The UK test in order to obtain a settlement visa. They can cost just a few pounds a week. If you're on a tight budget, there are free online English-language lessons available from a number of sources, including the British Council's online course (http://learnenglish.britishcouncil.org/en).

You may prefer to have private lessons, which are a quicker but generally more expensive way of learning a language. The main advantage of private lessons is that you learn at your own speed and aren't held back by slow learners or dragged along in the wake of the class genius. You can advertise for a teacher in local newspapers, on shopping centre or supermarket bulletin boards, university or school notice boards, and through your or your spouse's employer.

Many British universities hold summer and other holiday language courses for foreigners, e.g. Birmingham, London and Oxford, a list of which is available on Summer Schools Info (www.summer-schools.info/english-as-a-foreign-language). The British Chamber of Commerce provides an English tuition advisory service in many countries, and works closely with English schools, universities and other institutions. For information, contact your local British embassy, consulate or high commission abroad.

For an introduction to languages in the UK, see **Language** on page 28.

Glasgow Science Centre, Scotland

OXFORD ST. SELFRIDGES
OXFORD STREET
REGENT STREET
PICCADILLY CIRCUS
CHARING CROSS
529
DENNIS
XX 9591

10.
PUBLIC TRANSPORT

Public transport services in the UK vary from region to region and town to town. In some areas services are reasonable to good, while in others they're infrequent, slow and expensive (when not on strike!); in late 2016, after the latest round of fare increases, UK commuters were paying up to SIX times as much as their counterparts in Europe. The UK has no unified transport policy, especially no long-term strategy that balances the needs of the public transport user against those of the motorist. Consequently it has one of the most congested and ill-planned transport systems in Europe.

The disastrous rail privatisation in 1993 drove even more people onto the roads, although ironically, despite the astronomical cost and terrible service, the number of train journeys made has doubled since the late '90s. However, overall the percentage of travellers using public transport in the UK is fairly low, with some two-thirds of all journeys made by car. Nevertheless, it isn't always essential to own a car in the UK, particularly if you live in a city with adequate public transport (and where parking may be impossible in any case). On the other hand, if you live in a remote village or a town away from main train and bus routes, it's usually essential to have your own transport.

Despite more people using public transport in London – which has the world's largest rail and tube network – than in any other European city, it has the most expensive public transport of any capital city in Europe (six times as expensive as Paris and Rome). The UK killed off its trams many years ago – which in mainland Europe still perform an excellent role midway between a bus and a train – although a number of cities have introduced (or are planning) new metro, light rail transit and supertram systems, and are restricting car access to city centres (and encouraging cyclists). Many cities and counties promote the use of public transport over private cars, although trying to encourage people to travel by public transport has met with little success. One of the major problems (re road congestion) facing the UK is that it's usually cheaper to travel by car than use the railways.

Public transport is cheaper if you're able to take advantage of the wide range of discount, combination (e.g. rail, bus, underground and ferry), season and off-peak tickets available. Many regions offer combined bus, train, underground (metro) and ferry passes, and offer special rates for children, students, young people, pensioners, families, the unemployed and those receiving social security benefits, in addition to off-peak travel reductions.

A wealth of information is published by national and local public transport companies, local and county councils, and regional transport authorities, most of which provide a wide range of passes and fares for travellers. Public transport information is available via a wealth of websites, including www.traveline.org.uk, www.bbc.co.uk/travel and www.tfl.gov.uk (London).

TRAINS

The British railway system is the world's oldest, but has been the subject of controversy, scandal and tragedy in recent years. Privatised in 1996, the service went from boom (two years later) to bust when, in 2001, the operating company (Railtrack) went into liquidation. It also suffered several fatal crashes as a result of poor maintenance and inept management. The current not-for-profit operator, Network Rail, inherited something of a poisoned chalice, with unreliable services and an infrastructure badly in need of modernisation. Network Rail owns the infrastructure but the trains are operated by a number of regional companies.

There isn't a clear distinction between 'mainline' rail services between major cities and local services, and a train company may offer either or both services on its routes. Suburban or local trains stop at most stations along their route, while long distance trains are express services that stop only at major towns and often include first or 'executive' class carriages.

While it's usually possible to buy a meal on long-distance trains, either in a restaurant car or from a buffet, suburban trains usually offer nothing at all. Toilets are provided on trains on all but the shortest services and smoking is banned on all British trains.

In recent years services have been hit by a number of disputes and strikes which has led to services being severely curtailed on some networks, e.g. Southern.

☑ SURVIVAL TIP

Travel during peak periods is best avoided if at all possible, when packed trains (often standing room only) cause considerable discomfort for those commuting into major cities from the suburbs and provinces. It's also much more expensive to travel during peak times.

Types of Train

Most trains consist of first (shown by a '1' on windows) and standard class carriages. Services categorised as suburban or local are trains that stop at most stations along their route, many provided by modern diesel and electric-powered trains, including the Sprinter and Super Sprinter, Networker and Turbostar, with push-button operated or automatic doors. Long-distance trains are termed express and InterCity, and stop at major towns only.

Britain's first 'high-speed' train was the InterCity 125 (so named after their maximum speed of 125mph/201kph), the world's fastest diesel train in regular service; the more recent fast trains are electric or electric hybrid and many still operate on British main lines (although scheduled to be withdrawn in 2018). In recent years these have been replaced on many major routes by the InterCity 225 and Pendolino trains, which will be joined in 2018 by Virgin Rail's Japanese Azuma: all these trains are faster than the InterCity 125 but are currently restricted to 125mph for safety and signalling reasons. The only truly high-speed service is the Eurostar (HS1) – see below – from London to Europe via the Channel Tunnel. A second high-speed line (HS2 – see below)

is planned to link London with Birmingham, Manchester and Leeds.

All InterCity trains are air-conditioned. Restaurant cars is now very rare, and where they do exist they're restricted to first class passengers, but many trains offer catering from a buffet counter or a trolley service (timetables indicate services offering catering).

During rush hours (before 9.30am and from 4-7pm), trains are frequent on most routes, although it's best to avoid travelling during peak periods if possible, when trains are packed and fares are at their highest. Although travelling by train may not always compare favourably on paper with air travel, it's often quicker when you add the time required to get to and from town centres and airports. Many towns and cities are served by half-hourly or hourly services.

Eurostar

Eurostar is an international train service linking London, Brussels, Lille and Paris. The rail link between Folkestone and London Waterloo first opened in 1994 but only became a high speed route in 2003, reaching speeds of up to 186mph (300kmh) and making it possible to reach London from Paris (Gare du Nord) and Brussels in around two hours. In 2007, London's St Pancras station replaced Waterloo as the London Eurostar terminus, making journeys even faster (see box).

Fares vary considerably, according to the class (there are three: standard, standard premier and business premier), the day and time of travel, and the duration of your stay (for return trips). In late 2016, the lowest return fares from London to Paris were £54.50 in (very cramped) standard/economy, £99.50 in standard premier and £245 for a business premier class return. You need to book well in advance for the lowest standard/standard premier fares. For details, timetables and bookings, contact Eurostar (03432-186 186 or +44-1233 617 575 from outside the UK, www.eurostar.com).

Eurostar Journey Times

Journey	Time
London to Brussels	1hr 51mins
London to Lille	1hr 20mins
London to Paris	2hrs 15mins

St. Pancras International is situated at the heart of central London, with more underground connections than any other London station. There are four main overground services from the station: Eurostar, East Midland Trains, Southeastern and First Capital Connect. For more information call 020-7843 7688 or see http://stpancras.com.

Crossrail

Crossrail is a 73-mile (118km), £15 billion railway line under development in London and the counties of Berkshire, Bucks and Essex, running from Reading and Heathrow in the west, through 26 miles (42km) of new tunnels under London to Shenfield and Abbey Wood in the east. The central section between Paddington in central London and Abbey Wood is due to open in December 2018, while the western section beyond Paddington to Reading in Berkshire and London's Heathrow Airport is due to enter operation in December 2019. The project includes the construction of 10 new stations and upgrading 30 more, while integrating new and existing infrastructure. The new railway, which will be known as the Elizabeth line when services begin in 2018, will be fully integrated with London's existing transport network and will be operated by Transport for London.

Begun in 2009, the £15 billion project is Europe's largest infrastructure project and is expected to be delivered on time and within budget. It will improve journey times across London, ease congestion and offer better connections, while providing easier, quicker and more direct travel opportunities across the capital. New state-of-the-art trains will carry an estimated 200 million passengers per year and bring an extra 1.5 million people to within 45 minutes of central London.

For more information see www.crossrail.co.uk, which includes an interactive map that allows you to explore the route and obtain information about each of the new stations under construction.

Crossrail Construction

High Speed 2 (HS2)

High Speed 2 (HS2) is a planned high-speed railway linking London, Birmingham, the East Midlands, Leeds, Sheffield and Manchester. It would be only the second high-speed rail line in Britain after High Speed 1 (HS1), the Eurostar (see above) line that connects London to the Channel Tunnel and continental Europe. The line is to be built in a 'Y' configuration, with London on the bottom of the 'Y', Birmingham at the centre, Leeds at the top right and Manchester at the top left. If given final approval, work on the first phase is scheduled to begin in 2017, reaching Birmingham by 2026, Crewe on the left leg of the 'Y' by 2027 and full completion by 2033.

The line is highly controversial for a number of reasons, not least the cost, which is estimated at £55 billion (and is likely to be much higher by the time it's completed) or up to ten times the cost per kilometre of some comparable global counterparts. In fact HS2 isn't about speed so much as providing extra capacity, as the estimated time saving between London and Birmingham will be just 32 minutes, and one hour between London and Manchester. It could even be obsolete by the time it's built!

Tickets & Fares

Although a number of companies may be involved, you can buy 'through' tickets to stations on a different company's network; the price shouldn't vary, irrespective of where you purchase your ticket, although individual train companies sometimes offer reduced fares on their own routes. Depending on the special offers available, you may obtain a better deal by purchasing separate tickets for different 'legs' of a long journey.

There's a bewildering array of discount tickets available, including child and youth discounts (up to 25-year-olds), family and group tickets, and discounts for the over 60s (known as 'seniors') and the disabled, as well as special 'advance' tickets. Some tickets require the purchase of an annual 'railcard' that entitles you to discounts each time you buy a ticket, e.g. a 16-25, Senior or Family and Friends (group) Railcard (all £30 per year), which provide a discount of one-third off normal adult fares. Anyone can purchase a Network Railcard (£30 a year) but it only provides discounts on fares in the southeast of England. There's a summary of railcards at www.railcard.co.uk.

If you're a regular train traveller, you can buy a weekly, monthly or annual (point-to-point) season ticket, for which you need a passport-size photo. Less frequent travellers can make use of Travelcards which provide off-peak travel on suburban trains and are sometimes valid on other forms of transport, e.g. in London.

Rail fares in the UK are the highest in the world and are routinely increased each year well above inflation. However, despite the high fares, passengers aren't guaranteed a seat unless it's specifically reserved and many passengers on commuter trains are forced to stand for the whole journey.

The three main types of ticket are anytime (the most expensive), off-peak (valid outside rush hours and at weekends) and advance, which are for longer journeys and must be purchased at least a day in advance. Note that these are inflexible and can only be used on between specific stops on a specific train – and if you get off the train at an earlier station you risk being charged the full (much higher) fare.

Information about tickets is available from information and ticket offices at stations. To check timetables, book tickets and obtain other information, you can consult the Network Rail website (www.networkrail.co.uk) or go to the National Rail Enquiries website (www.nationalrail.co.uk), 'the gateway to the UK's national rail network' operated by the Association of Train Operating Companies.

Alternatively, you can visit www.thetrainline.com, probably the best for cheap tickets, or www.raileasy.co.uk, www.mytrainticket.co.uk and www.redspottedhanky.com, which all offer savings for advance bookings.

Station Facilities

Most main railway stations have restaurants, buffets and snack bars, although the quality of food generally leaves much to be desired (there are a few exceptions) and can be expensive. Smaller stations sometimes have vending machines for snacks, sweets and drinks. A majority of train stations have toilet facilities (sometimes for a fee – usually 20p) and many have baby changing facilities. Many stations have waiting 'lounges' and free wi-fi internet access within the station.

Most large stations have luggage lockers or left luggage offices, and you can usually find a trolley to wheel your bags around; porters are rare these days, and lifts (elevators) aren't provided at many stations.

There are shops at most central London stations and other main stations, and some termini have extensive shopping centres with banking facilities; e.g. London's Liverpool Street station is particularly well served with shops and other services, as is the new St Pancras International station.

Disabled Passengers

Wheelchairs are available at major railway stations and most trains have special facilities for their storage. Special arrangements can be made for disabled or mobility-impaired passengers when travelling by train, e.g. station staff can usually help passengers on and off trains, but cannot lift disabled passengers or heavy items such as mobility scooters.

When booking a journey, disabled passengers should provide as much information as possible regarding their needs. On services with seat reservations, you can reserve a seat or wheelchair space free of charge. Most trains can accommodate wheelchair users and new trains also have facilities to assist sensory impaired people, for example public information systems that are both visual and audible. Ramps for disabled access are provided at train stations, but you must ensure that your give staff sufficient notice if you require assistance.

UNDERGROUND TRAINS

There are underground (metro) urban railway networks in Glasgow, London and Newcastle (Tyne and Wear), and Manchester has a Metrolink light rail (tram) system. The best-known is in London: the London underground (see below) and the Docklands Light Railway (DLR) – a modern light rapid transit (LRT) system 25mi (40km) in length serving 45 stations in east and southeast London. Many other cities have plans for LRT or supertram systems (see **Trams & Lightrail Systems** below), although some have been delayed or put on hold due to lack of funds.

> In most European countries, an underground rail system is called a metro system, while in the US it's the subway. In London the underground vernacular is the 'tube' – a term derived from the tube-shaped tunnels through which the trains run under the city.

London Tube System

The London underground (tube) system is the oldest (parts of it have been around since the 1860s) and largest in the world, with some 500 trains and over 270 stations handling over 3.5 million passenger journeys a day. Given the congestion above ground, London without its tube would be unthinkable, and it's easily the fastest and most convenient way to get around the city and its suburbs (provided stations and lines aren't closed for engineering work – an increasing occurrence in recent years, particularly at weekends). Outside the central areas, and even within some of them, trains actually run above ground – something which, not surprisingly, many first-time visitors to the city find confusing.

If you've reached retirement age or have an eligible disability and are a permanent London resident, you can apply for a Freedom Pass from your borough council. This entitles you to free travel on all London's public transport including buses, tube, trains, Docklands Light Railway and trams. Enquire at your borough council offices or visit the Freedom Pass website (www.freedompass.org).

Transport for London (TfL) centres provide comprehensive information about the tube network (plus bus services and the DLR). TfL centres are located throughout central London and there's also a 24-hour hotline (0343-222 1234) and an in-depth journey planner on the website (http://tfl.gov.uk/plan-a-journey). It also publishes a range of guides, including audio guides, large print maps and details of accessibility at station, which can be ordered or downloaded from the TfL website (https://tfl.gov.uk/forms/12387.aspx).

TRAM & LIGHT RAIL SYSTEMS

There are eight tram or light rail systems in the UK in Birmingham, Blackpool, Edinburgh, London, Manchester, Newcastle, Nottingham and Sheffield. Other new light rail schemes are in the planning stage and systems have also been proposed for Leeds and Liverpool, although funding has been refused by the government, making them unlikely to proceed.

BUSES

In the UK, there are two main types of bus service: town and city services and long-distance buses, often referred to as coaches. Each region has its own local bus companies providing local town and country services. In large towns and cities, most bus services start and terminate at a central bus station, and it can be confusing trying to find the right connection. If you need assistance, ask at a bus station information office. Most bus companies provide free timetables and route maps, and many local district and county councils publish a comprehensive booklet of timetables and maps (possibly for a small fee) for all bus services operating within their region. In many cities, night bus services are in operation. Timetables are also posted at major bus stops and are available online.

The deregulation of bus services in 1986 allowed any bus company to operate on any route, and led to cut-throat competition and many companies going out of business. In more recent years, the 'big five' operators – Arriva, First Group, Go-Ahead Group, National Express and Stagecoach – have swallowed up most of their competitors (amid numerous claims of dirty tricks) and on many routes have established a monopoly or near monopoly. Some also operate train services.

When you reach the female pension age (which because of pending changes varies according to your year of birth), you're entitled to a free bus pass that allows free travel on buses throughout the UK, but normally only at certain times of day (and frequently not before 9am). You can apply at your local council offices or online via Gov.uk (www.gov.uk/apply-for-elderly-person-bus-pass).

Long-distance Buses

A number of companies provide long-distance bus services. The main operator is National Express (08717-818181, www.nationalexpress.com) that provides a nationwide service in England, Wales and Scotland. Some local bus companies operate express bus services (which make a limited number of stops) within their area, e.g. Green Line commuter coaches, owned by Arriva, which serve Greater London and the home counties. There are also some budget coach companies, such as Megabus (http://uk.megabus.com/), which provides a nationwide service, and EasyBus (www.easybus.co.uk) that's part of the EasyJet stable and links London through its main airports.

National Express serves 1,000 destinations nationwide (daily, with the exception of Christmas Day), and carries over 18 million passengers more than a billion miles a year. It operates a fast and reasonably priced hourly service to the most popular destinations. Express buses are the cheapest form of long-distance travel within the UK and, although journeys take up to twice as long as trains, fares are often 50 per cent lower. National Express coaches arrive and depart from Victoria Coach Station in London, which is a ten-minute walk from Victoria railway station.

☑ SURVIVAL TIP

The Brit Xplorer (www.nationalexpress.com/offers/brit-xplorer.aspx) allows non UK residents unlimited travel around the UK on National Express coaches and costs from £79 for seven days travel up to £219 for 28 days.

Tickets can be purchased in advance at around 2,000 National Express agents (most travel agents) throughout the UK or from departure points, and can be bought by phone (08717-818181) or online (www.nationalexpress.com). Advance bookings are subject to a £1 or £2 booking fee but are recommended at busy times, on overnight services, when boarding at a suburban point, or when it's important that you travel at a particular time. Tickets are available as e-tickets or m-tickets (direct to your mobile phone), or you can collect them from an agent or have them mailed to you. Allow at least seven days if you want to receive tickets by post.

The cheapest tickets, known as Funfares, are up to 50 per cent cheaper but cannot be amended or exchanged. You're asked to limit yourself to no more than two bags (each up to 20kg) on National Express buses (plus hand luggage), and excess baggage may be subject to extra charges.

International bus services are provided by Eurolines (www.eurolines.co.uk), a group of coach companies that travel to over 500 destinations across Europe. Eurolines UK departs mostly from London Victoria Coach Station, although some operate directly from the provinces. International services usually have domestic nationwide connections.

Local bus services are provided at all international and regional airports, including inter-airport bus services. Some local bus companies provide saver cards for the young, e.g. those aged under 24, offering discounts of around 50 per cent for travel after 9am. Many other reduced fare tickets are available, including cheap day returns, season tickets, rover tickets and family tickets.

Rural & City Buses

Most counties and regions are served by one or more local bus companies (e.g. London and its suburbs are served by Transport for London), which often operate single and double-decker buses (including London's world-famous red buses). In many towns and cities, bus companies also use mini-buses.

Services usually operate from around 6am to midnight, and in major cities there's also a night bus service, e.g. London has an excellent night bus service (with slightly higher fares than day buses) operating from around midnight to 6am. Like national bus companies, local bus companies organise local, national and international day trips and tours, with pick-up points in local towns and villages.

Buses are often slow during the day due to traffic congestion, particularly in major towns and cities, and it's often quicker to take a train or, in London (and a few other cities), the tube (see **London Tube System** above). In rural areas, buses run infrequently and rarely directly to where you want to go; they usually follow a circuitous route that takes in the surrounding villages and towns. A direct journey taking, say, 15 minutes by car, can easily take an hour or more by bus!

FERRIES

Regular car and passenger ferry services to the southeast of England operate from ports in Belgium, France, the Netherlands and Spain. Some services operate year round, while others run only during the summer (usually May to September), and the frequency of services varies from dozens a day on the busiest route (Calais/Dover) during the summer, to a few a week on longer routes out of season.

Most ships have a restaurant, self-service cafeteria, children's play area and shops, and some have 'executive' lounges, where for a few pounds extra you can enjoy superior facilities and a more relaxing atmosphere. Generally, the longer the route, the better and more comprehensive the facilities. Although Calais-Dover is the shortest (and cheapest) route and offers the most frequent crossings, ships on longer routes are generally less crowded and more comfortable.

On the longer routes (i.e. to Spain from Portsmouth/Plymouth, the Hook of Holland from Harwich and most Brittany ferries' routes to France), there are overnight services with sleeping accommodation.

Information about services is available via ferry operator's websites: Brittany Ferries (www.brittany-ferries.co.uk), Condor Ferries (www.condorferries.co.uk), DFDS Seaways (www.dfdsseaways.co.uk), Irish Ferries (www.irishferries.com), Manx Ferries (www.manxferries.com), P&O Ferries (www.poferries.com) and Stena Line (www.stenaline.co.uk).

UK & Ireland Ferries

Within the UK, there are regular ferry services to the Isle of Wight, i.e. Portsmouth to Fishbourne and Ryde, Southsea to Ryde and from Lymington to Yarmouth. Car ferry services operate from England to Douglas (Isle of Man) from Heysham, Fleetwood and Liverpool. From Douglas there are regular services to Belfast and Dublin. Regular services operate from the west of Scotland to the Western Isles, and to the Orkney and Shetland Isles from the north and east of Scotland. Regular ferry services to the Channel Islands are operated from Poole, Portsmouth and Weymouth throughout the year.

Services to the Republic of Ireland operate between Fishguard-Rosslare, Holyhead-Dun Laoghaire (for Dublin), Liverpool-Dublin, Pembroke-Rosslare and Swansea-Cork. There are also services to Larne in Northern Ireland from Cairnryan and Troon (both in Scotland) and Fleetwood (England), and to Belfast from Douglas (Isle of Man), Liverpool and Stranraer (Scotland).

Fares

Ferry companies offer a range of fares, including standard single and (unrestricted) return fares, and three- and five-day returns. Fares vary enormously, and you should check for offers, which are numerous and unpredictable. If you're able to book several months in advance, you can often pay up to 50 per cent less than the standard fare. It's worth shopping around for the best deal – bear in mind that most travel agents have no access to 'special' fares or 'privileged' information, and you'll do as well (or better) to trawl the online ferry booking sites, such as www.aferry.co.uk, www.directferries.co.uk, www.ferrybooker.com and www.ferrysavers.com (there are many more).

EUROTUNNEL

If you want to travel to the UK through the Channel Tunnel by car, you must drive to Coquelles, near Calais and board a special train, which takes you to Folkestone near Dover (there's no road tunnel between France and the UK). This service is operated by Eurotunnel, whose trains run every 20 minutes and cross the Channel (running through the rock beneath the sea) in just 35 minutes. There are no services, other than toilets, on trains but you can stretch your legs inside the carriages. Trains carry all vehicles, including cycles, motorcycles, cars, trucks, buses, caravans and motorhomes.

> Eurotunnel booking doesn't guarantee you a particular time, and you may have to wait for the next train at peak times, although if you arrive early you may be able to take an earlier train.

Fares can be higher than those for the Calais-Dover ferry crossing (e.g. £68-86 one way for an average vehicle and up to four passengers in late 2016), although prices drop to ferry levels out of high season, and off-peak, short break and 'frequent traveller' reductions are available. For details and bookings, contact

Eurotunnel (0844-335 3535, www.eurotunnel.com).

TAXIS

Taxis are usually plentiful in all towns and cities (except when it's raining, you've lots of luggage or you're late for an appointment!). Taxis are relatively expensive in the UK – around the same as in many other European countries – and certainly aren't a cheap form of transport. There are two kinds of taxis, licensed taxis or cabs (abbreviation of cabriolet) and private hire cars (including Uber or minicabs, both covered below). All taxis must be licensed by the local municipal or borough council and have a registered licence number. Minicabs don't always need to be licensed, although most are. The main difference, from the passenger's point of view, is that taxis can usually be hailed in the street and minicabs (and Uber – see below) can only be booked by phone.

In addition to taxi services, many taxi and minicab companies operate private hire (e.g. weddings, sightseeing), chauffeur and courier services, and provide contract and account services, e.g. to take children to and from school. Many taxi and minicab companies provide a 24-hour service with radio-controlled cars.

London is famous for its purpose-built taxis or 'black cabs' which cover a vast area of around 610mi² (1,580km²) stretching well into the outer suburbs, and which are obliged to undertake journeys of up to 12mi (19km) from anywhere in Greater London (or 20 mi/32km from Heathrow Airport). London taxis have a strictly regulated scale of fares and charges (see www.tfl.gov.uk/gettingaround/taxisandminicabs/taxis/1140.aspx), to which it's customary to add a tip of around 10 per cent (although it isn't obligatory).

Minicabs

As an alternative to a licensed taxi, you can use a minicab, which, unlike a black cab, cannot be hailed in the street and must be booked by phone. It's illegal for minicabs to ply for hire in the street like licensed taxis. Minicabs are cheaper than licensed taxis, but you've no guarantee that the driver will be reliable, honest or know his way around. There's no official training scheme for minicab drivers and there are dozens of companies available, so the best way to find a good one is to ask someone for a recommendation. The good news is that you may be able to negotiate the fee, which may be lower than for a black cab. You must phone for a minicab in advance, and agree the price to your destination before starting your journey, as they don't have meters.

Minicabit (www.minicabit.com) is an app – and a rival to Uber (below) – that allows you to compare and book minicab & taxi quotes online.

Uber

Uber (www.uber.com/en-GB) operates an inexpensive taxi service in many UK cities using private drivers operating private cars that can be booked via a mobile phone using a special app. To start using Uber as a passenger you must signup and create an account, after which you download and install an app on your mobile phone. Bookings are made via the app and payment is via a debit or credit card, so you don't need to pay (or tip!) the driver. You must be aged 18 to use Uber (or 21 to be a driver).

Drivers are self-employed and Uber allows them to work when they want and as few or as many hours as they want (up to the permitted maximum per day). However, the average earnings claimed by Uber are disputed by many drivers, many of whom earn less than the minimum wage per hour.

Needless to say, regular taxi services (and minicabs) have been hard hit by Uber – which is allegedly already worth some $60 billion! (it operates worldwide) – and licensed taxi drivers have staged protests in London and other cities, so far to no avail.

Currently Uber only operates in a dozen cities and areas in the UK, but the network is constantly growing. For details, see www.uber.com.

AIRLINE SERVICES

The airline business is extremely competitive in the UK and fares are among the lowest in the world and the lowest in Europe (the UK is the main hub for the world's long-haul airlines). In addition to low long-haul fares, cheap flights are available to most European destinations throughout the year.

The UK's budget airlines have revolutionised air travel in the UK and Europe, particularly Ryanair (www.ryanair.com – actually an Irish airline based in Dublin) – the second largest airline by passenger numbers in Europe in 2015 – and Easyjet (www.easyjet.com), Europe's fifth-largest airline. The other major budget airline is Flybe (www.flybe.com). Budget airlines offer little or nothing in the way of extras and charge for every little thing, but offer incredibly low fares (see below).

British Airways (BA, www.britishairways.com) is the UK's national airline and one of the world's largest airlines with flights to over 165 international destinations; it's a member of the Oneworld alliance that includes American Airlines, Cathay Pacific, Finnair, Iberia, Japan Airlines and Qantas. In 2011, BA merged with Iberia to form the International Airlines Group (IAG), the third-largest airline holding company in the world, although both airlines have retained their own branding. They have since been joined by Irish airline Aer Lingus and Spanish airline Vueling (the leading airline at Barcelona's El Prat airport).

> **☑ SURVIVAL TIP**
>
> Nowadays, most airlines allow you to check-in online – indeed some charge you extra to check in at the airport. This may save time, but you're still expected to arrive at least two hours before the departure time for a long-haul flight (e.g. to the USA), and at least one hour before a European flight – if you arrive late you can lose your seat.

The main long-haul British competition to BA comes from Virgin Atlantic (www.virgin-atlantic.com), which is consistently rated one of the best airlines in the world, e.g. by readers of *Business Traveller* magazine (www.businesstraveller.com), the leading magazine for frequent flyers. Virgin has pioneered new customer values, and its first and business class services include an on-board bar and lounge, a choice of three meals, individual seatback screens with a choice of on-demand films, and seats that convert into full-length 'beds'. Domestic air services are also provided between British international and provincial airports (see below) by a number of smaller airlines.

Check with your airline regarding flight information and allow time for traffic delays, accidents and security checks when travelling to airports. If you're flying to the continent during a public holiday period or at any time during the summer, you should be prepared for a delay.

Airports

There are over 100 licensed civil airports in the UK, including many international airports, the most important of which are London-Heathrow, London-Gatwick, London-Stansted, Manchester, Luton, Edinburgh, Birmingham, Glasgow and Bristol (all handling over 5 million passengers a year). Many regional airports also operate international flights (excluding flights to Ireland, which are widespread), including Aberdeen, Belfast, Cardiff, Durham-Tees Valley, Humberside, Leeds-Bradford, Liverpool, London-City, Nottingham-East Midlands and Southampton. A number of smaller airports operate scheduled domestic flights to both regional and international airports.

London's Heathrow airport (southwest of the city centre) is one of the world's busiest airports, handling over 75 million passengers a year. Over 90 airlines are based there, spread among its five sprawling terminals. Gatwick airport, south of London, is the UK's second-busiest airport, and the busiest single-runway airport in the world. It has two terminals (North and South) linked by a monorail system. Heathrow and Gatwick have good bus and rail connections to central London, the provinces and other British airports (including each other). Heathrow can also be reached by tube and the high-speed Heathrow Express direct rail connection from Paddington station, taking just 15 minutes. It will also be connected to Crossrail (see page 141) in 2019.

Flight information is available direct from airports and via many websites, such as the UK Airport Guide (www.ukairportguide.co.uk).

Fares

Air fares to and from the UK are among the cheapest in the world, thanks to deregulation and increased competition. BA and Virgin routinely match each other's prices on long-haul fights, and stiff competition from US airlines has also shaken up the transatlantic fare structure. However, the best deals are on short-haul European flights.

> ☑ **SURVIVAL TIP**
>
> If you're planning a trip abroad during school holidays or a public holiday weekend, book well in advance, especially if you're going to a popular destination such as Paris or New York.

Deregulation in 1997 led to a spate of new budget airlines such as Ryanair (www.ryanair.com), Easyjet (www.easyjet.co.uk) and Flybe (www.flybe.com), which have hit the profits of the major airlines and cemented the UK's position as Europe's low-cost, air travel hub. Easyjet and Ryanair have revolutionised air travel in the UK and Europe, with fares starting from as little as £15 – they also routinely 'give away' thousands of tickets on selected routes during special promotions – although once you've paid for 'extras' such as baggage and administration fees, fares are usually much higher. Always book online for the lowest fares (often you've no option).

Budget airlines offer a no-frills service (most operate without tickets) and undercut other airlines by charging for seats only – meals, drinks (even tea and coffee), entertainment (films, headphones) and even baggage must be paid for separately – Ryanair has even 'threatened' to charge passengers £1 to use a toilet on its planes! Note also that many flights are to secondary, less popular airports that may be some way from the local city.

Most airlines provide a vast range of tickets, depending on when you want to fly, how many nights you want to stay, how much notice you give, and whether you fly on a fixed (pre-booked) flight or an open ticket.

Whatever your destination, it pays to shop around for the best deal – one of the best is a round-the-world ticket, the price of which depends on the class and number of stops (make sure that ticket/flights are valid for a year). You can compare ticket prices via numerous websites, including Expedia (www.expedia.co.uk), Flightline (www.flightline.co.uk), Money Saving Expert (http://flightchecker.moneysavingexpert.com), Skyscanner (www.skyscanner.net), Travel Republic (www.travelrepublic.co.uk) and Travel Supermarket (www.travelsupermarket.com).

Always make sure that you fully understand any ticket restrictions, as some flights cannot be changed, while others allow you to change flights for a fee, e.g. £50 or US$100. Always book and pay for flights with a credit card, which provides extra protection from your credit card company if an airline or operator goes bust.

11. MOTORING

British roads are amongst the most crowded in Europe, and the southeast of England is the most congested region in Europe – among western European countries, only Italy has more vehicles per road mile than the UK. Traffic density in the major cities and towns is particularly high, and results in frequent traffic jams. During rush hours – from around 7.30 to 9.30am and 4.30 to 6.30pm Mondays to Fridays – the traffic flow is painfully slow in many areas, particularly on busy motorways; e.g. anywhere on the M25 London orbital motorway, motorways into and out of London, and in and around most major cities.

Most town centres are chaotic during rush hours, particularly in central London, where the average traffic speed is around 10mph (it takes as long to cross most city centres in a car as it did 200 years ago in a horse and cart!). Journey times have more than doubled since the mid-'90s, and the UK's motorists spend an average of around ten days a year in jams over their working lives, which are estimated to cost British industry billions of pounds a year.

There are around 1,750 deaths a year on British roads, and over 200,000 injuries. However, these figures, although unacceptably high, are decreasing due to safer car design and better road management, and are among the lowest of any developed country (it's difficult to have an accident when you're stuck in a traffic jam!). A quarter of deaths in road accidents involve drivers under the age of 25 and thousands of young drivers and their passengers are maimed each year. The UK has no additional speed restrictions for young and inexperienced drivers, who can also drive high-performance cars immediately after passing their driving tests. Women drivers have half as many accidents as men, but usually drive fewer miles.

Road and traffic information is available from many websites, including www.aaroadwatch.co.uk, www.bbc.co.uk/travelnews and www.trafficengland.com.

LONDON CONGESTION CHARGE

In an effort to reduce traffic and improve the flow in central London, a 'congestion charge' was introduced in February 2003, which although successful is (not surprisingly) unpopular with motorists, who must pay £11.50 a day to enter the restricted area. In the early days of the congestion charge, Transport for London claimed that it had reduced the number of cars entering central London by some 70,000 a day, although more recent figures suggest that London is now just as congested as it was before the charge was introduced.

The majority of vehicles must pay this fee to enter the Congestion Charge Zone between 7am and 6pm, Mondays to Fridays, but some ultra low emission cars, motorcycles, scooters and mopeds and blue badge holders are

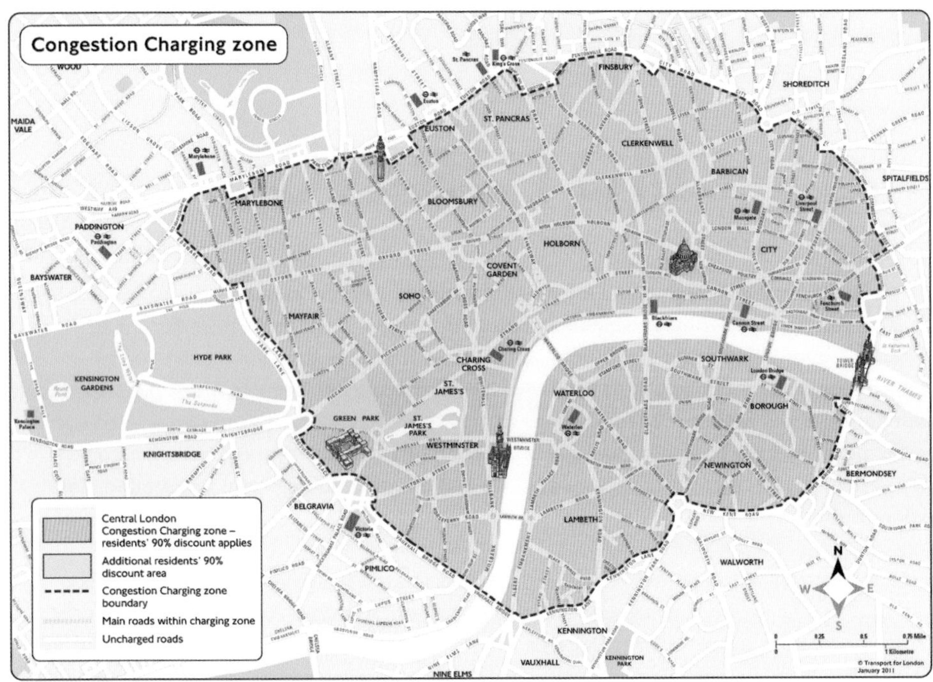

exempt. There's no charge at weekends and on local public holidays, which are designated non-charging days (also between 25th December and January 1st), and between the hours of 6pm and 7am. For more information, see www.tfl.gov.uk/modes/driving/congestion-charge.

VEHICLE IMPORTATION

If you wish to import a vehicle into the UK you must do the following (or pay an importer or shipping company to do it for you):

- Inform the nearest HM Revenue & Customs (HMRC) office within 14 days that the vehicle has arrived in the UK.
- Pay duty and VAT as instructed by HMRC.
- Obtain vehicle approval to show that the vehicle meets UK safety and environmental standards (this is automatic for vehicles sold in the EU).
- Register and tax the vehicle with the DVLA (see below), who will issue you with a registration number so that you can get number plates made.
- Insure the vehicle before you drive it on UK roads.

See the Gov.uk website (www.gov.uk/importing-vehicles-into-the-uk/overview) for more information.

When you import a vehicle into the UK (either free of tax and duty or when duty and tax have been paid on importation) you need to obtain an 'import pack' (new or used, as applicable) from the DVLA available from www.gov.uk/dvlaforms (or contact DVLA Customer Enquiries, 0300-790 6802).

VEHICLE REGISTRATION

A vehicle registration document (V5) shows the registered keeper (the person who keeps the vehicle on public roads and not necessarily the legal owner) of a vehicle. It gives the keeper's name and address, the registration mark (number or tag) and other details about the vehicle. A new registration document must be issued each time there's a change in the details printed on it, e.g. a change in the name or address of the keeper.

If you import a vehicle, the DVLA allocates a registration number (corresponding to the year of manufacture of your vehicle) and provides an authorisation certificate which you take to a garage to have British registration plates made and fitted to your vehicle. Your vehicle registration document (V5) is sent to you a few weeks later. If the vehicle has been admitted without duty and tax being paid, the registration document is endorsed with the words 'Customs Restricted Until (date)'. This can be exchanged for a standard registration document when you've paid the duty or tax or after the one-year restriction period has expired.

All cars registered in the UK and over three years old must undergo an annual serviceability test known as the MOT (see **Test Certificate** on page 156).

If you buy a new car from a garage or dealer in the UK, they will apply for a registration number on your behalf and fit registration plates. When you buy a used vehicle in the UK, you should always be given the registration document. However, the document doesn't prove legal ownership, and you should satisfy yourself that the seller either owns the vehicle or is authorised to offer it for sale. When you buy a used vehicle, you must complete the back of the registration document ('Notification of Changes') and send it to the DVLA.

The Department for Transport issues new registration numbers twice a year, on 1st March and 1st September. Thus you can (usually) tell the age of a car from its registration number, which usually remains with it throughout its life.

BUYING A CAR

After years of decline, the British car industry is now highly profitable, although most major manufacturers are foreign-owned (American, French, German, Indian or Japanese). Cars are more expensive in the UK than in many other European countries, although you can obtain a discount off the list (book) price of most new cars. Electric and hybrid vehicles are also available, although charging points are few and far between.

There are numerous magazines for new car buyers, and most newspapers include ads for used cars. One of the best websites for used car buyers is *Auto Trader* (www.autotrader.co.uk), which allows you to find cars by make and model, seller's distance from your home, price, and a wealth of other features such as colour, mileage, transmission (manual/auto), fuel, etc. Another good option for used cars is visiting a car auction, such as those held by British Car Auctions (www.british-car-auctions.co.uk), and online auctions on Ebay (http://motors.ebay.co.uk).

New and used car reports are available from the AA (www.theaa.com/cbg/home.jsp), *Auto Express* (www.autoexpress.co.uk/buying-advice) and numerous magazines.

If you're planning to buy a car privately, be sure to check that it isn't on credit (hire purchase) or has not been stolen or 'written off' in an accident and later repaired (see www.autocheck.co.uk or www.hpicheck.com). These websites contain checklists of things to look out for when buying a car, such as inspecting a car, test driving it and verifying that the vendor has the authority to sell it.

TEST CERTIFICATE

All vehicles (cars, motorcycles, motor caravans, light goods and dual-purpose) over three years old must have an annual Driver and Vehicle Standards Agency (DVSA) test. This was previously called the Ministry of Transport test or 'MoT' and the name has stuck. Passenger-carrying vehicles with more than eight seats, and taxis (excluding private hire cars), must be tested after they're one year old and there are separate rules for larger vehicles (contact the DVSA for information – see www.gov.uk/government/organisations/driver-and-vehicle-standards-agency).

Tests are performed by officially approved test centres, including local authorities and most large garages, many of which will test your car while you wait (although you may need to make a booking). Some garages do tests seven days a week and even provide a free collection and delivery service. The test usually takes around 30 minutes, depending on the condition and cleanliness of your car, and includes lights; steering and suspension; brakes (including the handbrake); tyres and wheels; seat belts and general items such as windscreen washers and wipers; horn; exhaust system and silencer; plus the exhaust emissions and vehicle structure, e.g. soundness of the bodywork. Tyres require 1.6mm of tread over 75 per cent of their width. The test has been made more stringent over the years and it's now difficult to get an old car to pass.

Recently, certification has been computerised, with all records held on a central computer. The official (maximum) cost of the test (for a car) in 2016 was £54.85 (£29.65 for a standard motorcycle), although some garages charge less. When your car passes the test, you're given a Test Certificate (VT20); if it fails, you're given a red refusal form (VT30) listing the defects that must be corrected. If your car fails, you're only permitted to drive it home, to a garage for repairs or to another testing station after repair, although many MoT stations will fix the faults and re-test the car the same day. Faults which don't constitute a failure are listed as 'advisories' which may warrant attention before the next test is due. You can appeal against a test failure by completing form VT17 (available from any testing station) and sending it to the DVSA with the appeal fee within 14 days of failure.

> ☑ **SURVIVAL TIP**
>
> A valid test certificate shouldn't be taken as a guarantee of a car's roadworthiness, particularly as many aspects of a car's operation aren't tested, e.g. engine and gearbox.

You can have your car tested anytime, for example if you want to sell it. However, if it fails the test, even when it isn't due, you're unable to drive it until it has passed. It's an offence to use a vehicle on public roads without a valid test certificate. You're permitted only to drive it to a testing station where you've pre-booked a test. Without a test certificate, you cannot renew your vehicle (road) tax (see page 160). If you lose your test certificate, you can get a duplicate from the testing station that carried out the test, provided you've the serial number or the approximate date of issue.

The standard of testing is variable, owing mainly to a wide variation in the interpretation of test standards. It's unlikely that two testing stations will find the same faults on an old car, e.g. one that's five years old. It's unwise to buy a vehicle without a recent test certificate, even at a bargain price (which should make you even more suspicious), as many old cars fail the test. Even buying a car with a new test certificate doesn't guarantee that it's in good condition. It's easy for someone to obtain a false test certificate and many testers lose their licences each year for issuing false certificates.

If you're buying a car privately without a guarantee, you would be advised to have an independent inspection carried out by a motoring organisation (see page 168). If you ask a garage (or anyone) to do a pre-test check on your car, don't ask them to repair it to test standard to get it through the test, as this could result in unnecessary expense. Ask them to take it for the test to find out what (if anything) needs fixing. Essential repairs recommended by a garage may not be the same as those officially required after a test. Police carry out roadworthiness spot checks on vehicles, and if your vehicle is found not to be roadworthy, the fact that you've a valid test certificate is irrelevant.

DRIVING LICENCE

The minimum age for driving in the UK is 17 for a motor car (up to 3.5 tonnes laden) or a motorcycle over 50cc and 16 for a motorcycle (moped) up to 50cc, an invalid carriage and certain other vehicles. For commercial vehicles up to 7.5 tonnes laden, the minimum age is 18, and for heavy goods vehicles (HGV) it's 21. Driving licences are issued for certain categories of vehicles, e.g. category A is for a motorcycle, B is for a car, C is for a truck and D is for a bus. Holders of a full foreign driving licence or an international driving permit can drive in the UK for one year using a foreign licence.

If you hold a licence from a EU member state you can drive in the UK on your foreign licence until the age of 70 or for three years after becoming a resident, after which you must exchange your licence for a British one. Those with a licence issued in Andorra, Australia, Barbados, British Virgin Islands, Canada, Falkland Islands, Gibraltar, Faroe Islands, Hong Kong, Japan, Monaco, New Zealand, Singapore, South Africa, South Korea, Switzerland or Zimbabwe, can exchange their foreign licence for a British driving licence in their first year in the UK without taking a driving test. If a British licence isn't obtained they must stop driving, but have up to five years in which to exchange their licence.

If you hold a licence issued by a country that isn't listed above, you must take a driving test during your first year in the UK. If you don't pass the driving test during your first year, you must apply for a provisional licence, and drive under restricted conditions (e.g. with a qualified driver) until you've passed your test.

Some foreign licences (for example those printed in Arabic or Japanese) must be translated into English, or an international driving permit must be obtained before arrival. To apply to exchange your licence for a British driving licence, obtain an application form (D1) from any post office or download one from www.gov.uk/dvlaforms. An eye test

certificate isn't required, although you must be able to read a number plate at 66 feet (20m) in daylight, with glasses or contact lenses if necessary. British licences contain a photograph and come in two parts; a plastic, credit-card size identity card and a paper licence. Complete form D1 and send it to the DVLA with the appropriate postcode (shown on the form) and the following:

- Your foreign driving licence and, if applicable, an international driving permit (which are returned to you);
- Your permanent address in the UK;
- Documents proving your identity, e.g. your passport, and a passport-style colour photograph;
- A cheque or postal order for the fee (£43 in 2016).

Your British driving licence is sent to you around one week later and is valid until the age of 70. At the age of 70 it must be renewed and every three years thereafter, provided you remain fit to drive. You must declare any health problems which may make you unfit to drive at any time, and not just when applying for a licence. An international driving permit is required if you plan to drive in some countries. Check with one of the motoring organisations (see page 168).

An international driving permit, valid for one year, is obtainable from motoring organisations for £5.50 by post (a postage fee may apply) or from major post offices. You must provide a passport-size photograph, a photocopy of the identity page of your passport, the fee and a copy of your driving licence, and enclose these with the completed form. Holders of a British or foreign car driving licence can ride a motorcycle of up to 125cc in the UK without obtaining a separate licence. For motorcycles over 125cc, you must have a motorcycle licence (see **Motorcycles** on page 163). Foreign licences issued by EU member states and certain other countries can be exchanged for a British licence within five years of becoming resident in the UK.

If you change your permanent address within the UK, you must notify the DVLA as soon as possible by completing the section on the back of a paper licence (if applicable) and returning it to the address shown. A new licence is issued free of charge. You can be fined if you fail to notify the DVLA of a change of address.

A provisional licence is exchanged free of charge for a full licence after passing your driving test. A police officer can ask to see your driving licence at any time, and you must either produce it immediately or take it personally to a police station (named by you) within seven days. Driving without a licence or while disqualified attracts a heavy penalty.

> **▲ Caution**
>
> If you accumulate 12 or more penalty points within three years, you're usually automatically disqualified from driving for a minimum of six months.

Court convictions for many motoring offences result in an 'endorsement' of your licence, whereby you receive a number of penalty points. Most offences 'earn' a fixed number of penalty points, e.g. speeding usually merits three penalty points, but some are at a court's discretion.

If you already have points on your licence, and a new offence would bring your points total to 12 or more, you must appear in court (as only a court can disqualify you from driving). If you've been disqualified in the past three years, you usually lose your licence for a minimum of one year (two previous disqualifications normally lead to a two-year ban). You can be disqualified for a single offence, such as drunken or reckless driving, which can also result in a prison sentence when injury or death resulted. If you drive while disqualified, you can receive a prison sentence and have your car confiscated.

Further information about driving licences can be obtained from the Driver and Vehicle Licensing Agency/DVLA (0300-790 6801, www.gov.uk/government/organisations/driver-and-vehicle-licensing-agency).

CAR INSURANCE

There are three categories of car insurance available in the UK – third party, third party fire & theft and comprehensive – as described below.

Third Party: This is the minimum legal cover which includes insurance against claims for injury to other people caused by your passengers. Third party insurance provides the minimum legal cover in all EU countries, plus Andorra, Iceland, Norway and Switzerland, without a green card. Not all insurance companies offer third party car insurance.

Third Party, Fire & Theft: Third party, fire and theft (TPF&T) includes loss or damage caused to your car and anything fitted to it by fire, lightning, explosion, theft or attempted theft. It usually includes broken glass.

Comprehensive: Comprehensive insurance covers all the risks listed under the two categories above, plus damage to your own car, theft of contents (usually limited to £100 or £150), broken glass (e.g. windscreen replacement), personal accident benefits and medical expenses (e.g. £100 or £200). It also usually includes damage from natural hazards, e.g. storm damage. Extra cover may be offered free or for an additional fee, and may include the cost of hiring a car if yours is involved in an accident or stolen; legal assistance; no-claims discount protection; and extra cover for a car stereo system.

Comprehensive insurance may also cover you against loss when your car is in a garage for repair after an accident. Check a policy for any restrictions; for example, you may not be covered against theft if your car isn't garaged and locked overnight. Most lenders usually insist on comprehensive insurance for leasing, contract hire, hire purchase and loan agreements.

Any insurance policy can (at extra cost!) include other people to drive your car (either individually named or any driver), but comprehensive insurance is generally reduced to third party when you're driving a car that doesn't belong to you. Not all policies allow you to drive another car, so check the wording first.

Cost of Insurance

The cost of car insurance has soared in recent years, with premiums doubling between 2007 and 2014. The primary reason is fraudulent claims, particularly for whiplash and other injuries – the so-called 'cash for crash' scams. The UK has seen a compensation epidemic in recent years, and many drivers now fit a dashboard camera (dashcam) in their cars to provide evidence of their innocence in the event of an accident caused by a third party.

Accidents among the young (one in five suffer an accident in their first year and teenagers have almost double the risk of death from a road-traffic accident than the general population) drivers have also soared, which has led to their premiums rocketing, with some facing premiums of several thousand pounds – in fact some first-time drivers receive quotations of £20,000-25,000! Young drivers can save money on insurance by having a 'Smartbox' installed in their car that monitors how they drive (see www.co-operativeinsurance.co.uk/youngdriver).

There are a number of websites that allow you to compare the cost of insurance policies, although you need to bear in mind that these sites are paid commissions by insurance companies, so aren't always impartial. It's advisable to obtain quotes direct from insurer such as Admiral (www.admiral.co.uk/car-insurance), Aviva (www.aviva.co.uk/car), Churchill (www.churchill.com/car-insurance) and Direct Line (www.directline.com/car-insurance), some of which don't appear on comparison sites. One of the best value for money companies for the over 50s is Saga (www.saga.co.uk/insurance/car-insurance).

Green Card Insurance

British motor insurance is valid in Andorra, Austria, Belgium, Bulgaria, Croatia, Cyprus, Czech Republic, Denmark, Estonia, Finland, France, Germany, Greece, Hungary, Iceland, Ireland, Italy, Latvia, Lithuania, Luxembourg, Malta, Netherlands, Norway, Poland, Portugal, Romania, Slovak Republic, Slovenia, Spain, Sweden and Switzerland. In order to extend your comprehensive cover to these countries you require a Green Card (contact your insurance company for information). This is usually available for a maximum period (e.g. three months a year) and can be expensive.

It's mandatory to have a green card when driving in some countries, including Albania, Belarus, Bosnia and Herzegovina, Former Yugoslav Republic of Macedonia (FYROM), Islamic Republic of Iran, Israel, Moldova, Morocco, Russia, Serbia and Montenegro, Tunisia, Turkey and Ukraine.

VEHICLE TAX

Vehicle tax (commonly called 'road tax') is required for all cars and motorcycles, although the old road tax disc (which was affixed to the windscreen) was phased out in 2014. Vehicles registered before March 2001 are taxed according to their engine size: vehicles with engines of 1,549cc or less are taxed at £145 per year and those with engines of 1,550cc and over at £230 per year. (It's possible to pay six-monthly, but it works out at around 10 per cent more expensive.) Vehicles registered after March 2001 are taxed according to the number of grams of carbon dioxide (CO_2) their engines emit per kilometre driven and their fuel type – from £0 to £515 per annum – as shown on the Gov.uk website (www.gov.uk/vehicle-tax-rate-tables/rates-for-cars-registered-on-or-after-1-march-2001). Motorcycles are taxed according to engine size, from £17 for up to 150cc to £80 for over 600cc.

Newly registered cars are subject to a higher first year tax rate. Rates vary from £0 for cars with up to 130g/km emissions up to £1,120 for those with higher emissions. These don't apply to imported vehicles unless they're deemed to be new, i.e. purchased

within six months of import or with less than 3,600mi (6,000km) on the clock.

Road tax can be paid at a post office, where forms and information leaflets are available. To tax a vehicle you must complete a Vehicle Licence Application Form (V10) and take it to a post office with your vehicle registration document; a valid MoT test certificate, if applicable (see **Test Certificate** above); a disabled exemption certificate, if applicable; and the payment, e.g. cash or cheque. Alternatively, you can tax your car online at www.gov.uk/vehicle-tax if you're the registered keeper of the vehicle and your name, address and any changes you've made to your vehicle have been updated on DVLA records. A receipt for payment will be sent to you within five working days.

Road tax cannot be transferred from one vehicle to another or from one owner to the next. You receive a refund of any full months of pre-paid tax and this is sent automatically when the DVLA receives notification that the car has been sold, scrapped, exported or officially taken off the road.

The authorities have clamped down on untaxed cars in the past few years. In the mid-2000s there were an estimated over 2 million untaxed vehicles on British roads, but the number is now thought to be around 250,000.

GENERAL ROAD RULES

A booklet published by the Department for Transport entitled *The Official Highway Code* (The Stationery Office) contains advice for all road users, including motorists, motorcyclists and pedestrians. It's available for £2.50 from bookshops and British motoring organisations and is essential reading, particularly for foreigners and anyone unused to driving on the left. A free online version is available on the Gov.uk website (www.gov.uk/highway-code).

A more comprehensive explanation of road signs is given in a booklet entitled *Know Your Traffic Signs*, available from bookshops for £4.99.

BRITISH DRIVERS

Like motorists in all countries, British drivers have their idiosyncrasies and customs. In general, Britons have a reputation for being good drivers, and most are courteous. Unlike many other Europeans, they're usually happy to give way to a driver waiting to enter the flow of traffic or change lanes. However, tempers are rising on the UK's overcrowded streets, and 'road rage' is becoming more common. It's often provoked by tailgating, headlight flashing, obscene gestures, obstruction and verbal abuse, so be careful how you behave when driving.

Many drivers are nervous of motorways and have little idea how to drive on them; common faults include poor lane discipline, undertakers (motorists who overtake on the inside), driving too fast in poor conditions (e.g. fog and heavy rain), and driving much too close to the vehicle in front. One thing most foreigners immediately notice when driving in the UK is the speed people at which drive, which may be well above the prevailing speed limit. The exception to this rule is the ubiquitous 'Sunday driver', so-called because he rarely drives on any other day of the week and is never actually going anywhere, but just enjoying the scenery (hence his maximum 20mph speed). You'll also notice that many motorists are reluctant to use their lights in poor visibility or until it's completely dark at night; even then, they may use only parking lights in areas with street lighting.

Take it easy when driving in winter. Although heavy snow is rare, particularly in the south, the UK experiences a lot of fog and ice which make driving extremely hazardous (it also gets dark at around 4pm or even earlier in the north). Black ice is also common, and is the most dangerous sort because it cannot be seen. When road conditions are bad, allow two to three times longer than usual to reach your destination.

BRITISH ROADS

There are some 225,000mi (360,000km) of roads in the UK, including around 1,950mi (3,100km) of motorways. In general, the quality of British roads is excellent, although some main roads and motorways are in a poor condition through being constantly chewed up by juggernauts. Many suburban roads are full of potholes, as councils simply cannot afford to repair them. The UK has a smaller motorway network than many other western European countries, most of which are toll-free (see www.cbrd.co.uk/motorway).

There's a toll charge of £6.60 for cars when crossing the Severn Bridge westwards into Wales (crossing eastwards doesn't incur a charge). In London, there's a toll for the Dartford Crossing, which is an integral part of the M25 orbital motorway around London and crosses the Thames to the east of the capital. The toll, termed the Dart Charge, can no longer be paid when crossing and must be paid by midnight on the day you cross (see www.gov.uk/pay-dartford-crossing-charge). Travel north is by tunnel, south by bridge, and the toll for a car in either direction is £2.50 (although it's free between 10pm and 6am).

Motorway travel in the UK is generally fast, although it's often slowed to a crawl by road works and the ubiquitous contra-flow, where two-way traffic occupies a single carriageway. However, despite their high traffic density, motorways are the UK's safest roads, accounting for around 6 per cent of all road deaths. Casualties on town and rural roads are proportionately much higher.

Emergency SOS telephones are located on motorways, where arrows on marker posts at the roadside indicate the direction of the nearest telephone. The hard shoulder on motorways is for emergencies only, and you mustn't stop there simply to have a rest (for which you can be fined). In fact, the hard shoulder is a very dangerous place to stop, and many fatal accidents on motorways involve vehicles stopped there.

TRAFFIC POLICE

Police must have a reason to stop motorists in the UK, e.g. erratic driving or a defective bulb, although they can usually find a pretext if they want to stop you. They have access to a sophisticated automatic number plate recognition (ANPR) system linked to central computers and can easily identify drivers who've broken the law, e.g. uninsured vehicles. Police cars sometimes display messages to motorists behind them via a panel inside their rear windscreen, e.g. 'Seatbelt', 'Reduce Your Speed', 'Do Not Pass', 'Accident Ahead' or 'Follow Me'.

> If you don't have your papers with you when stopped by the police, you must take them personally to a police station (named by you), usually within seven days. They mustn't be sent by post.

Undercover police also wear plain clothes and drive unidentified cars. If someone in plain clothes stops you, wait for identification to be shown before unlocking your car door or winding down your window. If you think you haven't committed an offence and wish to contest it in a court of law, don't accept a fixed penalty notice, but ask for a full charge to be

brought against you. You'll never be asked to pay a fine on the spot.

You aren't required by law to carry your car or motorcycle papers when motoring in the UK. However, if you're stopped by the police (for any reason) while driving, they may ask to see your diving licence (British if held), vehicle registration document, test certificate and/or insurance certificate.

MOTORCYCLES

Motorcycling is popular in the UK, both as a means of transport and as a pastime (scooters and motorcycles have become fashionable again in recent years), with over 1.3 million motorcyclists on the road. In recent years, motorcycle accidents have been greatly reduced by the compulsory wearing of helmets, safer bikes and protective riding gear, and better training and defensive riding by bikers. In general, laws that apply to cars also apply to motorcycles. However, there are a few points that apply to motorcyclists in particular, as wearing crash helmets and the use of dipped headlights at all times.

Motorists with a full motor car licence (British or foreign) may ride a motorcycle (up to 125cc) without passing a test or obtaining a special licence, although they must take a course of compulsory basic training (CBT) – this is necessary even to ride a moped. Drivers who passed their test before February 1st 2001 only need undergo CBT if they're riding a bike between 50 and 125cc. An 'L' (learner) plate must be displayed if riding a motorbike but not a moped.

Insurance for motorcycles is high, and similar to that for cars (see **Car Insurance** on page 159). The cost of insurance depends on your age (riders aged under 25 pay much more), the type and cubic capacity of your motorcycle, and the length of time you've held a licence.

Information for motorcyclists is available from the Department for Transport's Think! road safety campaign (http://think.direct.gov.uk/motorcycles.html), which has downloads on bike maintenance and further training. Info for bikers is also provided by a number of independent websites, including www.bennetts.co.uk, www.bikersadvice.com and www.motorcycle.co.uk.

DRINKING & DRIVING

As you're no doubt well aware, drinking and driving make a dangerous cocktail. In 2013, over 8,000 people were injured in drink drive accidents (where at least one driver was over the legal limit), including around 260 fatalities. On Friday and Saturday nights between 10pm and 4am, around two-thirds of drivers and riders killed are over the legal alcohol limit.

In England, Wales and Northern Ireland, you're no longer considered fit to drive when your breath contains 35 micrograms of alcohol per 100ml, or your blood contains 80mg of alcohol per 100ml or 107mg per 100ml of urine. In Scotland the limits are significantly lower: 22, 50 and 67 respectively.

For someone of average body weight, the recognised maximum they can drink and still remain under the limit is two pints of average

strength beer or its equivalent. Anything over two small beers or even a large glass of wine may be too much however for someone of slim build or someone unused to alcohol. Random breath tests aren't permitted. However, the police can stop any car under any pretext (e.g. to check that it isn't stolen) and ask the driver to take a breath test. This involves simply blowing into a device which turns red if you fail the test. It's an offence to refuse to take a breath test, for which the penalty is the same as failing the test.

If you fail the breathalyser test, you're taken to a police station and are given a further test on a special analyser after around 20 minutes. If you're still over the limit, you've the right to request a blood or urine test, which may also be requested by the police. The police and most people choose blood tests. If you insist on a test and are then found to be over the limit you must pay a fee. Samples of blood or urine are put into separate containers, one of which is sealed and given to you for private analysis (should you so wish). Note that you can still be over the legal limit the morning after a heavy night's drinking.

You can also be disqualified for driving while under the influence of drugs; cannabis smoked days before a test can show up in specimens and can result in a disqualification for driving while under the influence of drugs. You can also be convicted of being drunk if you're 'in charge of a vehicle' even though you weren't actually driving it. This carries the same penalties as drunken driving. Fines and penalties are dependent on how much over the limit you are. If you're convicted of driving or attempting to drive while drunk, you lose your licence for a mandatory 12-month period, and receive a heavy fine and/or six months imprisonment.

CAR CRIME

Although car crime has fallen significantly to the lowest level for 50 years thanks to better security systems, if you drive an expensive (or valuable) car it's wise to have it fitted with an alarm, engine immobiliser and a tracker device. Favourite targets (often stolen by professional crooks to order) include premium German cars (such as Audi, BMW and Mercedes) and British makes such as Aston Martin, Bentley and Range Rover. (Thefts of new Range Rovers in London is so high that some insurers will only insure them if certain precautions are taken.)

The best (and most expensive) security for a valuable car is a tracking device, such as Securicor Trakbak and Tracker Network, that's triggered by concealed motion detectors. The vehicle's movements are tracked by radio or satellite, and the police are automatically notified and recover over 90 per cent of vehicles. Some systems can immobilise a vehicle while it's on the move (which might not be such a good idea!). Many insurance companies offer a discount on comprehensive insurance (e.g. 20 per cent) when you've a tracking system fitted.

Many websites provide advice on preventing car crime, including https://crimestoppers-uk.org/keeping-safe/vehicles and www.police.uk/crime-prevention-advice/vehicle-crime.

If your car is stolen, report it to the police and your insurance company as soon as possible.

FUEL

Fuel costs around twice as much in the UK as it does in the US, and Britain is also one of the most expensive countries in Europe in which to fill up your car. In October 2016, the average price for a litre of unleaded petrol and diesel was around £1.16, according to the Petrol Prices website (www.petrolprices.com), while super-unleaded cost £1.26 and premium diesel £1.31 per litre.

UK fuel costs vary depending on the area or town, and aren't standard throughout the country for the same brand (it can depend on local competition). Supermarkets are the cheapest outlets and have around 40 per cent of the market. Prices must be displayed on garage forecourts. You can find the lowest petrol prices in your area at www.petrolprices.com.

The cleanest fuels are compressed natural gas (CNG) and liquefied petroleum gas (LPG), which costs from around 57p per litre. Most petrol engines can be converted to use both petrol and CNG/LPG, and can be switched between them. However, its availability is limited. For a list of outlets, contact UKLPG (www.uklpg.com). It's worth noting that gas-powered cars aren't allowed on the Eurotunnel or in some underground car parks.

Electric cars and hybrids (which have a battery powered electric motor and small petrol engine which charges the battery) are gaining in popularity, although they're better suited to town driving as charging points aren't always easy to find (and you need to be able to charge a vehicle while at home).

Most petrol stations also have a shop selling a wide range of motoring accessories and other goods. In fact, the main business of many petrol stations isn't selling fuel, on which profit margins are minimal (except for the government!). Today's petrol stations are more like convenience stores and sell a wide range of confectionery, snacks, drinks (even beer, wine and spirits), pizzas, newspapers and magazines, and take in dry-cleaning; some even have cafés and bake bread.

SPEED LIMITS

The following speed limits are in force for cars and motorcycles throughout the UK, unless traffic signs show otherwise:

Local speed limits set by councils often reduce speeds in built-up areas (with street lighting) to 20pmh (32kph), especially close to schools. There may also be limits of 40mph (64kph) on the outskirts of towns and villages, and 50mph (80kph) on winding stretches of single-lane rural roads (both will be as signposted).

Type of Road	Speed Limit
Motorways and dual-carriageways	70mph (113kph)
Unrestricted single carriageway roads	60mph (97kph)
Approach roads to towns	40mph (64kph)
Built-up areas (towns)	20/30mph (32/48kph)*

* Applies to all traffic on all roads with street lighting, unless otherwise indicated by a sign. Some cities and towns have imposed a 20mph limit.

Speed limits are indicated in miles per hour, not kilometres. When towing a caravan or trailer, speed limits on all roads (except those in built-up and residential areas) are reduced by 10mph (16kph). Speed limits for buses, coaches and goods vehicles not exceeding 7.5 tonnes are the same as when towing, except that the permitted speed limit on motorways is 70mph. Heavy goods vehicles (exceeding 7.5 tonnes) are permitted to travel at 50mph on single/duel carriageways and 60mph on motorways.

Speed cameras (both fixed and mobile) are in use throughout the country and over a million motorists a year are prosecuted for speeding, resulting in fines of over £100m. However, the use of a speed camera alert device isn't illegal and they're widely sold and used; however, the best models (such as Road Angel and Novus) – which use Global Positioning Satellite (GPS) to detect cameras – cost up to £300 (there's also an annual fee of around £50 to update the system). Many local authorities are now using average-speed cameras, which average a drivers' speed on all routes across a wide area (with up to 50 cameras operating in a network). It's almost impossible to evade detection, as the digital cameras cover every entry and exit point in an area.

A national speed camera database publishes locations of speed cameras across the UK, although it relies on users to keep the information updated (www.speedcamerasuk.com).

There's a maximum fine of £1,000 for speeding (£2,500 on motorways) and a penalty of 3-6 penalty points. Speeding fines usually depend on an offender's previous convictions and your speed above the limit. Fines for speeding vary from a fixed penalty of £60 for marginal speeding (e.g. up to 15mph above the limit), to hundreds of pounds for speeding of 30mph or more above the limit, when you're usually prosecuted in court and may be disqualified from driving for a period.

If you're stopped for marginal speeding you've the choice of paying a fixed penalty or going to court. You may also have the option of taking a speed awareness course which costs around the same as the minimum speeding penalty (£100), but means you don't get the penalty points. Note that if you go to court and lose, your fine is likely to be higher, and you must also pay costs (so make sure that you've a good case).

In some areas (e.g. residential areas, private roads, school and university grounds, and car parks) there are speed bumps, known as 'sleeping policemen', designed to slow traffic. These are sometimes indicated by warning signs and, if you fail to slow down, it's possible to damage your suspension or even turn your car over (accidents have even resulted in fatalities).

CAR HIRE

There are a number of multinational car hire (which is usually used in preference to 'car rental' in the UK) companies in the UK, including Avis, Budget, Enterprise, Europcar and Hertz, plus a number of large independents. Major companies have offices in towns throughout the country and at major airports. Cars can also be hired from many garages and local car hire companies in most towns, which may have much lower rates than the nationals. Check out some of the comparison websites, e.g. www.carrentals.

▲ Warning

Some rental companies (or their managers) operate a scam that involves charging renters for damage that existed when a vehicle was hired. To avoid this you should take photos of any damage (body dents, broken lights, windscreen chips, scuffed bumpers, etc.) as evidence when you hire a car. Another scam is charging excessively for repairs (£500-1,000 for a replacement tyre!), so it's worth taking out full insurance.

co.uk, www.rentalcars.com/en/country/gb or www.travelsupermarket.com: you can also look in local newspapers, search online, or look under *Car Hire* in the Yellow Pages (www.yell.com).

Rental costs vary considerably between rental companies, particularly over longer periods (weekly and monthly rates are lower). You need to ensure that rates include unlimited mileage, collision damage waiver insurance, personal accident and baggage insurance, plus VAT. Rental cars usually mustn't be driven outside the UK unless prior arrangement is made with the hire company and continental insurance (a green card) obtained.

To hire a car in the UK, you require a full British or European driving licence or an international driver's permit, which must have been held for a minimum of one year (or two years if aged under 23). You may be asked for some form of identification in addition to your driving licence. The minimum age is usually between 18 and 23, although those aged 18 to 21 must normally provide their own fully comprehensive insurance or purchase collision damage waiver (CDW) insurance at a special (high) rate. Drivers under 21 are usually restricted in their choice of cars, and some hire companies insist on a higher minimum age (e.g. 25) for some categories of cars; you must usually be aged 23 to 25 to hire a minibus or motor caravan. The maximum age for hiring a car may be 70 or 75.

A minimum deposit of £50 to £75 (or equal to the total hire charge) is usually required if you don't pay by credit card, and may be much higher if you don't take out CDW insurance. When paying by credit card, check that you aren't charged for erroneous extras or for something for which you've already paid, e.g. petrol. In fact, paying by credit card usually means that you give the hire company a 'continuous authority' (or blank cheque) to debit your card account.

Vans and pick-ups are available from major rental companies by the hour, half-day or day, or from smaller local companies (which once again, are cheaper). You can also hire a motor caravan, a caravan or trailer, or a minibus from a number of companies (prices vary with the season). In addition to self-drive car hire, in many cities you can hire a car with a chauffeur for business or sightseeing.

Car Clubs & Private Hire

An alternative to traditional car hire companies is offered by car clubs and private hire. With car clubs (also called 'car sharing') you join a club and pay a membership fee that allows you to hire cars across the UK from as little as 30 minutes up to 6 months. Unlike traditional car hire, you pay only for the time you use. Rates include insurance, a free fuel allowance (e.g. 20 miles per day), a limited number of miles free per week (e.g. 500) and the congestion charge (in London), with hire fees from around £5 per hour. The major players have cars in a number of major cities across the UK, with London being the best served.

There are a number of companies with national schemes including www.citycarclub.co.uk and www.zipcar.co.uk. Carplus (0113-373 1757, www.carplus.org.uk) is a national charity that works independently and in partnership with car clubs to reduce over-dependency on private cars by promoting sharing and accessible, affordable and low-carbon alternatives.

MOTORING ORGANISATIONS

There are four major national motoring organisations in the UK: the Automobile Association/AA (0800-085 2721, www.theaa.com), Britannia Rescue (0800-022 3948, www.britanniarescue.com), Green Flag National Breakdown (0845-246 2766, www.greenflag.com) and the Royal Automobile Club/RAC (0800-0722 822, www.rac.co.uk). By far the largest organisation is the AA, followed by the RAC and Green Flag. All offer continental cover as an option. There are few essential differences between the services provided by the major British motoring organisations, although membership costs vary.

All organisations offer a range of membership levels (e.g. individual, couple and family), and different levels of service, which may include roadside assistance, relay (get you home), 72-hour European breakdown cover, home start and relay plus (which provides a free replacement car for up to 48 hours). Some organisations cover the car (for any driver), while others cover the driver (in any car). Organisations charge from around £20 a year for recovery only, and up to over £200 for their premium service, which includes European recovery. There's usually a discount when you buy online.

Many insurers offer breakdown cover, including Direct Line (0845-246 8702, www.directline.com), which operates a roadside-rescue service in partnership with Green Flag. Insurance companies often offer membership of a motoring organisation for a lower fee when you take out car insurance, while the major motoring organisations also offer car insurance. It's a confusing area and it's worth using a comparison website such as www.money.co.uk/breakdown-cover.htm to find the best deals. Most motoring organisations offer inducements to new members such as free mobile phones, free or reduced-cost MOT tests, free safety checks and 50 per cent off windscreen replacements.

Be wary of having your car repaired after it's towed away by a garage 'approved' by a motoring organisation – always obtain a quotation first and make sure that it's competitive.

PARKING

Parking in most cities and towns is often a problem, particularly on Saturdays when everyone's doing their shopping. On-street parking is a particular problem, and most roads without parking meters or bays have restricted or prohibited parking. British companies don't usually provide employees (except perhaps directors) with parking facilities in large cities and towns, so check in advance whether parking is available at your workplace (if it isn't, it could be very expensive). Outside cities and towns, parking is usually available at workplaces.

> You can pay for parking by phone virtually anywhere in the UK (see https://paybyphone.co.uk/how-it-works/parking).

Parking Restrictions

On-road parking (waiting) restrictions in the UK are indicated by yellow or red lines at the edge of roads, usually accompanied by a sign indicating when parking is prohibited, e.g. 'Mon-Sat 8am-6.30pm' or 'At any time'. If no days are indicated on the sign, restrictions are in force every day, including Sundays and public holidays. Yellow signs indicate a continuous waiting prohibition, and also detail times when parking is illegal, while blue signs indicate limited waiting periods. Loading restrictions for loading and unloading goods may be shown by one to three short yellow lines marked on the kerb (and indicated on a sign).

A summary of the road markings used to indicate parking and waiting restrictions in the UK is shown in the table below:

For more information, consult *The Official Highway Code*. In most towns, there are public and private off-road car parks, indicated by a sign showing a white 'P' on a blue background. Parking in local authority car parks can cost from around 20p for a half-hour, although it may become progressively more expensive the longer you stay, and can easily cost £1 or more an hour for short-term parking – or several times this in the increasing number of cities that are trying to discourage cars from entering city centres. However, parking is generally cheaper (per hour) the longer you park.

Parking in public car parks and at meters may be free on Sundays and public holidays (check the notice before buying a ticket). In many areas, there are 'park and ride' parking areas, where parking and/or public transport into the local town or city may be free (particularly around Christmas time). Many councils produce car park maps, showing local parking areas, available free from council offices, libraries and tourist information centres. You can use the website Parkopedia (en.parkopedia.co.uk) to check the cost of parking in the UK and worldwide.

Council & Private Car Parks

Parking in a private car park in a city (e.g. London) can cost over £7 an hour or over £50 per day, although monthly and annual season tickets are usually available for commuters. National Car Parks (NCP), the UK's largest car park operator, has 24-hour car parks in most cities; you can search for an NCP car park via the 'Car Park Finder' function on the NCP website (www.ncp.co.uk).

In many areas, there are both short- and long-stay car parks. Fees may be reasonable for short stays of up to two or three hours, beyond which rates at short-stay car parks are much more expensive. Some car parks, such as those operated by councils, have introduced a scheme which links fees to demand, with fees starting as low as 20p an hour, although a six-hour stay can cost £25.

If you commute into a city it may well be cheaper to drive to a convenient railway station

Road Markings

Road Marking	Meaning
White zigzag line	No parking or stopping at any time
Single red line*	No stopping between 7am and 7pm (or as indicated by a sign) from Mondays to Fridays, except for loading or unloading
Double red line*	No stopping, loading/unloading or parking at any time
Double yellow lines	No parking at most or all times (as indicated by signs)
Single yellow line	No parking between around 7am and 7pm on four or more days a week
Broken yellow line	Restricted parking (see sign for details)

* known as 'red routes'

(where parking usually costs around £2 to £6 a day) and take a train into the city centre. Weekly, monthly and annual parking season tickets are usually available at railway stations (and underground stations in outer London).

Parking Meters

The maximum permitted parking period at meters varies from 30 minutes to two hours. Meter-feeding (i.e. returning to a meter to insert more money) is illegal, although many people do it. You're supposed to vacate a parking space when the meter time expires, even if it was under the maximum time allowed, and you aren't supposed to use another meter in the same group. Meters are usually in operation from around 7am until 7pm, Mondays to Fridays, and from 7am to 6pm on Saturdays (check the sign on meters). Sundays are usually free, although meters at railway stations and airports may be in operation 24-hours a day. If you remain at a meter beyond the excess charge period, you're liable for a fixed penalty (fine) handed out by a police officer or a traffic warden.

Pay-and-Display

These are parking areas where you buy a ticket from a machine and display it behind your windscreen. It may have an adhesive backing which you peel off and use to stick the ticket to the inside of your windscreen or a car window. Parking costs anything from 30p an hour up to £5 an hour, e.g. in central London. When you've inserted sufficient coins for the period required, press the button to obtain your ticket. Pay-and-display parking areas tend to operate from around 7am until 6 or 7pm, usually excluding Sundays and public holidays. Note that machines usually don't give change.

Note that many parking meters and pay-and-display machines don't give change, so keep a supply in your car. Alternatively you can pay for parking by phone (see www.paybyphone.co.uk).

Parking Fines & Penalties

The fine for illegal parking depends on where you park. There's usually a fixed penalty ticket, e.g. £60 or up to £130 in London, for overstaying your parking period or parking illegally on a yellow line. Parking in a dangerous position or near a pedestrian crossing (i.e. on the zigzag lines or studded area) results in a higher fine, plus three penalty points on your driving licence. Penalties for non-payment or overstaying your time in a permitted parking area, e.g. at a parking meter or in a pay-and-display area, are set by the local authorities who issue parking tickets.

> You may have to pay up to £200 to have your car released from the pound (where towed cars are taken), and they won't release it until you've paid (in cash or by debit or credit card); and they charge a daily storage fee (e.g. £25-50) after the first 24 hours. You cannot be towed away from a pay-and-display area or a parking meter unless the parking bay has been suspended.

If your car is clamped, there will be a sticker on the windscreen – to prevent you inadvertently attempting to drive off and damaging your car, and to instruct you how to get the clamp removed. You'll need to pay a substantial fee (e.g. £100 or more) before your car is released, plus the parking fine. If you don't arrange for the release of the clamp within a certain period (e.g. four hours), it could be towed away.

Residents' Parking

Residents in most cities and large towns must obtain a parking permit from their local council in order to park on the street in central areas (e.g. anywhere in London) – you must provide proof of identity and residence, e.g. a Council Tax bill. Charges are set by local councils, and vary considerably, from nothing to £100 or more per year for the first car. The number of permits issued for an individual dwelling varies (usually up to three or four), as does the cost – a permit for a second car in some areas of London costs hundreds of pounds. There are also special permits for disabled drivers with a blue badge (see www.gov.uk/blue-badge-scheme-information-council), who can park in reserved spaces, free at meters and in most (but not quite all) car parks, and can ignore many on-road parking restrictions.

Note that using a mobile phone while driving is prohibited and can result in a £200 fine and six penalty points on your licence.

Bamburgh Castle, Northumberland

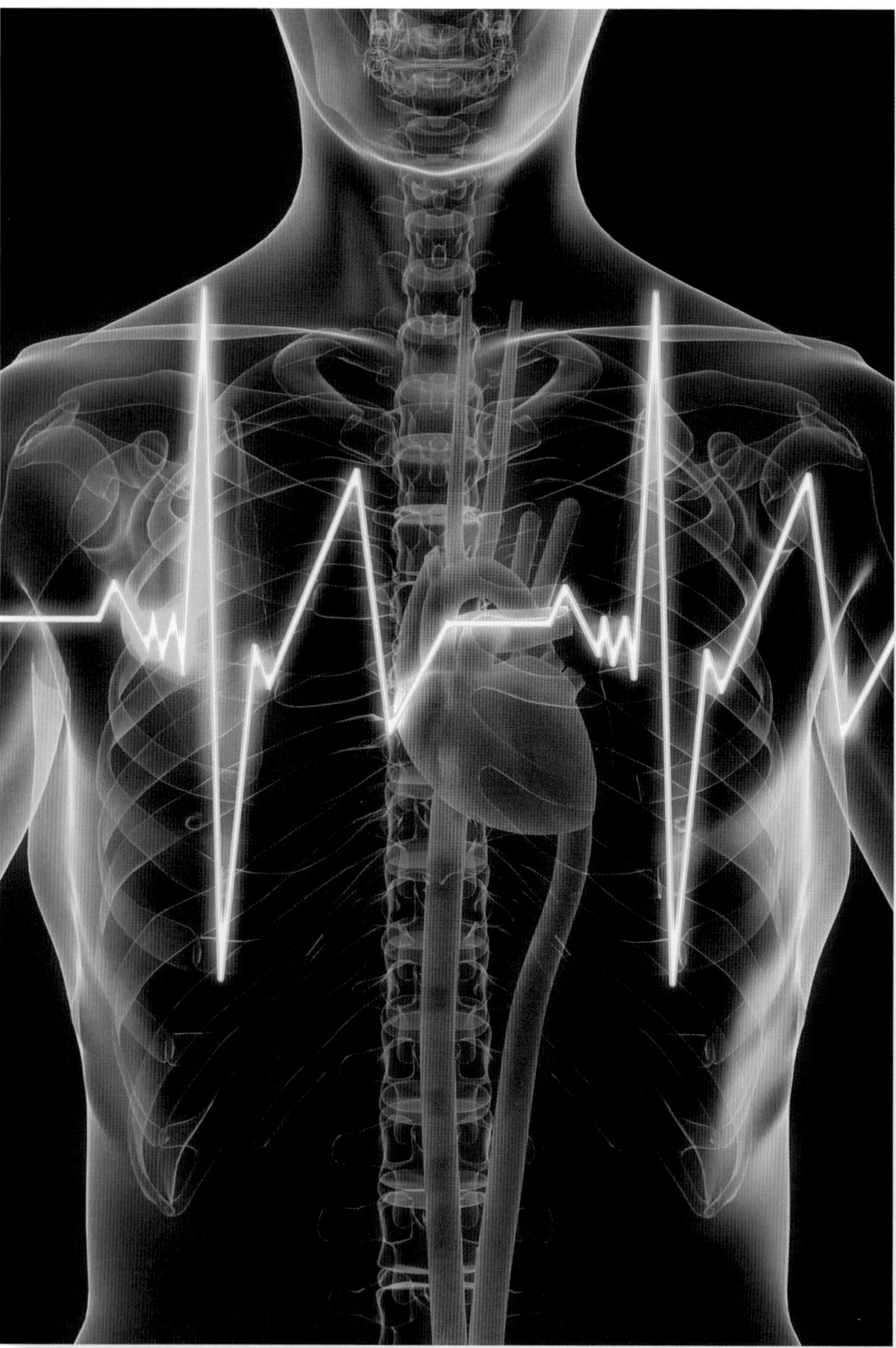

12. HEALTH

One of the most important aspects of living in the UK (or anywhere for that matter) is maintaining good health. The UK is famous for its National Health Service (NHS), which provides free or low-cost healthcare to all British citizens and most foreign residents. The standard of British-trained doctors and nursing staff is among the highest in the world, and British medical science is in the vanguard of medical technology and procedure (many pioneering operations are performed in the UK), and many foreigners visit the UK for private medical treatment. However, the under-resourced NHS (see below) is under increasing pressure, exacerbated by unhealthy lifestyles and an aging population.

If you're planning to take up residence in the UK, even for part of the year, you may wish to have a health check before your arrival, particularly if you've a record of poor health or are elderly. There are no unusual health risks in the UK and no immunisations are required unless you arrive from an area infected with yellow fever or somewhere there has been a serious epidemic.

EMERGENCIES

If you're unlucky enough to be involved in an accident, or suffer a sudden serious illness in the UK, you'll be somewhat relieved to know that emergency transport by ambulance and treatment at a hospital Accident & Emergency (A&E) department is free to everyone. In a medical emergency, simply dial 999 or 112 from any telephone (calls are free) and ask for the ambulance service. State your name and location and describe your injuries or symptoms (or those of the patient), and an ambulance with paramedics will be despatched to take you to hospital. Emergency calls (999 or 112) must be made in real emergencies only, and health authorities can levy a fee if an emergency ambulance is called unnecessarily. The UK doesn't have a national air ambulance service, although there are emergency helicopter services in some areas for critical cases.

For 'emergencies' that aren't life-threatening but still warrant urgent medical help, you can dial 111, a 24-hour service that's free to call. Advisors can check your symptoms and provide advice or refer you to the appropriate service – and can call an ambulance for you if they think it's needed.

If you're physically capable, you can go to the A&E department of an NHS general hospital, many of which provide a 24-hour service. Alternatively, there are minor injuries units (MIUs) and urgent care centres (UCCs) that treat less serious injuries such as cuts, sprains and burns, and walk-in centres where you can see a doctor or nurse if you cannot get an appointment with your GP. Police stations keep a list of doctors' and chemists' private telephone numbers in case of emergency, and there are also private 24-hour medical and dental services (search online or see the Yellow Pages, www.yell.com) in the major cities that make house calls – but check the cost before using them!

NATIONAL HEALTH SERVICE (NHS)

The National Health Service (NHS) was established in 1948 to ensure that everyone had equal access to health care. Providers of NHS services include family doctors, specialists, hospitals, dentists, chemists, opticians, community health services (e.g. district nursing and health visitor services), the ambulance service, and maternity and child health care.

Originally, all NHS medical treatment was free, the service being funded entirely from general taxation and National Insurance contributions. However, as the cost of treatment and medicines has soared, part of the cost has been passed on to patients via supplementary charges. While hospital treatment, the ambulance service and consultations remain free, most patients must now pay fixed charges for prescriptions, dental treatment, sight tests and NHS spectacles, although charges are usually below the actual cost. Family doctors, called general practitioners (GPs), theoretically still make free house calls (but are reluctant to do so), and community health workers and district nurses visit those at home who are convalescent, bedridden or have new-born babies.

However, NHS treatment and services isn't as universally available as they once were. The quality of service you receive depends very much on where you live, as waiting lists for specialist appointments and hospital beds vary from area to area and are getting longer. There are widespread and serious problems with getting a doctor's appointment (within a reasonable time frame) and even getting on a doctor's NHS list is difficult in some areas. This has resulted in an crisis in hospital A&E departments, where people turn up in their droves because they're unable to get timely GP appointments.

The NHS is facing a chronic shortage of staff (nurses, doctors, specialists, etc.) and serious underfunding and many operations and services are (unofficially) rationed or restricted. The treatments and drugs available may vary depending on your local health authority, some of which don't provide certain expensive treatment (e.g. for cancer) as they simply cannot afford it.

> If you don't qualify for healthcare under the NHS it's essential to have private health insurance (see page 196). This is wise in any case if you can afford it, owing to the inadequacy of public health services in many areas, and long waiting lists for specialist appointments and non-urgent operations. Visitors to the UK should have holiday health insurance if they aren't covered by a reciprocal arrangement.

The NHS provides free or subsidised medical treatment to all foreigners with the right of abode in the UK, and to anyone who, at the time of treatment, has been a resident for the previous year. Exceptions to the one-year qualifying rule include European Union (EU) nationals with a European Health Insurance Card (which replaced the old form E111), refugees or those with 'exceptional leave to remain' in the UK, students on a course of over six months, and foreign nationals coming to take up permanent residence in the UK.

Nationals of countries with reciprocal health agreements with the UK also receive free or subsidised medical treatment, although exemptions from charges is generally limited to emergency or urgent treatment (e.g. for a communicable disease) required during a visit to the UK. For a comprehensive list of treatments available for those from your country of origin see Gov.uk (www.gov.uk/

government/organisations/department-of-health).

Anyone who doesn't qualify under one of the above categories must pay for all medical treatment received, although some medical and dental emergencies are treated free of charge, e.g. emergency treatment at a hospital outpatients department as a result of an accident, or admission to hospital for no longer than one night.

PRIVATE TREATMENT

IN addition to NHS hospitals, hospital care in the UK is also provided in private clinics and hospitals, and in private wings or wards of large NHS hospitals. Increasingly, patients are being referred to private hospitals for NHS-funded treatment, while many NHS consultants also treat patients privately.

Private treatment includes health checks and screening, complementary medicine and cosmetic surgery (see below), some of which aren't available on the NHS. If you need to see a GP or specialist privately, you (or your insurance company) must pay the fee. Fees vary considerably, but you should expect to pay at least £50 for a routine consultation with a GP.

The quality of private treatment isn't superior to that provided by the NHS, and you shouldn't assume that because a doctor (or any other medical practitioner) is in private practice he's more competent than his NHS counterpart. In fact, often you'll see the same specialist or be treated by the same surgeon on the NHS and privately. If you see a private doctor, his offices will be plush and welcoming, you'll be greeted courteously by his receptionist, he'll have more time to spend with you and his bedside manner will be impeccable. However, he won't necessarily be a better doctor than the one in the high street community clinic.

When selecting a private specialist or clinic, you should be extremely cautious and only choose someone who's been recommended by a doctor or organisation that you can trust. It's sometimes wise to obtain a second opinion, particularly if you're diagnosed as having a serious illness or requiring a major operation. According to some reports, unnecessary operations are becoming increasingly common in the UK, even under the NHS!

Always make sure that a medical practitioner is qualified to provide the treatment you require, as (surprisingly) anyone can call himself a doctor in the UK.

DOCTORS

There are excellent family doctors, (usually referred to as GPs, short for general practitioners), in all areas of the UK. The best way to find a doctor, whether as an NHS or a private patient, is to ask your colleagues, friends or neighbours if they can recommend someone. GPs are listed under Doctors (Medical Practitioners) in the Yellow Pages (www.yell.com) and you can also search for an NHS GP practice in your area via the NHS Choices website (www.nhs.uk). Lists of doctors are also available at libraries, tourist information offices, police stations and citizens' advice

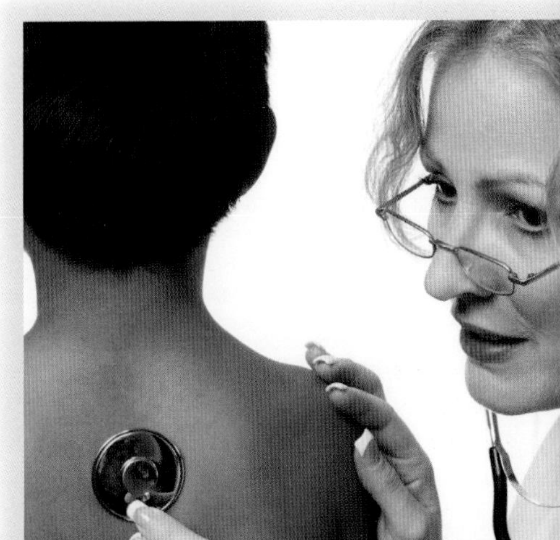

bureaux. Some universities and colleges have a health centre where students should register; otherwise, doctors' offices are known in the UK as surgeries.

Surgery hours vary considerably, with some surgeries open from 8 or 8.30am to 6 or 7pm, Mondays to Fridays, while others close at 3pm or may not open at all on certain afternoons. Surgeries may also be held on Saturday mornings.

The government would like all surgeries to open 12 hours a day, seven days a week, as the long waiting times to get a doctor's appointment (typically 7-14 days) are blamed in part for the huge increase in people turning up at A&E departments.

NHS GPs

NHS doctors are contracted by the Department of Health – through public bodies such as NHS England – to look after a number of patients in their 'catchment' area. As so many doctors now work in group practices, it's normal to register with a practice rather than with an individual doctor; this means that you can see whichever GP is available, but you may have to wait longer to see a specific GP. Doctors/practices can refuse to register you as a patient if they have no vacancies or you live outside their catchment area.

GP-led health centres, sometimes called walk-in centres, provide medical care to patients irrespective of whether they're registered with another doctor. They provide a backup service to patients without a GP or who cannot get an appointment with their own GP. They're generally open from 8am to 8pm seven days a week. To find your nearest centre, contact your Area Team or search via the NHS Choices website (www.nhs.uk).

If you've trouble getting onto an NHS doctor's list, contact your NHS Area Team (in England visit www.nhs.uk/servicedirectories/pages/areateamlisting.aspx#trl) which has a duty to find you a doctor. If you're living in a district for less than three months or have no permanent home, you can apply to any doctor in the district as a temporary resident. After three months, you must register with a doctor as a permanent patient. An NHS doctor must give 'immediate necessary treatment' for up to 14 days to anyone without a doctor in his area, until the patient has been accepted by a doctor on a permanent basis.

All NHS GPs must produce practice guides for patients, containing the names of the doctors, times of surgeries and any special services provided, such as ante-natal, family planning and well woman (well man) or diabetic clinics.

An NHS number is issued when you first register with a GP, which you must give to any NHS practitioner who requires it. If you don't have an NHS number, the receptionist will give you a form to complete. If you're registering with a new NHS doctor, your medical records will be transferred to your new GP.

Around 80 per cent of GPs work in a partnership or group practice, around 25 per cent of which are in health centres, that provide a range of medical and nursing services. Health centres may have facilities for blood tests, immunisation, cervical smears, health education (known as 'well person clinics'), family planning, speech therapy, chiropody, hearing tests, and physiotherapy and other remedial treatment. Many also offer dental, ophthalmic, hospital outpatient and social work services. Most health centres and group practices have district nurses, health visitors, midwives and clinical psychologists in attendance at certain times.

Most doctors operate an appointment system. You cannot just turn up during surgery hours and expect to be seen, although if you're an urgent case (but not an emergency) your doctor will usually see you immediately. Standard appointment times are short and patients often overrun, so you may have to wait well past your appointed time to see a doctor.

NHS doctors make free house calls and emergency visits outside surgery hours (at their discretion) in cases when patients are house bound or too ill to visit the surgery. In fact, a doctor is responsible for his patients 24 hours a day and, when he's unavailable, must make alternative arrangements, whether through his partners in a group practice, by means of a voluntary rota between individual doctors or via a deputising service.

COMPLEMENTARY MEDICINE

Growing fears about the side-effects of medicines, and general disillusionment with the NHS have led to a huge growth in complementary (or alternative) medicine in the last few decades, although the UK is still way behind many other EU countries, particularly France and Germany. Complementary treatments are chosen by millions of Britons a year, although most aren't covered by the NHS or private health insurance in the UK.

The most popular complementary practices include acupuncture, chiropractic, holistic medicine, homeopathy, osteopathy and reflexology.

London is home to Europe's largest provider of complementary medicine, the Royal London Hospital for Integrated Medicine.

CHEMISTS & MEDICINES

Medicines ('drugs' in British English normally refers to illegal drugs or narcotics, although the word 'medication' is sometimes used instead of medicine) are obtained from a chemist (pharmacy), most of which provide free advice regarding minor ailments and suggest appropriate medicines.

There are three categories of medicine in the UK:

- Medicines that can be prescribed only by a doctor (via an official form called a prescription) and purchased from a chemist (see **Prescriptions** below);
- Medicines that can be sold only with the approval of a chemist (e.g. travel sickness pills);
- Medicines (such as aspirin and paracetamol) that can be sold 'over the counter' in chemists, and are available from other retail outlets such as supermarkets.

If you're taking regular medication, you should bear in mind that the brand names of medicines vary from country to country, and should ask your doctor for the generic name. If you wish to match medication prescribed abroad, you'll need a prescription with the medication's trade name, the manufacturer's name, the chemical name and the dosage. Most medicines have an equivalent in other countries, although particular brands may be difficult or impossible to obtain in the UK. It's also advisable to bring some of your favourite non-prescription medicines (e.g. aspirins, cold and flu remedies, and lotions) with you, as they may be difficult to find or may be much more expensive. If applicable, you should also take spare spectacles, contact lenses, dentures or hearing aids.

Some medicines requiring a doctor's prescription (see below) in the UK are sold freely in other countries, although other medicines that are controlled elsewhere are freely available in the UK. Some medicines aren't recognised (i.e. reimbursed) by the NHS, in which case your doctor will usually inform you and may offer to prescribe an alternative. If you insist on having an unrecognised medicine, you must usually pay for it yourself. Requests for repeat prescriptions may be accepted by your doctor by post, telephone or online. Most chemists use a computer to store information about the health problems of regular customers and the medicines prescribed or sold to them.

If you need medicines after normal chemist opening hours, there's usually a chemist in towns and city suburbs that's open after hours to prescribe emergency medicines. Chemists operate a duty roster that's posted in chemist windows and published in local newspapers, indicating the local chemist on duty. If you require medicine urgently when all chemists are closed, you should contact your GP or a local police station. You can also search for a pharmacy on the NHS Choices website (www.nhs.uk).

Most chemists also sell toiletries, cosmetics, health foods and cleaning supplies. Some, such as Boots, may have departments selling everything from CDs and books to electrical, photographic and kitchen equipment (in addition to those items mentioned above). A health food shop sells anti-allergy and diet foods, homeopathic medicines and eternal-life-virility-youth pills and elixirs, which are popular in the UK (even though their claims are usually in the realms of fantasy).

Prescriptions

To obtain medicines prescribed by a doctor you simply take your prescription form to any chemist. Your prescription may be filled immediately if it's available off the shelf, or you may be asked to wait or to come back later. NHS prescriptions for medicines are charged at a fixed rate of £8.40 per item (2016), although some people qualify for free medicines (see below). Those who need to pay for more than four prescription items in three months or 14 items in 12 months can save money by buying a prepayment certificate (PPC), which costs £29.10 for three months or £104 for 12 months. You can obtain a PPC from some chemists, by phone (0300-330 1341) or online (https://apps.nhsbsa.nhs.uk/ppcwebsales/patient.do).

> **☑ SURVIVAL TIP**
>
> Some medicines prescribed by a doctor (e.g. certain painkillers) can be replaced by substitute medicines that can be purchased over the counter for less than the prescription charge. Boots, the UK's largest chain of chemists with almost 2,500 stores (including Alliance Pharmacy), and supermarkets are often the cheapest places to buy non-prescription medicines.

Many people qualify for free prescriptions, including hospital outpatients and day patients; children aged under 16 and full-time students under 19; pensioners (aged over 60 in 2011); expectant mothers and those who've had a baby in the last year; people with certain medical conditions (e.g. diabetes, epilepsy and cancer) or a permanent disability that prevents them getting around without help; and those receiving certain state benefits. There are also reduced charges for people on low incomes.

With the exception of children under 16 and pensioners, anyone entitled to free prescriptions must apply for an exemption certificate or a refund (forms are available from Jobcentre Plus, GPs, hospitals, dentists and opticians). When you're exempt you must complete and sign the declaration on the back of the prescription form.

HOSPITALS & CLINICS

All large towns and cities have one or more NHS hospitals or clinics, indicated by road signs with a white 'H' on a blue background. There are many kinds of hospital in the UK, including community hospitals, district hospitals, teaching hospitals and (unlikely as it may seem) cottage hospitals – small, localised institutions.

Major hospitals are called general hospitals, and provide treatment and diagnosis for inpatients, day patients and outpatients. Most have a maternity department, infectious diseases unit, psychiatric and geriatric facilities, and rehabilitation and convalescence units, and cater for all forms of specialised treatment. Some general hospitals are designated teaching hospitals, which combine treatment with medical training and research. In addition to general hospitals, there are specialist hospitals, e.g. for children, the mentally ill and disabled, the elderly and infirm, and the treatment of specific complaints or illnesses. There are also dental hospitals, where dental surgery is performed.

Only major hospitals have an Accident & Emergency (A&E) department, while some just have an urgent care centre or minor injuries unit. Some NHS hospitals have sports' injury clinics, although you must usually be referred by your GP. In many areas there are NHS 'well woman' clinics, where women can obtain medical check-ups and cervical smear tests, and NHS family planning clinics. You can be referred to these clinics by your GP or can refer yourself, and you can also refer yourself to an NHS genito-urinary medicine (GUM) clinic for sexual health.

Most hospitals are managed by trusts that manage secondary care health services on behalf of the NHS. Since 2004, hospitals have been assessed for quality by the Health Commission (now the Care Quality Commission) and the 'best' hospitals have received Foundation status, which means that they receive extra funding and enjoy greater autonomy from the NHS.

NHS Hospitals

NHS hospital accommodation is usually in wards of various sizes, e.g. four, six or 12 beds, although single rooms are available in some newer hospitals. Some wards are mixed, i.e. men at one end and women at the other, usually divided by a central administration area – men and women aren't treated side by side in the same ward. Many NHS hospitals have rooms for private patients (known as 'pay beds') and they're permitted to charge for extras such as a telephone, TV or a wider choice of meals. In most hospitals you choose your meals the day before and provision is made for vegetarian and other diets. Some wards have dining rooms for those who are sufficiently mobile and most have day rooms for patients.

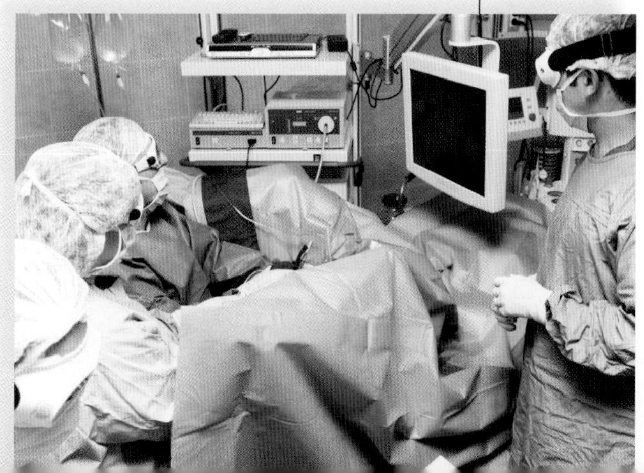

The service, facilities and standards of NHS hospitals vary considerably, with the best comparing favourably with private hospitals (apart from a possible lack of 'luxury' faculties). On the other hand, some NHS hospitals are dingy and depressing – hardly the place you would wish to be when you're ill. However, there's one consolation to being in an NHS general ward: just think how lonely and bored those poor private patients must be, ensconced in their luxury rooms with nobody to talk to all day!

Note that many UK hospitals have a serious problem with deadly infections, i.e. superbugs such as MRSA, E.coli and Clostridium difficile (C-diff), which are resistant to antibiotics. You would be wise to check which hospitals have the lowest infection rates in your area and choose one of them if possible.

Private Hospitals & Clinics

In addition to NHS hospitals, there are private hospitals and clinics in all areas, many providing only specialist services (e.g. health checks and sports injuries) and which usually don't cater for accidents or emergencies (or anyone without private health insurance or a large bank balance). Some provident associations (e.g. BUPA and AXA PPP – see **Private Health Insurance** on page 196) operate their own hospitals and clinics throughout the UK. Private patients are provided with single rooms equipped with all the comforts of home, including a radio, TV, telephone, en suite bathroom and room service (a visitor can also usually enjoy a meal with a patient in the privacy of his room).

CHILDBIRTH

Childbirth in the UK normally takes place in a hospital labour ward or a birth centre – the latter is smaller and puts the emphasis on natural birthing techniques. If you wish to have your child at home you must find a doctor or midwife (see below) who's willing to attend you. Some doctors are opposed to home births, particularly for first-time mums or where there's a higher than average risk of complications and when specialists or special facilities (e.g. incubators) may be required. The Which? Birth Choice website provides a wealth of useful info on the pros and cons of different birthing choices (www.which.co.uk/birth-choice).

For hospital births, you can usually choose (with the help of your GP or midwife) the hospital where you wish to have your baby, although a shortage of midwives and maternity units means that you may have little choice. The best units are oversubscribed, therefore you should book your hospital bed as early as possible. Your GP will also refer you to an obstetrician. Find out as much as possible about local hospital methods and policies on childbirth, either directly or from friends or neighbours, before booking a bed. UK hospitals don't routinely allow caesarean births on demand – at least, not on the NHS – unless there's a valid medical reason.

The policy regarding a father's attendance at a birth varies with the hospital. A father doesn't have a legal right to be present during labour or childbirth (which is at the consultant's discretion), although some doctors expect fathers to attend. Women are encouraged to make a 'birth plan' stating their wishes regarding pain relief, birthing positions and who they want with them at the birth, and most

☑ SURVIVAL TIP

If the presence of the father is important to you, you should check that it's permitted at the hospital where you plan to have your baby and any other rules that apply.

hospitals will follow the plan unless there's a medical emergency.

In the UK, midwives are responsible for educating and supporting women and their families during the childbearing period. Midwives can advise women before they become pregnant, in addition to providing moral, physical and emotional support throughout a pregnancy and after the birth. Your midwife may also advise on parent education and antenatal classes for mothers. After giving birth, mothers are attended at home by their midwife for the first ten days or so, after which they see a health visitor and their GP to monitor their child's health and development.

Registration

Births in the UK must be reported to your local Registrar of Births, Deaths and Marriages (see your local telephone directory). Either parent can register a birth by simply going to the registrar within six weeks of the birth and giving the child's details. You don't have to provide proof of the birth, although it's useful to bring your hospital discharge summary if you have one. The health authority or hospital where a child was born will also notify the registrar of the birth.

Both parents must report to the registrar if they aren't married and they both want their details to be included on the birth certificate; if this isn't possible then the parent who cannot attend must fill out a form declaring their interest. If only the mother registers the birth, only her details are listed, although it may be possible to add the father's details later. A birth is usually registered in the area where the baby was born, but can be registered with another office. Births to foreigners in the UK may also need to be reported to a consulate or embassy – for example, to obtain a national birth certificate and passport for a child.

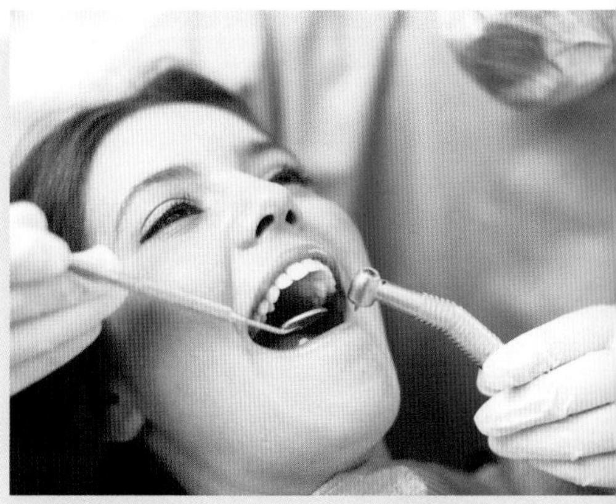

DENTISTS

Britons' annual consumption of over around a million tonnes of sweets (some 15kg per person) ensures that dentists (and sweet manufacturers) remain financially healthy. Despite the efforts of dentists to promote preventive dentistry, millions of Britons never go near a dentist (mostly out of fear) unless they're 'dying' from toothache. Fortunately, when you need help there are excellent dentists in all areas, although the number of dentists providing treatment on the NHS has dwindled in recent years (see **NHS Treatment** below).

The best way to find a good dentist, whether as an NHS or a private patient, is to ask your colleagues, friends or neighbours (particularly those with perfect teeth) if they can recommend someone. Dentists are listed under Dental Surgeons in the Yellow Pages (www.yell.com) and are permitted to advertise any special services they provide, such as an emergency or 24-hour answering service, dental hygienist, and evening or weekend surgeries. Some even offer minor cosmetic surgery such as tooth whitening and Botox injections. You can also search for a dentist on the NHS Choices website (www.nhs.uk). The British Dental Association (020-7935 0875, www.bda.org/

public) can also provide a list of dentists in your area.

In some areas, community clinics or health centres provide a dental service for children, expectant and nursing mothers, and disabled adults. Some hospitals provide a free emergency service, e.g. on Sundays and public holidays. Dental hospitals in London provide a free emergency service on most days. Around 50 per cent of dentists hold an evening surgery one day a week or on Saturday mornings.

Many family dentists in the UK are qualified to perform specialised treatment, e.g. periodontal work, although you must usually see a specialist. In the UK, false teeth (dentures) are made (and repaired) by a dental technician and prescribed and fitted by a dentist.

Fees vary considerably depending on the area and the dentist. The cost of dental treatment has risen considerably in recent years and you can pay £80 for more for a private check-up. Many people now delay having a check-up for up to two years, rather than biannually or annually.

NHS Treatment

In theory, dental care is covered by the NHS, although it's only completely free to those under the age of 18 (19 if in full-time education), pregnant women, mothers with a baby under one year of age and those who receive certain state benefits (e.g. Income Support, income-based Jobseeker's Allowance, income-based Employment and Support Allowance, Pension Credit guarantee credit and some levels of Universal Credit). There's also help for those on low incomes.

Patients who don't qualify for free treatment must pay 80 per cent of the set NHS fees for 'normal' dental treatment, e.g. fillings, extractions, hygiene work, and standard bridges and dentures, according to a fixed scale of fees (see www.nhs.uk/nhsengland/aboutnhsservices/dentists/pages/nhs-dental-charges.aspx). Note that you can still be charged more than the schedule figure under certain circumstances, particularly for crowns, bridges or dentures.

In practice, dentists are over-stretched in the UK, and many are unwilling to accept new NHS patients if their quotas are already full (which they usually are). If you're fortunate enough to find an NHS dentist, you should ensure that the dentist knows that you expect NHS treatment when you register. To remain entitled to NHS-subsidised treatment you need to have regular check-ups, otherwise you may find yourself dropped from the dentist's NHS list.

Dentists aren't obliged to treat you if you aren't a registered patient, even in an emergency. If you miss a dental appointment without giving 24 hours' notice, your dentist may charge you a standard fee.

Many dentists operate an emergency service, and in some areas an emergency dental service is operated by the local health authority. If you're suffering from agonising toothache and you cannot find a dentist who will treat you, there may be a local dental hospital that provides an emergency service.

OPTICIANS

Opticians are listed under 'Opticians-dispensing' or 'Opticians-ophthalmic (optometrists)' in the Yellow Pages (www.yell.com) and may advertise their services, such as

contact lenses or an emergency repair service; you can also simply search online for one in your area. Opticians (like spectacles) come in many types and sizes. Your sight can be tested only by a registered ophthalmic optician (or optometrist) or an ophthalmic medical practitioner, who tests eyesight, prescribes glasses and diagnoses eye diseases. Most 'high street' opticians are both ophthalmic opticians and dispensing opticians, who make up spectacles.

Many opticians (such as Boots) collect old spectacles and donate them to Vision Aid Overseas which provides eye tests and glasses to people in developing countries (www.visionaidoverseas.org).

An ophthalmologist is a senior specialist or eye surgeon; an orthoptist is an ophthalmologist who treats children's eye problems. If you need to see an ophthalmologist or orthoptist, you must usually be referred by your GP. The Eye Care Trust (0845-129 5001, www.eyecaretrust.org.uk) can provide advice, and direct you to an appropriate eye specialist.

The 'eye business' is competitive in the UK and, unless someone is highly recommended you should shop around for the best deal. The last decade has seen a flood of 'chain store' opticians such as Boots, Specsavers and Vision Express opening in high streets and shopping centres, and these may have lower prices than independent opticians. Supermarket chains Asda and Tesco also have opticians in some of their larger out of town stores, and their prices are highly competitive. You can also buy spectacles online from companies such as Glasses Direct (www.glassesdirect.co.uk).

Prices for both spectacles and contact lenses vary considerably, so it's wise to compare costs before committing yourself to a large bill. The prices charged for most services (spectacle frames, lenses and contact lenses) are often lower in the UK than elsewhere in Europe, although higher than North America.

Sight Tests

Some people receive free sight tests under the NHS, including children under 16, full-time students under 19, those aged over 60, the registered blind and partially sighted, diagnosed diabetics and glaucoma sufferers, those at higher risk of glaucoma (e.g. close relatives of someone who has the disease) and those receiving certain state benefits.

If you aren't entitled to a free sight test under the NHS, you must pay around £20 although many chemists offer vouchers which reduce the price, and many offer a free eye test in the hope that you'll buy your glasses from them. Sight tests are valid for two years, although you should be aware that your eyesight can change considerably during this time.

You don't need to buy your spectacles (lenses or frames) or contact lenses from the optician who tests your sight, irrespective of whether you're an NHS or private patient, and you've the right to a copy of the prescription resulting from an NHS or private sight test. Many opticians try to hold on to eye test customers by promoting special offers such as two pairs of glasses for the price of one or free sunglasses.

DRUG & ALCOHOL ABUSE

Drug and alcohol abuse are serious health problems in the UK, where drug-related deaths hit an all-time high in 2015. Almost one in three British adults (15 million people) has taken an illegal substance – including hard and 'recreational' soft drugs such as cannabis/marijuana – and a fifth of those still do so, with some 40 per cent of drug takers in the higher echelons of society. (There has long been a public debate about the possible long-term harmful effects of smoking cannabis and its effects on the brain, which include schizophrenia.) While it's illegal to possess, grow, distribute or sell cannabis in the UK, if an adult is found in possession of a small amount for personal use – which accounts for around two-thirds of all police recorded drug offences in the UK – they're likely to receive only a warning.

The UK has the highest number of legal high – a substance with stimulant or mood-altering properties that isn't on the current list of illegal drugs – users among young people in Europe. In 2016, the production, distribution, sale and supply of legal highs was made an offence punishable by up to seven years in prison. It isn't, however, an offence to possess legal highs, but the police have the power to confiscate and destroy it.

For help and advice regarding drug abuse, contact the Talk to Frank Helpline (formerly the National Drugs Helpline, 0300-123 6600, www.talktofrank.com) or Narcotics Anonymous (0300-999 1212, www.ukna.org).

Alcohol Abuse is widespread in the UK – where it's directly responsible for over 8,500 deaths a year – it's estimated that some 10 million Britons have a drink problem, many of whom are unaware of it. The consumption of alcohol is also a serious problem among Britain's children and young people (especially women), many of whom drink large amounts in a short amount of time with the express intention of getting drunk – a phenomenon known as 'binge drinking'. Excessive drinking is an increasing problem among the middle aged (over 55s) and retirees, many of whom drink much more than the recommended levels.

A national alcohol helpline known as Drinkline (0300-123 1110) operates from 9am-8pm weekdays and 11am-4pm at weekends, to advise those concerned about their own or someone else's drinking, and Alcoholics Anonymous (0800-9177 650, www.alcoholics-anonymous.org.uk) has support groups in all areas. The Drink Aware charity (www.drinkaware.co.uk) provides a wealth of useful information about alcohol and its effects, as does Alcohol Concern (www.alcoholconcern.org.uk).

SMOKING

As in most countries, smoking contributes to a huge loss of life and working days, although the number of smokers has steadily decreased over the last 20 years, from some 45 per cent in 1975 to less than 20 per cent today. Some smokers have moved from smoking to 'vaping – inhaling nicotine vapour from an electronic (e)cigarette. Some 2 million smokers and ex-smokers puff away on these devices, sold in many corner shops and 'vape' stores, although the jury is still out regarding whether they're a lifesaver or a health risk.

Smoking is banned in most public places and on most public transport, and since 2007 has been prohibited in all enclosed public spaces such as pubs, restaurants and private clubs. Since 2015 drivers in England have been banned from smoking in cars when they're carrying children.

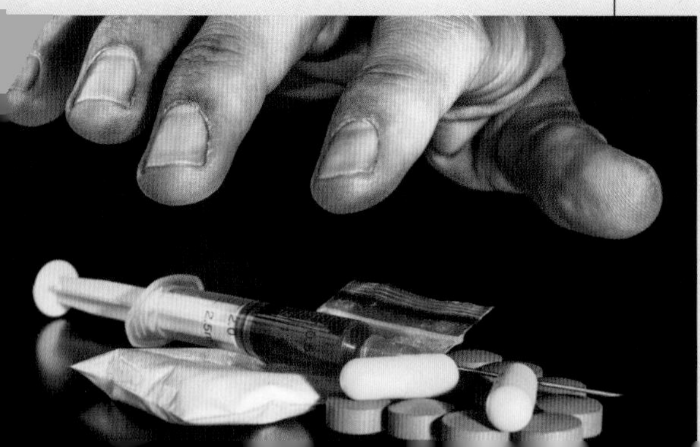

Organisations that help smokers quite include Action on Smoking and Health (020-7404 0242, www.ash.org.uk) and QUIT (020-7553 2100, www.quit.org.uk). There are also non-smoking clinics and self-help groups throughout the UK to help those wishing to quit. You can also obtain advice from your GP regarding free support services provided by the NHS.

DEATHS

Like births (see above), deaths in the UK must be reported to your local Registrar of Births, Deaths and Marriages (see your local telephone directory). When someone dies, a medical certificate must be completed by a doctor and taken to the registrar within five days. If someone dies suddenly, accidentally, during an operation or in unusual circumstances, or if the cause of death is unknown, the doctor will notify the police and/or a coroner, who will decide whether a post-mortem is necessary to determine the cause of death.

In any case, the registrar will need certain information about the deceased, including his date and place of birth and death, details of marriage (if applicable), and whether he was receiving a state pension or any welfare benefits. The registrar then issues a death certificate and a certification for burial or cremation (a 'green form') which authorises a funeral to take place. These documents must be given to a funeral director (also known as an undertaker) to arrange the burial or cremation, or for the body to be shipped to another country. If you wish to remove a body from the UK, permission must be obtained from a coroner at least four days before shipment.

You may wish to announce a death in a local or national newspaper, giving the date, time and place of the funeral, and your wishes regarding flowers or contributions to a charity or research. In the UK, the traditional dress for a Christian funeral is black or dark clothing.

Donor Cards

You may wish to carry a Donor Card, so that in the event of your death your organs can be used to save or dramatically improve (such as giving sight to a blind person) someone's else's life. Cards are available from chemists, libraries, doctors' surgeries and supermarkets, or you can join the NHS Organ Donor Register (0300-123 2323, www.organdonation.nhs.uk).

Moves are afoot to change the present law to an opt-out scheme, so that you'll have to register if you don't want to donate your organs, otherwise consent will be implied. Such a scheme (called 'deemed consent') has existed in Wales since December 2015; if you die in an accident there and haven't registered your desire not to donate an organ you'll be treated as having given consent.

GENERAL INFORMATION & HELP

There are many health 'helplines' in the UK covering a broad range of medical and related problems, many operated by volunteers. Some helplines provide a 24-hour service, although many have limited hours of operation, so if there's no reply, try again later. Some of the most useful helplines are listed below.

- Childline (0800-1111, www.childline.org.uk): a free, confidential, 24-hour national helpline for children and young people in danger or trouble;
- Medical Advisory Service (020-8995 8503 or 020-8994 9874 for the helpline 6-8pm only, www.medicaladvisoryservice.org.uk): can offer help with almost any health-related problem;

- NHS 111 (111): a 24-hour health advice and information service staffed by NHS nurses, who can advise on particular symptoms or health conditions and refer you to local healthcare services such as doctors, dentists, late night chemists, and self-help and support organisations;
- Samaritans (0845-790 9090, 24 hours, www.samaritans.org): will help you talk through any emotional problem and isn't, as many believe, purely for those contemplating suicide;
- The Silver Line (0800-470 8090, 24 hours, www.thesilverline.org.uk): a confidential free helping for older people.

Useful websites on UK health issues include:

- BBC Health News (www.bbc.co.uk/news/health): part of the encyclopaedic BBC site;
- NHS Choices (www.nhs.uk): the official NHS site;
- Surgery Door (www.surgerydoor.co.uk): provides information on a wide range of family health topics, from pregnancy to immunisation.

Warning

Note that information obtained from recorded telephone helplines, websites and books – although usually recorded, written or approved by medical experts – must be viewed with caution and should not be used as a substitute for consulting your doctor.

13. INSURANCE

In the UK, you can insure practically anything, from your car to your camera, the loss of your livelihood to your life. You can also insure against most eventualities, such as rain on your parade or village fete, the possibility of twins (or sextuplets) or cancelling your holiday due to an emergency. For particularly unusual requests, you may be required to obtain a quote from Lloyd's of London, the last resort for unusual insurance needs, not only within the UK, but also worldwide. However, if an insurance requirement is particularly unusual or risky, you may find that premiums are prohibitively high and there may be restrictions on what you can and cannot do.

The UK is renowned as a nation of gamblers, which is reflected in the relatively low levels of insurance, not only for such basic requirements as loss of income or life insurance, but also insurance for homes and their contents. After serious flooding caused millions of pounds of damage in recent years, it was revealed that as many as half of all households in some areas had no building or home contents insurance, or were under-insured. Many people tend to rely on state 'insurance' provisions, which come under the heading of social security (and are often referred to as 'Benefits'). These include sickness and unemployment payment, income support (for families on low incomes) and state pensions. Social security usually provides only for the most basic needs and those who are reduced to relying on it often exist below the poverty line.

It isn't necessary to spend half your income insuring yourself against every eventuality from the common cold to a day off work, but it's important to be covered against an occurrence that could precipitate a major financial disaster.

☑ SURVIVAL TIP

As with everything to do with finance, it's important to shop around when buying insurance. It bears repeating – always shop around when buying or renewing insurance. Simply picking up a few brochures from insurance brokers, making a few telephone calls or comparing premiums online can save you a lot of money.

If you're coming to the UK from abroad, you would be wise to ensure that your family has full health insurance during the period between leaving your last country of residence and your arrival in the UK. This is particularly important if you're covered by a company health insurance policy that terminates on the day you leave your present employment. If you aren't covered by the National Health Service (see page 174), it's important to have private health insurance.

There are just a few cases in the UK when insurance for individuals is compulsory, which include buildings insurance if you've a mortgage (because your lender will insist on it) and third party motor insurance which is required by law. You may also need compulsory third party and accident insurance for high-risk sports such as hang-gliding, mountaineering and parachuting. Voluntary insurance includes pensions, accident, income protection, health, home contents, personal liability, legal expenses, dental, travel, motor breakdown, pet and life insurance.

INSURANCE COMPANIES

Insurance is big business in the UK, and there are numerous insurance companies to choose from, many of which provide a wide range of insurance services, while others specialise in certain fields only. You can buy insurance from many sources, including traditional insurance companies selling through their own salesmen, independent brokers, direct insurance companies (selling direct to the public), banks and other financial institutions, post offices, motoring organisations, travel agents, supermarkets and chain stores. Policies offered by banks are generally the most expensive and don't usually offer the best cover. Most brokers will provide a free analysis of your family's insurance needs.

In recent years, direct marketing and direct response insurance companies (bypassing brokers) have resulted in huge savings for consumers, particularly for car, buildings and home contents insurance. Direct marketing companies provide quotations over the telephone or via the internet, and often you aren't even required to complete a proposal form. The leading direct sales insurance companies include Direct Line (www.directline.com), Churchill (www.churchill.com) and Zurich (www.zurich.co.uk).

It's worth comparing the cost of insurance online using comparison sites which allow you to compare policies from various insurers, including www.comparethemarket.com, www.confused,com, www.gocompare.com, www.google.co.uk/compare and www.moneysupermarket.com. However, you should still shop around as comparison websites are paid to promote certain insurers or policies. If you're aged over 50 it's worth comparing the rates and policies offered by Saga (www.saga.co.uk).

INSURANCE CONTRACTS

Read all insurance contracts before signing them. If you don't understand everything ask a friend or colleague to 'translate' it or take legal advice. If a policy has pages of legal jargon and gobbledegook in very small print you've a right to be suspicious, as it's common practice nowadays to be as brief as possible, and write clearly and concisely in language which doesn't require a legal degree. Always check any exclusions or conditions and have them explained if you don't understand them.

European Union (EU) directives on unfair terms and legal-speak in consumer contracts have curbed insurance companies' discretion to increase future charges. Take care how you answer questions in an insurance proposal form as, even if you mistakenly provide false information or omit to mention something, an insurance company can refuse to pay out when you make a claim.

> ☑ **SURVIVAL TIP**
>
> Before agreeing to an insurance contract you should shop around and take a day or two to think it over. Never sign on the spot as you may regret it later. With some insurance contracts, you've a 'cooling off' period of up to 14 days, during which you can cancel a policy without penalty.

Most insurance policies run for a calendar year from the date on which you take out a policy. Note that insurance policies aren't automatically renewed in the UK – as they are in many European countries – and you aren't liable to pay for another year if you fail to cancel a policy before the term expires.

SOCIAL SECURITY

Social security is the name given to state benefits paid to residents of the UK, e.g. unemployment and sickness benefits, maternity pay, income support and family benefit. The cost of social security was some £230 billion in 2015-16 (or 35 per cent of all government spending), which includes benefits and tax credits, personal social services such as child protection and pensions paid to former public sector employees.

Some benefits are dependent on your National Insurance contributions (see below), others on your circumstances, income or savings, while some have no preconditions. Almost one-third of the population receives some form of state benefit, including around 13 million who receive the State Pension (see below) and some 2.5 million people (a three-fold increase in the last few decades) who receive some kind of incapacity benefit, a large percentage of whom 'allegedly' aren't entitled to it. On the other hand, it's estimated that as many as 2 million people don't claim the benefits to which they're entitled, particularly pensioners, therefore it's important to know your rights.

The UK welfare system is very complicated – there are over 50 benefits and payments that people can claim – and they're subject to frequent change. The most common benefits include:

- **Disability Living Allowance:** paid to disabled people and children who need care. Pensioners needing care may qualify for Attendance Allowance.
- **Employment & Support Allowance:** formerly called Incapacity Benefit, this is paid to people with an illness or disability although they're still encouraged to find work.
- **Housing Benefit:** help with rent for people on low incomes; some people also get help paying their Council Tax (see page 211).
- **Income Support:** paid to people in employment but on low incomes (in effect subsidising employers who don't pay a living wage!).
- **Jobseeker's Allowance:** the main benefit for people of working age who are out of work, or work fewer than 16 hours a week on average and who are looking for work.
- **Pension Credit:** tops up state pension payments to guarantee a minimum income for people over retirement age.
- **Tax Credits:** extra money for working people on a low wage; it includes an extra payment for those who have children or childcare costs.

In 2011, the government announced a major welfare overhaul that was intended to simplify the system by replacing many benefits (such as Jobseeker's Allowance, Income-related Employment and Support Allowance with a single Universal Credit. Its implementation has been much delayed, but it's scheduled to begin full operation in 2017 (although further delays are possible). For a full explanation see www.gov.uk/universal-credit/overview. Reforms are also planned to reduce fraud and errors, including stricter tests on eligibility, e.g. checking whether those claiming Employment and Support Allowance are fit to work. It isn't necessary to be a British citizen to claim benefits, although you do have to be 'habitually resident'.

Social security payments are generally paid directly into a bank, building society or post office account. Benefits and national insurance contributions are reviewed annually, and increased in line with the retail price index (RPI). Increases are paid from 6th April, which is the start of the UK tax year.

Detailed information about all social security benefits and how to claim them is available from the Gov.uk website (www.gov.uk/browse/benefits). Other sources of information and advice are the Debt Advice Foundation (www.debtadvicefoundation.org/benefits), the Child Poverty Action Group (020-7837 7979, www.cpag.org.uk) and Age UK (0800-169 2081, www.ageuk.org.uk), publishes a wide range of guides and factsheets about claiming benefits for the elderly (and also sells **very expensive** services, insurance and products!).

If you're refused social security or receive less than you think you're entitled to, you should challenge the payment and take independent advice, e.g. from a Citizens Advice Bureau (www.citizensadvice.org.uk/benefits).

National Insurance

National insurance (NI), called social security in most countries, is mandatory for most working people in the UK aged from 16 to the state pension age of 65. National Insurance contributions (NICs) entitle you to state benefits such as the State Retirement Pension, contribution-based Jobseekers Allowance and Employment and Support Allowance, Maternity Allowance and various bereavement benefits. You qualify for these benefits only if you've already paid (or have been credited with) enough of the right class of contributions at the right time.

When you arrive in the UK, you must apply for a national insurance number by contacting Jobcentre Plus (0345-600 0643) or visiting the Gov.uk website (www.gov.uk/apply-national-insurance-number). You may be called for an interview and the number can take six to eight weeks to be allocated. You receive a plastic NI number card with your personal number on it, which usually remains the same all your life. You must give your NI number to your employer if you're an employee, or to HM Revenue and Customs if you're self-employed, so that your NI contribution record can be kept up to date.

Your contributions and those of your employer depend on your income and status, e.g. employee or self-employed, which determines your 'class' of contribution as detailed below. NI rates are normally increased in April at the start of the tax year, and sometimes change during the tax year.

Once you reach state pension age, you aren't required to pay NI contributions, whether or not you've retired from work, although if you continue to work as an employee, your employer must still pay contributions for you. There are five classes of NI contributions. For more information about NICs, see the Gov.uk website (www.gov.uk/national-insurance/overview).

Class 1

Class 1 contributions (2016-17) are paid on earnings between £112 (known as the 'lower earnings limit') and £827 per week (the 'upper earnings limit'). The standard rate is 12 per cent. You don't pay NI contributions if you earn less than the lower earnings limit, and on earnings above the upper limit you pay contributions at 2 per cent. Your employer also contributes, according to your earnings.

Class 1A

Class 1A contributions are for employers who provide their employees with a car or petrol for private use. The employer pays class 1A contributions, not the employee.

Class 2

Class 2 contributions are for self-employed people whose earnings are over £5,965 per year (2016-17). Your contribution is £2.80 per week, which entitles you to claim most state benefits except Jobseeker's Allowance and Statutory Sick Pay. If your profits are above a certain amount, you may need to pay profit-related class 4 contributions (see below) in addition to class 2 contributions.

In the March 2016 Budget, the government announced plans to abolish Class 2 NICs from April 2018 and reform Class 4 NICs to introduce a new contributory benefits test. This means that instead of paying two classes of NICs (Class 2 and Class 4), the self-employed will pay just one (Class 4) in the future.

Class 3

Class 3 contributions are voluntary contributions for anyone without a full record of NI contributions or who isn't liable to pay class 1 or class 2 contributions, e.g. someone working abroad, a self-employed person with low profits, or someone who stopped working voluntarily. Class 3 contributions can also be paid if you've been excluded from class 2 contributions. Class 3 allows you to make voluntary payments, at a flat rate of £14.10 per week in 2016-17, at any time during the six years following a break in payments (after which it's too late). By filling the gaps in your NI contributions, you can protect your retirement pension or widow's benefits. Payment can be via a lump sum in addition to those methods listed under class 2 above.

Class 4

Class 4 contributions are also for the self-employed. In addition to class 2 contributions, you must pay a further 9 per cent of any profits between £8,060 and £43,000 per year (2016-17), and 2 per cent extra on earnings above the upper profits limit. Class 4 contributions are assessed and collected by HMRC when you pay income tax on your profits, and you receive tax relief on contributions.

From April 2018, Class 2 NICs will be abolished and class 4 NICs will be the only contributions made by the self-employed.

State Pension

Everyone who pays national insurance (see above) is entitled to a state retirement pension, although for most people this barely provides sufficient income to pay for their basic needs, let alone maintain their standard of living in retirement. The value of the state pension has fallen considerably in real terms in the last few decades, and many state pensioners live in poverty. Many people rely on the state pension to live on in their later years, rather than joining a company pension fund or taking out a personal pension plan. It's estimated that

around 80 per cent of Britons make far too little provision for retirement.

The state pension age is currently 65 for men and is gradually rising for women. Between April 2016 and December 2018 it will rise to 65 for women, after which the retirement age for both men and women will rise to 66 between December 2018 and October 2020. From 2026 to 2028 the state pension age for both men and women will start rising to 67. You can calculate the age when you'll receive the state pension by using the State Pension Calculator on the Gov.uk website (www.gov.uk/calculate-state-pension/y/age).

In 2016-17 the basic state pension was £119.30 per week for those who reached the state pension age before 6th April 2016 and have been credited with sufficient national insurance contributions. You may also be entitled to an additional state pension, called State Earnings-Related Pension Scheme (SERPS) before 2002 or the State Second Pension (S2P) after 2002. From 6th April 2016, the state pension was simplified by combining the current elements (state pension and additional state pension) into a single flat-rate payment. The maximum state second pension was around £160 per week in 2015-16, which is added to the basic state pension. You can obtain a estimate of how much your pension will be from www.nidirect.gov.uk/articles/getting-state-pension-statement.

The reluctance of people to invest for their retirement led the government to introduce automatic enrolment in a work pension scheme from 2012, which applies to anyone aged between 22 and pension age and earning over £10,000 a year. For more information, see www.gov.uk/workplacepensions.

The state pension is usually paid every four weeks into an account of your choice. You're paid 'in arrears', which means you're paid for the last four weeks, not for the coming four weeks.

For more information about state pensions, see the Gov.uk website (www.gov.uk/state-pension/overview), Independent Age (www.independentage.org) or the Citizens Advice Bureau (www.citizensadvice.org.uk/debt-and-money/pensions/types-of-pension/state-pension).

PRIVATE PENSION

Many people have a private pension, whether through their employer or a private pension fund (called variously a personal pension, self-invested personal pension or stakeholder pension scheme). You or your employer can usually pay up to £40,000 a year into your pension fund, but there are limits on how much tax relief you can receive. The actual amount you can pay in a tax year for tax relief purposes is the greater of a gross contribution of £3,600 or 100 per cent of your earnings, subject to the annual allowance.

You receive tax relief on all pension contributions at the highest rate paid on your earned income, and can pay contributions into a personal pension fund, net of income tax. The gains on investments from a pension are tax-free, but your pension on retirement is taxed as earned income.

It's worth noting that no other form of savings provides more tax breaks than a pension, e.g. free of income and capital gains tax, although most pension funds have performed VERY badly in recent years.

You can save thousands of pounds with a do-it-yourself (DIY) or 'execution-only' pension by cutting out the middleman and choosing your own investments – and there's little or no commission to pay. The savings on pension payments of just £100 per month can be almost £1,000 in the first year alone. A number of companies offer execution-only services.

Important

Bear in mind that pensions are the most expensive, mis-sold, misunderstood, poorly performing financial product you can buy, and the one most people need most of all!

The investment fund accrued by your pension can be invested in an annuity to pay your pension in your retirement years or you can draw down (take out) some of the funds to spend as you like. New rules in 2015 mean that from the age of 55 you can start accessing your pension funds – be it for an investment in rental property (an increasingly popular option), a world cruise or to buy a Ferrari. The government is understandably nervous at the prospect of pensioners going on a spending spree and has introduced a free and impartial advice service, called Pension Wise (www.pensionwise.gov.uk), to help you evaluate your options.

Most retirees wish to take some cash and invest the rest, either in an annuity – an insurance policy that gives you an income for the rest of your life – or in more flexible investments which allows you to keep your pot invested but take money from it as and when you need to.

If you opt for an annuity can shop around for the best deal from any insurance company. Many people fall into the trap of opting for an annuity recommended by their insurance company, which often costs them thousands or even tens of thousands of pounds. Retirees can now buy annuities at different times during their retirement, up to the age of 75, when they must buy a conventional annuity. See the Citizens Advice Bureau (www.citizensadvice.org.uk/debt-and-money/pensions/nearing-retirement/choosing-an-annuity) for independent advice.

If you retire abroad, British pensions are paid gross, but you must obtain a declaration from the foreign country's taxation authorities that you're a resident for tax purposes and are taxed on your worldwide income there.

Information

Before making any decisions regarding your pension, you should thoroughly investigate the various options available and obtain professional advice, e.g. from a member of the Society of Pension Consultants (020-7353 1688, http://the-spp.co.uk), the Association of Consulting Actuaries (020-3102 6761, www.aca.org.uk) or the Pensions Advisory Service (0300-123 1047, www.pensionsadvisoryservice.org.uk).

The Pension Wise service aims to provide phone and face-to-face guidance and has a lot of useful information on its website (www.pensionwise.gov.uk).

ACCIDENT INSURANCE

Accident insurance, although not common in the UK, is available from a number of companies. It includes lump-sum payouts in the event of death or permanent disability (e.g.

£100,000 to £250,000) or hospitalisation as the result of an accident, and usually provides hospital (e.g. £50 to £125 per day) and convalescence benefits (e.g. £200 per week) after a minimum period in hospital. The cost of accident insurance is usually between £10 and £25 per month depending on the number of people insured and the cover provided. You may be able to choose higher cash payments by increasing your premiums.

Accident insurance can often be combined with income protection insurance. Occupational accident insurance is compulsory and is paid by your employer. It covers accidents or illness at work and may also cover accidents that occur when travelling to and from work or when travelling on company business.

You can also take out critical illness insurance, which pays a lump sum or a regular income (usually until the state retirement age) should you be unable to work due to illness or an accident – but you must be aware of policy exclusions! Income protection insurance (IPI) or permanent health insurance (PHI) – which supposedly pays you an income when you're off work sick or unemployed long-term – is usually a complete waste of money and riddled with exclusions. It's also one of the most mis-sold insurance policies – UK banks have been forced to repay billions of pounds to policyholders in the last five years or so.

PRIVATE HEALTH INSURANCE

If you aren't covered by the NHS or a reciprocal agreement (see page 174) you should take out private health insurance, as private medical treatment in the UK can be very expensive (see **Private Treatment** below); the cost of an operation and hospitalisation run into thousands of pounds.

Long-stay visitors from countries without a reciprocal health insurance scheme should have long-stay health insurance or an international health policy, which covers you when travelling in the UK and abroad. A health insurance policy should cover you for essential healthcare necessary as a result of an accident and injuries (e.g. a sporting injury), whether they occur in your home, at your place of work or when travelling.

Even if you're eligible for NHS treatment, you may wish to consider taking out supplementary private health insurance, the main advantage of which is the much reduced waiting time for non-emergency operations. Around 10 per cent of the population has private health insurance – around half provided by their employer – and one in five operations in the UK is performed privately. If you're taking a job in the UK, check whether your employer provides private health insurance.

Most people with private health insurance are insured with provident associations such as BUPA and AXA PPP, which pay for specialist and hospital treatment only, and don't include routine visits to doctors and dentists (which are covered by the NHS). However, private patients are free to choose their own specialists and hospitals.

Most health insurance policies fall into one of two main categories: those providing immediate private specialist or hospital treatment (e.g.

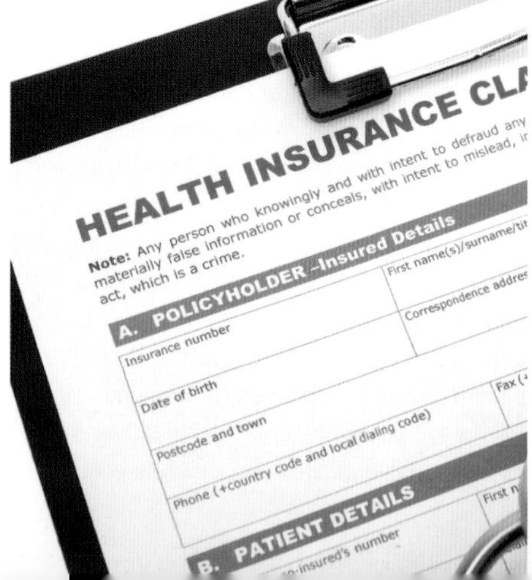

BUPA, AXA PPP and WPA) and so-called 'budget' or 'waiting-list' policies, where you're treated as a private patient only when waiting lists exceed a certain period. Under waiting-list policies, if you cannot obtain an appointment with an NHS specialist or an NHS hospital admission within a certain period (e.g. six weeks), you can do so as a private patient.

The cost of private health insurance depends on your age and the state of your health. There are maximum age limits for taking out health insurance with some insurers, which may be increased if you're willing to accept some restrictions. Some companies have (expensive) policies for those aged over 50 or 55. Once you've a policy, there are generally no restrictions on continuing membership, irrespective of age, although premiums are usually increased every five years, e.g. at the ages of 50, 55, 60, etc.

Treatment of any medical condition for which you've already received medical attention, or were aware existed up to five years before the start date of a policy, may not be covered. However, existing health problems (often referred to as 'pre-existing' conditions) may be covered after two years' membership, provided no further medical attention has been necessary during this period. Some group policies do, however, include immediate cover for existing or previous health problems for a higher premium. Other exclusions are listed in the policy rules, and may include chronic conditions requiring ongoing treatment, e.g. diabetes, kidney dialysis, arthritis and emergency treatment (at which the NHS still excels).

If you need treatment, you may be required to pay in advance and reclaim the cost from your insurance company later, although some insurers will pay bills directly.

DENTAL INSURANCE

Dental treatment that isn't covered by the NHS isn't usually included in private health insurance policies, although it may be available as an extra. Plans provided by BUPA and Denplan (a subsidiary of AXA PPP) have an average premium of from around £20 per month, but don't pay for routine treatment and only pay a contribution towards the cost of expensive treatments such as crowns, bridges and dentures.

> **☑ SURVIVAL TIP**
>
> If you've healthy teeth and rarely pay for more than an annual check-up and a visit to a hygienist, dental insurance offers poor value.

You can also obtain dental insurance (usually optional) under some foreign health insurance policies or a worldwide health scheme. Emergency dental treatment and treatment required as the result of an accident may, however, be covered by a standard health insurance policy or an accident policy. If you're in doubt, contact your health or accident insurance company. For details of dental treatment covered by the National Health Service (see page 174).

BUILDINGS INSURANCE

For most people, buying a home is the largest financial investment they will ever make. When buying a home, you're usually responsible for insuring it before you even move in. If you take out a mortgage to buy a property, your lender usually insists that your home (including most permanent structures on a property) has buildings insurance from the time you exchange contracts and are legally the owner. If you buy the leasehold of an apartment, your buildings insurance is arranged by the owner of the freehold. Even when not required by a lender, you would be extremely unwise not to have buildings insurance.

Buildings insurance usually includes loss or damage caused by fire; theft; riot or malicious acts; water leakage from pipes or tanks; oil leakage from central heating systems; flood, storm and lightning; explosion or aircraft impact; vehicles or animals; earthquake, subsidence, landslip or heave; falling trees or aerials; and cover for temporary homelessness, e.g. up to £10,000. Some insurance companies also provide optional cover that includes trees and shrubs damaged maliciously or by storms. There's often an excess (deductible), e.g. £100, which is intended to deter people from making small claims. Buildings insurance should be reviewed annually; insurance companies are continually updating their policies, therefore you must take care that a policy provides the cover required when you receive a renewal notice.

Lenders fix the initial level of cover when you first apply for a mortgage, and usually offer to arrange the insurance for you, but you're free to make your own arrangements. If you arrange your own buildings insurance, your lender will insist that the level of cover is sufficient. Most people take the easy option and arrange insurance through their mortgage lender, which may be the most expensive option. Some direct insurance companies guarantee to cut buildings insurance costs for the majority of homeowners insured through banks and building societies.

The amount for which your home must be insured isn't the current market value, but the cost of rebuilding it, should it be totally destroyed. There's generally no deduction for wear and tear, and the cost of redecoration is usually met in full. Buildings insurance doesn't cover structural faults that existed when you took out a policy, which is why it's important to have a full structural survey done when buying a property.

Buildings insurance is often combined with home contents insurance (see below), when it may be termed household insurance, although it may be cheaper to buy buildings and home contents insurance separately.

Many people pay far too much for their buildings insurance, as many insurance companies greatly over-estimate the cost of rebuilding. In many cases, building costs were calculated using the Royal Institute of Chartered Surveyors (RICS, www.rics.org) Rebuilding Costs Index rather than the correct Tender Price Index, which takes into account actual building prices. The RICS produces a table (http://calculator.bcis.co.uk) to calculate the cost of rebuilding your home, which should be used when assessing the cost. If you're in doubt, check how the rebuilding cost of your home was calculated and whether it's correct.

Most lenders provide index-linked buildings insurance, where premiums are linked to inflation and building costs (premiums are usually added to your monthly mortgage payments). It is, however, your responsibility to ensure that your level of cover is adequate, particularly if you carry out improvements or extensions which substantially increase the value of your home. All lenders provide information and free advice. If your level of cover is too low, an insurance company is within its rights to reduce the amount it pays out when a claim is made, in which case you may find that you cannot afford to have your house rebuilt or repaired should disaster strike.

The cost of buildings insurance varies according to the insurer, the type of building and the area, and is calculated per £1,000 of insurance. Premiums vary considerably from around £100-200 for a small two-bedroom property valued at say £100-200,000, up to double or more for a four-bedroom detached house. Shop around, as premiums vary considerably and many people pay too much. However, don't believe the advertising blurb, as some companies that claim to save you money actually charge more! Using comparison websites such as www.comparethemarket.com/home-insurance and www.moneysupermarket.com can help you find the best deal, although you should also obtain quotes from direct insurance companies.

Many insurance companies provide emergency telephone numbers for policyholders requiring urgent advice. Should you need to make emergency repairs, e.g. to weather-proof a roof after a storm or other natural disaster, most insurance companies allow work up to a certain limit (e.g. £1,000) to be carried out without an estimate or approval from the insurance company, but check first. If you let your house (or part of it) you should have should have landlord's insurance. If you intend leaving it unoccupied for a period of 30 days or longer you must usually inform your insurance company.

HOME CONTENTS INSURANCE

Home contents insurance (also called house insurance) is recommended for anyone who doesn't live in an empty house. Burglary and house-breaking are a major problem (particularly in cities) and there's a burglary every minute somewhere. Although there's a lot you can do to prevent someone breaking into your home, it's often impossible or prohibitively expensive to make your home totally burglar-proof without turning it into a fortress. However, you can ensure that you've adequate contents insurance and that your most precious possessions are locked in a safe or safety deposit box.

Types of Policy

A basic home contents policy covers your belongings against the same sort of 'natural disasters' as buildings insurance (see above). You can optionally insure against accidental damage and all risks. A basic contents policy doesn't usually include items such as credit cards (and their fraudulent use), cash, musical instruments, jewellery (and other valuables), antiques, paintings, sports equipment and bicycles, for which you must normally take out extra cover.

You can usually insure your belongings for their secondhand value (indemnity) or their full replacement value (new for old). This covers everything except clothes and linen (for which wear and tear is assessed) at the new cost price. Replacement value is the most popular form of contents insurance. It's best to take out an index-linked policy, where the level of cover is automatically increased by a percentage or fixed amount annually.

Premiums

Premiums depend largely on where you live, and on your insurer. All insurance companies assess the risk by location, based on your postcode. The difference between premiums charged by companies for the same property can vary by 100 per cent or more. Annual premiums are usually calculated per £1,000 of cover, and range from around £3 to £4 in a low-risk area but can be much higher in high-risk area where burglaries are commonplace. Your premiums are also higher if you live in a flood-prone area.

Combining your home contents insurance with your buildings insurance (see above) may save you money, although it's often cheaper to buy separate insurance. However, it can be advantageous to have your buildings and contents insurance with the same insurer, as this avoids disputes over which company should pay for which item, as could arise if you have a fire or flood affecting your home and its contents. Those aged over 50 (and possibly first-time homeowners) are offered discounts or special rates by some companies (e.g. Saga, www.saga.co.uk, who specialise in insurance for those aged over 50). Some companies also provide special policies for students in college accommodation or lodgings (ask an insurance broker).

PERSONAL LIABILITY INSURANCE

Although common on the continent of Europe and in North America (where people sue each other for millions at the drop of a hat), personal or legal liability insurance is unusual in the UK. However, home contents policies (see above) usually include personal liability insurance up to £1 million, and it's usually included in a travel policy (see below). Personal liability insurance covers individuals and members of their families against compensation for accidental damage, injury or death caused to third parties or their property. It usually covers anything from spilling wine on your neighbour's Persian carpet to your dog or child biting someone. If you run a business (even from home) you'll need liability insurance to cover your staff and clients.

HOLIDAY & TRAVEL INSURANCE

Holiday and travel insurance is recommended for all who don't wish to risk having their holiday or travel ruined by financial problems or arrive home broke. The following information applies equally to residents and non-residents, whether they're travelling to or from the UK or within the UK.

Travel insurance is available from many sources in the UK, including the Post Office, travel agents, insurance companies and agents, banks, automobile clubs and transport companies. Package holiday companies and tour operators also offer insurance policies, some of which are compulsory, too expensive and don't provide adequate cover. Before taking out travel insurance, carefully consider the range and level of cover you require, and compare policies.

Short-term holiday and travel insurance policies should include cover for holiday cancellation or interruption; missed flights; departure delay at the start and end of a holiday (a common occurrence); delayed, lost or damaged baggage; personal effects and money; medical expenses and accidents (including evacuation home); flight insurance; personal liability; legal expenses and default or bankruptcy insurance, e.g. against a tour operator or airline going broke.

Medical expenses are one of the most important aspect of travel insurance and you shouldn't rely on insurance provided by reciprocal health arrangements, credit card companies, household policies or private medical insurance (unless it's an international policy), none of which usually provide adequate cover overseas.

The cost of travel insurance varies considerably, depending on where you buy it, how long you intend to stay abroad and your age (many policies have a maximum age of 70). Generally, the longer the period covered, the cheaper the daily cost, although the maximum period covered is usually limited, e.g. six months. With some policies, an excess must be paid for each claim. As a rough guide, travel insurance for the UK (and most other European countries) costs from as little as £5 for one week although £15 to £20 buys you much more comprehensive cover; a family of four (two adults and two children under 16) usually pay between £10 and £40, depending on the options chosen (insurance companies usually offer different levels of insurance). Premiums may be higher for those aged over 65 or 70. Those who travel abroad frequently, whether on business or pleasure, may find that an annual travel policy provides the best value, but you should check exactly what it includes.

If you need to make a claim you should provide as much documentary evidence as possible to support it. Travel insurance companies gladly take your money, but they aren't always so keen to pay claims, and you may need to persevere before they pay up. Always be persistent, and make a claim irrespective of any small print, as this may be unreasonable and therefore invalid in law. Insurance companies usually require you to obtain a written report, and report a loss (or any incident for which you intend to make a claim) to the local police or carriers within 24 hours. Failure to do so may mean that a claim won't be considered.

20
SUM OF TWENTY POUNDS

14. FINANCE

Competition for your money in the UK is fierce and in addition to numerous British and foreign banks, financial services are provided by building societies, investment brokers, insurance companies, the post office and even large chain stores, supermarkets and service organisations. London is the most important financial market in Europe and one of the most important in the world, along with Frankfurt, Hong Kong, New York and Tokyo.

The tax burden on individuals is around average for the EU when direct and indirect taxes are taken into account, with deductions from gross salary, including income tax, social security and other benefit contributions, totalling an average of around 30-40 per cent. However, taxes (particularly income tax) are lower than in many other European countries and the cost of living is similar, with the notable exception of London, which is one of the most expensive cities in the world.

There are numerous books and magazines published to help you manage your finances, including *Money Observer*, *What Investment* and *Moneywise*. Personal finance information (including the best loan and mortgage interest rates) is published in the financial pages of the Saturday and Sunday editions of national newspapers, and is also available from many websites, including www.moneysavingexpert.com, www.moneywise.co.uk, www.thisismoney.co.uk and www.which.co.uk/money. However, bear in mind that newspapers and websites are often paid to promote certain companies or deals and are therefore not necessarily independent!

The figures and information contained in this chapter are based on current law and HM Revenue and Customs practice, which in the UK are subject to change.

☑ SURVIVAL TIP

The most important thing to bear in mind when seeking financial services is to shop around for the best deal and not to believe everything that comparison websites tell you – they're paid to promote certain companies and deals!

COST OF LIVING

No doubt you would like to know how far your pounds will stretch and how much money (if any) you'll have left after paying your bills. The UK has a similar cost of living to most other Western European and North American countries, although there are high rates of duty on petrol, tobacco, alcohol and cars. London is one of Europe's most expensive cities and rents and property prices in London and the southeast (anywhere within commuting distance of the capital) can be astronomical. Food prices are relatively low and similar to (or lower than) most continental countries – there's a seemingly endless price war between supermarkets – and the cost of consumer goods is also very competitive (thanks in no small part to fierce internet competition).

However, inequality is a huge and growing problem. In recent years the wealthy have never been better off, while the real incomes of the poor and working class have been static or have fallen. The gap between rich and poor in the UK is the largest since records began in 1886, and millions of state pensioners are unable to afford basic comforts such as a healthy diet, a car, heating or an annual holiday.

The UK's inflation rate is based on the Consumer Price Index (CPI), which measures changes in the price level of a market basket of consumer goods and services. The UK's official inflation rate in late 2015 was just 0.05 per cent, which was bad news for savers and investors, although excellent news for consumers. A report by the Joseph Roundtree Foundation in 2016 calculated that a single person in the UK needed an annual salary of £17,200 to enjoy just the minimum income standard of living, up from £13,500 in 2008, while a family of four needed at least £37,800 (£18,900 for each parent), compared to £27,800 in 2008.

The fundamental flaw with most cost of living surveys is that they convert local prices into $US, which means that ranking positions are as much the result of currency fluctuations as price inflation.

In the Mercer 2016 Cost of Living Survey (www.mercer.com/costofliving) of 211 cities worldwide – one of the most respected annual surveys – London was ranked 17th, a fall from 12th place the previous year. Hong Kong topped the list of most expensive cities for expatriates, followed by Luanda (Angola), Zurich, Singapore, Tokyo, Kinshasa (Democratic Republic of the Congo), Shanghai, Geneva, N'Djamena (Chad), and Beijing.

It's also possible to compare the cost of living between various cities, using various websites such as the Economist Intelligence Unit (www.worldwidecostofliving.com/asp/wcol_WCOLHome.asp), for which a fee is payable. There are numerous websites that give you an idea of costs in the UK, such as www.expatistan.com/cost-of-living/london, www.numbeo.com/cost-of-living/country_result.jsp?country=united+kingdom and www.workgateways.com/working-in-the-uk/cost-of-living. However, you need to take cost of living data with a pinch of salt, as it may not be up to date, and price comparisons with other countries are often wildly inaccurate and often include irrelevant items which distort the results.

It's difficult to estimate an average cost of living, as it depends very much on where you live and your lifestyle. There are also large differences in prices (and above all rents) between the major cities and rural areas. If you live in London, drive a BMW and dine in expensive restaurants, your cost of living will be much higher than if you live in a rural area, drive a Ford Fiesta and eat mostly at home!

However, the cost of living needn't be astronomical. If you shop wisely (buying local produce whenever possible and avoiding expensive imported goods), compare prices and services before buying, and don't live too extravagantly, you may be pleasantly surprised at how little you can live on – and still enjoy life!

BRITISH CURRENCY

As you're probably aware, the British unit of currency is the pound sterling, The pound had been very strong for the decade or so prior to the banking meltdown in 2008, which saw the value of the pound fall as low as US$1.40 in January 2009. However, the pound fell even

lower in late 2016 after the UK decided to leave the EU, standing at a 31-year low of $1.25 to the US dollar, despite the fact that the economy and stock market remained strong.

The British pound has a number of colloquial names, including quid and smacker, and terms fiver (£5) and tenner (£10) are also commonly used. The pound is divided into 100 pence and British coins are minted in 1p and 2p (bronze); 5p, 10p, 20p and 50p (cupro-nickel); and one (nickel-brass) and two (bronze outer rim, cupro-nickel centre) pounds. The 20p and 50p coins are seven-sided, while all other coins are round (although new 5p and 10p coins are planned, along with a 12-sided £1 coin). Smaller, lighter coins have been introduced in recent years, although British coins are still heavier than those in many other countries.

Banknotes are printed in denominations of £5, £10, £20 and £50 pounds; the higher the denomination, the larger the note. Forgery is a problem in most western countries, and there are a 'significant number' of forged notes in circulation, so be on your guard if someone insists on paying a large bill in cash (the £20 note was redesigned in 2007 to thwart counterfeiters). A new polymer (plastic) £5 note was introduced in 2016 that's allegedly indestructible, which will be followed by £10 and £20 notes.

The latest innovation is contactless payments (maximum £30), whereby a mobile phone or debit card can be used to pay for items via readers in shops (no pin required). This is expected to be the future of paying for small purchases.

FOREIGN CURRENCY

The UK has no currency restrictions, and you may bring in or take out as much money as you wish, in practically any currency. The major British banks change most foreign bank notes (but not coins), but usually give a better exchange rate for travellers' cheques than for bank notes (although travellers' cheques have been rendered virtually obsolete by debit and cash cards, according to most travel experts).

In addition to banks, many travel agents, hotels and shops in major cities change or accept foreign currency, but usually at a less favourable exchange rate than banks. Always shop around for the best rate as far in advance as possible.

When using a credit card abroad, for example in Europe, always pay bills in euros or the local currency and NEVER in £sterling (you may be offered a choice), when a mark up of 5 per cent or more may be added to your bill.

BANKS & BUILDING SOCIETIES

The major British banks with branches throughout the UK (termed 'high street' banks) include Barclays (www.barclays.co.uk), HSBC (www.hsbc.co.uk), Lloyds (www.lloydsbank.com), National Westminster (www.natwest.com), Santander (www.santander.co.uk) and TSB (www.tsb.co.uk). The banking world has been in a state of turmoil since the 2008 financial crisis with the government pumping in over £500 billion in a series of 'rescue' packages to bail out banks and quantitative easing (basically printing money) with huge amounts of debt.

Some banks and building societies were nationalised or part-nationalised – the UK government still owns around 25 per cent of Lloyds Banking Group and over three-quarters of the Royal Bank of Scotland group – and there have been a number of mergers and takeovers. Some well-known banking brands are now in foreign hands, e.g. Abbey National and Alliance & Leicester, which are now owned by Spanish banking giant Santander.

Banking is controlled by a few major players that have swallowed up many of the smaller independent banks. There are also private banks (mainly offering 'portfolio management' services for the wealthy), foreign banks (over 500 in the City of London alone) and internet only 'banks' such as Cahoot (www.cahoot.co.uk) and First Direct, www2.firstdirect.com), although all major banks also offer online banking.

In recent years, banking services have been provided by an increasing number of institutions including internet banks – usually aligned with or owned by one of the major high street or foreign banks – supermarkets (Co-op, Sainsbury and Tesco) and stores such as Marks & Spencer.

British banks provide free banking for personal customers who remain in credit, pay (negligible) interest on account balances and offer a range of financial services (although they aren't usually the best place to buy insurance or pensions). If you do a lot of travelling abroad, you may find the comprehensive range of services offered by high street banks advantageous. Many services provided by British banks are also provided by building societies (see below), which often offer better deals on financial 'products'.

In the mid-2000s, investigations by the Office of Fair Trading and Financial Services Authority revealed that banks had been levying excessive charges and selling unnecessary services (such as payment protection insurance or PPI) and the public have been compensated to the tune of £billions in recent years.

If you've a complaint against a British bank and have exhausted the bank's complaints procedure, you can apply for independent arbitration to the Financial Ombudsman Service (0800-023 4 567, www.financial-ombudsman.org.uk). Failing this, publicising your complaint via a TV programme, newspaper or online forum often achieves results.

Building Societies

Building societies date back to 1775 and were originally established to cater for people saving to buy a home. Savers would deposit 5 or 10 per cent of the cost of a home with the building society, which then lent them the balance. A building society would rarely lend to anyone who wasn't a regular saver, although this changed many years ago. In 1987, the regulations governing institutions offering financial services were changed, which resulted in banks and building societies competing head-on for customers.

Nowadays, building societies offer practically all the services provided by banks, including current and savings accounts, cash cards, personal loans, credit cards, insurance and travel services (but not business banking).

Business Hours

Normal bank (and building society) business hours are from 9 or 9.30am until 4.30 or 5pm (some are open until 5.30pm) Mondays to Fridays, with no closure over the lunch period. Most branches are open late one day a week until 5.30 or 6pm and some open on Saturdays, e.g. from 9.30am until 12.30pm (some are open until 3.30pm). All banks are closed on public holidays, historically referred to as 'bank holidays'.

Opening an Account

If you're new to the UK one of your first acts should be to open a current account with a bank or building society, like over 80 per cent of the British working population. Your salary is usually paid directly into your account by your employer (most will insist on this) and your salary statement (payslip) is sent to your home address or given to you at work.

Many people have at least two accounts, a current account for their out-of-pocket expenses and day-to-day transactions, and a savings account for long-term savings. Before opening an account, compare bank charges, interest rates (e.g. on credit cards) and other services offered by a number of banks.

To open an account, you simply go to the bank or building society of your choice and tell them you're living in the UK and wish to open an account. You'll be asked for proof of identity, e.g. a passport or driving licence, plus proof of address in the form of a utility bill. Foreign residents may be required to provide a reference from their employer or a foreign bank. After opening an account, don't forget to give the details to your employer (if you want to get paid).

Current Accounts

The facilities you should expect from a current account (equivalent to a US checking account) include a cheque book, a paying-in book and a debit card. Other features may include interest earned on credit balances, no charges or fees when in credit, monthly statements, an authorised overdraft facility and the availability of credit cards.

Most people pay their bills from their current account, either by standing order, direct debit, bank transfer or cheque. Bank statements are usually issued monthly (optionally quarterly) but can usually be consulted at any time online (banks are trying to phase out printed statements and replace them with online statements).

Most banks don't levy charges on a current account provided you stay in credit, although

 **Caution**

NEVER respond to a phone call purporting to be from your bank or any financial institution with whom you do business (or even someone claiming to be the police). If you feel it necessary you should telephone your bank for verification (or call in person), if possible using a different phone from the one you received the call on (sometime the crooks keep the line open!). Note that a bank will **NEVER** ask you for your account password!

Barclays and the Metropolitan Police publish *The Little Book of Big Scams* available from Barclays' branches or online (https://beta.met.police.uk/advice-and-information/fraud).

some accounts have a monthly fee but include extras such as travel insurance. Some banks or building societies allow free overseas cash withdrawals from some of their current or savings account.

A number of banks issue account holders with a security card reader where you insert your account card into the reader which generates a random number that must be entered when logging onto your account.

Savings Accounts

All banks and building societies provide a range of savings accounts, also called deposit, term deposit or high-interest accounts, which are intended for short or medium-term savings rather than a long-term investment. When opening an account, the most important considerations are how much money you wish to save, whether it's a lump sum or a monthly amount, how quickly you might need access to it and whether you're a taxpayer.

> ☑ **SURVIVAL TIP**
>
> **Deposit Protection**
>
> All banks and building societies, including branches and subsidiaries of foreign banks accepting sterling deposits in the UK, must be licensed by the Bank of England and contribute to the Financial Services Compensation Scheme (FSCS), which guarantees that deposits up to £75,000 (which covers over 95 per cent of savers) will be repaid if a bank goes bust.

The best savings interest rates are published in Saturday and Sunday newspapers such as *The Times* and *The Sunday Times*, and in financial magazines such as *Money Observer*, *Moneywise* and *What Investment*. Both *Which? Money* magazine and the financial section of the Which? website (www.which.co.uk/money) website offers invaluable advice and surveys, although some access requires a subscription, and you can also check rates on comparison websites such as www.moneysupermarket.com and www.thisismoney.co.uk.

MORTGAGES

Mortgages are available from a large number of lenders, including building societies, high street and foreign banks (including offshore banks), finance houses and credit companies, insurance companies, developers, local authorities, supermarkets and major stores, and even some employers. The UK has a competitive mortgage business, with over 100 lenders offering thousands of different mortgage products, although since 2008 mortgage providers have toughened their lending criteria and most insist on buyers putting down a 10 per cent deposit, while for the best deals you may need to fund up to a quarter of the purchase price.

Mortgage interest rates are often pegged to the Bank of England's base lending rate which fell to an all-time low of 0.5 per cent in March 2009 and was reduced further to 0.25 per cent in 2016. Since 2011 mortgage rates have been at their lowest since records began and in 2016 many lenders were offering a two-year fixed-rate mortgage at below 4 per cent interest, although most came with a hefty arrangement fee.

Four factors determine whether you can obtain a mortgage, and its size: your income, your credit history, the size of the deposit you can make, and the type and condition of the property itself. If you're an employee in steady employment with a good deposit, you should have no problem obtaining a mortgage – although whether it will be enough to buy the home you want is another matter entirely!

Lenders cannot require you to buy expensive building (or contents) insurance from them, but

will insist that you have building insurance and will require evidence.

Types of Mortgage

Once you've calculated how much you need or can afford to borrow and the term of the loan, you must decide what kind of mortgage is best for you. The most common type of mortgage offered in the UK is a repayment mortgage, where you repay the original loan and interest over the period of the mortgage, as with most personal loans. Your monthly payment includes both interest and capital payments – mostly interest at the start and mostly capital towards the end of the term.

One advantage of a repayment mortgage is that the term of the loan can be extended if you've trouble meeting your monthly repayments. A disadvantage is that you must take out a form of life insurance called a 'mortgage protection policy' to ensure that your loan is paid off if you die. This policy isn't expensive, as it pays off the mortgage only if you die before the term of the loan is completed (and both the term and amount owed decrease over time).

For the majority of people, a repayment mortgage together with adequate life insurance is the best choice, as it's the only loan that guarantees to pay off your mortgage by the end of the term (provided you maintain regular payments). Interest-only loans – where you pay only the interest and the capital owed remains the same – were popular some years ago (particularly with buy-to-let mortgages), but are rare nowadays and are usually restricted to around 60 per cent of a property's value.

Interest Rates

Generally, you'll have a choice between a fixed-rate loan and a variable-rate loan. Fixed-rate loans, where the interest rate is fixed for a number of years (possibly as little as one year), no matter what happens to the base rate in the meantime, are increasingly popular, especially if you fix them when interest rates are low. They offer some protection if rates begin to rise and for those on tight budgets who cannot afford an increase in their mortgage repayments, fixed-rate mortgages are a good choice.

With a standard variable rate (SVR) mortgage, the interest rate goes up and down in line with the base rate (set by the Bank of England). The variable rate is usually at least 2 per cent above the base rate. Theoretically, when the base rate changes, the variable rate should rise or fall by the same percentage, although a low base rate doesn't necessarily translate into lower mortgage rates for borrowers, as banks don't always pass on the cuts or pass on only part of the cut (they're under no obligation to do so).

Many current mortgages are variations on the fixed or variable theme. Tracker mortgages move up and down with the base rate but are usually lower than the SVR – banks must pass on interest rate falls to borrowers with a tracker mortgage. Capped mortgages can go up when the rate increases but the rise is limited (capped) during the duration of the deal. Discounted mortgages mean that the SVR is discounted, i.e. lower, for a period of time. However, if you switch lenders during the fixed period of the deal (from two years to the duration of the mortgage), there are high penalties. When the period ends the rate reverts to the SVR.

Equity Loans & Shared Ownership

If you're a first time buyer and cannot afford to buy a suitable home, you may be entitled to assistance through the government-backed Help to Buy scheme (see www.helptobuy.org.uk and www.gov.uk/affordable-home-ownership-schemes/overview), although you'll still need a 5 per cent deposit in most cases.

You can apply if you're a first time buyer with a household income of less than £60,000 a year and you cannot afford to buy a suitable property on the open market. You may also be eligible if you've previously owned a home but cannot now afford to buy one, for example your relationship with your partner has ended or because you rent your home from a local council or housing association.

A similar option is shared ownership, whereby you buy a 'share' of a property, e.g. 50 per cent, and pay a low fixed rent on the remainder. You've the option of buying further shares and increasing your ownership when you can afford it.

Mortgage Fees

There are various fees associated with mortgages. All lenders charge a fee for setting up a loan (variously called an arrangement, completion, booking or reservation fee), which is either a fixed amount or a percentage of the loan. This used to be from £150 to £400, but since 2008 it has risen fast and is usually at least £1,000. For buy-to-let mortgages, taken out by investor landlords, it can sometimes be a percentage of the loan, e.g. 2.5 per cent. This fee must be paid when you apply for a loan or when you accept a mortgage.

Mortgage brokers don't usually levy a fee, as they're paid a fee or commission by lenders. In addition to mortgage fees, there's usually a valuation fee of around £200 and the lender's legal fees, although some lenders waive these. Other fees to watch out for are early redemption fees (when you end a deal before the end of a fixed term) and exit fees which are charged when you pay off (or switch) your mortgage.

Advice & Information

Whatever kind of mortgage you're seeking, you should shop around and take time to investigate all the options available. One way to find the best deal is to contact an independent mortgage broker. Mortgage advice offered by lenders is often misleading and biased and not to be trusted (surveys have found that the mis-selling of mortgages is widespread among high street lenders). The best independent advice is found in surveys carried out by publications such as *Which? Money* magazine (see www.which.co.uk), which accept no advertisements, and daily newspapers (which do).

The best available mortgage rates are published in Sunday newspapers such as *The Sunday Times*, *The Sunday Telegraph* and *The Observer*, and in monthly mortgage magazines such as *Your Mortgage Magazine*. You can also make comparisons via the internet, e.g. www.moneyextra.com, www.moneyfacts.co.uk and www.moneynet.co.uk. Many websites include mortgage calculators and tips on finding the best deal, including www.moneyadviceservice.org.uk and www.moneysavingexpert.com.

COUNCIL TAX

Council tax is levied by local councils on local residents to pay for services such as further education, roads, waste disposal, libraries and community services, including local police, fire and civil defence forces. Each council fixes its own tax rates, based on the number of residents and how much money they need to finance their services. The amount payable depends on the value of your home, as 'rated' by your local council (not necessarily the market value). Properties in England are divided into the following bands:

Council Tax Bands

Band	Property Value
A	Up to £40,000
B	£40,001 to £52,000
C	£52,001 to £68,000
D	£68,001 to £88,000
E	£88,001 to £120,000
F	£120,001 to £160,000
G	£160,001 to £320,000
H	Over £320,000

The government hasn't changed these bands since their introduction in 1993 and there were no plans to revalue in 2016, so the tax doesn't reflect the true value of the properties or most UK property would be paying their tax in Bands F, G and H! Tax bands are different in Scotland and Wales (see www.which.co.uk/money/tax/guides/council-tax/council-tax-bands), while in Northern Ireland property tax is based on the rateable value of property.

The full council tax assumes that two adults are living permanently in the dwelling. If only one adult lives in a dwelling (as their main home), the bill is reduced by 25 per cent. Even if a dwelling isn't a main home, e.g. it's unoccupied or is a second home, most councils still charge full council tax on it after the first month, and some even charge an additional 50 per cent on long-term uninhabited homes. Note that some councils levy a surcharge for owners of holiday homes, i.e. homes that are only occupied for part of the year.

Certain people aren't counted when calculating the number of adults resident in a dwelling, e.g. full-time students, apprentices and trainees, or under-20s who've just left school. If you or someone who lives with you has special needs arising from a disability, you may be entitled to a reduction in your council tax bill. Those receiving certain benefits may pay no council tax or have their bills reduced. You can appeal against the assessed value of your property and any errors due to exemption, benefits or discounts.

Council tax can usually be paid by direct debit from a bank or building society account, by post with a personal cheque, in person at council offices, by credit card, or at a bank or post office. Payment can be made in a lump sum (for which a reduction may be offered) or in instalments.

All those who are liable for council tax must register with their local council when they take up residence in a new area, and are liable to pay council tax from their first day of residence. A register is maintained by councils containing the names and addresses of all those registered for council tax, which is open to public examination. If you don't want your name and address to appear on the register you can apply for anonymous registration.

If you're renting accommodation in some cases (e.g. short term rentals, bedsits, student accommodation, etc.) your landlord may pay the council tax for your property and include the cost in your rent. Some landlords do this to ensure that tenants don't build up debts for unpaid tax with the council without their knowledge.

When moving to a new county or borough, you may be entitled to a refund of a portion of council tax paid for the current year.

VALUE ADDED TAX

Value Added Tax (VAT) is payable at a standard rate of 20 per cent on all goods and services, with the exception of domestic fuels, the installation of energy saving materials, grant-funded installation of heating equipment or security goods, connection of gas supply, renovation of or alterations to dwellings, residential conversions, women's sanitary protection products (although their removal from this category is planned for 2017), children's car seats, contraceptives and products to help people quit smoking, on which the rate is 5 per cent.

Many goods and services are zero-rated, including most food (but not catering); young children's clothing and footwear; books and newspapers; mobile homes and house boats; prescriptions and the supply of many aids for disabled people; domestic water and sewerage; and public transport (and others).

Certain business transactions are exempt from VAT (not the same as being zero-rated). Exempt supplies include most sales, leases and lettings of land and buildings; postal services; insurance; betting, gaming and lotteries; the provision of credit; certain education and training; health and welfare; burial and cremation; subscriptions to professional bodies; works of art; sports services; charity fund-raising; cultural services, etc.; supplies of goods where tax cannot be recovered; investment gold; and the services of doctors, dentists and opticians.

If you're self-employed and your annual turnover (not just profits) is over £83,000 annually in 2016 (which rises by around £2,000 per annum), you must be registered for VAT. A business that makes exempt supplies only cannot register for VAT, but a company making zero-rated supplies can. An individual is registered for VAT, not a business, and registration covers all the business activities of the registered person. The VAT you're charged on goods and services purchased when setting up a business can be reclaimed, subject to certain conditions.

If you're in any doubt regarding your registration or VAT declarations, you should contact HMRC (0300-200 3700 or see www.gov.uk/government/organisations/hm-revenue-customs/contact/vat-enquiries). Many VAT publications and leaflets are available, including *VAT Notice 700: the VAT Guide*, copies of which are sent to you when you register. VAT publications can be downloaded from the Gov.uk website (www.gov.uk/government/publications/vat-notice-700-the-vat-guide).

INCOME TAX

It's hardly surprising that the British don't always see eye to eye with the French. After all, it was because of Napoleon that income tax was introduced in 1799 (the 'good' news is that it was introduced as a temporary measure only and may be rescinded at any time!). (Another Frenchman, William the Conqueror, was to blame for the introduction of the budget).

> Among the many British eccentricities is the government's financial tax 'year', which runs from 6th April to 5th April the following year.

Liability

Your liability for British taxes depends on where you're domiciled and whether you're a British resident. Your domicile is the country which you regard as your natural and permanent home. A person can be resident in more than one country, but at any given time he can be domiciled in one only. To be regarded as resident in the UK for a given tax year (6th April to 5th April of the following year, and not a calendar year), you must normally be physically present there for at least part of that year. You'll always be regarded as resident in the UK with respect to income tax if you spend six months (183 days) or more there in any one year (whether in one continuous period or during a number of visits).

If you're a new permanent resident in the UK (i.e. someone not ordinarily resident), you're considered resident only from the time of your arrival (the same rule applies to anyone leaving the UK for permanent residence abroad, who becomes not ordinarily resident in the UK from the time they leave). If you're classified as a resident, you're liable to British income tax on all income arising from a source in the UK. If you're a British resident and domiciled in the UK, you're liable for taxation in the UK on your worldwide income, including capital gains tax.

The UK has double taxation agreements with around 80 countries, which, despite the name, are to prevent your paying double taxes, and not to ensure that you pay twice. Under double taxation treaties, certain categories of people are exempt from paying British tax. If part of your income is taxed abroad in a country with a double taxation treaty with the UK, you won't have to pay British tax on that income. If you're a British citizen living abroad, you won't usually be liable for British tax, provided your absence from the UK covers a complete tax year and you don't remain in the UK for 183 days or more in any tax year.

For information about double taxation agreements, see the online *Double Taxation Relief Manual* (www.hmrc.gov.uk/manuals/dtmanual/index.htm).

Tax Rates

The rates of income tax payable in the UK are around average for the EU. Your taxable income is your income after all allowances and deductions have been made from your gross income (from all sources). The UK has three income tax rates (2016-17):

Like many things in the UK, there's a two-tier tax system, first class for the self-employed and a second class system, called Pay As You Earn (PAYE), for employees. The self-employed pay their tax in arrears (as all employees do in many European countries), whereby an employee's income tax is deducted at source, weekly or monthly from his salary by his employer. Although HM Revenue and Customs (HMRC) may give individuals a hard time when it comes to paying their tax bills, British and foreign companies withhold or avoid £billions in tax each year over disputed corporation tax bills, plus billions more contested by the self-employed and those owing capital gains tax.

Pay As You Earn (PAYE)

Income tax is collected by HM Revenue and Customs (HMRC). All employees pay direct income tax or Pay As You Earn (PAYE) income tax that's deducted from gross salaries at source by employers. PAYE isn't a separate tax, but simply the name given to the system of direct (income) taxation. Any additional income, whether tax is deducted at source or not, must be declared to HMRC. This may include part-time self-employment or income from investments or savings. PAYE tax applies to all income tax which is payable on earnings to which the scheme relates, and includes tax at the basic and higher rates.

Income Band	Tax Rate
£0-11,000	0 per cent
£11,001-43,000	20 per cent
£43,001-£150,000	40 per cent
over £150,000	45 per cent

Tax on Jobseeker's Allowance and other social security benefits, such as Maternity Pay and Statutory Sick Pay, also comes within the PAYE scheme. The PAYE scheme is disadvantageous to many employees, who would be entitled to claim larger and more allowances if they were classified as self-employed, and would also have the benefit of paying their tax in arrears.

PAYE Tax Code

The level of tax for those taxed under the PAYE system is denoted by a tax code. When you receive a new code, your notice of coding shows how the calculations have been made. You should check that the deductions, allowances and the total are correct. You don't receive a notice each year, but your current tax code is always given on your pay or wage slip (which you receive with your weekly or monthly salary). Your pay slip also shows your gross pay (your salary without any deductions) to date and the amount of tax you've paid to date.

If your circumstances change you should inform HMRC who'll send you a new income tax return to complete (see below) or simply change your tax code. You must inform them of any changes in your tax status – e.g. marriage, a dependent relative, divorce or separation (which entitles you to an additional allowance) – or a change in your income (maybe from a part-time job) or company benefits, e.g. a company car. It's in your interest to do this as, should the taxman find out later, you won't only be liable for any tax owed, plus interest, but can also be fined up to 100 per cent of the amount of unpaid tax.

Self-employed

Some 15 per cent of people in the UK (over 4.5 million) are self-employed, either as a 'sole trader' or in partnership with others. You're generally much better off from a tax point of view if you're self-employed, as you can claim more in the way of expenses than employees (paying PAYE tax). Another advantage for the self-employed is the delay between making profits and paying tax on them. To be classified as self-employed you must convince your tax office that you're genuinely self-employed and in business for yourself. You can check whether you're entitled to be self-employed via HMRC's guidance notes and calculator at

> **☑ SURVIVAL TIP**
>
> If you're self-employed, you'll almost certainly find it pays to hire an accountant to complete your tax return.

Gov.uk (www.gov.uk/government/collections/employed-or-self-employed).

If you're self-employed you pay class 2 national insurance contributions (see page 193) and also class 4 contributions at 9 per cent on profits between £8,060 and £43,000 per year (2016-17), plus 2 per cent on earnings above £43,000. You shouldn't hesitate to claim for anything that you believe is a legitimate business deduction. The IR will delete them if they don't agree, but what they will never do is allow you a deduction that you're entitled to and have forgotten to claim.

HM Revenue and Customs publish a raft of information for the self-employed (www.gov.uk/business-tax/self-employed) and also provides webinairs, e-learning and online chat forums. A number of business support helplines are available (www.gov.uk/business-support-helpline) and there's a helpline for the newly self-employed (0300-200 3504).

Personal Allowance

Before you're liable for income tax, you're allowed to earn a certain amount of income tax-free. If you earn below your taxable limit you aren't liable for tax. Everyone has a tax-free personal allowance, and a married couple is entitled to an additional married couple's allowance, both of which are increased for those aged 65 and over (even more for the over-75s). Under independent taxation for married couples, each partner is wholly responsible for his or her own tax affairs, including income and capital gains tax. The tax-free personal allowance for the 2016-17 tax year was £11,000, irrespective of age.

Income Tax Returns

If you're self-employed or a higher-rate taxpayer, you should be sent a tax return annually, although if you pay your income tax through PAYE and your tax affairs are fairly simple, you'll rarely receive one. Similarly, if you aren't paying tax on part of your earnings it's up to you to tell the tax authorities. If you don't receive a return (or all the forms required) and need one, it's your responsibility to request it, either by phone or online (www.gov.uk/government/organisations/hm-revenue-customs/contact/self-assessment-forms-ordering).

Self-assessment

A self-assessment system was introduced in 1997, and was the most far-reaching tax reform for 50 years. Under the old system, the Inland Revenue issued estimated assessments which could then be challenged by individual taxpayers. Self-assessment affects some 9 million self-employed people, company directors and taxpayers with substantial investment income or complex tax affairs, who must calculate their own tax liability. In theory, it's a simpler method of calculating tax, although there are hidden complexities and harsh penalties for late filing, and reservations

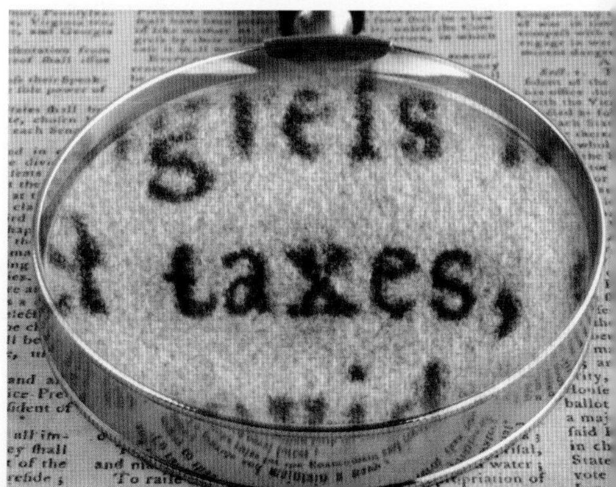

have been expressed about HMRC forcing people to become tax 'experts'. Many reports indicate that the first few years of self-assessment were chaotic, to say the least, with many people wrongly fined, and over 1 million sent incorrect bills.

If you've tax liabilities that aren't covered by PAYE you must register for self assessment using form SA1 which can be downloaded from the HMRC website. Self-employed people can register online (www.gov.uk/register-for-self-assessment). Once registered, you receive a Unique Taxpayer Reference (UTR) number, which must be quoted when contacting the tax authorities.

There are heavy fines for late filing and late payers under the self-assessment scheme. If you miss the deadline for filing your tax return by a single day, you must pay an automatic £100 fine (incurred by hundreds of thousands of people each year). You can appeal against a penalty for filing a late return.

Tax payments are due by January 31st of the following year – the same date as the deadline for online filing – and you can settle your tax bill in a number of ways, e.g. by post, at a bank or post office, online (via bank transfer) or by direct debit. A budget payment plan is available, allowing you to make voluntary payments towards future tax bills.

Income Tax Information

HM Revenue and Customs publishes a large number of leaflets about tax, which are listed on the Gov.uk website (www.gov.uk/government/collections/hm-revenue-and-customs-leaflets-factsheets-and-booklets#tax-help). Copies of tax leaflets can be downloaded from the website or ordered by telephone from tax offices and HMRC tax enquiry centres.

There are many books published about how to reduce your income tax bill, including J.K. Lasser's *Your Income Tax 2017: For Preparing Your 2016 Tax Return* (updated annually) and the *Daily Telegraph Tax Guide*. Many independent organisations provide online income tax information, including The Consumers' Association (www.which.co.uk/money/tax) and Citizens Advice (www.citizensadvice.org.uk/tax/income-tax-how-much-should-you-pay/income-tax-rates).

If you've a home or business computer, a number of tax computer programs are available, such as *ProTax* (Forbes) and *TaxCalc* (Acorah), designed to make it easier to calculate and check your income tax payments.

CAPITAL GAINS TAX

Capital Gains Tax (CGT) is applicable whenever you sell or otherwise dispose of (e.g. lease, exchange or lose) an asset which, broadly speaking, is anything you own. Anything you sell, from a second home to shares or antiques, that reaps profits above £11,100 per year (2016-17) is liable to CGT, payable at 18 or 28 per cent, depending on your highest rate of income tax (companies pay corporation tax at their normal rate).

CGT liability must be included in your income tax return. You don't have to pay CGT on your car; your main home; household goods and possessions worth less than £6,000 when you sell them; National Savings certificates;

premium bonds; betting winnings; most life insurance policies; government securities; and personal injury compensation.

If an asset disposed of was acquired before 31st March 1982, no capital gains tax is usually payable. To work out your gain (or loss), you deduct the purchase price and any costs from the sales price, e.g. if the asset is a property you can deduct costs such as the purchase costs and any improvements from your eventual profit.

If you've two homes, living part of the year in one and part in another, you must choose which is your main residence for capital gains tax purposes. It's best to choose the one on which you think you'll make the largest profit as your main home. You should inform the tax office within two years of buying a second home (otherwise they may decide which property is your main home for you), although you can change your mind at any time by informing your tax office.

HM Revenue and Customs publishes a number of leaflets about capital gains tax and provides information on its website (www.gov.uk/personal-tax/capital-gains-tax). If you're liable for CGT, you should obtain advice from an accountant, as you may be able to reduce your tax liability.

INHERITANCE TAX

Inheritance tax (IHT) at 40 per cent is payable in the UK on any bequests above £325,000 when left to anyone other than your spouse or a registered charity. The tax-free threshold has been frozen at £325,000 since 2009 but before that it increased annually and is likely to be much higher when you die (but then so will the value of your estate). The best way to reduce your IHT liability is to simply give some of your money away to family or friends or to a deserving cause (my account number is...), provided it doesn't adversely affect your standard of living.

Your liability for inheritance tax can be avoided by judicious financial planning and transferring assets, which is one of the most effective forms of tax planning. One way to avoid IHT is with a trust or an insurance policy that pays the tax liability (with your children or grandchildren as beneficiaries), although you must live for seven years after setting it up.

Couples can benefit from a 'double' threshold, as if you leave all your worldly goods to your spouse or civil partner they pay no inheritance tax, and they also inherit any unused portion of your allowance, thus a widow or widower could in theory leave a tax-free inheritance of up to £650,000. Certain gifts are also exempt.

☑ SURVIVAL TIP

It's best to make your beneficiaries the executors, who can instruct a solicitor after your death if they need legal assistance.

Those liable for inheritance tax must submit an account to HMRC detailing the assets they've inherited and their value, within six months of receiving them. There's a fine for anyone who makes a late declaration and there are heavy fines for providing fraudulent or incorrect information.

The Gov.uk website (www.gov.uk/inheritance-tax) provides information about CGT, and there's also a Probate and Inheritance Tax helpline (0300-123 1072). However, before making any gifts or transfer of property or any bequests in your will (see below), it's advisable to obtain legal advice from a solicitor who specialises in inheritance tax.

WILLS

It's an unfortunate fact of life, but you're unable to take your worldly goods with you when you take your final bow (even if you've plans to come back in a later life), so it's better to leave them to someone or something you love, rather than to HM Revenue & Customs – or leave a mess which everyone will fight over (unless that's your intention!). Surprisingly, over two-thirds of Britons die intestate – i.e. without making a will – which means that the inflexible laws of intestacy dictate how the estate is divided. It's estimated that over £2 billion in inheritance tax could be avoided if more people planned their taxes and made wills. Most married people imagine that when they die, everything they own will automatically be inherited by their partner. This isn't true. Under the laws of intestacy, common law (i.e. unmarried) partners have no legal rights.

The major problem with leaving no will is the delay in winding up your estate (while perhaps searching for a will), which can cause considerable hardship and distress at an already stressful time. When someone dies, an estate's assets cannot be touched until inheritance tax (see above) has been paid and probate (the official proving of a will) has been granted.

All adults should make a will, irrespective of how large or small their assets. If your circumstances change dramatically you must make a new will; for example if you get married, marriage automatically revokes any existing wills under English law; similarly, divorce means that gifts in a will to an ex-spouse are invalid. Spouses should make separate wills. So if you separate or are divorced, you should consider making a new will (but make sure that you've only one valid will). A new bequest or a change can be made to an existing will through a document called a 'codicil'. You should check your will every few years to make sure that it still meets your wishes and circumstances (your assets may also increase dramatically in value).

If you're a foreign national and don't want your estate to be subject to British law, you may be eligible to state in your will that it's to be interpreted under the law of another country. To avoid being subject to British death duty and inheritance laws, you must establish your country of domicile in another country. If you don't specify in your will that the law of another country applies to your estate, then British law will apply. If your estate comes under British law, your dependants will be subject to British inheritance laws and tax. Inheritance law is slightly different in Scotland from the rest of the UK, where part of the estate must be left to any children.

☑ SURVIVAL TIP

Keep a copy of your will in a safe place such as a bank, and another copy with your solicitor or the executors of your estate. You should keep information regarding bank accounts and insurance policies with your will(s), but don't forget to tell someone where they are!

You can draw up your own will (which is better than none), but it's wise to obtain legal advice from a specialist will writer or solicitor who will draw up a simple will for around £100 for a single person, or £200 for a couple (fees vary considerably and you should shop around). For those who would rather do it themselves, a simple will kit can be purchased from stationers for around £10, which also provides guidance on writing your will. You must have two witnesses (to your signature, not to the contents of the will) who cannot be beneficiaries or your spouse. If you wish, you can list all your 'valuables' and who's to get what (the list can be kept separate from the will and be changed without altering the will itself).

You also need someone to act as the executor (or personal representative) of your estate, which can be particularly costly for modest estates. Your bank, building society, solicitor (the least expensive, but far from cheap), or other professional will usually act as the executor, although this should be avoided if at all possible, as the fees can be astronomical.

15. LEISURE

Tourism is one of the UK's largest and most profitable industries, employing over 3 million people directly or indirectly, and earning the country more than £125 billion annually (predicted to double by 2025). The UK is the world's eighth most popular tourist destination and welcomes over 35 million overseas visitors annually. The diversity of leisure opportunities in the UK is enormous, with London providing more cultural activities than any other city in the world. Whatever your favourite leisure pursuits, you'll find them represented in abundance. There's a profusion of art galleries, museums, gardens, stately homes, zoos, sports facilities, sporting events, children's entertainment, cinemas, theatres, dance and music events, casinos, pubs, restaurants and much more.

The country has many aspects ranging from picturesque country towns and villages to bustling modern cities, all exuding a sense of history that's found in few other countries; people are drawn to it for many reasons, not least its rich traditions, quality of live entertainment (particularly in London) and the lively arts scene. Nowhere provides a more varied and vibrant nightlife for the young (and young at heart) than London, which is besieged by the youth of the world. It's also home to some of the world's best hotels and restaurants.

However, don't make the mistake of only visiting London and neglecting the UK's magnificent provincial cities and countryside, where a wealth of historic sites and spectacular natural beauty awaits you – including fishing villages, national parks, moors, castles, wild heathland, country inns, charming villages, bleak and rugged mountains, ancient cathedrals, sandy beaches, broads and marshlands. Whether you're a country or city lover, there's something for everyone in the UK. It's a small country, so no matter where you live you can regard most of it as your playground.

Good road and rail connections ensure that a huge area is accessible for day excursions, and practically anywhere is within reach for a weekend trip, particularly if you travel by air. The cost of air travel, both within the UK and to most European countries, is low by European standards, making weekend breaks affordable to most destinations.

TOURIST INFORMATION CENTRES

There are Tourist Information Centres (TICs) in all major towns and principal railway stations and airports, where staff can provide you with a wealth of information and book you a hotel room. Centres are signposted by the National Tourist Information sign of a red 'i' on a white background, and are often housed in public libraries. Maps and information is also provided on the Visit Britain websites (see above).

TICs have no standard opening hours, although 9.30 or 10am to 5 or 5.30pm, Mondays to Saturdays is usual. Later closing times and Sunday opening may operate in summer. Some close from September to Easter or open in the mornings only in winter, e.g. from

November to March. Many rural TICs close from 24th December to 1st January inclusive. Always telephone to check the opening hours in advance – an answer-phone service may provide information when centres are closed.

As well as the services mentioned above, TICs provide local and regional guides and public transport information; act as box offices for local theatre and concert halls; take bookings for local and city tours, excursions, guided walks and congresses; and arrange car hire or guide services.

General Information

A wealth of information is published about leisure activities in Britain. In most cities, there are numerous websites devoted to entertainment, e.g. *Time Out*, which provides comprehensive guides to London (www.timeout.com/London) as well as guides to other UK cities such as Glasgow and Manchester. Other magazines of interest include *This England*, *The Scots Magazine*, *Welsh Country* and *Ireland* magazines, plus an array of county magazines. Arts and entertainment programmes and information about special events are available from tourist offices in all major towns. Many local authorities also publish maps and brochures highlighting local places of interest and leisure facilities.

Many councils publish free directories listing local sports clubs, leisure facilities, arts and community centres, and opportunities for countryside and outdoor activities. A good source of general tourist information is Visit Britain, which has a comprehensive website extoling destinations, attractions and forthcoming events (www.visitbritain.com). Visit Britain is also the hub for four regional tourism websites: Visit England (www.visitengland.com, Visit Scotland (www.visitscotland.com), Visit Wales (www.visitwales.com) and Visit London (www.visitlondon.com). The Visit Britain online shop allows you to buy everything from theatre tickets to guidebooks (www.visitbritainshop.com).

The main aim of this chapter (and indeed the whole book) is to provide information that isn't found in standard guide books, of which there are literally hundreds. Some of the best include the *Michelin Green Guide to Great Britain*, *Lonely Planet England* (plus books on Scotland, Ireland, Wales) and the *Rough Guide to Britain*.

 **Caution**

Tourists and day-trippers should take care not to become victims of rip-off prices in tourist areas (particularly in central London) and attractions. If prices aren't displayed, always ask the price before ordering or buying anything, and check for minimum prices, service charges and other extras in restaurants.

HOTELS

British hotels range from international five-star luxury establishments, castles and converted stately homes, to budget hotels, guesthouses and B&Bs. Don't judge the rest of the UK by the standards and rates in London, where demand outstrips supply, allowing even the worst hotels to charge exorbitant rates (and where the best, such as Claridges, the Ritz and the Savoy charge a king's ransom). If you're planning to stay in London, always book well in advance, and spend as much as you can afford if you want a half-decent hotel (rooms cost from around £100 per night after discounts). If you don't need to be in the middle of town, out-of-town hotels (except those at Heathrow airport, which charge near London rates) offer better value for money.

British hotels are Europe's most expensive and often offer a poor standard of accommodation (tiny rooms, hard beds/pillows, etc). A survey conducted by the Department of National Heritage some years ago (little has changed since) found that they were the most expensive and worst value for money in Europe, and that around a quarter of visitors were dissatisfied with their accommodation. Inexpensive hotels (e.g. around £40-50 per night) are particularly difficult to find, and budget travellers must usually settle for bed and breakfast (B&B) accommodation rather than a 'proper' hotel, although this is often just as expensive.

The tourist board, motoring organisations and guidebooks use varying hotel grading systems. Rates vary, depending on the location, season and amenities provided, as well as the quality of accommodation offered, but the following table can be used as a *rough* guide:

Hotel Ratings

Rating	Price Range
1	£35-60
2	£50-75
3	£80-130
4	£100-150
5	£150+

The prices quoted (see box) are for two people sharing a double room with bath (prices are usually quoted per room and not per person). Single rooms may be available at a slightly lower rate, but usually a single person occupies a double room and there's no reduction. Always check whether the price quoted includes value added tax (VAT), which at 20 per cent can make quite a difference. Look out for extras such as telephone calls (calls from rooms are prohibitively expensive), internet fees, mini-bar/water costs and breakfast. During off-peak periods and at weekends you can usually haggle over room rates, particularly late at night at large hotels (which frequently offer reduced rates, but may not tell you unless you ask).

Many hotels offer special weekend rates (usually for Friday and Saturday), particularly during off-peak periods, which may include dinner, bed and breakfast. Some hotels with restaurants offer half-board (breakfast and evening meal) or full-board (breakfast, lunch and evening meal) at advantageous rates. A cooked (English) breakfast may be included in the price, although nowadays it's usually an extra and can cost up to £20. It's usually served 'buffet style' (self-service) and consists of fruit juice, cereal, a hot main course (i.e. English breakfast), croissants, toast and marmalade/jam, and coffee or tea.

Most top class hotels provide air-conditioned rooms with tea and coffee-making facilities; room service; radio and television (possibly with on-demand films and satellite TV); en suite bathroom or shower; telephone; iPod dock; mini-bar; hair dryer; and a trouser press. Many hotels have specially equipped rooms for the disabled. Large hotels may offer a choice of restaurants and bars; secretarial, business and conference facilities; a health and leisure centre with swimming pool, gymnasium, solarium, sauna and spa; hairdressing salon; and a range of shops.

Due to the high price of most traditional British hotels, budget hotel chains, such as Premier Inn (over 700 locations, www.premierinn.com) and Travelodge (over 500 locations, www.travelodge.co.uk) are extremely popular with price-conscious travellers. They usually follow a two-star format, and provide reasonable, inexpensive accommodation. Premier Inn and Travelodge room rates start from around £30 per night excluding breakfast if you book well in advance, but can reach £100 if you book at the last minute in a popular town or region (like airline ticket, prices vary depending on the demand at the time of booking).

> **☑ SURVIVAL TIP**
>
> Unless you're **absolutely certain** you won't need to change or cancel your booking, you should avoid booking a non-refundable room (normal bookings can be cancelled with a full refund with 24 hours notice).

Travelodge rooms usually have a king-size bed, and they also have family rooms for two adults and two children; rooms include an en suite bathroom, TV, radio and tea-making facilities. A lunch-bag style breakfast can be ordered and eaten in your room for around £5, and there's also usually a 'restaurant' (although nothing grand) in the building or nearby. Rooms with facilities for the disabled are also available. Hostelries are located near motorways and A roads (and increasingly in city centres and near tourist attractions), and are open seven days a week from 7am to 10pm. Some are open 24 hours.

The best place to compare prices is via the internet, where there's a wealth of hotel websites, including Booking.com (www.booking.com), Expedia (www.expedia.co.uk), Hotels (www.hotels.com), London Town (www.londontown.com), Trivago (www.trivago.co.uk) and Trip Advisor (www.tripadvisor.com).

Hotel Information

Apart from the wealth of information provided on its website, Visit Britain (www.visitbritain.com/gb/en) also publishes guides to bed & breakfast, self-catering and pet-friendly accommodation. General hotel guides include *The Good Hotel Guide Great Britain & Ireland* and the *AA Hotel Guide* and *AA Bed and Breakfast Guide*.

Accommodation is rated by regional tourist boards according to its accessibility for wheelchair users and others who have difficulty walking or climbing stairs. Information and advice about accommodation for the physically disabled is available from Visit Britain and Tourism for All (0845-124 9971, www.tourismforall.org.uk).

BED & BREAKFAST

Bed and breakfast (B&B) accommodation consists of a room in a private house, country pub, farmhouse or even on a university campus, and is found throughout the UK, from cities to remote hamlets. It's more informal than a hotel and provides an opportunity to meet the British in their own homes. Many ordinary homes providing B&B accommodation are shown by a *Bed & Breakfast* sign hanging outside or in the window. Guest house accommodation is similar in price and standard to B&B, but is usually available only in towns. A few B&Bs won't accept children and many don't cater for disabled people.

Although it's advisable to book in advance for public holiday weekends or at any time in London, it's usually unnecessary, particularly if you're touring and need a room for just one or two nights. If you don't book in advance, you've more freedom to go where you please, but you should bear in mind that some B&Bs have a minimum stay of two or three nights. If you're staying for more than one night, you may be expected to vacate your room for most of the day and to leave by noon (or earlier) on your last day.

Like hotel accommodation, standards vary greatly from a basic single room sharing a bathroom to a luxury double room with en suite bathroom (possibly in a country house). Many B&Bs are graded by regional tourist boards using Visit Britain's star rating system (see above), with room rates ranging from around £40 to £50 per person, per night. Rates in country house hotels are similar to first class hotels. There may be a reduced rate for stays of a week or longer.

As the name suggests, bed and breakfast always includes breakfast (usually a full cooked English breakfast). Some B&Bs also offer an optional evening meal (dinner) for a reasonable price, which must usually be ordered in advance. Most B&Bs provide tea and coffee-making facilities in rooms.

A number of guides to B&Bs are published, including the *AA Bed & Breakfast Guide* and *Alastair Sawday's Special Places to Stay British Bed & Breakfast*. B&B accommodation can be booked via numerous website agencies, including www.bedandbreakfasts-uk.co.uk, www.bedandbreakfast-directory.co.uk and www.visitus.co.uk. The Visit Britain website (www.visitbritain.com) and its offshoots also include bed and breakfast accommodation, as well as agencies representing a number of hosts.

Airbnb

Although most readers will be familiar with AirBnB (www.airbnb.co.uk), it only started business as recently as 2008 (in San Francisco). It began as a way of putting individuals with a spare room or rooms in their home in touch with people looking for an inexpensive place to stay for a few days or weeks. The informality and simplicity of the arrangement struck a resounding chord around the world: in the UK alone some 80,000 homeowners advertise on the site. The 'BnB' in the name means, of course, bed and breakfast, but the "air" is nothing to do with air travel – it comes from 'air mattress'.

One reason for its popularity in the UK is that under the rent-a-room scheme, homeowners (and tenants) can earn up to £7,500 gross each year tax-free from letting a room or rooms in their home. This was supposed to ease the housing shortages. However, the downside (there's always a downside) is that many landlords who would otherwise let their properties long-term have signed up with AirBnB, thus reducing the number of properties available for tenants and exacerbating the already critical shortage of accommodation in many towns and cities, particularly London.

 **Caution**

If you're thinking of letting your own home, bear in mind that some owners have had their homes trashed and property stolen by AurBnB guests.

SELF-CATERING

Self-catering cottages, bungalows, apartments (flats), houseboats, houses, chalets and mobile holiday homes are available for rent in holiday areas and major cities. An apartment is often a good choice for a family, as it's usually cheaper than a hotel room, provides more privacy and freedom, and allows you to prepare your own meals as and when you please. Standards, while generally high, are variable, and paying a high price doesn't always guarantee a well-furnished or well-appointed apartment. Many self-catering establishments are classified by regional tourist boards using the Visit Britain rating system.

Studios (for two people) in cities are available from around £75 per night, one-bedroom apartments (for four people) from £100 per night and two-bedroom apartments (for up to six people) from around £125 per night (rates may be much higher in London and other major cities). There may be lower rates for stays of a week or longer and rates are also reduced outside peak periods.

The weekly rent of a country cottage varies considerably from around £250 to £1,000 per week for four people, depending on its location, size, amenities and the season. Before booking any self-catering accommodation, you should check the holiday changeover dates and times; what's included in the rent (e.g. cleaning, linen); whether cots or high chairs are provided or pets are allowed; if a garden or parking place is provided; and what sort of access there is to public transport (if applicable). Self-catering accommodation is usually let on a weekly basis from Saturday to Saturday, often for a minimum of one or two weeks.

Many useful fact sheets and booklets are available from Tourist Information Centres and self-catering accommodation is also advertised in holiday magazines and national newspapers, particularly the Saturday and Sunday editions. You can book self-catering accommodation via a plethora of websites, including www.cottages4you.co.uk, www.holidaycottages.co.uk, www.hoseasons.co.uk, www.independentcottages.co.uk, http://lovingapartments.com, www.ownersdirect.co.uk and www.sykescottages.co.uk.

YOUTH HOSTELS

If you're travelling on a tight budget, one way to stretch your financial resources is to stay in youth hostels, which may vary from a castle to a camping pod, a hunting lodge to a city apartment block. There are some 300 youth hostels in Britain, most affiliated to the Youth Hostelling Association (England and Wales), including around 60 in Scotland run by the Scottish Youth Hostel Association (SYHA). Many open all year round, while others close during the winter.

All YHAs publish handbooks and accommodation guides, and excellent maps (usually free) showing hostel locations, opening dates and facilities. Websites also provide plenty of useful info and enable you to book online.

Membership is open to all, although the permitted minimum age of children accompanied by an adult is generally five, or 14 when unaccompanied. Children aged between 5 and 15 receive free membership when their parents (or a single parent) are members. Annual YHA Membership is £20 for an adult, £10 for those aged under 26 and £30 for a family (there's a £5 discount if you pay by direct debit). Non-members pay a £3 per night supplement. Membership fees of the SYHA (Scotland) and HINI (Northern Ireland) are similar to the YHA.

Overnight rates in England and Wales vary, depending on the particular hostel, which are graded from one to five stars. Prices range from around £15 to £25 per night for a bed in a shared dormitory, £25 to £60 for a double room and from around £50 for a family room (rates may be higher in July and August). Hostels in Scotland are graded from one to four stars (rates are similar to those in England and Wales).

For further information about youth hostels in England and Wales, contact the YHA's national office (0800-0191 700 or 01629-592 700, www.yha.org.uk). For information about Scottish and Northern Ireland youth hostels, contact the Scottish Youth Hostel Association (01786-891400 or 0845-293 7373, www.syha.org.uk) or Hostelling International Northern Ireland (028-9032 4733, www.hini.org.uk).

CARAVANS & CAMPING

Camping is no longer all about damp tents and baked beans eaten from the tin. There's a new variant known as glamping (glamorous camping), where you can stay in cosy camping pods, shepherd's huts, canvas yurts and safari-style tents. Caravanning is perennially popular with the Brits, and some caravans and chalets offer almost five-star luxury.

The UK has around 4,000 licensed caravan (trailer), chalet and camping parks, some 3,000 of which are graded under a quality scheme operated by the British Holiday and Home Parks Association (www.bhhpa.com) and the National Caravan Council (www.thencc.org.uk), in co-operation with local tourist boards. A database of inspected sites can be found at www.ukparks.com. In addition to the main caravan parks, the Camping and Caravanning Club maintains a list of over 1,400 certificated locations, which are generally small and secluded sites often located in the grounds of a house or farm. Permission is required to camp anywhere outside official sites.

The cost of parking a touring caravan is from around £10 to £30 a night, depending on their length and the particular caravan park. An electricity hook-up costs an additional £3 to £5 per night, depending on the number of people. The cost of pitching a tent at a camping site is usually from £5 to £10 a night, depending on the tent size and the site, plus usually a similar fee per person. Many caravan parks also have static caravans that can be hired for £250 to £500 per week, depending on the size, amenities and number of berths required. In addition to buying your own caravan, which costs anything from £5,000 to £25,000 depending on its size (e.g. two to six-berths), quality and fittings, you can also hire touring caravans in all areas.

Useful camping and caravanning guides include *Alan Rogers – the Best Campsites in Britain & Ireland* (www.alanrogers.com) and *Camping & Caravanning Britain* (the AA). A number of magazines for caravanners, motor caravanners and outdoorsmen are published in the UK, including *Practical Motorhome* and *Trail*.

Various organisations for caravanners and motor caravanners exist, including the Camping and Caravanning Club (0845-130 7631, www.campingandcaravanningclub.co.uk), the Motor Caravanners' Club (01684-311 677, www.motorcaravanners.eu) and the National

Caravan Council (01252-318251, www.nationalcaravan.co.uk). For more upmarket options, take a look at www.glamping-uk.co.uk and www.love-glamping.co.uk.

MUSEUMS & ART GALLERIES

The UK has numerous museums and art galleries, which include some of the most important collections to be found anywhere in the world (the British have been looting and pillaging for centuries to fill them). London is home to the UK's most celebrated collections, and admission to many of them is free – a great British tradition. However, visitors are invited to make a donation and a charge is made for entry to 'special' temporary exhibitions.

London institutions that charge fees range from around £5 to £25 and £1 to £15 for children (usually under the age of 16); students generally receive a reduction on production of a student identity card. Some museums and art galleries provide free admission on one day a week and annual season tickets. Leading museums and galleries are open seven days a week (including most public holidays) from around 10am to 5 or 6pm, Mondays to Saturdays, and 2 or 2.30pm to 6pm on Sundays – some also stay open late one evening a week. Many museums and galleries provide reductions for disabled people and some have wheelchair access. There's lots of information on the www.visitlondon.com website.

Opening times vary, so check in advance, particularly when planning to visit the smaller London and provincial museums and galleries, some of which open on only a few days a week.

In addition to the great national collections, there are also many excellent smaller museums, galleries and displays in stately homes and National Trust properties throughout the UK, many of which are well worth a visit. Most councils publish free directories of local arts organisations and provide information about activities.

GARDENS, STATELY HOMES, PARKS & ZOOS

Lists of gardens, stately homes, castles, theme parks, zoos, botanical gardens and national parks are available from tourist offices, and can be found in any good guide book. Most are open throughout the year, although many have reduced opening hours in winter, e.g. October to March.

Kenwood House, Hampstead, London

The National Trust (NT) is a privately funded charitable organisation that looks after over 300 historic buildings and over 600,000 acres of countryside in England, Wales and Northern Ireland. Many gardens, landscaped parks, and prehistoric and Roman sites are also in its care. Membership costs £63 a year for an individual, £105 for a couple, £111 for a family (including all children aged under 18) and £1,555 for life membership. There's a 25 per cent reduction for seniors, but only if you've held either an individual or joint membership for at least five of the last ten years. Membership includes free access to all NT buildings and sites and an annual handbook – you can join at any National Trust property. For further information, contact the National Trust (0844-800 1895 or 0344-800 1895, www.nationaltrust.org.uk). The National Trust for Scotland is a separate organisation (0131-458 0200, www.nts.org.uk).

English Heritage has broadly similar aims to the NT. Membership costs £52 a year for adults, £92.50 for a family and £43.50 for a senior. Membership allows you to visit over 400 English Heritage properties free of charge and you receive a property guidebook, maps, an events diary, a quarterly magazine and free entry to special events. For information, contact English Heritage's Customer Service Department (0370-333 1181, www.english-heritage.org.uk).

If you're a keen gardener you may be interested in joining the Royal Horticultural Society (0845-260 5000, www.rhs.org.uk). Adult membership costs from £57 (less by direct debit) and £83 for a family, and entitles you to free entry to many beautiful gardens and a range of other benefits.

The UK has a number of internationally acclaimed zoos, including London and Whipsnade (50km/30mi north of London), plus many others throughout the UK including Bristol, Chester, Edinburgh, Glasgow and Manchester. There are also a number of safari parks (e.g. Longleat) where animals are allowed to roam free. Zoos are open most days of the year (some close only on Christmas Day), and you should expect to pay around £15 per adult and £12 per child (although family rates and other concessions may apply).

The UK also has around 100 theme parks which are very popular (some 100 million visitors annually) and an excellent place for a special (i.e. expensive) day out for children. The most popular include Alton Towers (Staffordshire), Pleasure Beach (Blackpool), Thorpe Park (Surrey), Chessington World of Adventures (Surrey), Pleasure Island (Lincolnshire) and Legoland (Windsor).

CINEMAS

There has been a renaissance in the cinema in the last few decades, following a decline in the '60s to '80s, when many cinemas were turned into shops, bingo halls and even places of worship. Today, over 3,500 separate screens are in operation, and cinemas are thriving, with attendances doubling in the last decade. The mainstream cinema scene is dominated by the major chains, which include Cineworld, Odeon and VUE. In the last decade, many multiplexes have been built (often in new out-of-town leisure and shopping complexes) generally with ten or more screens, Dolby or THX surround sound – some have enormous IMAX screens and show films in 3D – plus comfortable, extra-wide seats with ample leg-room in air-conditioned auditoriums. Free parking plus cafés, restaurants, bars and games rooms may also be provided. Cinemas also show classics and foreign-language films, which are usually screened with their original soundtracks and subtitles.

Film Classifications

Classification	Age Restriction
U	None
PG	Parental guidance advised
12a	No one under 12 admitted unless accompanied by an adult
15	No one under 15 admitted
18	No one under 18 admitted

Ticket prices range from around £3 for children's matinees in provincial cinemas up to around £20 for first-run films in London's West End; the average price is around £9 or £10. Most cinemas offer reductions (usually half price or less) for children and pensioners, although you should check in advance, as some reductions only apply to certain performances. Many cinemas have a reduced price day, usually Mondays or Wednesdays, when admittance is cheaper, although discounts may be available on any afternoon. Many modern cinemas have facilities for the disabled.

All films on general release are given a classification by the British Board of Film Censors (shown below), which denotes any age restrictions, as shown below:

Most cinemas accept telephone bookings and tickets can also be purchased in advance, online or in person. All the major cinema chains have websites where you can view trailers and book tickets to collect from a machine at the cinema (and avoid queuing).

There are private film clubs in the major cities and local film societies in all areas, and a number of magazines for film buffs are published. National and local newspapers publish cinema programmes, and most also review the latest films.

THEATRE, OPERA & BALLET

The UK is world-renowned for the quality and variety of its theatre, opera and ballet companies, and London arguably has the world's most vibrant theatre scene, with over 150 commercial and subsidised venues, including around 50 in the West End alone. Between five and ten new major productions open each week, and a much greater number when smaller and fringe venues are included.

Theatre embraces modern drama; classical plays; comedy; musicals; revue and variety; children's shows and pantomime; opera and operetta; ballet and dance. London's fringe theatre is lively and extensive, and provides an excellent training ground for new actors, companies and playwrights. Many venues nationwide support youth theatres, and people of all ages who see themselves as budding Laurence Oliviers and Katherine Hepburns can audition for local amateur dramatics' societies. The theatre is well patronised throughout the country, and is one of the delights of living in the UK, particularly if you live within easy reach of London.

> The cost of tickets for most London musicals and plays ranges from around £25 to over £100 (the most expensive seats for some shows can top £200) and from £10 to £50 for provincial theatres, although agencies such as www.discounttheatre.com sell tickets at reduced prices.

Excellent theatre and musical entertainment isn't, however, confined to London. Many provincial towns also have acclaimed theatres, concert halls and arts centres that attract international stars (and they usually charge only a fraction of London's West End prices). The arts are subsidised by the Arts Council which, among other things, funds a repertory company touring programme that ensures the arts reach areas without permanent theatres.

Opera and ballet are mostly patronised by only a small minority of the middle and upper classes. Ticket prices for performances at the Royal Opera House in Covent Garden partly explain why: a seat in the orchestra stalls costs around £190 to see international stars, despite the fact that it's subsidised by the National Lottery to the tune of some £70m. Prices vary with the production and the particular seats; tickets at the top end of the price range are cheaper for ballet than for opera performances.

In mid-2016, the best seats cost well over £200 for some performances, but if you're prepared to watch from up in 'the gods' or even stand – and book early enough – you can buy a ticket for as little as £10.

Provincial ballet and opera tickets cost far less, e.g. those for the English National Ballet on tour are between £10 and £67, while tickets to the Glyndebourne Touring Opera cost between £17 and £60. Dance performances in general tend to be cheaper than opera. In addition to classical ballet, dance companies are popular and numerous throughout the UK, specialising in everything from contemporary dance to traditional forms from all corners of the globe.

There are usually evening performances from Mondays to Saturdays, and often a matinee performance on one weekday, usually a Wednesday, and Saturdays. There are no performances on Sundays (even actors and actresses are entitled to a day off!).

Most theatres have a number of spaces for wheelchairs, induction loops for the hard of hearing, and toilets for wheelchair users (but mention any special needs when booking). Some theatres produce Braille programmes and brochures, and most allow entrance to guide dogs for the blind. Some theatres have signed performances for the deaf and hard of hearing, but usually only on certain dates. Restaurants and/or bars are a feature of almost all major theatres, and some London and most provincial theatres have private or public car parks nearby. If you wish to have a drink during the interval, it's best to order it in advance before the show starts to avoid the crush.

Free programmes for provincial and London theatres are available from Tourist Information Centres and London theatres also have a number of excellent websites, e.g. www.officiallondontheatre.co.uk and www.londontheatre.co.uk. The official tourist board's Visit Britain Shop has a section devoted to theatre deals, including 2-for-1 tickets (www.visitbritainshop.com).

Most British newspapers contain reviews of London and provincial shows, particularly the quality daily and Sunday newspapers, which have their own theatre critics. London's entertainment magazine, *Time Out,* carries comprehensive reviews and details of all London's shows, as does the *Evening Standard*'s free weekly *ES* magazine.

CONCERTS

Classical concerts are staged regularly throughout the UK by British and international performers, and celebrated international festivals cover orchestral, choral, opera, jazz, folk, rock and world music. London's unrivalled concentration and variety of music venues, and its four major orchestras – the London Symphony Orchestra (LSO), the London Philharmonic Orchestra (LPO), the Royal Philharmonic Orchestra (RPO) and the Philharmonia – make it the music capital of the world. Acclaimed provincial orchestras include those in Birmingham, Manchester and Bournemouth, along with the BBC National Orchestra. The most celebrated classical music season is 'the Proms' (promenade concerts), performed at the Royal Albert Hall, and culminating in the famous 'Last Night of the Proms' concert, which is screened internationally.

Local music societies or music clubs regularly organise concerts and recitals, for which members (or 'friends') receive priority bookings; reduced seat prices; savings on meals, holidays and special events; a free mailing list; and you can even take part in programme planning. Tickets usually range from around £10 to £20. You can become a member or friend of a music society, orchestra or theatre for as little as £10 a year. Free lunchtime organ and choral concerts are performed in cathedrals and churches throughout the year, and free outdoor concerts are staged in summer (a collection is usually made to help meet expenses).

In addition to classical and choral music, just about every other kind is performed regularly somewhere in the UK, including brass and steel band music, country & western, folk, heavy metal, hip hop, house, jazz, indie, medieval, reggae, rock, rhythm and blues, rap and soul music, to mention just a selection. Fans of certain kinds of music, e.g. folk or jazz, can find clubs in most cities, usually with low membership fees. The UK is a world leader in the popular music industry, and London is again the centre of attraction, with more gigs in one night than most provincial cities stage in a month. These range from pub sessions to concerts by mega rock stars who fill Wembley Stadium or the O2 Arena.

Concert ticket prices are generally lower than in many other western countries, although the prices for superstars can be astronomical, costing from £50 to over £200, depending on who's performing, and the venue.

The UK also plays host to some major music festivals in summer, such as Glastonbury and the Reading Festival, although they're attended for the atmosphere as much as for the music, and the British weather means a pair of wellington boots is an essential accessory.

Many publications are dedicated to the popular music industry, most prominently the *New Musical Express*. Classical music magazines have burgeoned in recent years, and include *Classical Music, Gramophone,* and *Early Music Today*.

The online entertainment magazine, *Time Out* (www.timeout.com) provides comprehensive music reviews and lists all concerts in the London area. There are also editions covering Edinburgh and Manchester. Information about provincial concerts is available from local TICs and libraries. Among the many websites of interest to music fans are London Net (www.londonnet.co.uk – all kinds of music, including a free email magazine), Folk and Roots (www.folkandroots.co.uk – folk music) and London Organ (www.londonorgan.co.uk), for organ recitals in and around London.

SOCIAL CLUBS

There are numerous social and other clubs in the UK, including Rotary clubs, working men's clubs, business clubs, church groups, Conservative clubs, Freemasons, international friendship clubs, Kiwani clubs, Labour clubs, Lion and Lioness clubs, Royal Antediluvian Order of Buffaloes (RAOB) clubs, Round Table clubs, ex-servicemen's clubs, sports clubs and women's clubs. Expatriates from a multitude of countries also have their own organisations in major cities and elsewhere (ask at your country's embassy for information), notably American Men's and Women's clubs. The many famous, exclusive and upper crust gentlemen's clubs in London principally exist to enable members to escape from their wives! (There are also exclusive clubs for ladies.)

Clubs exist almost everywhere, focusing on pastimes such as chess, bridge, whist, art, music, theatre, photography, cinema and local history (etc.). If you want to integrate into your local community, one of the best ways is to join a local club. In major cities, there are also singles clubs, some of which operate nationally and organise a comprehensive range of social activities throughout the week. If you're retired, you may find your council publishes a programme of recreational activities for your age group. Most also publish calendars of sports and social events, and information about local groups and associations is available from libraries.

DANCE CLUBS & NIGHTCLUBS

There are dance clubs and nightclubs in all major centres, open until between 2am and 7am, with entrance fees ranging between £10 and £30; admission is often cheaper if you arrive early (before the real action starts). In some clubs, you may not be admitted unless you're a member, on the guest list or have celebrity status. London has one of the most cosmopolitan nightlife scenes to be found anywhere, with venues to suit every taste in music, fashion and atmosphere. As well as clubs specialising in musical genres, e.g. house, reggae, '70s soul, '80s pop, there are salsa and Latin dance clubs, and lapdancing clubs for 'gentlemen' seeking entertainment. There's also a huge variety of gay clubs – information is available from gay websites such as the *Pink News (*www.pinknews.co.uk) and *Time Out* (www.timeout.com)

The dress code is usually smart casual, which usually excludes jeans, leather, T-shirts and trainers, although in some establishments this may be *de rigeur* (fashion usually dictates, depending on the venue). Only clubs with a music or dancing licence can sell alcohol after 11pm.

'Alternative' comedy provides cheap and exciting entertainment, and is popular in London (which has more comedy clubs than any other city in the world) and many provincial cities. Observational, spontaneous and surrealist comedians vie with impressionists and sketch teams nightly for the limelight. Admission is around £5 to £25.

GAMBLING

Gambling is one of the UK's favourite pastimes (sometimes it's an occupation) and embraces horse and greyhound racing; football pools; sweepstakes; the National Lottery; bingo halls; casinos; slot machine (or amusement) arcades; card games; raffles; betting on the results of general elections, public appointments, football matches or other sports events; and forecasting the names of royal babies or ocean liners. You can bet on almost anything, although one bookmaker refused to quote on the date of the end of the world (the punter wanted to pay with a post-dated cheque!).

Your chance of landing the lottery jackpot is 14 million to one against (or 116 million to one for EuroMillions); in fact there's a much greater likelihood you'll be struck down dead by lightning in your own home, although this doesn't prevent millions of Britons playing regularly.

National Lottery: Launched in 1994, the national lottery is operated by Camelot, for whom it has proved a licence to print money. It's the UK's answer to the state lotteries staged by European countries and most US states (the previous national lottery in the UK was suspended in 1826 when the operator absconded with the takings). Lottery tickets cost £2 each and jackpots can be over £20 million when 'rolled over' for a few weeks, while EuroMillions tickets are £2.50 and the jackpot sometimes builds up to over £100 million. 'Rollovers' happen when no one has chosen the six main numbers in the draw and the prize money is added to that of the following week, thus allowing a larger jackpot to build up.

☑ SURVIVAL TIP

If you've a gambling problem, you can get help from Gamblers Anonymous (020-7384 3040, www.gamblersanonymous.org.uk), Gamble Aware (0800-8020 133, www.gambleaware.co.uk) or Gamcare (www.gamcare.org.uk).

Betting Shops: Some of the UK's 10,000 or more turf accountants (usually called betting shops or bookies, short for bookmakers) can be found in just about any town in the country. They were legalised in the '60s to allow off-course betting on horse and greyhound races. You can also bet on horse and greyhound races by post, telephone or online, while on-course tote betting is also popular.

Football Pools: Until the National Lottery was launched, the football pools were the UK's major weekly 'flutter' with a weekly turnover of £900m, and participants can still win huge cash prizes by forecasting (i.e. guessing) the results of football matches. The treble chance is the most popular bet, involving punters guessing which matches will be score draws (matches which end in a draw with each team scoring at least one goal) and prizes can run to around £2 million. Many millions of people, within the UK and around the world, have a weekly flutter on the pools. If you don't want to fill out a coupon each week, you can arrange a regular bet using the same numbers.

Casinos: London is one of the world's most popular gambling centres among the seriously rich, and it comes as no surprise to discover that it's home to over 25 of the UK's some 140 casinos. London casinos have a turnover of over £2 billion a year, although it's much smaller in provincial casinos, where gamblers generally play more often but for smaller stakes. There's a surfeit of online bingo, poker and other gambling websites, which are the equivalent of crack cocaine for gambling addicts.

Premium Bonds: Premium Bonds aren't an investment, as no interest is paid. They're similar to a ticket in a lottery, except that you cannot lose your original investment and can cash in your bonds at any time. The 'possible' premium is in a monthly draw (made by ERNIE, the Premium Bonds computer), which offers prizes ranging from £25 to £1 million (around 1.6 million prizes, totalling over £60 million a month). The minimum initial purchase is £100 after which you can invest £1 at a time, with the maximum holding of £50,000.

Premium bonds can be purchased at any post office, by post or online (www.nsandi.com), and are entered into the next draw after purchase. Results are announced in the national press and are available at main post offices, including a list of unclaimed prizes. You can also check if you're a winner on the website.

Other Forms of Gambling: Other forms of popular gambling include bingo (casinos for housewives, where around 5 million have a weekly flutter in 1,000 commercial bingo clubs), slot-machine arcades (the poor man's Las Vegas) and sweepstakes (the most popular of which is the Irish Sweepstake).

PUBS

The UK is noted for its pubs (an abbreviation of public house), which are a British tradition going back to Roman and Saxon times (drunkenness isn't a new phenomenon – the British have been sots for millennia), when inns were established to meet the needs of travellers. A pub is one of the most welcoming places in the UK, particularly on a freezing winter's night when many have inviting open fires, and represents the heart of many local communities.

According to licensing statistics, there are some 48,000 pubs in the UK (and falling), and every town and many villages have at least one, although numbers have been falling – there were more than 67,000 in the early '80s. A pub is the local meeting place for business and pleasure and, if you arrange to meet a stranger anywhere in the UK, it's invariably at a pub. In recent years, pubs been under increasing pressure, with margins on beer cut to the bone, and falling sales as more people choose to buy cheap alcohol from supermarkets and drink it at home or defect to more fashionable café-bars.

Traditional pubs often have two bars: a 'posh' bar called a 'lounge', 'saloon' or 'private' bar, and a public bar for the riff-raff and those in dirty working clothes (which are sometimes barred from lounge bars by a dress code). The public bar is usually where the darts board, slot machines and other games are to be found. Most modern pubs have only a single large lounge bar.

Most pubs provide reasonably priced hot and cold food at lunchtimes (usually self-service from the bar) and some have excellent *à la carte* restaurants in the evenings. An increasing number serve decent wine and imaginative meals from around £15 (but, alas, too few), although quality is extremely variable. In recent years, so-called gastro pubs have appeared in increasing numbers, serving gourmet food with prices to match. Pub restaurants operate in the same way as any others, and credit cards are usually accepted. Lunch is normally served from noon to 2 or 2.30pm and dinner from 6pm to 9.30pm, although some serve (fast) food all day. A reservation may be necessary for dinner in a popular pub.

British pubs serve a multitude of beers and alcoholic beverages, from continental lagers to traditional British ales, with a total of over 1,000 brands available nationwide. In the last few decades, there has been a revival in traditional or 'real ales', brewed from fresh barley, hops and oats. The British produce the widest range of beers in the world, including many draught beers (on tap) drawn from casks or kegs, such as the ever popular bitter, stout (e.g. Guinness), mild, and a wide variety of continental lagers (many brewed in the UK under licence). In addition to draught beers, numerous bottled and canned beers are also available, including brown ale (Newcastle is the most famous brand name), pale ale, light ale and many more. A recent development has been the spread of 'boutique' beers – beer for connoisseurs that are produced in small quantities by local microbreweries.

Although the UK pays lip service to the metric system, beer is still sold in pints (568ml) and not litres (a small beer is half a pint). Wine is sold by the glass, but there's no law regarding the quantity or size of measures, and many pubs' standard measures are 175ml or even 250ml (one third of a bottle!), rather than the traditional 125ml. Spirits are sold in measures of one-sixth of a gill (24ml) in England and Wales – in Scotland and Northern Ireland, they're larger (free pouring without a measure is virtually unheard of in the UK).

One major difference between the UK and other countries is that in the UK you usually order drinks and bar food at the bar, and pay in cash when you order. You cannot usually 'run a tab' and pay when you leave (or when you fall off your chair), as is common on the continent. Receipts aren't usually provided unless you ask for one, which would be considered very unusual in any other establishment.

Some British pubs are owned by brewery conglomerates and therefore sell beer produced only by their owners. Most, however, are now owned by operating chains, and even those still brewery-owned must, by law, offer 'guest beers'. If you want a pub with a wide selection of the best beers, choose a free house, which is a pub with no brewery ties and therefore free to sell whatever beer it chooses (which usually means the pick of the most popular brands). Most pubs sell an average of around 20 different draught and bottled beers, plus a large variety of spirits, cocktails, soft (non-alcoholic) drinks and a (usually limited) selection of wines.

The Licensing Act 2003, which came into force in 2005, allows pubs in England and Wales to apply to the local council for opening hours of their choice. Bars in restaurants, hotels and other buildings, are generally governed by the same licensing laws as pubs, except when a special licence has been granted.

Many traditional games are played in pubs, including darts, bar billiards, pool, skittles (nine pins), dominoes, and cards. Pinball and similar machines may also feature. You aren't permitted to play games for money, as betting and gambling are illegal in pubs. Some pubs also have full-size snooker tables. Another popular diversion is the pub quiz, which many people take very seriously! Many pubs also have large-screen TVs, where major sports events, particularly soccer matches, are screened. Karaoke evenings are also popular in many pubs, where frustrated would-be pop stars 'perform' their favourite songs.

The legal age for buying and consuming alcohol in a pub is 18, although children aged over 14 are admitted at the discretion of the landlord, and can consume non-alcoholic drinks. Children under 14 are admitted to beer gardens, family rooms, pub restaurants and an increasing number of pub lounges. Pubs can apply for a 'children's certificate' until 9pm or 9.30pm, which allows children to join their parents in the bar for a meal.

The law regarding driving and drinking is strict (see page 163) and the police are particularly active over weekends and holiday periods, such as Christmas and the New Year. If you've had more than a couple of drinks, you would be well advised to hitch a ride with a sober friend or use public transport – for your own safety and that of others.

A wealth of pub guides is published in the UK including *The AA Pub Guide*, the *Good Beer Guide* (CAMRA) and *The Good Pub Guide* (Ebury Press), containing details of over 5,000 pubs (a very long pub crawl), including the type of food served, its quality and price, atmosphere, service, facilities for children and much more. You can also trawl through websites such as www.beerintheevening.com, www.fancyapint.com and www.pub-explorer.com. See also our sister publication, *London's Secrets: Pubs & Bars* (Survival Books).

RESTAURANTS & CAFÉS

The standard of restaurant food in the UK varies considerably, probably more so than almost anywhere else in the world. Most foreigners are familiar with the infamous (and previously well-deserved) image of a country full of 'greasy spoon' establishments (specialising in fried food and overcooked vegetables), which still lingers on in some places.

However, there has been a revolution in UK catering in the last few decades and there's now a plethora of excellent restaurants offering a quality and variety of culinary delights hardly bettered anywhere in the world. In fact, top class restaurants are usually excellent, and sometimes outstanding. You need only to open the pages of the latest *Michelin Red Guide Great Britain & Ireland* to realise that British food doesn't always live up (or down) to its dreadful reputation.

On the negative side, prices for good food are often astronomical (wine can also be *very* expensive), and even modest food can be costly, particularly in London. UK restaurant prices are routinely twice as high as what you would expect to pay in other western countries.

Despite being synonymous with junk food, 'fast' or 'take-away' (take out) food can be very good, and comes in an amazing variety. Most take-away establishments accept telephone orders, and an increasing number make home deliveries (e.g. pizzas).

> **☑ SURVIVAL TIP**
>
> The British are notoriously bad tippers and many would like to see the practice officially abolished. Many restaurants now include a voluntary service charge (10 to 20 per cent), all or part of which may go to the staff. Feel free to ask staff whether they receive the service charge, and if not, have it removed from the bill and pay a tip in cash. The same applies when adding a tip to a credit card payment – staff **ALWAYS** prefer customers to give tips in cash.

Britain doesn't have a café culture like most other major European countries – drinking coffee in the rain doesn't have the same appeal as it does on a sunny sidewalk in Paris or Rome – but nevertheless, British towns have plenty of places where you can enjoy a coffee and croissant and watch the world go by.

There has been a flood of café openings in recent years, with large chains such as Starbucks (www.starbucks.co.uk), Costa Coffee (www.costa.co.uk) and Caffé Nero (www.caffenero.com) having outlets on almost every street corner. Smaller, owner-operated cafés may provide a more cosmopolitan environment to relax in, usually with pavement seating; and many offer homemade food (rather than the plastic fare dished up by the chains), although it can be hit and miss – but once you've found your local café heaven it's likely to become a regular haunt.

The best bets for those wishing to eat well and cheaply are British pubs (pub grub, or bar food, is usually served at lunchtime only, e.g. noon to 2pm) and ethnic restaurants, particularly Chinese, Indian, Greek, Turkish and Italian, where the standard of food, although not uniform, is usually high, and a meal costs around £10 to £20 a head (without wine). A medium-priced restaurant will set you back around £30 a head, plus drinks.

London is now one of the world's great eating capitals, rivalling Paris and New York for quality and ethnic variety, although not for value for money. When you find really good food, it's usually outrageously expensive, and paying £75 to £150 (or more) a head for a meal isn't unusual if you want the very best. The UK has a lot to learn from the continent about good food that doesn't cost the earth.

Most restaurants are licensed to serve alcohol, but only with meals. The cost of wine can also be astronomical, with a mark-up of 200 per cent commonplace. Many restaurants charge up to three times the shop price for branded wine, or offer cheap plonk in make-believe, own-label bottles or in carafes. Unfortunately, 'bring your own' (BYO) restaurants are rare in the UK (where are all the enterprising Aussies?).

Many restaurants offer set-price menus at lunchtime (usually from noon to 2pm), usually offering a choice of two or three courses for £10 to £15. Some offer half-portions for children or have a children's menu. Children of all ages are usually admitted to licensed restaurants, although few restaurants cater particularly for children (without their own credit cards). Some restaurants provide separate vegetarian and diabetic menus (some even provide healthy low-fat meals). Cafés in the UK, unlike those in most continental countries, aren't usually licensed to sell alcohol unless they're one of the burgeoning numbers of café-restaurants.

Many department stores, galleries and museums have excellent value-for-money restaurants, often providing breakfast and lunch menus. Cheap meals are also provided by the YWCA and YMCA, the YHA, community centres and leisure centres. It's advisable to make a reservation for popular restaurants, particularly for Friday and Saturday evenings, and at any time for parties of more than four people.

All restaurants and cafés are obliged by law to display their tariffs where customers can see them before entering. If an establishment has an extensive *à la carte* menu, the prices of a representative selection of food and drink available must be displayed, in addition to any *table d'hôte* menu. All service or cover charges must also be clearly stated, and prices shown must be inclusive of VAT.

If you've a complaint regarding anything stated (or not stated) in a menu, or there's a big difference between what's stated and what you're served or charged, you can make a complaint to a local Trading Standards Officer.

Your best bet is to reach a compromise with the manager or owner, and negotiate a reduction to take into account your complaint. You can legally refuse to pay for anything inedible, and insist on leaving, but must leave your name and address (and show proof of identity). If you do this, the management cannot prevent you leaving, or call the police, as you've committed no offence.

There are plenty of good restaurant guides published in the UK. However, many (like most hotel guides) charge restaurants for entry, including *Les Routiers*, the AA and the RAC, which has led critics to question their impartiality. Even some motorway service stations are included in *Les Routiers*! Among those that don't charge for inclusion are the *Michelin Red Guide, Harden's London Restaurants and Harden's UK Restaurant Guide* (Harden Ltd) and the *Waitrose Good Food Guide* (www.thegoodfoodguide.co.uk). See also our sister publications, *London for Foodies, Gourmets & Gluttons* and *London's Best Cafés, Coffee Shops & Tearooms.*

London by night

16. SPORTS

Sports facilities are generally excellent throughout the UK, whether you're a complete novice or an experienced competitor. Among the most popular sports are soccer (football), rugby (union and league rules), cricket, athletics, fishing, snooker, horse racing, motor racing, golf, hiking, cycling, squash, badminton, tennis, swimming and skiing, many of which were British inventions. Most water (sailing, windsurfing, waterskiing, canoeing, yachting) and aerial sports (hang-gliding, parachuting, ballooning, gliding, light aircraft flying) also enjoy a keen following.

The sports industry is big business, and new sports facilities and complexes, including golf clubs, yacht marinas, indoor tennis clubs, dry-slope ski centres, fitness and country clubs have sprouted in all areas. They're all part of a huge growth market which is expected to gain even greater momentum in the coming years, as more people retire early and have more time for leisure and sport (ironically, many other people won't be able to afford to retire at all). Many sports owe their popularity (and fortunes) to television and the increased TV coverage and competition for TV rights from cable and satellite TV stations. Both professional and amateur sports have benefited hugely in recent years from the increase in the commercial sponsorship of individual events, teams and league competitions.

The vast majority of sports facilities are 'pay-as-you-play', which means you don't need to join a club or enrol in a course to use them, although there are also many private clubs where you pay an annual membership fee. Participation in most sports is inexpensive, and most towns have a community sports or leisure centre, financed and run by the local council. District, borough and county councils publish free directories of clubs in their area, and regional sports councils provide information about local activities.

Sports results are given on various websites such as the BBC (see below), and published widely in daily newspapers (which also have excellent websites); the Sunday broadsheet newspapers provide comprehensive cover and a nationwide results service (particularly for soccer and rugby). Numerous magazines are published for all sports, from angling to yachting, most of which are available (or can be ordered) from any newsagent.

The names and addresses of sports associations and federations can be obtained from Sports England or the Sport and Recreation Alliance (see box). Good general websites for sports information and results include the BBC (http://news.bbc.co.uk/sport) and Sporting Life (www.sportinglife.com).

For information about sports facilities, contact Sport England (0845-850 8508, www.sportengland.org) or the Sport and Recreation Alliance (020-7976 3900, www.sportandrecreation.org.uk), which is the national association of governing bodies of sport and recreation in the UK.

AERIAL SPORTS

Most aerial sports have a wide following, particularly gliding, hang-gliding, paragliding, hot-air ballooning and microliting. The main thing most aerial sports enthusiasts have in common is madness and money, both of which are usually required in abundance to fulfil man's ultimate ambition, although there are a number of inexpensive options available. One of these is hang-gliding, which has become increasingly popular in recent years, with hang-gliding schools in all regions.

Paragliding is one of the cheapest and easiest ways to 'fly', and entails launching yourself off a steep mountain slope with a paraglider, or being tow-launched by a vehicle. Paragliding equipment costs from around £750 secondhand to £4,000 new. It's as well to bear in mind that every landing is a 'controlled crash' and to have insurance to cover all eventualities.

Hot-air ballooning has a small, but dedicated band of wealthy followers due to the high cost of balloons, although the sport has never enjoyed greater popularity. A flight in a balloon costs around £100 and is a marvellous experience, although there's no guarantee of distance or duration, as flights are dependent on wind conditions and the skill of your pilot (not to mention a safe landing).

Aircraft and gliders (sailplanes) can be hired with or without an instructor (provided you've a pilot's licence) from most small airfields. A new plane can cost anything from £50,000 to £100,000, although shared-ownership schemes are bringing the joys of flying to a much wider audience. There are many gliding clubs, and parachuting and free-fall parachuting (sky-diving) flights or jumps can be made from most private airfields.

Microlights and ultralights (a go-cart with a hang glider on top and a motorised tricycle below) are an excellent alternative to 'real'

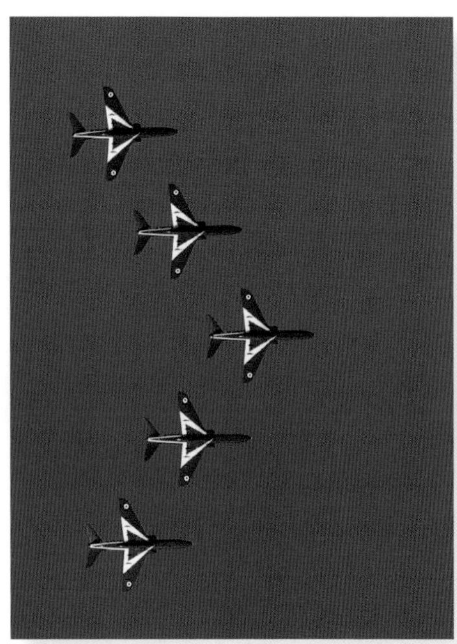

aircraft, as they can be assembled and disassembled quickly, are easily transported and cheap to run. It's one of the cheapest and most enjoyable ways of experiencing real flying, costing from around £3,000 for a secondhand machine up to £40,000 for a new dual-seat, top-of-the-range craft. Fliers require a private pilot's licence that costs up to £2,000 in tuition fees and normally takes up to six months and 40 hours of instruction to obtain, including classroom training and written examinations.

CRICKET

Cricket is a peculiarly English sport which usually takes foreigners some time to understand. (Many British people don't understand the finer points, including your author). If you don't know the difference between a stump and a bail, or an over and a wicket, you may as well skip this bit, as any attempt to explain would take around 100 pages and almost certainly end in failure.

The first-class cricket season in England runs from April to September, when the main competition is for the County Championship, competed for by 18 county teams organised into two divisions. Matches are played over four days, many of which are drawn, owing to the vagaries of English weather. In addition to the County Championships, county teams also compete in the Royal London One-Day Cup, where limited-over matches are played in one day; and in a one-day knockout competition, the Friends Life t20. Limited-over cricket has become increasingly popular in recent years.

In addition to the first-class County Championship, there's a Minor Counties Championship (Eastern and Western Divisions), a Second XI Championship and a multitude of village, school, university, pub and women's teams, who compete at all levels throughout England and Wales. Scotland and Ireland also have cricket teams, although they (wisely) don't take the game seriously. There's an England ladies cricket team (who've been doing rather well lately but have a difficult job getting men to take them seriously), and the game is played at all levels by women and girls throughout the UK. For those who wish to play with a straighter bat or brush up on their googly technique, there are cricket schools and coaching courses in many areas.

Cricket is played at international level (called test matches) by a number of Commonwealth countries, including Australia, India, New Zealand, Pakistan, South Africa, Sri Lanka, the West Indies and Zimbabwe. During the English cricket season the England cricket team is usually engaged in one or two minor series of international matches (three tests) or a major series (five or six tests). If you think four days (county matches) is a long time for a single match to last, a test match lasts five days, usually with a rest day after two or three days' play. One-day internationals are also played.

The England cricket team also undertakes overseas tours during the English winter, when it plays a series of test matches. The old enemy (in cricketing terms) are the Aussies (Australians), with whom England compete every few years for the Ashes (which aren't human, but the burnt remains of an old cricket bail from the early days of international cricket). A world cup knockout competition also takes place every four years.

One of the best cricket websites is Wisden (www.bloomsbury.com/uk/special-interest/wisden), publishers of *Wisden Cricketers' Almanac* since 1864, while that of the England and Wales Cricket Board (www.ecb.co.uk) is equally indispensable.

CYCLING

Cycling is not as popular in the UK as it is on the continent, and not much more than 2.5 per cent of journeys are made by bicycle in the UK, compared to an average of around 20 per cent in Denmark and over 25 per cent in Holland. Most people buy cycles for shopping or getting around towns, rather than cycling purely for pleasure, exercise or sport, e.g. touring or racing. However, the sport of cycling has undergone something of a renaissance in recent years, since the successes of British cyclists in the 2012 and 2016 Olympic games and, especially, of Sir Bradley Wiggins who won the Tour de France in 2012 and Chris Froome who won the Tour in 2013, 2015 and 2016. Competitive cycling embraces road and track racing, cycle speedway, time-trialling, cross-country racing, touring, BMX, bicycle polo, mountain biking and bicycle moto-cross.

> **▲ Caution**
>
> The growing popularity of cycling in recent years has led to an increase in the number of accidents with motor vehicles, particularly lorries (trucks), and especially in cities. It's important not to underestimate the dangers of cycling (especially for children) on the UK's overcrowded roads.

A wide range of cycles is available to suit all pockets and needs, ranging from a basic shopping bike costing around £100 to a professional racing bike costing thousands. In between these extremes are commuter or town bikes, touring bikes, mountain bikes, BMX bikes, tricycles, tandems and bicycles with folding frames. Before buying a bike, carefully consider your needs, both present and future, obtain expert advice (e.g. from a specialist cycle store) and shop around for the best deal. Ensure that you purchase a bike with the correct frame size. Mountain bikes have become increasingly popular in recent years, and cost from around £150 up to £4,000 (expect to pay around £200 to £300 for an adequate bike).

Bicycles can also be hired by the day or week from cycle shops in cities and tourist areas; costs vary considerably, but are usually from around £5 to £10 per day, depending on the type of bike (town, touring or mountain) and the area. Boris Bikes – the nickname for London's bike sharing scheme – are especially popular in the capital where four-wheel transport often grinds to a halt. Tandems, tricycles and folding bikes can also be hired in some areas.

There are an increasing number of cycle paths in the UK, from traffic-free routes, e.g. canal side towpaths, to cycle lanes on local roads. Sustrans, a charity devoted to sustainable transport, runs the National Cycle Network which was first set up in 1995 using funding from the National Lottery 'Millennium Fund' and now maintains more than 14,000mi (20,530km) of cycling and walking routes around the UK; check out the Sustrans website (www.sustrans.org.uk/ncn/map/national-cycle-network) to buy a route map or find maps of local routes near you.

If you're interested in joining a cycling club, your local library can provide information about local clubs or you can contact British Cycling (0161-274 2000, www.britishcycling.org.uk). Keen cyclists may be interested in joining the Cyclists Touring Club (0844-736 8450 or 01483-238 337, www.ctc.org.uk), which is the UK's national cyclists' association with local groups throughout the UK. The CTC campaigns for the rights and safety of cyclists on the road, and publishes a range of booklets to help get you on the road. Membership includes free third party insurance, legal aid, technical advice, touring information and a bi-monthly magazine. The CTC also operates a bicycle insurance scheme.

An interesting magazine for those who live in the London area is *The London Cyclist*, published bi-monthly by the London Cycling Campaign (020-7234 9310, www.lcc.org.uk). Other useful books include *Cycling for Dummies* by Gavin Wright & Ben Williams and the *Big Book of Cycling for Beginners* by Tori Bortman (Rodale), while Ordnance Survey publishes a series of local touring maps suitable for cyclists.

Local cycling guides and maps are published by councils, conservation and cycling groups in many areas, who also publish safety booklets and brochures for children. Many magazines are published for cyclists, including *Cycling Plus*, *Cycling Weekly*, *Cycle Sport* and *Mountain Biking UK*.

FISHING

Fishing (or angling) facilities are superb in the UK, where fishing is the largest participant sport in the country with over 4 million anglers. The country has a huge variety of well-stocked waters, and some of the best salmon and trout (brown, sea and rainbow) fishing in the world. In addition to the many rivers and lakes (or lochs in Scotland), trout fishing is possible at over 160 reservoirs. Scotland is world-famous for its salmon fishing (and its scotch).

There are three types of fishing in the UK: sea, game and coarse fishing. Sea fishing is simply fishing in the open sea, while game fishing takes place at managed fisheries stocked with trout or salmon. Coarse fishing is the most popular form of fishing, and is common in designated rivers or man-made waters for many species of fish, including bream, carp, perch, pike, tench and trout. Coarse fishermen use live bait such as maggots and worms, and none of the fish caught are killed, but are returned to the water (after being weighed and recorded in the case of competitions).

The close season, which is the period when fishing isn't permitted, varies for different species of fish, and between the various River Authorities who are responsible for recreational fishing. Always check when the close season is before fishing anywhere in the UK.

In England and Wales, you must obtain a fishing permit (called a rod licence) for fresh-water fishing. A non-migratory trout and coarse fish rod licence for the full 2016-17 season costs £27 for an adult and £5 for a junior, and a one-day licence £3.75. An adult's salmon and sea trout licence costs £72. Licences are obtainable from fishing tackle suppliers, hotels and online from the Environment Agency (www.environment-agency.gov.uk). Once you've obtained a rod licence, you must obtain permission to fish from the owner of the water, which usually entails paying a membership fee or buying a ticket (a day permit costs around £2 or £3 a day in some areas), while in some ponds or lakes, fishing may be free. Shops selling angling equipment should be able to advise on the possibilities to be found locally. You can find UK fisheries on the Fisheries website (www.fisheries.co.uk).

Deep-sea and coastal fishing are free, apart from sea trout and salmon fishing, which is only permitted with a licence. In some areas, 24-hour recorded telephone information is provided about fishing conditions and river levels, and fishing platforms are provided for disabled anglers. Ask at Tourist Information Centres for details.

When sea fishing from the shore (e.g. from rocks), be careful where you position yourself, as in some areas it's possible to be stranded by rising tides or swept out to sea and drowned!

Rod licences aren't required in Scotland, although written permission must be obtained from the water's owner to fish for salmon or sea trout, or to fish in freshwater for other species. Each district in Scotland has its own close season for salmon fishing, which is generally from the end of August to the end of February. Information regarding permits can be obtained from local Tourist Information Centres. In

Northern Ireland; a licence is required for each rod for game fishing (see www.nidirect.gov.uk/angling). Permission to fish is also required from the owner of the water, which usually means taking out short-term membership of a local fishing organisation or buying a day ticket.

Many monthly or bimonthly magazines are published for anglers in the UK and there are numerous websites, including Go Fishing (www.gofishing.co.uk), a joint venture by some of the leading magazines, including the *Angling Times*, with news, tips and an anglers' forum.

FOOTBALL (SOCCER)

Soccer (or Association Football, as it's officially called) is the UK's national spectator and participation sport. All major British cities have a professional or semi-professional soccer team, and most towns and villages have a number of amateur clubs (well over 40,000 in total) catering for all ages and standards. Most professional clubs and leagues are sponsored, and professional players wear the name of their sponsor on their shirts. The league season in the UK officially runs from August to May, although professional soccer seems to be expanding continually in one way or another, and there's no mid-season winter break (unlike in most other European countries).

Most matches are played on Saturdays, although some clubs play regularly on Friday evenings, and there are also mid-week matches (Tue-Wed) and Sunday and Monday evening Barclays Premier League and Football League Championship matches, many of which are televised live on Sky TV or BT Sport (see **Chapter 8**). It isn't necessary to buy a ticket in advance for most matches, although Premier League games, local derbies (matches between neighbouring clubs) and cup matches are usually 'all-ticket', meaning that tickets must be purchased in advance.

In England, the English Football League (EFL) is the world's oldest league competition (instituted in 1888), which now consists of three divisions (the Championship, Division 1 and Division 2) with a total of 72 clubs (24 in each division). However, the top league is the FA Premier League, consisting of the top 20 clubs, formed when the first division clubs in the EFL broke away in 1992. The bottom three Premier League clubs are relegated to the Championship each season and the top three Championship teams promoted in their place. The Premiership has created a huge gulf between its top clubs and those in the lower leagues; relegation from the Premier League costs a club over £50 million in lost revenue from TV, sponsorship, advertising and ticket sales (and also the loss of a club's best players).

David Beckham

In Scotland, a Premier division was established in 1975/76 to improve competition and increase gate receipts by restricting the league to the top ten clubs, who play each other four times a season (a total of 36 matches each).

The cost of tickets in England has risen at well over double the rate of inflation in recent years, to fund expensive new all-seat stadia, and superstars costing £50 million or more (in 2016 Paul Pogba cost

Manchester United some £100 million including agent's fees), and tickets now average well over £50 for Premier League games, with tickets to watch the top teams fetching the largest premium. Season tickets are even more expensive, and prices vary wildly. English Premier League fans pay from around £300 to over £1,000 (Arsenal), or up to four times that of some of their continental counterparts. However, the high price of tickets doesn't seem to deter supporters, and many Premier League clubs sell out every home game, although it has priced many traditional working class fans out of the game.

Thanks to the millions pumped into soccer by sponsors and TV companies in recent years, top British clubs now compete with the richest Italian and Spanish clubs for the best foreign players. British football has been revitalised over the past decade, although it has had a detrimental effect on the development of home-grown stars (some Premier League teams regularly field only one or two English players). It's often cheaper to buy top-class players abroad than in the UK, and many clubs have resorted to doing this, as prices for home-grown (British) players have skyrocketed.

Transfer fees of £10-20 million are commonplace, and top players command fees in excess of £30m. This has also put severe pressure on clubs' wage bills: salaries have gone through the roof since the Bosman ruling removed transfer fees for players who've reached the end of their contracts. Premier League salaries are typically £25,000 to £50,000 per week, but many players receive over double this, and the top players can earn £200,000 a week or more (nice work if you can get it!).

The Scottish League has three divisions, each with ten clubs. Northern Ireland has the semi-professional Irish League, and Wales the amateur Welsh League (although two Welsh teams, Cardiff and Wrexham, play professional football in the English Football League and Swansea City play in the Premiership).

In addition to national league football, the UK also has a number of national cup competitions. In England, the main knockout competition is the FA Cup, instituted in 1871 and open to amateur clubs, the final of which is played at Wembley Stadium. Cup final tickets cost from £50 to £115 but can easily go for around £1,000 or more a pair on the black market. Other national cup competitions in England include the English Football League (EFL) Cup, in which all league clubs take part, and various other competitions for professional teams in the lower divisions of the Football League.

There are dozens of websites devoted to football, including www.football.co.uk, www.bbc.co.uk/football, www.premierleague.com and the Scottish Premiership website (http://spfl.co.uk).

The FA Community Shield is competed for in an annual match between the FA Premier League champions and the FA Cup winners at Wembley on the weekend before the start of the English football season. In Scotland, teams compete for the Scottish FA Cup and the Scottish League Cup, which opens the Scottish football season. There are also cup competitions in Northern Ireland and Wales. British clubs also participate in European cup competitions, including the Champions League (for national league winners and other top–placed teams) and the EUFA Europa League for top-placed teams that don't qualify for the Champions League and domestic cup winners.

The English football league is among the most competitive in the world, and even matches between teams from the top and bottom of divisions are usually keenly contested. English teams have had considerable success in Europe the last few decades, despite the fact that top English clubs usually play many more matches than clubs in other European countries.

GOLF

There are over 3 million golfers and around 2,500 courses in the UK, including private and practice courses. Scotland, where golf originated in the 15th century, has many of the UK's most beautiful courses (including links courses) and boasts no fewer than seven world-famous championship courses. There are public (municipal) and private courses throughout the UK, and although golf is a relatively expensive sport, you don't have to be a millionaire to play (unless you spend all day at the 19th hole!). No membership is required to play on a public golf course, although it's advisable to book in advance. In some areas there are few public courses – or indeed none at all – but private clubs may allow visitors to play, although usually only during weekdays (and provided they're members of a club elsewhere and have a handicap certificate).

Green fees (the cost of a round) are reasonable at most public clubs, averaging around £10 per round (18 holes), although fees at top courses are between £30 and £50 per round. Fees are usually increased by around 20 to 25 per cent at weekends and on public holidays. The Direct Tee Times UK website (www.direct-teetimes.co.uk) allows you to book a round of golf online at courses throughout the UK.

The top private golf clubs are often difficult to join and expensive (there's huge snob appeal in belonging to a fashionable club), running into £thousands a year for the best clubs. They usually have strict dress rules, both on the course and in the clubhouse. Many private golf clubs are part of a larger country club or hotel sports complex, which may include a luxury hotel, restaurant, bar, tennis, squash, swimming pool, snooker and clay pigeon shooting.

Many golf clubs have driving ranges and most also have professionals (instructors) to help reduce the number of balls you lose. Driving ranges are also provided in most areas, with all-weather floodlit bays, practice bunkers and putting greens.

Crazy golf, approach golf, pitch and putt and putting greens are provided in many areas for those who set their sights a little lower than winning The Open, and are often features of public parks.

Numerous golf books are published, including the *Golf Course Guide* (AA Publishing), *Golf is not a Game of Perfect* by Robert J. Rotella (Pocket Books) and *Finally: The Golf Swing's Simple Secret* (JT & SM). Good websites include www.golf.co.uk, www.golfingguides.net and www.ukgolfguide.com.

GYMNASIA & HEALTH CLUBS

There are gymnasia and health and fitness clubs in most towns, where sadists are employed and masochists go to torture themselves. Working out is popular and some companies provide their own health and leisure centres or pay for corporate membership for staff. In addition to many private clubs, most public sports and leisure centres have tons (or

> Health and fitness clubs are a huge growth market, which includes chains such as Fitness First (www.fitnessfirst.co.uk), Nuffield Health (www.nuffieldhealth.com/gyms) and Virgin Active (www.virginactive.co.uk), although they can be expensive. Cheaper alternatives include Pure Gym (www.puregym.com), a no-frills chain open 24 hours with low monthly membership charges and no contract tie-in, Xercise4Less (www.xercise4less.co.uk) and The Gym Group (www.thegymgroup.com).

tonnes) of expensive bone-jarring, muscle-wrenching apparatus, designed to get you into shape or kill you in the attempt. A good gymnasium or health club will carry out a physical assessment before letting you loose (dead punters aren't good for business).

When choosing a gym there are many factors to take into account which may include ambience, spaciousness, architectural wow-factor, cleanliness, experience and friendliness of staff, range and quality of equipment, variety of fitness classes, sports facilities on offer, range of spa facilities and treatments, social events, level of care for the well-being of members, and many more.

Most local sports and leisure centres have a health and fitness club, or circuit training and exercise rooms, where supervised weight training sessions are held (single sex and mixed). Membership isn't usually necessary, although it may include preferential booking facilities and the free use of equipment at certain times. Peak use of the fitness room is around £5 per session on a casual basis, and there's often a lower charge during off-peak times (usually 9am to 5pm, Mondays to Fridays).

Many sports and leisure centres also provide a huge variety of exercise classes, including t'ai chi and other martial arts; high impact (energetic) and low impact (gentle) aerobics classes (e.g. callanetics); Pilates and yoga; spinning (cycling classes); aqua-aerobics (in the swimming pool); and various dance classes. Some centres organise dance and exercise classes for all ages and levels of fitness (from beginners to triathlon competitors), during the daytime (including weekends) and evenings. Always check the class standard before enrolling.

Many local authorities are investing in outdoor gym equipment set up in public parks. These are generally well equipped and maintained and are free to use. Check with your local council or search for your nearest outdoor gym with the Great Outdoor Gym Company website (www.tgogc.com). Many local authorities also have reasonably priced indoor gyms and swimming pools, with membership from around £25 per month, as do the YMCA (www.ymca.org.uk).

The cost of membership of a private club varies considerably, depending on the area, the facilities provided and the local competition. Exclusive private members' clubs are eye-wateringly expensive – £thousands a year – while others are very reasonable, although you can easily pay £20 per session (e.g. in London). Nowadays many gyms don't even require you to be a member with no sign-up or monthly fees, and you can pay-as-you-go or pay for a number of sessions. Clubs are usually open seven days a week from 6-8am until around 10pm (or even 24 hours), with reduced hours at weekends.

HIKING

Whether you call it walking, rambling, hiking or orienteering, getting from A to B for fun and pleasure is extremely popular, and is the most common form of exercise; what's more, it's free! In England and Wales, there's a total network of over 137,000mi (220,000km) of public footpaths, bridleways (paths fit for horse riders, but not vehicles) and byways, which is more than in any other country in the world. Many paths have been joined to form continuous well-marked, long-distance routes or national trails, as they're known in England and Wales (the longest is 600mi/1,000km). In Scotland, the law differs for the moment (see below); walkers there generally have an absolute right of access to uncultivated land, unless there's proven danger to walkers or wildlife.

General information about walking is provided by a wealth of websites, including www.walkingbritain.com, www.walking-routes.co.uk, www.walking-uk.com and www.walkingworld.com. An excellent source for walking books is www.walking-books.com.

Public rights of way grew up as part of the ancient communications system, in use long before any form of transport was invented; and landowners must, by law, give walkers the right of passage across their land, which is fine in theory. Recent campaigns by walkers have led to clashes with landowners and farmers, some of whom will go to any lengths to deny walkers access to their land. The government reluctantly decided that the Country Landowners Association and its 50,000 members (who are estimated to own over half of the countryside in England and Wales) would never allow access to their land voluntarily, and passed the Countryside and Rights of Way Act 2000, giving people more rights to roam.

In addition to the thousands of miles of public footpaths, there are 14 national parks in England and Wales, established to protect the UK's finest landscapes from developers and provide people with the opportunity to use and enjoy the open countryside. There are no national parks in Scotland (the whole country is practically a national park), but it has 40 National Scenic Areas, occupying one eighth of the country, and offering some of the most beautiful and unspoilt walking in Europe.

Hiking paths are signposted (or waymarked as it's called in 'hiking talk') by signs showing the destination and sometimes the distance. In England and Wales, national trails are waymarked with an acorn symbol, while in Scotland, long-distance footpaths are waymarked by a thistle symbol. When following a path, you should look out for waymarks and use a map (see below). In England and Wales, paths are often signposted where they join roads, but many footpaths or tracks may be indicated only by arrows (yellow for footpaths, blue for bridleways and red for byways), or by special markers if the path is used as a recreational route.

Orienteering is popular, and is a combination of hiking and a treasure hunt or competitive navigation on foot. It isn't necessary to be super fit, and the only equipment that's required (in addition to suitable walking attire) is a detailed map and compass. For information, contact British Orienteering (01629-583037, www.britishorienteering.org.uk).

If you're interested in joining a walking club, contact the Ramblers Association (020-7339 8500, www.ramblers.org.uk), which promotes rambling, protects rights of way, campaigns for access to open country, and defends the beauty of the countryside against those who would destroy it for financial gain. It has over 300 local groups throughout the UK and members receive a quarterly magazine, a yearbook, equipment discounts, free membership of their local ramblers group, and the opportunity to participate in numerous walks with experienced guides. Its Go Walking search facility (www.ramblers.org.uk/go-walking.aspx) enables you to find walking events, groups and routes in your area.

In many towns and country areas, guided local walks are conducted throughout the year (which may be part of a comprehensive programme of walks), ranging from sightseeing tours of towns to walks around local beauty spots, for which there may be a small fee.

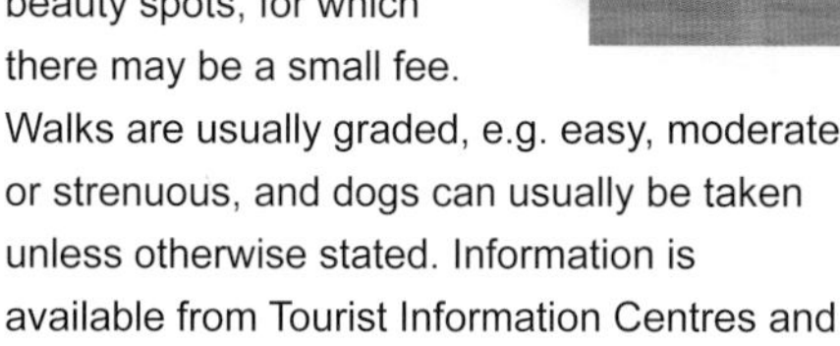

Walks are usually graded, e.g. easy, moderate or strenuous, and dogs can usually be taken unless otherwise stated. Information is available from Tourist Information Centres and local libraries.

MOTORSPORTS

Motor racing has a huge following, and embraces everything from Formula One (F1) grand prix to stock car racing. Among the many classifications of motor racing in the UK are Formulas One, Two and Three; Formula 3000; sports car and Formula Ford racing; rallying; hill-climbing; historic sports car racing; competitions among special one-make series (such as Mazda MX-5); autocross; go-karting; and bantam racing for kids.

The most famous British motor racing venues include Brands Hatch (01474-872331, www.brandshatch.co.uk), Donington Park (01332-810048, www.donington-park.co.uk), Goodwood (01243-755060, www.goodwood.com) and Silverstone (01327-320280, www.silverstone.co.uk), host of the British Grand Prix. The British Grand Prix is one of the UK's most expensive sporting events; entrance and a grandstand seat will cost hundreds.

Regular race meetings are also held at Caldwell Park, Castle Combe, Donington Park, Oulton Park, Snetterton and Thruxton Park. National hot rod, saloon, stock car and banger racing also arouse enthusiasm among the young. Meetings are held on most Saturdays during the main season, which runs from April to October at stadia throughout the country.

Motorcycle racing is almost as popular and includes grand prix racing for 125cc, 250cc, 350cc and 500cc bikes and superbikes over 1,000cc. The Isle of Man Tourist Trophy circuit is the UK's most famous (or infamous) race. It takes place on public roads around the island and lacks the safety features (and the fast-acting emergency services) found at purpose-built circuits, which has led to the deaths of many riders over the years. Other forms of motorcycling with a large following include sidecar and speedway racing, scrambling and moto-cross. Speedway is held at stadia around the UK from March to August.

A number of magazines are dedicated to motorsports in the UK, such as *Autosport* (www.autosport.magazine.co.uk) and *Motorsport* (www.motorsportmagazine.co.uk), and many websites, including www.autosport.com, www.fia.com, www.motorsport.co.uk and www.f1-racing.org.

RACKET SPORTS

There are excellent facilities for most racket sports, particularly badminton, squash, racketball and tennis. There are two main types of racket sport centres: public leisure centres and private clubs. Many leisure centres have around six squash courts (also used for racketball) and a number of badminton courts. Some have indoor tennis courts, although these aren't usually permanently available as halls are also used for other sports.

There are also private clubs for most racket sports, particularly squash and tennis. Court fees are reasonable, although annual membership fees may be high. Some private clubs are highly exclusive (e.g. Queens Club and Wimbledon), and it's difficult to join unless you've excellent connections, pots of money or are famous (preferably all three). If you're an advanced player, you may find the level of competition is higher at private clubs than at community leisure centres.

To find the racket clubs in your local area, search online, look in the Yellow Pages (www.yell.com, or enquire at your local library.

Andy Murray

Tennis

Despite the popularity of tennis as a spectator sport (particularly Wimbledon), actually playing tennis isn't very popular in the UK, largely because it isn't much fun in the cold and rain. Indoor tennis courts are relatively scarce and prohibitively expensive, and are a necessity in the depths of a British winter. More indoor courts are, however, being built all the time. The cost of hiring an indoor tennis court at a sports centre is from £10 to £20 an hour, depending on the time of day (short tennis on a reduced size court can also be played in some sports centres).

Most local councils and some private sports centres provide a number of outdoor hard and grass courts (clay courts aren't common), which can be hired for around £5-£10 an hour (adults) or from around £2 an hour for under-16s. Some centres have outdoor courts with artificial surfaces which can be used in all weathers, and some parks and most sports centres have floodlit outdoor courts.

If you're a serious tennis player you may be interested in joining a private club. Costs vary, but can be relatively high, e.g. an enrolment fee plus an annual subscription (or a monthly fee) for membership of an exclusive tennis club, with indoor and outdoor courts. Many private clubs also have gymnasia and swimming pools that can be used by members for an increased payment. Sports centres and private clubs usually have coaches available for private or group lessons. National, county and local tennis competitions are held at all levels for both sexes.

For further information about tennis in the UK, contact the Lawn Tennis Association (020-8487 7000, www.lta.org.uk).

Squash

Squash (or more correctly squash rackets) has been declining in popularity since its heyday in the '80s, but is still widely played and there's an abundance of courts in leisure centres and private squash clubs in all areas. England has a larger number of players and courts than any other country in the world and boasts many of the world's top players. Private clubs usually cater exclusively for squash, and clubs combining squash and tennis (or some other sport) are rare. Many private squash clubs have a resident coach.

The cost of hiring a court in a sports centre is from around £10 for a 40-45 minute session (off-peak rates may be lower). Annual membership of a private squash club varies from around £50 to £150 a year; off-peak, family and junior membership may also be available. Court fees are usually around the same or a little lower than municipal courts, although there may be an extra charge for guests.

Racquetball, an American version of squash, can be played on squash courts in the UK, and rackets and balls can be hired from some squash clubs.

Squash is an energetic sport and you should think twice before taking it up in middle age, particularly if you're unfit, have high blood pressure, or a heart or respiratory problem (many sports deaths in the UK occur on squash courts!). Players of any age should get fit to play squash and shouldn't play squash to become fit. Tennis and badminton are better choices for the middle-aged, as they aren't as frenetic as squash, although singles badminton can be a hard slog.

Useful websites include www.squashplayer.co.uk and www.englandsquashandracketball.com, which has a search facility for finding your nearest courts.

Badminton

Badminton is more popular than tennis in the UK with over one million adults playing it each month. Most badminton facilities are provided by community sports centres and schools, and private clubs are rare. The cost of hiring a badminton court in a sports centre is around £10 an hour, or around £5 an hour at off-peak times.

Courts in public sports and leisure centres can be booked up to two weeks in advance, while private clubs may allow bookings to be made further in advance. Rackets, shoes and towels can usually be hired (or purchased) from public sports centres and private clubs. Most centres and clubs organise internal leagues, ladders and knockout competitions, and also participate in local and national league and cup competitions. There are clubs in most areas which usually meet one evening a week and may play all year round or just for a limited season, e.g. autumn to spring. Fees may be as low as £15 a season or up to £100 a year at a leisure centre.

For information about badminton, see www.badmintonengland.co.uk.

Table Tennis

Table tennis is popular, and is played both as a serious competitive sport and as a pastime in social and youth clubs. Most leisure centres have a number of table tennis tables for hire for as little as £2 an hour, and bats can be hired for a small fee. If you want to play seriously there are clubs in most areas. Costs vary, but it's an inexpensive sport with little equipment necessary. For further information, contact the national association, Table Tennis England (01908-208860, https://tabletennisengland.co.uk).

ROCK-CLIMBING & CAVING

Those who find walking a bit tame may like to try abseiling, rock-climbing, mountaineering, caving or pot-holing (subterranean mountaineering). The UK has a distinguished record in international mountain climbing and few mountains in the world haven't been climbed at some time by British mountaineers – who were often the first to climb them. If you're

> **Caution**
>
> It's extremely foolish, not to mention highly dangerous, to venture off into the hills (or holes) without an experienced guide or proper preparation, being in excellent physical condition and having sufficient training and the appropriate equipment. It's also essential to tell someone where you're going and when you expect to return.

an inexperienced climber, you would be well advised to join a climbing club (over 300 are affiliated to the British Mountaineering Council) before heading for the hills. There are climbing schools in all the main climbing areas, and many local clubs have special indoor training apparatus (e.g. a climbing wall) for aspiring mountaineers. Some leisure centres also provide facilities for climbing training, such as climbing walls.

A number of climbers, cavers and potholers are killed each year in the UK, many of whom are inexperienced and reckless. Many more owe their survival to rescue teams who risk their own lives to save them.

A good map is vital for those who venture into remote areas, such as Ordnance Survey maps (printed in 1:25 and 1:50 scales) available from bookshops and newsagents.

For information about climbing in the UK, contact the British Mountaineering Council (0161-445 6111, www.thebmc.co.uk).

RUGBY

There are two separate codes of rugby (or rugby football) in the UK, rugby union and rugby league. The main difference between the codes is that rugby union (which used to be strictly amateur) is played with teams of 15 players, and rugby league, which is played by amateurs and professionals with 13 players to a team (two less to pay!). Rugby union became a professional sport in 1995, as it was in danger of losing its best players to new rival professional organisations (and to rugby league), and many countries had been secretly paying their top union stars for years anyway. Despite initial concern that it wouldn't attract sufficient supporters, the game has grown in popularity in recent years.

Rugby union is played in all regions of the UK and has a wider following than rugby league, with the top 12 clubs in England playing in the Aviva Premiership (www.premiershiprugby.com). Below the Aviva Premiership is the RFU Championship comprising a further 12 teams, from which the top team can be promoted to the Premiership, followed by the National Leagues and the geographically based Regional Leagues. Other leagues include the Pro12 involving 12 professional clubs from Ireland, Italy, Scotland and Wales.

Main cup competitions are the LV= Cup (formerly the Anglo-Welsh Cup), a knock-out competition between the Aviva Premiership clubs and top Welsh teams that compete in Pro12, and the British and Irish Cup which pits England's RFU Championship teams against top clubs from Wales, Ireland and Scotland. The top 20 European rugby union clubs also compete in the European Rugby Challenge Cup, which includes teams from the English Premiership, the French Top 14 and Pro12.

There's intense competition between England, Scotland, Wales and Ireland for supremacy on the rugby union pitch and the four nations compete each year for the Triple Crown – awarded to the team which wins all their games against the other three countries. The home nations also compete with France and Italy in the Six Nations Championship. The ultimate achievement is the Grand Slam, when a team wins all its championship matches.

Within the Six Nations, England also plays Scotland for the Calcutta Cup.

Rugby union is also played internationally at the highest level by Australia (the Wallabies), New Zealand (the All Blacks) and South Africa (the Springboks), and a number of other nations including Argentina, Fiji, Romania and Western Samoa. Every four years, the Rugby World Cup is staged in a different country.

Rugby league is played professionally in the UK mainly by teams in the north of England who compete in the Super League and Challenge Cup, the final of which is played at Wembley Stadium in London. There are also many amateur rugby league teams for players of all ages, including a number of teams in the London area dominated by Australian expatriates. Rugby league is played internationally by Great Britain, Australia, New Zealand, France and Papua New Guinea. Most towns, schools and universities have rugby teams competing in local league and cup competitions, in one or both rugby codes.

Rugby websites include www.premiershiprugby.com, www.englandrugby.com, the official site of Rugby Union, and the Rugby League website, www.therfl.co.uk.

SKIING

Skiing is a popular sport with the British despite the fact that there are only a few ski resorts in the British Isles (in Scotland), and these could never hope to cater adequately to the country's over two million skiers. Scottish ski centres include Aonach Mor, Cairngorms (Aviemore), Glencoe, Glenshee and Lecht. However, for most British skiers, skiing in Scotland is of little interest and isn't a viable alternative to a skiing holiday in the Alps or North America. In comparison with the Alps, Scotland suffers from a lack of atmosphere, and skiing conditions early in the season are unpredictable, with storms and strong winds often causing lifts to be closed, and badly affecting the state of the snow.

The British, however, have made up for their lack of snow (and mountains) with dry-slope skiing. There are around 75 centres in the UK (see www.natives.co.uk/whatsnew/dryski.htm) catering for over 300,000 skiers a year. Learning to ski on a dry-slope can save you time and money when you arrive in a winter resort, and also helps experienced skiers find their ski-legs before arriving. A dry-slope consists of around 2,000m² (ca. 21,500 ft²) of ski-matting, usually with separate areas for beginners and advanced skiers. The maximum descent of 'pistes' is around 500 metres (1,640ft), although most are 200-300 metres (650-1,000 feet).

Skiing can also be practised indoors on a new type of artificial snow, which feels just like the real thing. There are a number of such centres offering this, including the Snow Centre in Hemel Hempstead (Herts.), the Snowdome in Tamworth, Staffordshire, in the Midlands,

and Snozones in Milton Keynes, close to London, Castleford in Yorkshire and Braehead near Glasgow. Bear in mind that, in contrast to dry slopes, these places get really cold – the temperature is never more than -3ºC, and with the wind-chill factor it can feel like -15ºC!

SNOOKER & BILLIARDS

Snooker is a popular sport in the UK, and most large towns boast at least one snooker or billiards club. Many hotels, bars and sports clubs also have snooker tables. Snooker clubs, most of which have bars and many also with restaurants, often open from around 10am to midnight daily. In the last few decades the popularity of snooker has increased enormously due largely to the success of televised championships, which have transformed what was once a minority pastime with a seedy image into a successful national sport with a huge following.

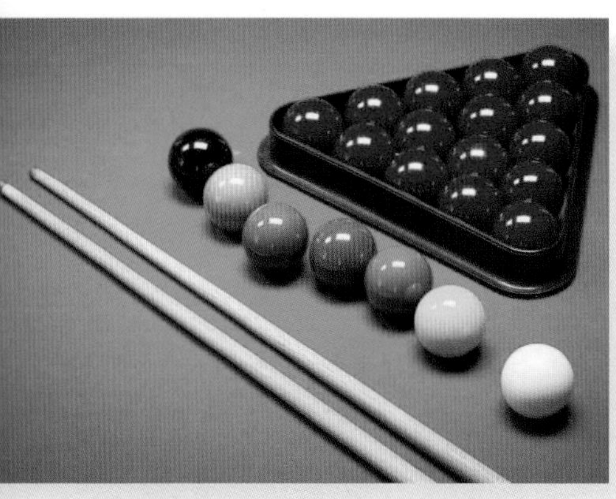

Professional competitions are staged throughout the world and top players are millionaire celebrities. Snooker is also increasingly played by women, professionally as well as for fun, and they make up a large percentage of TV audiences.

Billiards, however, is waning in popularity, although it still arouses considerable interest elsewhere in the world. American pool is also played fairly widely, although it's very much the poor cousin of snooker, and, to a lesser extent, billiards. A game called 8-ball is also popular (commonly played in pubs, with teams competing in local leagues), as is bar billiards.

SPORTS & LEISURE CENTRES

Most towns have a community sports or leisure centre (also called recreation centres), usually run and financed by the local council. Some cities and towns also have modern commercial sports centres, which, although more expensive than municipal centres, offer unrivalled sports facilities (and some charge minimal membership fees). A huge range of sports and activities are catered for, including badminton, basketball, netball, swimming and diving, squash, indoor soccer (five-a-side), rollerskating, BMX bikes, gymnastics, yoga, weight training, table tennis, tennis, racketball, aerobics, cricket, climbing, canoeing (in the swimming pool), archery, bowls, hockey, trampolining, martial arts and snooker. Councils publish information about local sports and leisure centres.

Some centres have ice rinks and dry-slope skiing facilities, while most have one or more (e.g. main and learning) indoor swimming pools, squash courts, badminton courts, sports halls (which are available for hire), general activity and fitness rooms, and a games room. Many sports centres have a health and beauty salon, which may include a sauna, Turkish bath (or steam room), Jacuzzi, solarium, spa bath, massage and a beauty treatment room.

Centres usually provide meeting rooms, nursery facilities, a shop, a reasonably-priced restaurant or café and a licensed bar. All centres provide parking, although there may be a fee. In addition to sports activities, some centres also organise a range of non-sporting leisure activities, e.g. art, bingo, bridge, chess, dancing, music, photography, Scrabble and whist.

Sports and leisure centres are usually open seven days a week from around 9am to 11pm, although some smaller centres use school sports facilities, and are available only from early evening (e.g. 5pm) Mondays to Fridays and at weekends. Membership, for which there's usually a fee of around £30-50 a year, is usually necessary, although this may not be required if you want to just book courts or equipment.

In some centres, particularly in London and other major cities, annual membership costs from £10 to £60 a year and may be higher for non-residents. Season tickets, block bookings and subscriptions are usually available for some facilities. Most centres charge spectators an entrance fee of around £1, and all have reduced rates for children (or juniors) at around half the adult rates. They also have daytime off-peak rates (usually before 5pm) for most facilities.

All sports and leisure centres have clubs and club nights for a variety of sports, and also organise leagues, tournaments, ladders, knockout competitions and special events. Most centres run fitness training and sports courses throughout the year for juniors and adults, and also offer individual and group coaching. Holiday sports sessions and play schemes are held during school holidays (e.g. in summer) and at weekends, and most centres organise special sports and games' parties for children on request. All centres have changing rooms and showers.

SWIMMING

You can swim at numerous beaches throughout the UK; some have a dubious reputation for cleanliness, although in general they're improving. Details are provided in the MCS *Good Beach Guide* (www.goodbeachguide.co.uk), which includes surveys of over 1,100 beaches. There are even naturist and non-smoking beaches in some resorts.

There are public heated indoor and outdoor swimming pools in most towns, many located in leisure centres (see above) – although if you like to swim regularly all year round, you may wish to check out the local facilities before buying or renting a home.

A more widely accepted standard is that of the Blue Flag organisation (www.blueflag.org), which rates beaches and marinas for cleanliness and a number of other criteria in 49 countries.

In 2016, England, Scotland, Wales and N. Ireland had a combined total of 199 Blue Flag beaches. See also the Beach Guide (www.thebeachguide.co.uk/best-beaches/blue_flag.htm).

The temperature of indoor pools is generally maintained at 23-30°C (74-80°F). Many centres have a main pool and a teaching pool, often with a waterslide (jet slide, water chute), flumes, wave machine, whirlpool or waterfall – great fun for kids. Some centres provide diving boards at certain times and paddling pools for toddlers. Many also have sunbeds, saunas, solaria and Jacuzzis. Separate sessions are arranged for various groups and ages, focusing on early morning swimming, lane swimming, diving, senior citizens, mums and babies, over 25s, school holidays and aqua-aerobics. Aqua-natal sessions for expectant or post-natal mothers may also be held.

Pools are usually busy at weekends and on public holidays, and it's best to visit during the week if you can. If you're going along for a general swim, check in advance whether the pool has been booked for a special session. The cost is usually from £2.50-£5 for adults and

£1-£3 for juniors under 16 and senior citizens. There are generally reduced rates for family groups. Most centres provide annual season tickets, for around £40 to £120 a year, allowing you to swim at any time.

Before entrusting your children to the care of some swimming pools, you should check the safety standards, as they vary considerably and some are unsafe (public pools must have adequate lifeguard cover). This also applies to beaches, many of which fail to meet basic safety standards owing to a lack of emergency equipment, lifeguards and warning flags. Most leisure centres provide swimming lessons (all levels from beginner to fish) and run 'improver' and life-saving courses.

Excellent websites for UK swimmers include www.britishswimming.org and www.swimming.org.

WATERSPORTS

All watersports – including sailing, windsurfing, waterskiing, rowing, power-boating, canoeing, kayaking, surfing and subaquatic sports – are popular in the UK, which is hardly surprising considering it's surrounded by water and has hundreds of inland lakes and rivers where these sports can also be enjoyed. Boats and equipment can be hired at coastal resorts, lakes and rivers, and instruction is available for most watersports in holiday areas. Jet and surf skis can also be hired.

Rowing

Rowing is a sport at which the British excel, its competitors having won many gold medals at world championships and the Olympic Games. There are around 500 rowing clubs in the UK and over 300 regattas, the most famous of which is Henley Regatta. The most famous single race held in the UK is the University Boat Race (inaugurated in 1836), held on the Thames around Easter time between eight-oared crews from Cambridge and Oxford universities – it's world-famous and is shown live on TV. Canoeing for children is sometimes taught in indoor swimming pools in winter. Budding canoeists must be able to swim 50 metres before being admitted to a canoe club, and the wearing of life jackets is compulsory (see www.britishrowing.org).

Caution

No experience, test, safety training or equipment is compulsory to take to the waters in and around the UK, and many people needlessly risk their lives and carry no safety equipment. e.g. flares, life jackets or radios. Don't get caught unprepared and make sure you observe all warning signs on waterways.

Surfing, Windsurfing, Waterskiing & Sub-aqua

Wetsuits are almost mandatory for surfing, windsurfing, waterskiing and sub-aquatic sports, even during the summer months (the water is freezing in and around the UK at almost any time of the year). Surfing is popular, and is centred at Newquay in Cornwall, which has staged a number of world-class events.

Scuba diving is another popular sport. Participants must pass a medical examination and undergo an approved training course to obtain the PADI open water diving certificate. Courses are run at many swimming pools and cost from around £300-£400. Equipment can cost hundreds or even thousands of pounds, although secondhand equipment is available. The season runs from April to September – the best diving areas in the British Isles are Cornwall and the Scilly Isles.

Sailing

Sailing has always been popular in the UK, which has a history of producing famous sailors, from Sir Francis Drake and Admiral Horatio Nelson to Sir Francis Chichester and Ellen MacArthur. There are sailing clubs (around 1,500) and schools in all areas, and boats of all shapes and sizes can be hired, from ocean-going racing yachts to dinghies. In recent years there has been a marina boom, especially in the southeast, and if you're a sailing enthusiast it's possible to purchase a home where you can moor your boat outside your front door. Websites such as www.sail.co.uk can provide detailed information about brokers.

The Royal Yachting Association (RYA) runs excellent courses for sailors wishing to become safe and proficient skippers. The Coastal Skippers and Yachtmaster courses lead to qualifications for commercial and racing skippers, but there are also courses for power-boaters and coastal 'potterers'. For details see the RYA website (www.rya.org.uk).

Many magazines are dedicated to boating and yachting, plus another ten to various other water sports.

Information

For the addresses and telephone numbers of national sports associations, contact Sport England (www.sportengland.org) or the Sport and Recreation Alliance (www.sportandrecreation.org.uk).

Many foreign sports and pastimes have a group of expatriate fanatics in the UK, including American football, baseball, boccia, boules (and pétanque), Gaelic sports (hurling, Gaelic football), handball and softball. For information, enquire at council offices, libraries, Tourist Information Centres, expatriate social clubs, embassies and consulates.

Burlington Arcade, London

17. SHOPPING

The choice, quality and variety of goods on sale in British shops is excellent, particularly in London, one of the great shopping cities of the world. Not only is the UK, in the words of Napoleon, 'a nation of shopkeepers', but it's also a country of compulsive shoppers, shopping being the number one 'leisure' activity (after watching television). In the UK, you often hear references made to the 'high street' (e.g. high street shops and high street banks), which isn't usually a reference to the name of a street (although many towns do have a High Street), but a collective term for businesses commonly found in most town centres.

Shops in town centres vary from huge department stores selling just about everything (e.g. Harrods and Selfridges in London), to small high-class specialist retailers in Georgian or Victorian-style arcades. The traditional high street – now slipping into history in many areas – encompasses a number of small shops, including a butcher, baker, greengrocer, grocer (general store), newsagent, chemist (pharmacy), bank/building society, post office and the inevitable pub (or two).

In larger towns shops may include a ironmonger (hardware, household wares), launderette (laundromat), off-licence (alcoholic beverages), betting shop, fish and chip shop, dry cleaners, hairdresser, bookshop, health food store, ladies' and men's fashion/shoe stores and take-away food outlets. Larger centres also have one or more supermarkets and department stores, and most country towns also have a (food) market on at least one day a week. Outside main shopping centres there are 'corner shops', which are general or convenience stores selling a wide range of food and household products.

There's usually no bargaining or bartering in the UK although, if you plan to spend a lot of money or buy something expensive (e.g. a television, computer or major appliances), you should shop around and shouldn't be shy about asking for a discount (except in most department stores, chain stores and supermarkets, where prices are usually fixed). Many shops (especially John Lewis) will also match any genuine advertised price (but excluding internet prices).

Value Added Tax (VAT– see page 212) at 20 per cent is included in the price of most goods with the exception of food, books and children's clothes, and the advertised price is usually the price you pay. Most shops accept major credit cards, although in some stores they may accept only cash, debit cards and their own account or credit cards.

Always shop around for the best deal, particularly when buying expensive items such as home appliances. The best way to do this is online via a search engine such as Google: simply enter the name and model number of the product and you'll get a list of buying options.

Shopping guides can be obtained from Tourist Information Centres in many areas, and for those who live in or around the capital, our sister guide *London's Best Shops & Markets* will prove invaluable. Websites focusing on shopping in London are many, including www.21stcenturyvillage.com, www.streetsensation.co.uk and www.timeout.com/london/shopping.

OPENING HOURS

There are no hard and fast rules for opening hours in the UK. In smaller towns and villages, shops generally open between 9 and 9.30am and close around 5.30 or 6pm, Mondays to Saturdays. In larger towns and cities, larger shops often stay open until 7pm or 8pm. In smaller towns and villages shops may close at lunchtime for an hour or two, and some stores close on Mondays or Wednesday afternoons. Thursday is traditionally 'late night' shopping, when many shops open until 8pm or later. Some large supermarkets are open 24-hours a day, seven days a week.

Under the 1994 Sunday Trading Act, shops are permitted to open on any Sunday with the exception of Easter Sunday. Small shops under 280m² (ca. 3,000ft²) may open all day, and larger shops can open for a maximum of six hours, only between 10am and 6pm. Many shops also open on public holidays, with the exception of Christmas Day and Easter Sunday.

Queuing is an English institution and is as carefully observed in shops as anywhere else. In any establishment where there's more than one person waiting to be served, people usually form a neat line behind one another. Turns are strictly observed and queue jumpers are frowned upon. In some stores and supermarket counters you need to take a number from a dispenser and wait for it to come up on a display.

SALES

Given the British love affair with shopping it isn't surprising that the British love a bargain, and sales are extremely popular. Most stores hold sales at various times of the year, the largest of which are held in January and July, when bargains abound (many newspapers publish sales' guides). Sales are also held in the spring and autumn – some shops will hold one at the drop of a hat – and some seem to have a permanent sale. However, retailers aren't permitted to describe goods as reduced when they've never been sold at the quoted 'normal' price, although they may have been advertised at a higher price for a relatively short time simply to get around the law.

The largest sales take place after Christmas, with some shops starting their 'New Year' sales on Boxing Day (26th December), although most begin around the 27th December, and last for up to six weeks. The sales after Christmas are actually 'New Year' sales, which traditionally started on the 2nd January, but retailers have brought them forward over the years, originally to offset lower than expected sales over the Christmas period. A growing trend over the last decade has been for some sales to start even before Christmas.

Sales also take place in the summer, usually beginning in July. It isn't unusual to find people camping outside shops overnight before the first day of the summer sales to ensure that they're first in line to grab the best bargains. Sales are a good time to stock up on otherwise expensive goods such as designer clothes and shoes, home furnishings and electronics, and there are some genuine bargains to be had.

Outlet Centres

The UK was the site of the first European factory outlet centre (Cheshire Oaks in the northwest of England) and today it's home to a

wide range of centres across the country. Variously called factory outlets, outlet centres/malls and designer outlets, these centres are where retailers (especially fashion chains) and manufacturers ostensibly sell end-of-line (and unpopular) stock at a discount on high street prices. However, you need to know what you're buying as not everything is the bargain it purports to be.

Many centres are now tourist attractions in their own right, such as Bicester Village (www.bicestervillage.com), a designer outlet that's home to over 130 fashion and lifestyle boutiques offering (allegedly) savings of up to 60 per cent. It's very popular with the Chinese and reportedly numbers the Duchess of Cambridge among its regulars. You can find other centres via numerous websites, including www.outlet-malls.eu/united-kingdom, www.outletsheet.com/uk/malls and www.realm.ltd.uk/outlet-centres.

FAMOUS STORES

The following is a selection of Britain's favourite and most famous High Street stores. Many also offer online shopping via their websites.

Boots: Boots Company plc, widely known as simply Boots or Boots the Chemists, is one of the UK's most ubiquitous chain stores, with outlets in most high streets throughout the country – a total of 2,500 no less. In recent years, they have diversified their business from a traditional pharmacy to one offering home appliances, kitchenware and spectacles (opticians) in their major stores. They also stock a wide range of cosmetics, hair products and perfumes. For further information, see www.boots-uk.com.

Debenhams: A chain of some 150 department stores in the UK and Ireland, Debenhams is best known for its fashion, and sells a range of designer and own-label clothes at affordable prices. Part of Debenhams' appeal is its concessions, which are 'shops-in-shops' that can be found in most Debenhams stores, although they have gone down market in recent years. For further information, see www.debenhams.com.

Fenwick: Founded in 1882 in Newcastle-upon-Tyne (still its flagship store and headquarters), Fenwick is an independent chain of stores with outlets in Canterbury, Leicester, London (Bond Street and Brent Cross), Tunbridge Wells, Windsor and York. It also owns the Bentalls stores in Bracknell and Kingston-upon-Thames, and Williams and Griffin in Colchester. Most stores (the exception is Newcastle) focus on fashion and household goods. For more information, see www.fenwick.co.uk.

Fortnum & Mason: Fortnums is one of England's oldest and most renowned department stores; founded in 1707, it celebrated its 300th anniversary in 2007. Situated in Piccadilly, London, its fame rests almost entirely on its upmarket food hall, although only one of its several floors is devoted to food. It also has a celebrated tea shop. It's famous for its luxury food hampers – just the job for the races (Ascot, Epsom, etc.), polo, Glyndebourne and fête champêtre (garden parties). For further information, see www.fortnumandmason.com.

Harrods: The most famous department store in the world and one of the largest. Situated

Harrods, London

in Knightsbridge in London, Harrods occupies 4.5acres (1.82ha), with over one million ft² (305,000m²) of selling space, and over 330 departments. Harrods caters to upmarket customers and is said to be able to provide anything a customer wants – its motto is Omnia Omnibus Ubique – 'All Things for All People, Everywhere'. Of particular note is its world-famous Food Hall, where you can try many products before buying. For more information, see www.harrods.com.

Harvey Nichols: Founded in 1813 as a linen shop, Harvey Nichols ('Harvey Nicks') is an upmarket department store chain with its original store in London's Knightsbridge, and other stores in Birmingham, Bristol, Edinburgh, Leeds, Liverpool and Manchester (plus a number overseas). It offers many of the world's most prestigious brands in womenswear, menswear, accessories, beauty, food, and homewares, and attracts younger shoppers than its main rival Harrods, which tends to be more expensive. The London store also has a renowned restaurant, bar and café, which have become destinations in their own right and are a favourite meeting place for savvy shoppers. For further information, see www.harveynichols.com.

John Lewis: The UK's favourite department store chain, John Lewis scores highly with customers on its range of products and customer service. It offers solid good value (its motto is 'Never knowingly undersold'), an unconditional returns policy, and a general feeling of good taste rather than showy fashion. One of the John Lewis Partnership's most unusual aspects is that it's a limited public company that's held in trust on behalf of its employees (called 'partners'), who have a say in the running of the business and receive an annual share of the profits.

John Lewis stores sell a wide range of goods including upholstery, lighting, electrical items, clothes, toys, beauty products and kitchenware. It's also one of the UK's favourite electrical retailers, the owner of Peter Jones and Waitrose (see below), and one of the UK's foremost internet retailers. The only downside to John Lewis is that it has only some 45 stores nationwide, although you can shop online via its excellent website (www.johnlewis.com).

Liberty: A celebrated store in Regent Street, London, founded by Arthur Lasenby Liberty in 1875 to sell ornaments, fabrics and miscellaneous art objects from Japan and the Far East. Nowadays Liberty sells fashions, cosmetics, accessories and gifts, in addition to homewares and furniture. Liberty has a distinctive style and is famous for producing its own beautiful and luxurious fabrics. The shop is noted for its intimate feel, being unlike a typical large department store, with stairs and decorative elevators instead of escalators. For more information, see www.liberty.co.uk.

Marks & Spencer: Variously known as M&S, Marks and Sparks or simply Marks, Marks & Spencer is a British institution, with a reputation for good quality products and customer service. M&S lingerie is particularly popular and most English women own at least some items of M&S underwear. It's one of the most widely-recognised chain stores in the UK and the largest clothing retailer, as well as being a multi-billion pound food retailer. Their food range is more expensive than most supermarkets but offers high quality and reliability. It also sells homewares such as bed linen, but this is a smaller part of the business than the other two ranges. For further information, see www.marksandspencer.com.

Cashback

In many shops, when you're paying with a debit card, you can request some 'cash back'. You can ask for an amount (the limit is £50) to be added to your bill and the cash is then given to you with your receipt. If you only need a small amount of cash, this saves you going to an ATM (fee-free ATMs are rare in some areas).

Peter Jones: Known as PJs to its many fans, Peter Jones in Sloane Square is one of London's largest and best-loved department stores (part of the John Lewis Partnership since the '20s). It's seen as a rather exclusive store, although its stock and decor are no different from other John Lewis stores, and a cut above the partnership's other central London department stores. For more information, see www.johnlewis.com/our-shops/peter-jones.

Selfridges: A chain of department stores founded by American entrepreneur Harry Gordon Selfridge, who opened a large store in London's Oxford Street in 1909. Selfridge was a pioneer in terms of department store marketing and retailing, and is popularly held to have coined the phrase 'the customer is always right', which he used regularly in his advertising. In addition to its London flagship store in Oxford Street, one of London's largest, Selfridges also has stores in Birmingham and Manchester. For further information, see www.selfridges.co.uk.

WH Smith: Named after William Henry Smith, WH Smith was created in 1828 (although the original store opened in 1792) and was the world's first chain store company. Today, it sells books, newspapers, magazines, stationery and entertainment products from over 600 UK High Street stores, with another 600 located at airports, train stations, hospitals and motorway services. It also operates internationally in Australia, South East Asia, India and the Middle East. For further information, see www.whsmith.co.uk.

Waitrose: The supermarket division of the John Lewis Partnership. Although one of the UK's smallest supermarket chains, with over 320 branches, Waitrose is highly rated and is consistently voted the UK's best supermarket by members of the Which? consumer group. Like the partnership's department stores (see above), Waitrose is targeted at the middle class market, emphasising quality food and customer service, rather than low prices (their slogan is 'Quality food, honestly priced'). Waitrose offers a number of special services including home deliveries, a party service and online shopping. For further information, see www.waitrose.com.

SHOPPING CENTRES

Over the last twenty years numerous vast out-of-town, indoor shopping centres (malls) have sprung up throughout the UK normally, but not always, out of town, where it's possible to do your weekly shopping under one roof (nirvana or shopping hell, depending on your viewpoint). Centres usually contain a huge selection of shops, including all the famous high street names.

Among the most popular UK shopping centres are Bluewater in north Kent, (www.bluewater.co.uk), Merry Hill in the West Midlands (http://intu.co.uk/merryhill), Lakeside in the southeast (http://intu.co.uk/lakeside), Meadowhall in Yorkshire (www.meadowhall.co.uk) and Manchester's Arndale Centre (www.manchesterarndale.com), which draw shoppers from up to 50mi (80km) around and day-trippers from even further afield. The UK's largest mall is the Trafford Centre in Manchester (http://intu.co.uk/traffordcentre), with more than 180,000m^2 of retail space.

More recent developments include Westfield (http://uk.westfield.com/london), opened in 2008 in Shepherds Bush (West London), with 265 shops, 50 eateries and 4,500 parking spaces (including valet parking), and Liverpool One (www.liverpool-one.com), which is the UK's largest open-air shopping centre and includes a 36-hole golf adventure centre. In September 2011, Westfield opened their latest shopping centre in Stratford, East London (http://uk.westfield.com/stratfordcity), site of the 2012 Olympics. It claimed over 47 million shoppers that year, making it the most visited mall in the UK.

Smaller but no less popular are retail parks, which group a number of stores together, each with its own entrance and free shared parking. There's usually a supermarket, plus stores selling furniture, electrical goods, DIY and pet merchandise, clothes and discount goods. There has also been a proliferation of out-of-town supermarket superstores (which exceed 1,000), similar in size to continental hypermarkets, and often selling everything from food and clothes, to home furnishings and electrical goods (see **Food & Supermarkets** below).

The largest shopping centres incorporate a wide range of leisure attractions, including multiplex cinemas, ten-pin bowling, games arcades, children's play areas, and lots of restaurants and bars. Like American malls, most are designed for people with cars, although most are served by bus services from nearby towns.

An unequal battle has raged between high streets and out-of-town centres for many years, which towns have been losing hands down, although some are belatedly fighting back. Malls have turned many towns into virtual ghost towns.

MARKETS

Most small towns have markets on one or two days a week (Fridays and Saturdays are most popular) and in cities there may be a permanent daily market. Markets are cheap, colourful and interesting, and often a good place for shrewd shopping, although you must sometimes be careful what you buy and be wary of counterfeit goods. Items on sale include fresh fruit and vegetables, foods from specialist retailers, clothes, handicrafts, household goods, secondhand books, records, antiques and bric-a-brac. Farmers' markets (see below), where producers sell directly to the public, are popular and are held weekly in many towns.

Check with your local library, town hall or Tourist Information Centre (TIC) for information about local markets.

'Food miles' is a recent buzzword coined to describe the distance food travels before it reaches a retailer. Nowadays, an increasing amount of the produce sold in supermarkets has flown half way round the world, so that shoppers in the UK can eat, for example, asparagus and strawberries all year round.

Farmers' Markets

A farmers' market is a market where farmers, growers or artisan producers from the local area sell their own produce direct to the public. Quality is generally good although prices can be high. All products sold should have been grown, reared, caught, brewed, pickled, baked, smoked or processed by the stallholder.

Some of the best farmers' markets are certified by FARMA, the National Farmers' Retail & Markets Association (www.farma.org.uk), who independently assess and certify farmers' markets throughout the country to make sure that they're the 'real deal'. To find farmers' markets in your area, see www.localfoods.org.uk and www.local-farmers-markets.co.uk.

FOOD & SUPERMARKETS

Some three-quarters of food in the UK is purchased from supermarkets and the country is home to several large chains. The largest is Tesco, followed by Asda, Sainsbury's, Morrisons, Waitrose, and newcomers Aldi and Lidl. Most of these sell their own brands of clothing as well as food. Waitrose is the most expensive of these, but has a reputation for high quality. All the 'traditional' supermarkets have made efforts to cut prices in recent years to compete with the incomers.

Revealingly, it's the German no-frills chains Aldi and Lidl – derisively dubbed 'discounters' by the main supermarket chains – which have been aggressively expanding in the last decade. They offer not only low prices – not offers but permanently low prices – and have increasingly been winning awards for their quality, particularly own brands. The low prices are partly possible by their offering less choice of products than other supermarkets, which enables them to benefit from bulk buying: for example, they may only send one brand of tomato ketchup instead of a choice of ten.

The quality and variety of food in British supermarkets has increased in leaps and bounds in recent years and they're among the world's best. They excel in hygiene, safety standards, efficiency and choice, offering produce from every corner of the globe. The major supermarkets have also branched out into other fields such as banking and financial services.

Some department and chain stores are also famous for their food halls, including Harrods, Selfridges and Fortnum and Mason in London, and Marks and Spencer (M&S) nationwide. The latter offers a smaller grocery range than supermarkets (mostly fresh foods), but is renowned for its quality, particularly their range of convenience meals (now copied by other supermarkets).

The major supermarket chains also operate smaller convenience stores in towns and cities, such as Tesco's 'Metro' and Sainsbury's 'Local' stores. There are also reasonably priced convenience store chains such as the Co-op, Costcutter, Nisa and Spar, which have outlets in most towns.

You can compare the prices at supermarkets via websites such as My Supermarket (www.mysupermarket.co.uk), which provides a comparison between prices at a wide range of supermarkets and discount stores, including Aldi, Asda, Iceland, Lidl, Marks & Spencer, Morrisons, Poundland, Sainsbury's, Tesco and the online retailer Ocado.

Superstores

The largest supermarket chains such as Tesco, Asda, Sainsbury's and Morrisons have built over 1,000 huge out-of-town superstores in the last few decades, which in addition to the traditional supermarket offerings contain a range of shops-within-a-shop. These may include a newsagent, chemist, optician, florist, delicatessen, cheese counter, bakery, fishmonger, butcher and market-style stalls, fresh pizza counters and a petrol station – even an in-store sushi bar. To avoid long queues it's best to avoid shopping around 6pm on Friday evenings and on Saturday and Sunday mornings. Some of the superstores operated by Asda, Tesco and Sainsburys are large enough to qualify as true hypermarkets, as found on the continent.

Quality & Choice

Whatever you may have heard about the British junk food diet, it can hardly be laid at the door of the supermarkets. Their fresh food range is as good (if not better) as that available in most European counterparts (although many Europeans shop in street markets). They also offer a wide range of wholesome fare produced using traditional methods. Many foreign foods can be found in supermarkets, which often have a separate delicatessen where these predominate, and the growth of a foodie culture has seen what were once exotic ingredients twenty years ago become mainstream.

The high turnover of stock ensures that produce is fresh (although it may have been stored for up to a year in special 'bunkers' to prevent spoilage), and many supermarkets bake their own bread on the premises. Most have fresh fish, meat and dairy counters, and offer a wide choice of frozen products. However, many towns also have a freezer shop (e.g. Farmfoods and Iceland), which generally offers a wider choice and lower prices than supermarkets if you buy in bulk. In many towns a 'milkman' will deliver milk to your door, along with other groceries, although they must be ordered in advance and you pay more for the convenience.

Alcohol

Most supermarkets stock a wide selection of wine (including own label) and other alcoholic drinks. Their buying power allows them to undercut independent drinks' retailers and they've been blamed for putting off licences (liquor shops) – and pubs –out of business. However, you should shop around, as prices and choices vary considerably. Many supermarkets (e.g. Waitrose) and wine merchants (e.g. Majestic) make free home deliveries if you buy 6 or 12 bottles.

Major UK wine retailers include Averys (www.averys.com) and Majestic (www.majestic.co.uk), while Wines Direct (www.winesdirect.co.uk) allows you to compare prices.

Miscellaneous

All supermarkets provide trolleys and baskets that shouldn't be removed from supermarkets or their environs, e.g. car parks; some require a £1 deposit. Many supermarkets provide recycling collection sites at stores, where you can take bottles, paper, plastics and cans. Most supermarkets offer online shopping (see **Internet Shopping** on page 276), which can then be collected from a store (known as 'click and collect') or delivered locally; deliveries are free when you spend a minimum amount.

If you're having a party many major supermarkets provide a party service and can arrange a variety of prepared cold food trays, plus drinks, snacks, party-ware, gifts and prizes, sandwiches and sweets. Some also provide glasses on free loan (or for a nominal fee) if you buy alcohol from them.

There's a legally compulsory 5p fee for a basic plastic bag in all UK supermarkets and most other large stores, profits from which must go to charity, in order to discourage their use (plastic waste is a scourge on wildlife and the environment). You can purchase heavy-duty carrier bags ('bags for life') for a small fee.

POUND SHOPS

A couple of factors have led to an explosion of bargain shops over the last decade or so. The decline of most town and city centres as shoppers do more and more of their shopping online or in out-of town retailers means that shop rents are now comparatively low (which is why so many charity shops can afford decent locations – an increasingly common sight on British high streets): and the limited growth of wages in real terms over the last decade has led many shoppers to look for ways to stretch their money further.

Ahead of the pack of this new wave of shops is the well-established Poundland, which now has approaching 500 branches around the country: as you would expect, everything there costs £1 (or nearly so – they have started experimenting with a handful of more expensive items near their tills). Visiting their shops is a fascinating experience, and if very worthwhile for those setting up a new home on a budget. For £1 you can buy larger things than you might expect, such as mops, as well as tea bags, pregnancy testing kits and iPhone cases!

A number of similar shops can be found, including some that don't restrict themselves to a £1 price such as B&M and Bargain Buys (which was started by the founder of Poundland after he sold his original business). These shops are particularly useful if you want to put together a cheap tool kit, need stationary or get through a lot of alkaline batteries.

> ☑ **SURVIVAL TIP**
>
> If you need kitchen measuring equipment and cannot cope with decimal measures, you'll need to bring your own measuring scales, jugs, cups (US and British recipe cups aren't the same size) and thermometers. Note also that British pillows and duvets aren't the same size or shape as in many other countries.

DEPARTMENT & CHAIN STORES

The UK has many excellent department and chain stores. The major department store groups include Debenhams, House of Fraser and John Lewis. Among London's many department stores are the renowned Harrods and Selfridges, two of the largest stores in the world. (Harrods, by the way, has a dress code, and spending a penny there actually costs a pound.)

There are dozens of chain stores in the UK, selling everything from electrical goods to books and clothes. One of the most acclaimed is Marks and Spencer, noted for its clothes, home furnishings and excellent food halls. There are also catalogue shops (e.g. Argos, www.argos.co.uk), where you select your purchases from catalogues rather than a display.

Most department and chain stores provide customer card accounts (e.g. Debenhams, House of Fraser, John Lewis and Marks and Spencer) and allow balances to be repaid over a period, although this isn't wise as the interest charged is usually very high. However, some shops offer a period of free credit. Account customers can often take advantage of special offers and discounts, and some shops arrange special shopping evenings. Many department and chain stores sell gift vouchers that can be redeemed for goods at any branch.

Department stores (and many smaller shops) provide a gift-wrapping service, particularly at Christmas, and deliver goods locally or even worldwide.

CLOTHES

The clothing industry is extremely competitive, and London is one of the world's leading fashion centres, particularly for the young. What London lacks in *haute couture* houses, it more than makes up for by the sheer variety, energy, innovation and vitality of its fashion scene. It's renowned for its design schools, such as St Martin's and the Royal College of Art, which produce a stream of brilliant young designers.

Clothes shops offer a wide range of attire, from traditional bespoke tailoring to the latest ready-to-wear fashions, with prices ranging from a few pounds to a few thousand. Top quality and exclusive (i.e. expensive) British ladies' and men's fashion stores (many chains sell both ladies' and men's clothes) include Aquascutum, Burberry, Jaeger, Liberty and Paul Smith.

More middle-of-the-road fashions (with regard to price and quality) can be found at Benetton, Dorothy Perkins, Evans, Gap, Hennes (H&M), House of Fraser, Matalan, Monsoon, Next, TK Maxx, Wallis and Zara. Miss Selfridge, New Look, River Island and Topshop cater primarily for teenagers and those in their 20s and 30s. Clothes for the less affluent shopper can be found at Primark, Peacocks and major supermarkets; prices in Primark in particular can be staggeringly cheap.

Most clothes retailers have a website and some former chain stores now sell online only, e.g. Littlewoods (www.littlewoods.com). Online clothes-shopping has become big business and many e-Bay stores are turning a better profit than some high street shops. One of the success stories of the decade is ASOS (www.asos.com), now the UK's largest independent fashion e-store, selling cutting-edge clothes at high street prices. It has a reputation for producing and marketing the latest trends, often hot off the catwalk, in a glossy magazine style format.

Top quality men's clothing shops include Austin Reed, Gieves and Hawkes, Harrods, Selfridges and Moss Bros. For the young man about town, there's a wide range of fashion shops, including Burtons, Gap, Next for Men, River Island and Top Man. All cities also boast a profusion of independent shops covering the whole spectrum of fashion and for every price bracket. Markets are often a good place to shop for cheap clothes, and mail-order offers (e.g. in Saturday and Sunday newspaper magazines) also usually provide good value. Sports clothing is worn by people of all ages, including those who never set foot near a track or pitch, and there are some good sportswear chains, including JD Sports and Sports Direct.

British clothes are generally of good quality, particularly those from famous English manufacturers, who produce classic styles and traditional clothes that are made to last (and outlast ever-changing fashions). Cheaper clothes are largely made abroad (e.g. in the Far East), as it's simply too expensive to produce them in the UK, and although the quality of may occasionally be suspect you usually get what you pay for. Quality stores may provide an alteration service (for a small fee) and many also provide a made-to-measure tailoring service.

The most renowned men's tailors are to be found in London's Savile Row, while Jermyn Street is famous for handmade shirts, and Bond Street is one of Europe's premier locales for ladies' fashion. Unless you're wealthy, beware of shops that don't price their window displays – as when buying a Rolls-Royce, if you must ask the price you cannot afford it!

Although you can buy shoes in many clothes shops and some supermarkets, specialist retailers are varied and abundant. These range from the top quality (and top price) brands such as Russell & Bromley, Bally, Charles Jourdan, Dune, Jones Bootmaker and John Lobb, to the more affordable Barratts, Brantano, Ecco, Hotter, Office, Pavers, Schuh, Shoe Zone and Sole Trader. Like good quality English clothes, English shoes (famous makers include Crockett & Jones and Church's) are made to last, although few manufacturers remain. Two other famous English brand names are Clarks and Start-rite, both of which make excellent children's shoes in a wide range of fittings, as well as good quality, reasonably priced footwear for adults. Many younger people opt for trainers rather than shoes, which can be bought in all sportswear shoes as well as specialist stores such as Footlocker.

Shoe repair shops can be found in most towns and many department stores, which often have a Mister Minit concession (or similar) where repairs are carried out while you wait.

NEWSPAPERS, MAGAZINES & BOOKS

The British have long been a nation of inveterate newspaper readers, although sales have been falling since the '90s as more and more people get their news fix from television and, more recently, the internet. However, many are read by two or three people, suggesting that at least half the population reads a newspaper each day.

In addition to the national daily and Sunday papers there are around 70 regional dailies and 2,000 free or paid-for weekly papers, plus hundreds of magazines. Free newspapers such as *Metro* and the *London Evening Standard* have taken a large slice of the market – over 1.3 million copies of *Metro* are published daily – and many readers now subscribe to a news website rather than pick up a printed copy. Many national papers can be read for free online, while others require an online subscription (which works out much cheaper than buying the printed version). There's no tax on newspapers, magazines or books.

Many newspapers have a strong political slant. The majority have traditionally supported the Conservative party, although this changed somewhat in the late '90s after the election of a more centrist Labour government and loyalties are now slightly less clear-cut. Daily and Sunday newspapers range from the 'quality' press for serious readers to the popular tabloids for those who just like to scan the news.

A directory of British newspapers and magazines can be found online at www.britishpapers.co.uk and www.world-newspapers.com/uk.html.

Daily newspapers include (roughly in order of average sales, highest first), *The Daily Telegraph*, *The Times*, the *Financial Times* and *The Guardian*. The equivalents in Scotland are *The Glasgow Herald* and *The Scotsman*. Until recently, the description 'broadsheet' was used for the above newspapers, but *The Times* converted to tabloid format some years ago, and *The Guardian* to a demi-tabloid ('Berliner') format. The popular tabloid daily press includes *The Sun, The Daily Mail, The Mirror, the Daily Express, the Daily Star* and *the Daily Record* (which replaces its stable-mate *The Mirror* in Scotland).

On Sundays, the quality newspapers are *The Sunday Times*, *TheSunday Telegraph* and *The Observer*, and, in Scotland, *The Sunday Herald* and *Scotland on Sunday*. They're good sources of advertisements for quality cars, executive appointments, property (in the UK and abroad), entertainment, travel and holidays. The popular Sunday tabloids are *The Sun on Sunday*, *The Mail on Sunday*, *The Sunday Mirror* and *The Sunday Express*. Most Sunday and many daily newspapers (usually on Saturdays) include a colour magazine, some of which have earned a reputation for quality journalism in their own right, e.g. *The Sunday Times Colour Magazine*.

There are also regional daily and evening newspapers in most areas. Free weekly newspapers are delivered to homes throughout the UK, and numerous magazines are on sale, including many popular European and North American titles.

If you prefer to have publications delivered to your doorstep, most newsagents will do this for a small fee. You can also take out subscriptions to your favourite magazines, which is usually cheaper than buying them from newsagents, and some national newspapers (e.g. *The Times*) can be bought at less than half price if you join their subscription voucher schemes.

A selection of foreign newspapers, such as *The International Herald Tribune*, *The Wall Street Journal Europe*, *USA Today*, *Die Welt* and *Le Monde* is to be found on newsstands in urban centres, often on the day of publication, and European editions of *Newsweek* and *Time* are sold by at many city newsagents. If you're willing to wait a few days for delivery, many foreign publications can be bought on subscription at a large saving over newsagent prices.

BOOKS

Just as the internet has had a negative effect on newspaper circulation, so it has rocked the bookselling world. High street bookshops are an apparently dying breed as an ever increasing number of people buy their books online from stores such as Amazon (www.amazon.co.uk) or download them as e-books to read on laptops or e-readers. Since the closure of Borders in 2009 the only major national chains are WH Smith and Waterstones, although some excellent specialist bookstores remain.

In London, the area around Charing Cross Road is a Mecca for readers with a multitude of bookshops, including the world-famous Foyles, where you'll find books on just about everything. Some stores specialise in certain subjects such as art and design, feminist and ethnic interests, science fiction, sport, law, medicine, travel, politics, economics and foreign literature. The availability of foreign language books is otherwise limited to major cities. Cut-price bookshops, where 'remaindered' books that have been sold off cheaply by publishers can be bought at discount prices, are commonplace, while secondhand bookshops are relatively rare. Department stores, newsagent chains, convenience stores and supermarkets also offer a limited range of books, although some sell only paperback novels. In cities, bookshops are often open most days until around 8pm, possibly including weekends.

Although books may not be particularly cheap in the UK, they're often cheaper than in other countries (particularly textbooks). Prices, formerly fixed, are now widely discounted – at least as far as bestsellers are concerned. Cut-price books even appear on supermarket shelves (some are virtually given away as loss-leaders). One of the major sources of discounted books is Amazon, which sells books at up to 50 per cent discount with free UK delivery, as well as offering used books for as little as 1p each (plus postage!) via Amazon Marketplace. Car boot sales and markets are also a great place to buy secondhand books

FURNITURE

Furniture is usually good value in the UK, and top quality furniture is often cheaper than in many other European countries. There's a huge choice of modern and traditional designs in every price range although, as with most things, you generally get what you pay for. Exclusive *avant garde* designs from Italy, Denmark and other countries are available (usually with equally exclusive prices), but imports also include reasonably-priced quality leather suites.

Among the largest furniture chain stores in the UK are DFS, Dreams (beds), Furniture Village and Harveys, most of which offer a wide range of furniture from budget lines to quality products. High-end British manufacturers include Ercol, G-Plan and Parker Knoll. All large furniture retailers publish catalogues and have websites. If you want good quality furniture that will hold its value (and may even increase), you should consider buying antique or vintage furniture, which is excellent value for money, particularly Edwardian and later pieces.

Oak is the most common wood used for traditional British quality furniture (there's a well-known store called Oak FurnitureLand) and pine, which can be bought stained or unstained, is also popular. When ordering furniture, you may need to wait around six weeks for delivery. Many manufacturers sell directly to the public, although you shouldn't assume that this will result in huge savings, and should compare prices and quality before buying. There are also shops specialising in beds, sofas, reproduction and antique furniture, along with many companies manufacturing and installing fitted bedrooms, bathrooms and kitchens.

If you want reasonably-priced, good quality, modern furniture, there are a number of companies selling items for home assembly (which helps keep down prices), such as IKEA, the world's only global furniture chain. Assembly instructions are usually easy to follow (although some people think a Rubik's cube is easier), and some companies print instructions in a number of languages.

Furniture and home furnishings are highly competitive businesses and you can often reduce the price by some judicious haggling, particularly when spending a large sum. Another way to save money is to wait for the sales to come round. If you cannot wait, and don't want to pay cash, look for an interest-free credit deal. Some retailers offer buy now, pay later deals, although any savings are often 'costed' into the retail price. Check the advertisements in local newspapers and national home and design magazines, such as *Country Homes & Interiors*, *House & Garden*, *Ideal Home* and *Living*.

HOUSEHOLD APPLIANCES

Large household appliances, such as cookers and refrigerators, are usually provided in rented accommodation, and may also be included in new homes. Many vendors include fitted kitchen appliances such as a cooker, refrigerator, dishwasher and washing machine when selling a house or apartment, although you may need to pay for them separately. It isn't worthwhile shipping these items to the UK, as they may not fit into UK homes and can be purchased inexpensively locally. A wide range of household appliances is available, from British and foreign manufacturers, with many shops also selling American-style refrigerators and other appliances.

If you already own small household appliances it may be worthwhile bringing them to the UK, as usually all that's required is a change of plug, but check first. If you're coming from a country with a 110/115V electricity supply (e.g. the US) you'll need a lot of expensive transformers. Don't bring a television to the UK from the continent or the US as it won't work. Smaller appliances, such as vacuum cleaners, grills, toasters and electric irons, aren't expensive, and are usually of excellent quality. Before buying household appliances, whether large or small, you may like to check the test reports and surveys in *Which?* magazine (see Consumers' Association on page 279) at your local library or consult the Which? website (www.which.co.uk).

Shops such as Apollo, Currys and Euronics have branches across the UK and can offer good deals, while the major supermarkets and catalogue retailers such as Argos also offer good deals. Warehouse clubs such as Costco offer competititive prices for household goods, as do online vendors such as http://ao.com, www.appliancesdirect.co.uk and www.empiredirectappliances.co.uk, not to mention the ubiquitous Amazon.co.uk. Before buying any home appliances you should compare prices online, which vary considerably for the more expensive items. One you've decided what you want, if you enter the model identification into Google you'll easily be able to compare prices; you can also try dedicated price comparison sites such as www.pricerunner.co.uk.

SECONDHAND BARGAINS

There's a lively secondhand market for almost everything in Britain, from antiques to motor cars, computers to photographic equipment (the British spend billions a year on secondhand goods). You name it, and somebody will be selling it secondhand. The internet auction site eBay (www.ebay.co.uk) is particularly popular and is a source for anything you could ever think of. With such a large secondhand market there are often bargains to be found, particularly if you're quick off the mark. All towns have charity shops such as the British Heart Foundation, Oxfam and Sue Ryder (among others) that sell both new and secondhand goods.

There's a number of national and regional weekly newspapers devoted to bargain hunters, including *Loot* (www.loot.com) and *Bargain Pages* (www.bargainpages.co.uk), published in various editions for different areas (advertisements are usually free to non-traders). The online marketplace for secondhand goods is huge and it's worth looking at classified advertising websites such as Exchange and Mart (www.exchangeandmart.co.uk), Gumtree (www.gumtree.com), Preloved (www.preloved.co.uk) and Craigslist (http://london.craigslist.co.uk), some of which have editions for many UK cities.

There are many magazines dedicated to secondhand cars, such as *Auto Trader* (www.autotrader.co.uk). If you're looking for a particular item, such as a camera, boat or motorcycle, you may be better off looking through the small advertisements in specialist, rather than more general, publications. The classified advertisements in local newspapers are also a good source of bargains, particularly for furniture and household appliances. Shopping centre, newsagent and company notice boards can also prove fruitful.

Another place to pick up a bargain is at an auction, although it helps to be knowledgeable about what you're buying (you'll probably be competing with experts). Auctions are held throughout the year for everything from antiques and paintings to motorcars and property. The UK has some of the world's most famous auction houses, including Sotheby's, Christie's and Phillips, which hold free local valuation days throughout the country, as well as numerous local independent auctioneers (see www.auctionhouse.co.uk).

Antique shops are found in most towns, and antique street markets (e.g. Portobello Road in London) and fairs are held regularly throughout the country. For information about local events inquire at your local Tourist Information Centre or library. Car boot (trunk) sales, where people sell practically anything from the boots of their cars, are popular throughout the UK, and the best place to acquire real bargains (and loads of junk!) without any consumer protection. Sales are customarily held on Sundays, and are advertised in local newspapers and on billboards.

HOME SHOPPING

Shopping by mail-order and telephone has always been popular, and shopping via the internet (see below) is now enormous and has created a sea change in buying habits. Catalogue and television (TV) shopping by mail, telephone and the internet is big business and worth billions a year. Direct retailing by companies (cutting out the middleman) has become more widespread in recent years, particularly for computers, office equipment and services such as insurance. Along with the increasing importance of electronic shopping, TV shopping is becoming more popular.

Mail-order Catalogues

There are many companies in the UK selling exclusively by mail-order. Customers are provided with a free colour catalogue, and can often also act as agents, collecting orders from other customers and receiving a commission. The major mail-order catalogues contain almost everything you would expect to find in a department store (nowadays most companies also offer online shopping). The main attraction is that goods are bought on approval, and can usually be paid for over a period of 6 or 12 months at no extra cost. Shipping costs are usually paid by the mail-order company (including returns). Among the major mail-order companies are Freemans, JD Williams, K&Co and Littlewoods. Others include direct-selling clothes manufacturers such as Boden, Cotton Traders, Damart, Hawkshead, Lands' End, Le Redoute and Next Directory.

Some major shops and chains also publish mail-order catalogues and will send goods almost anywhere in the world, e.g. Fortnum & Masons, Habitat, Harrods and Selfridges. Most major food retailers accept orders by telephone or via the internet. Many charities, institutions and organisations, e.g. Amnesty International, the British Heart Foundation, the National Trust, the Natural History Museum, Oxfam, Save the Children, the Science Museum and the World Wildlife Fund, also publish mail-order catalogues. The added bonus for buyers is that, in addition to buying beautiful, exclusive and often unusual handmade items from around the world, you can also contribute to a good cause.

Internet Shopping

Shopping online is becoming ever more popular and in 2015 Britons spent over £114 billion online. There are numerous shopping site portals, including www.moneysavingexpert.com/shopping, www.shopguide.co.uk, www.shopping.net and www.google.co.uk/shopping. Amazon (www.amazon.co.uk) frequently has the lowest prices on a wide range of goods,

Caution

Although shopping via the internet is generally secure (see http://en.wikipedia.org/wiki/internet_security), you must take care and verify a company is kosher before paying – and always pay by credit card if possible (if it isn't you should be suspicious). A common fraud is to sell bogus holiday accommodation that doesn't exist.

especially as delivery is often free. Other useful sites include price comparison sites such as www.dooyoo.co.uk, www.kelkoo.co.uk, www.pricechecker.co.uk, www.pricegrabber.co.uk and www.pricerunner.co.uk.

Other sites of interest include those offering vouchers and discounts (www.groupon.co.uk, www.vouchercodes.co.uk, www.vouchercloud.com and www.wowcher.co.uk), cashback sites (www.topcashback.co.uk and www.quidco.com), group buying (www.incahoot.com) and auction sites (www.bumblebeeauctions.co.uk and www.ebay.co.uk).

With internet shopping, the world is your oyster and savings can be made on a wide range of goods, including music, clothes, sports equipment, electronic gadgets, jewellery, books, wine, computer software, and services such as insurance, pensions and mortgages. Savings can also be made on holidays and travel.

Buying Overseas

When buying goods overseas, ensure that you're dealing with a bona fide company and that the goods you're buying will work in the UK. If possible, ALWAYS pay by credit card when buying via the internet (or by mail-order), because for bills between £100 and £30,000, the credit card issuer is usually jointly liable with the supplier under the Consumer Credit Act 1974. When buying expensive goods abroad, make sure that they're insured for their full value during shipping.

VAT & Duty

When buying overseas, take into account shipping costs, duty and VAT. There's no duty or tax on goods purchased within the European Union or on goods from most other countries worth up to £390. Don't buy alcohol or cigarettes abroad (unless you import them personally), as the duty is usually too high to make it cost-effective. When VAT or duty is payable on a parcel, the payment may be collected by the post office or courier company on delivery. See Gov.uk for more information (www.gov.uk/goods-sent-from-abroad/overview)

SHOPPING ABROAD

Shopping abroad for most British people consists of a day trip to Calais and a visit to a French hypermarket (similar to a British superstore). Considerable savings can be made on a wide variety of goods, including food (e.g. cheese, ground coffee, chocolate, cooked meats and patés), alcohol (beer, wine and spirits), cigarettes and tobacco, toys, housewares (e.g. hardware, glassware and kitchenware) and clothing. Don't forget your passports or identity cards, car papers, foreign currency and credit cards. Many French shops accept sterling, but usually give you a poor exchange rate. It's best to use a credit or debit card (and pay in euros) when shopping abroad and on board ferries, as you receive a better exchange rate.

Since 1st January 1993, there have been no cross-border shopping restrictions within the European Union for goods purchased with duty and tax paid, provided all goods are for your personal consumption or use and not for resale. Although there are no restrictions, there are 'indicative levels' for certain items, above which goods may be classified as commercial quantities. For example, those aged 17 or over entering the UK may usually import the following amounts of alcohol and tobacco without question:

- 10 litres of spirits (over 22° proof);
- 20 litres of fortified wine such as port or sherry (under 22° proof);
- 90 litres of wine (or 120 x 0.75 litre bottles/10 cases) of which a maximum of 60 litres may be sparkling wine;

- 110 litres of beer;
- 800 cigarettes, 400 cigarillos, 200 cigars and 1kg of smoking tobacco.

The vast cross-Channel shopping business is made possible by cheap, off-season, day return ferry trips (the ferry companies make their money on ship-board sales rather than the fares). Cross-Channel shopping has led a number of British companies to open outlets in Calais, including Sainsbury's, Tesco, Victoria Wine and The Wine Society.

Important

Following the UK's decision to leave the European Union (due to be completed by March 2019 at the latest), the whole question of EU tariffs and duties will raise its ugly head and could result in the return of duty-free limits when importing goods, particularly alcohol and tobacco, from the European Union.

RETURNING GOODS & CONSUMER RIGHTS

Under UK consumer law, you're entitled to your money back if there's a fault with a product, or if goods are of unsatisfactory quality, not fit for their purpose or not as advertised. You must, however, be able to prove that the fault was present when the goods were sold, and the burden of proof is on you as the consumer.

Refunds: Shops aren't obliged to give you a refund if there's nothing wrong with a product, e.g. if you've changed your mind about the purchase, although many will as a goodwill gesture. If you're buying a present it's best to ask about refund policies before buying. During sales some shops will only provide credit note refunds unless a product is faulty.

Repairs, Replacements & Compensation: If you buy goods that you later find are faulty you're entitled to a repair as an alternative to a refund or replacement. If the goods cannot be repaired economically you're entitled to a replacement or a refund.

Sale Goods: You've the same rights when you buy goods in a sale as at any other time, unless a fault was specifically mentioned at the time of the sale. It's illegal for retailers to display notices stating 'no refunds on sale goods'.

Guarantees & Warranties: Under EU law all electronic items and appliances have a guarantee of two years, during which you're entitled to free repair, although you may have to pay a 'call-out' fee for an engineer. If the item goes wrong within a month of purchase you can take it back to the shop where you bought it, after which you usually have to take it to a service or repair centre. You're responsible for collecting an item when it has been repaired or paying for it to be shipped to you.

If you've any questions about your rights as a consumer, contact your local trading standards department (www.gov.uk/find-local-trading-standards-office) or the Citizens Advice consumer service (www.adviceguide.org.uk/england/consumer_e.htm). Most department and chain stores exchange goods or give a refund without question (although the British rarely complain or return goods), but smaller retailers aren't so enthusiastic.

Consumer Complaints

If you need to make a complaint you should act quickly. Contact the seller as soon as possible to explain the problem and to say what you want done about it. You should also make your complaint in writing to the customer services manager, confirming any promise or response made. If the shop is part of a chain then you should write to the head office.

> ☑ **SURVIVAL TIP**
>
> Extended warranties, which are beloved by stores, are almost never worth the money. The chances of most electrical and electronic equipment going wrong are remote, and when they do it's usually cheaper to throw them away and buy a new item.

Shops are legally obliged to give customers this information and businesses operating under a different name from their legal one must publicly display their corporate name and address.

If you aren't sure about where you stand legally you can check your rights before you confront the trader by contacting a consumer organisation such as the Citizens Advice consumer service (0345-404 0506, www.adviceguide.org.uk/england/consumer_e.htm) or Northern Ireland's Consumer Line (www.nidirect.gov.uk/consumerline). Contact the UK European Consumer Centre (www.ukecc.net) for help with problems buying from another EU country.

The Consumers' Association

The Consumers' Association (01992-822800, www.which.co.uk) is a highly acclaimed independent consumer organisation in the UK, with over a million members. It publishes an excellent monthly magazine, entitled *Which?*, and has a very informative website. Both contain invaluable information about a wide range of goods and services – just about everything is tested at some time or another – and are available on subscription only, although the magazine can be consulted in reference libraries in larger towns.

All tests are organised independently by the Consumers' Association and cover financial services (e.g. insurance, banking, pensions and investment); cars; leisure products; food and health; household and domestic appliances; and items of public interest. Dangerous products are highlighted, best buys are recommended and, most importantly, you're told how to obtain your legal rights when things go wrong.

The Consumers' Association also publishes other consumer magazines, including *Which? Computing, Which? Gardening, Which? Travel* and *Which? Money*.

Westminster Abbey, London

18. ODDS & ENDS

This chapter contains miscellaneous information. Although all the topics covered aren't of vital importance, most are of general interest to anyone living or working in the UK, including everything you ever wanted to know (but were afraid to ask) about tipping and toilets.

BRITISH CITIZENSHIP

Apart from those born to a foreign diplomat, anyone born in the UK before 1983 automatically qualifies for British citizenship. A person born abroad before 1983 whose father was born or adopted in the UK (or had become a British citizen in the UK) and who was married to their mother, is automatically a British citizen through descent from his father. A person born in the UK after 1982 becomes a British citizen automatically only if either parent was a British citizen or a permanent resident (settled) at the time of their birth. Anyone born after 1982 with a parent who was born or adopted in the UK (or who had become a British citizen in the UK) is automatically a British citizen by descent from either parent. If the parents weren't married at the time of birth, the mother's status is relevant.

Any foreign national aged over 18, including a Commonwealth or Irish citizen, can apply to become a British citizen (called 'naturalisation'). To qualify you must have been permitted to live as a permanent resident in the UK for a minimum of one year, have lived in the UK legally for a total of at least five years without being absent from the country for more than 450 days (with no more than 90 days' absence in the year prior to your application) and plan to continue living in the UK. You cannot apply for British citizenship in order to qualify to live elsewhere in the European Union. You must also have sufficient knowledge of the English, Welsh or Scottish (Gaelic) language, be of good character, e.g. no criminal record and pay a fee. Parents of non-British children who qualify under the above rules can apply on their behalf (called 'registration'), for which there's a reduced fee.

Anyone aged over 18 and married to a British citizen can apply for naturalisation, provided he's permitted to live in the UK as a permanent resident and has lived in the UK legally for a total of at least three years without being absent from the country for more than 270 days, and with not more than 90 days' absence in the year prior to the application. He must also plan to continue living in the UK, be of good character and pay a fee. It takes an average of 6 to 12 months to become a naturalised British citizen. For further details, contact the Home Office UK Border Agency (0845-010 5200, www.ukba.homeoffice.gov.uk).

You can apply for a passport online (see www.gov.uk/browse/abroad/passports), by mail or in person, which is the best option if you need a passport quickly as there are sometimes long delays (you should allow around six weeks for a first passport). Application forms are available from main post offices and should be sent by post to your local passport office with the fee, relevant documents (such as your birth certificate), two passport-size photographs and your old passport (if applicable). An application form for a British passport must be signed by a person of professional standing in the community who knows you well, e.g. a doctor, Member of Parliament or a justice of the peace.

For further information contact the passport advice line (0300-222 0000).

CLIMATE

The UK has a generally mild and temperate climate, although it's extremely changeable, and usually damp at any time of year. Because of the prevailing south-westerly winds, the weather is variable, and is affected mainly by depressions moving eastwards across the Atlantic Ocean. This maritime influence means that the west of the country tends to have wetter, but also milder, weather than the east.

The amount of rainfall also increases with altitude, and the 'mountainous' areas of the north and west have more rain (around 2,000mm per year in the Lake District and the western Highlands of Scotland, with almost as much in the Pennines) than the lowlands of the south and east, where the average is 700mm. Rain is fairly evenly distributed throughout the year in all areas. It may feel as though it rains most of the time, but in fact (according to the Meteorological Office) it does so only on one day in every three.

The driest months are usually March to June; and the wettest, September to January. For many, spring is the most pleasant time of year, although early spring is often very wet, particularly in Scotland.

In winter, temperatures are higher in the south and west than in the east, and winters are often harsh in Scotland and on high ground in Wales and northern England, where snow is usual. December and February are traditionally the severest months, when it's often cold, wet and windy. When it snows, the whole country comes to a grinding halt (except for the kids, who love it) and people routinely complain that the authorities were unprepared. Although temperatures drop below freezing in winter, particularly at night, it's rarely below freezing during the day, although the average temperature may hover around a cold 4°C (39°F). Regional variations are relatively small, e.g. 2°C (35.6°F) in Edinburgh, 3°C (37.4°F) in Manchester and at over 5°C (41°F) in London.

The most unpleasant features of British winters are freezing fog and black ice, both of which make driving hazardous. The 'pea-soup' fog that was usually the result of smog and pollution – and which many foreigners still associate with London – is a thing of the distant past. The warmest areas in summer are the south and inland areas, where temperatures are often around 26°C (75°F), and occasionally rise above 30°C (86°F), although the average is 15°C to 18°C (60°F to 64°F). Fine autumn weather is often is often preceded by early morning fog or mist, which may last until midday. Early autumn is often mild, particularly in Scotland. Average daily temperatures in London are: winter just over 5°C (41°F), spring 11°C (51.8°F), summer just below 18°C (64.4°F) and autumn just over 12°C (53.6°F).

The good news is that British winters are becoming milder, with snow rare and frost less frequent in most areas. British weather is also becoming drier, with the last decade experiencing some of the driest summers since records began in 1659. To add a little spice to the usual diet of cold and rain, in the last few decades the UK has been afflicted with gales and torrential rain, which has led to catastrophic flooding in some areas. There's an ongoing debate among weather experts and scientists as to whether climate changes (not just in the UK, but worldwide) is a result of global warming or just a periodic phenomenon.

Weather forecasts appear designed to be deliberately vague, as if the meteorologists are continually hedging their bets; therefore most forecasts include scattered showers and sunny periods at the very least. A fairly recent innovation is percentage forecasting such as a 70 per cent chance of rain, a 50 per cent likelihood of frost overnight and a 10 per cent probability of sunny periods (and a 100 per cent chance that it will all be wrong!).

Detailed forecasts for just about any country or region are available via the internet, but the best sites for the UK include www.metoffice.gov.uk, www.weather.org.uk, www.bbc.co.uk/weather and www.weatherweb.net. Weather forecasts are also available via daily newspapers and TV and radio broadcasts (usually after the news). Warnings regarding dangerous weather conditions affecting motoring, e.g. fog and ice, are broadcast regularly on BBC national and local radio stations.

During early summer, when pollen is released in large quantities, the pollen count is provided in radio and TV weather forecasts and in daily newspapers for hay fever sufferers.

CRIME

The crime rate in England and Wales has (officially) fallen for many years – by 40 per cent since 1984 – although homicides rose by 11 per cent (year-on-year) to 573 in 2015 (notably gun and knife crimes), which roughly equates to 10 homicides per million population in 2015. However, overall crime continued to fall (by 7 per cent), largely driven by a decline in thefts and criminal damage.

Caution

Barclays and the Metropolitan Police publish *The Little Book of Big Scams*, available from Barclays' branches or online (https://beta.met.police.uk/advice-and-information/fraud), to help you avoid becoming a victim of fraud.

In recent years there has been a rash of thefts of metal for scrap, including lead from the roofs of buildings and bronze statues (antique garden ornaments are also a popular target); farmers have also been hard hit as farm equipment and vehicles have been targeted. Fraud – which includes internet fraud, credit card fraud, income tax evasion and VAT fraud – is rising and costs billions of pounds a year, accounting for larger sums than the total of all other robberies, burglaries and thefts combined.

Although the crime figures may paint a depressing picture, it's all relative (an estimated 15,696 people were murdered in the US in 2015) and the UK is generally a safe place to live. Crimes of violence are still relatively rare in much of the country and you can safely walk anywhere in most cities day or night. If you take care of your property and take precautions against crime (including avoiding potential high crime areas), your chances of becoming a victim are small. The rate of crime varies hugely from area to area, and anyone coming to live in the UK should avoid high crime areas whenever possible. For information see www.ukcrimestats.com.

GEOGRAPHY

The title of this book may cause some confusion, particularly as there are occasional references to the United Kingdom, England, Scotland, Wales, Ireland and Northern Ireland. The term Britain, as used in this book, comprises Great Britain (the island which includes England, Wales and Scotland) and Northern Ireland, the full name of which is the 'United Kingdom of Great Britain and Northern Ireland', usually shortened to UK. The British Isles is the geographical term for the group of islands, which includes Great Britain, Ireland and a number of smaller islands surrounding Britain.

The UK covers an area of 93,600mi² (242,432km²) and is around the same size as New Zealand or Uganda and half the size of France. It's some 600mi (1,000km) from the south coast to the northern-most point of Scotland, and around 300mi (500km) across in the widest part. Nowhere in the UK is more than 75mi (120km) from the sea and the strikingly-varied coastline is one of the most beautiful in the world. The UK has a varied landscape; most of England is fairly flat and low-lying (particularly East Anglia), with the exception of the north and southwest, while much of Scotland and Wales is mountainous. If the most dire predictions of global warming become a reality, many regions of the UK will be flooded as the sea level rises.

The highest mountains are Ben Nevis in Scotland at 1,343 metres (4,406ft) and Snowdon in Wales at 1,085 metres (3,560ft). The country can roughly be divided into a highland region in the north and west, and a lowland region in the south and east, approximately delimited by the mouths of the River Exe (Exeter) in the southwest and the River Tees (Teesside) in the northeast. The UK has around 1,200mi² (1,931km²) of inland waters, the most famous and largest area being the Lake District in the northwest of England.

GOVERNMENT

The UK is a constitutional monarchy, under which the country is governed by ministers of the crown in the name of the sovereign (Queen Elizabeth II), who's the head of state and the government. Nowadays, the monarchy has no real power and its duties are restricted to ceremonial and advisory ones only, although there are certain acts of government that require the participation of the sovereign, such as the opening and dissolving of parliament and giving royal assent to bills. Parliament is the ultimate law-making authority in the UK and consists of two houses or chambers, the House of Commons and the House of Lords, which together comprise the Houses of Parliament.

> Parliament sits in the Palace of Westminster (opposite) in London, built in the 19th century after the previous building was destroyed by fire, and whose clock, Big Ben (actually the name of the large bell), is London's most famous landmark.

However, the Channel Islands and the Isle of Man make their own laws on island affairs, and a certain amount of legislative power has been devolved to the Scottish Parliament and the respective Assemblies of Wales and Northern Ireland (see below).

The UK's democratic traditions date from 1265, when King Henry III was forced to acknowledge the first Parliament. Westminster, which is often referred to as the 'mother of parliaments', is the model for many democracies around the world.

House of Commons

The House of Commons is the assembly chamber for the 650 Members of Parliament (MPs) who are commoners (i.e. not Lords or titled people), elected by the people of the UK in a general election that must be held every five years if parliament isn't dissolved earlier. Each MP represents an area called a constituency; at the 2015 general election there were 533 constituencies in England, 59 in Scotland, 40 in Wales and 18 in Northern Ireland (the number is due to change before the next general election in 2020). If an MP resigns, retires or dies during the term of a government, a by-election is held to choose a new MP.

All British and Commonwealth citizens (and citizens of the Republic of Ireland) over the age of 18 and resident in the UK can vote in parliamentary elections, provided they're registered voters. To be eligible to vote your name must appear in a register of electors, maintained and updated annually by councils. If you fail to register you're liable to a fine. Voting isn't compulsory and there's no penalty for not voting, but don't complain about the government if you don't vote! Between 70 and 80 per cent of people usually vote in general elections.

British citizens who've been living abroad for less than ten years also have the right to vote in parliamentary elections. While they're still eligible to vote in the UK, they can also vote there in local and European elections or they can opt to do so in their country of residence if it's in the EU. Anyone who's a registered voter and who's away from his constituency during parliamentary, European or local government elections, can vote by post or appoint a proxy to vote on his behalf.

There are three main national parties in the UK: the Conservatives or Tories (right wing leaning), Labour is left-wing and the Liberal Democrats (centre). There are a few other smaller parties, most of which contest seats in particular regions or constituencies only. These include the Scottish Nationalist Party (SNP); the Ulster Unionist Party, the Democratic Unionist Party, the Social and Democratic Labour Party (SDLP) and Sinn Fein, all of Northern Ireland; Plaid Cymru (Welsh

nationalists); the UK Independence Party (UKIP), the Green Party and the Communist Party of Great Britain.

The government is formed by the political party that wins the largest number of seats at a general election; if no party has a clear majority, i.e. 326 seats, then a coalition government may be formed between a number of parties. After the 2015 general election the Conservatives were the largest party with 331 seats, an overall majority of 12.

The highlight of the week in the House of Commons is question time, during which MPs can question ministers, and which often becomes heated when the PM and the Leader of the Opposition trade insults.

The head of the government is the Prime Minister (PM), who's the leader of the party with the majority of seats (or the leader of the principal party in a coalition) and who chooses an inner cabinet of around 20 ministers. In addition to the cabinet, the government also appoints around 80 junior ministers, of which there may be two to five in each ministry. Every few years (or months if cabinet members resign suddenly), a game of musical ministries takes place, in which the Prime Minister's more loyal supporters get promoted, and those who are lukewarm about his/her policies are consigned to the backbenches.

The Leader of the Opposition, who's the head of the largest defeated party (and not part of a government coalition), appoints a shadow cabinet of shadow ministers, whose job is to respond to government ministers in Parliament and to act as the party's spokespeople. MPs who are members of the cabinet or shadow cabinet sit on the front benches (on opposite sides) in the House of Commons. All other MPs are known as backbenchers.

The House of Commons is presided over by the Speaker, who's the spokesman and president of the chamber and who controls proceedings (or attempts to). The Speaker is an MP (of either party, but usually from the governing party) who's elected by the House at the start of each parliament or when the previous speaker retires or dies. He neither speaks in debates nor votes on a bill, except when voting is equal (when he has the deciding vote). The Speaker has an apartment in the Palace of Westminster.

House of Lords

The House of Lords is referred to as the 'Other Place' in the House of Commons, and is the geriatric ward of the constitution, where retired MPs and a declining number of blue-blooded landowners spend their days in retirement. The Lords consists of the Lords Spiritual (archbishops and bishops) and Temporal, which includes a fixed number of 90 hereditary peers and peeresses, all life peers and peeresses, and the Law Lords, with the precise total depending on the number of life peers the prime minister chooses to create.

Until the beginning of the 20th century, the House of Lords had extensive powers, and could veto any bill submitted to it by the House of Commons. It still retains powers to block government legislation temporarily, which sometimes has the same result in practice. It's no longer the highest court of appeal in the UK and has been replaced by the Supreme Court, which after Brexit (see page 18) will be the UK's final legal jurisdiction, as it will no longer come under the rule of the European Court of Justice.

The House of Lords was formerly presided over by the Lord High Chancellor, but the Constitutional Reform Act 2005 transferred these roles to the Lord Speaker and the Lord Chief Justice. Members of the House of Lords

and also decides on matters that differentiate Scotland from England in a number of areas. For example, student fees have been abolished and doctors in Scotland can prescribe drugs on the NHS that are unavailable to patients in England and Wales. Its system of election is a complicated mix of the 'first past the post' and proportional representation. The Scottish Nationalist Party (SNP), Conservatives and Labour are the main parties, while the Greens and Liberal Democrats each have a handful of seats.

are unpaid, although they receive generous attendance and travelling expenses when on parliamentary business.

Referendums

Referendums are rare in the UK and are usually reserved for matters of national importance and must be sanctioned by Parliament. The British people cannot demand a referendum, e.g. by collecting signatures in a petition, for which there's no precedent under British law, and referendums aren't held at the regional or local level.

There have been two national referendums on membership of the EU, the first in 1975 (when the EU was the European Economic Community or EEC), when over two-thirds of those who too part voted in favour of continuing EEC membership. However, as you'll know, in June 2016 the UK voted to leave the EU by 52 per cent to 48 per cent, which is expected to be finalised by the end of March 2019 at the latest.

This decision will have far-reaching political, legal and economic implications.

Devolution

In 1999, the 129-member Scottish Parliament came into existence and the Scottish Executive, which is formed by the majority party or a coalition based on a parliamentary majority, exercises power. The Scottish Parliament is responsible for local matters such as education, housing, health and tourism,

The Welsh Assembly has far more limited powers than the Scottish Parliament, and only limited tax-raising powers. Its main function is deciding how the funds formerly at the disposal of the Welsh Office in London and allocated to it by central government should be spent. This is significant, but as its creation was supported by only a quarter of Welsh people – another quarter were opposed, and half didn't vote – it has yet to convince them that it's worth taking seriously.

The Northern Ireland Assembly sits in the Parliament Buildings at Stormont (Belfast), and was established in 1973, since when it's been suspended on a number of occasions as a result of the 'troubles' in the last 30 years (when there was virtually a civil war between the Catholic and Protestant communities). However, following the Good Friday agreement of 1998 and the St Andrews agreement in 2006, full power was restored to the devolved institutions in 2007. It has the power to legislate on a wide range of matters which aren't explicitly reserved by the UK parliament, and to appoint the Northern Ireland Executive. Its electoral and procedural arrangements are highly idiosyncratic, reflecting the unusual situation of Northern Ireland.

Local Government

The administration of local affairs in the UK is performed by local government or local authorities. In most areas of England and Wales services are divided between two authorities, a district council and a county council, while in large cities, services are usually provided by a single authority, e.g. a borough council in London and a metropolitan district or city council elsewhere. London is divided into 32 boroughs and the Corporation of the City of London. In Scotland, services are usually divided between district, regional or island councils, and in Northern Ireland between district councils, area boards and central government.

England and Wales are divided into 53 counties, which are further subdivided into 369 districts. All districts and 47 of the (non-metropolitan) counties have locally-elected councils with separate functions. In Scotland, there are nine regions that are divided into 52 districts, each with its own area council.

LEGAL SYSTEM

England and Wales, Scotland and Northern Ireland all have their own separate legal systems and law courts and, although there are many similarities, there are also considerable differences. In Northern Ireland, procedure closely follows that of England and Wales, but Scottish law differs in many respects, and is based on a different legal tradition from English law. Differences include the buying and selling of property, consumer rights, inheritance and the rights of young people. Even so, much modern legislation applies throughout the UK and there's a common distinction between criminal law (acts harmful to others or the community) and civil law (disputes between individuals) in all regions. Under the British legal system you're innocent until proven guilty, although you may sometimes get the impression that not everybody is aware of this.

In the UK, less serious cases are dealt with by a magistrates' court (a 'people's court', although there are professional stipendiary magistrates), which handles civil and criminal cases. A magistrates' court normally consists of three lay magistrates, known as justices of the peace (JPs), who are advised on points of law and procedure by a legally-qualified clerk or assistant. Cases involving children under 17 are heard in juvenile courts. Minor civil claims such as small debts, are heard in a county court, of which there are around 300 in England and Wales.

Supreme Court Judges

A person convicted by a magistrates' court has the right of appeal to a crown court (criminal cases) or high court (civil cases) against the sentence imposed (if he pleaded guilty) or the conviction if he pleaded not guilty. Civil cases may be dealt with by a Queen's

Bench, Family division or Chancery division court, depending on the subject matter.

Magistrates are usually unpaid local volunteers, chosen for their character and judgment, and aren't usually legal professionals. Sentences in magistrates' courts often vary considerably for the same offences, and magistrates have considerable discretion in the fines they impose for certain offences, such as motoring offences. There's a chronic shortage of magistrates in some areas, particularly in blue-collar districts.

More serious criminal offences, such as murder, manslaughter, rape and robbery with violence, are tried by a crown court before a judge and a jury consisting of 12 people (15 in Scotland); or, in a civil case, a high court. Every local or parliamentary elector between the age of 18 and 65 who has been resident in the UK for at least five years since the age of 13, can be called on to serve on a jury unless ineligible or disqualified. If you're found guilty in a crown court or a high court, you've the right of further appeal against conviction or sentence to a court of appeal, criminal or civil division, depending on the case. All courts have a huge backlog of cases.

In criminal and civil cases involving a point of general public importance, you may be given leave to appeal to the Supreme Court, the highest and final court of appeal in the UK. In cases involving or conflicting with EU regulations or the European Convention on Human Rights, you can appeal to the European Court of Justice (Luxembourg) – at least while the UK remains a member of the EU – or the European Court of Human Rights (Strasbourg). Only one in four appeals in any court are successful, so that often the only winners are the lawyers.

As in most countries, the cost of taking anyone to court to obtain justice is a huge lottery, and invariably costs more than you could ever hope to gain, or ends in failure. The only winners are the legal profession, who charge astronomical fees.

Citizens Advice Bureau

The Citizens Advice Bureau (CAB) – sadly lacking an apostrophe – was founded in 1939 to provide an emergency service during the Second World War. It's an independent organisation that provides free confidential information and advice on almost any problem or subject. These include social security; consumer and debt problems; housing; family and personal difficulties; employment; justice; local information; health; immigration and nationality; and taxes. There are over 1,000 CAB offices in England, Wales and Northern Ireland.

For more information about the CAB, contact the National Association of Citizens Advice Bureau (020-7833 2181, www.citizensadvice.org.uk). In Scotland, there's a separate Citizens Advice Scotland (0131-550 1000, www.cas.org.uk) service.

Small Claims & Money Claim Online

If you've a claim of up to £100,000, you can use the simplified Small Claims procedure (www.hmcourts-service.gov.uk) or Money Claim Online (0845-601 5935, www.moneyclaim.gov.uk, customerservice.mcol@hmcourts-service.gsi.gov.uk). Note that the limit for small claims is £5,000, and the limit for money claim online is £100,000.

Under either system you take out the summons yourself and do your own prosecuting. No costs are awarded to either side as no lawyers are required, similar to private arbitration. (If you use a lawyer in a small claims court it can cost you thousands of pounds in legal fees.) The fee for making a claim varies depending on the size of your claim from £30 to £120, but if you win your fees are paid by the other party. Further information is available online (see above) and from county courts.

MARRIAGE & DIVORCE

In 1995, the law regarding where a marriage can take place was changed, and consequently, in addition to a church or register office (civil ceremony), you can get married anywhere that's licensed by the local authorities, including boats, stately homes, castles, hotels, restaurants and sports venues. The bride and groom must be at least 18 years old, or 16 if they have parental consent (which also applies to foreigners who get married in the UK).

Warning

'Marriages of convenience', where a foreigner marries a British subject in order to remain in the UK, are illegal, and subject to intense scrutiny by the Home Office.

Foreigners living in the UK who are married, divorced or widowed should have a valid marriage licence, divorce papers or a death certificate, which is usually necessary to confirm their marital status with the authorities, e.g. to receive certain legal or social benefits. A blood test isn't required to get married. Marriage according to the rites of the Church of England can be by banns, by licence (common or special) or under a superintendent registrar's certificate. If you get married in a church or place of worship, you must give notice to the local register office, but you aren't required to undergo a civil wedding service.

The average church wedding costs around £10,000. The alternative is to be married in a register office or another venue licensed to stage civil weddings under a superintendent registrar's certificate, which is much simpler and cheaper than a church wedding and without the religious significance. To be married in a register office, the bride or groom must live within its official area. Each partner must show his or her birth certificate and pay the fee to the local register office (if you've been married before you must produce a decree absolute or a death certificate) at least 21 days but not more than three months before the planned wedding date.

On the wedding day you must have two witnesses (anyone will do). A ring isn't required for a register office wedding, although most couples use one. The ceremony lasts around ten minutes, after which you both sign the register (when it's too late to change your mind!).

Same-sex ('gay') marriage was legalised in 2014 in the UK, with the exception of Northern Ireland where it isn't recognised. Same-sex partners can also enter into a legal civil partnership (since 2005), including in Northern Ireland, which offers the same legal rights and responsibilities as marriage – an option that isn't available to heterosexual couples!

To be divorced, a couple must have been married for at least one year. Under British law it's unnecessary to prove that a partner has committed an act which gives grounds for divorce (thus depriving private detectives of much lucrative work), but a marriage must have broken down beyond repair. To prove a marriage has 'irretrievably broken down' (in legal terminology) and obtain a divorce, a couple must fulfil certain legal requirements such as living apart for two years when both partners want a divorce (or five years when only one partner wants a divorce). There are many other grounds for divorce such as desertion, the behaviour of one partner in such a way that the couple cannot live together, or adultery.

When a divorce is granted, the court issues a decree nisi and an application for a decree absolute (which makes the divorce final) can be made six weeks later, and is usually a formality. Both partners receive a divorce certificate from the county court or divorce registry that proves the divorce, and which is necessary if you wish to remarry. Almost half of all marriages in the UK end in divorce and the UK is top of the European divorce league.

There are many organisations that provide marriage counselling (e.g. Relate – www.relate.org.uk) and advice for couples contemplating divorce. The Gov.uk website also provides information about marriage and divorce (see www.gov.uk/browse/births-deaths-marriages/marriage-divorce).

MILITARY SERVICE

There's no conscription (draft) in the UK, where all members of the armed forces are volunteers. To join the army applicants must be British citizens, British subjects under the Nationality Act, 1981, British Protected Persons or Commonwealth Citizens (who need to have lived in the UK for at least five years). As a general rule, all recruits enlist on an Open Engagement, which allows them to serve for 22 years from their 18th birthday, or date of attestation (whichever is the later date) and so qualify for a pension. A soldier enlisted on this engagement has a statutory right to leave after four years, calculated from his 18th birthday or from three months after attestation (whichever is the later). This right is subject to giving 12 months notice of intention to leave and provided the soldier isn't restricted from leaving in any way, perhaps due to a lengthy training course.

Discharge is also permitted for compassionate reasons, grounds of conscience (conscientious objection) or purchase. Reservists are entitled to register as conscientious objectors if called up for military service. Short, medium and long-term commissions (as officers) are based on educational and personal qualifications, and all services have a range of educational sponsorship schemes.

Conscription was abolished during the '60s, and there's little likelihood of it being reintroduced short of a major war. The UK is unusual in Europe in having no national service, the belief being that professional armed services are better equipped to cope in times of crisis. In addition to its full-time military services, the UK has a regular reserve force totalling over 200,000, and volunteer reserve and auxiliary forces of around 100,000 (who train at weekends and for a few weeks each year).

The UK is one of the main contributors to NATO, and spends almost £35 billion on defence, and a higher proportion of its GDP than most NATO countries except the US. The UK has reduced its armed forces in the last few years as part of the so-called 'peace dividend' resulting from the thaw in east-west relations. However, following the Iraq war and peacekeeping duties in Afghanistan and elsewhere, the armed forces are overstretched, which has been exacerbated by recruitment difficulties in recent years.

In 2015, the government committed to increase defence spending by 0.5 per cent above inflation every year until 2021 and continue to meet NATO's target to spend 2 per cent of GDP on defence for the rest of the decade.

THE MONARCHY

The British royal family is the longest reigning monarchy in the world, and certainly the most famous. Its continuity, apart from the period from 1649 to 1660, remains unbroken for a thousand years. The head of the royal family is the monarch or sovereign, currently Her Majesty (HM) Queen Elizabeth II, who's married to His Royal Highness (HRH) the Duke of Edinburgh, Prince Philip (who's the son of Princess Andrew of Greece). The monarch is head of state and head of the British Commonwealth, although these are ceremonial titles without any real power. The UK is governed by HM Government in the name of the Queen.

> Nowadays, the most popular members of the Royal Family (apart from the Queen) are the Duke and Duchess of Cambridge (William and Kate) and William's younger brother, Prince Harry.

The Queen and Prince Philip have four children: Prince Charles (the Prince of Wales), who's the heir to the throne (and who married Camilla, Duchess of Cornwall, after being divorced from the late Diana, Princess of Wales); Princess Anne (the Princess Royal, married to Timothy Laurence); Prince Andrew (the Duke of York, divorced from Sarah Ferguson, the Duchess of York); and Prince Edward (who married Sophie Rhys-Jones in 1999). The most popular member of the Royal Family was the late Queen Elizabeth, the Queen Mother, who died aged 101 in 2002. The Queen's sister, Princess Margaret (who was married to the Earl of Snowdon – formerly Anthony Armstrong-Jones), died in the same year. The Royal Family includes other major and minor royals, many of whom are descended from King George V's other children, Henry (the 1st Duke of Gloucester), George (the 1st Duke of Kent) and Mary.

The most important functions of the Queen are ceremonial, and include the state opening of Parliament; giving Royal Assent to bills; the reception of diplomats; entertaining foreign dignitaries; conferring peerages, knighthoods and other honours; the appointment of important office-holders; chairing meetings of the Privy Council; and sorting out family squabbles. She also attends numerous artistic, industrial, scientific and charitable events of national and local interest. The Queen and other members of the royal family are patrons or honorary heads of many leading charities and organisations, and the royal family undertake over 3,000 official duties each year. The Queen and other members of the royal family visit many areas of the UK each year, and undertake state visits and royal tours of foreign and Commonwealth countries.

Around 85 per cent of the cost of the royal family's official duties is met by the public purse, including the upkeep of royal palaces, the Queen's flight and the royal train. The Queen's public expenditure on staff, and the expenses incurred in carrying out her official duties, is financed from the Civil List approved by Parliament. Annual allowances are made in the Civil List to other members of the royal family, with the exception of the Prince of Wales, who, as the Duke of Cornwall, receives the net revenue of the estate of the Duchy of Cornwall. The Queen is estimated to be the richest woman in the UK, although much property attributed to her actually belongs to the state.

PETS

The UK is generally regarded as a country of animal lovers and has over 14 million pet owners, including some 7 million dog owners. This is attested to by the number of bequests received by the Royal Society for the Prevention of Cruelty to Animals (RSPCA), which far exceeds the amount left to the National Society for the Prevention of Cruelty to Children (NSPCC). The British are almost uniquely sentimental about animals, even those reared for food, e.g. battery hens. Protests about various forms of commercial cruelty to animals make headline news at regular intervals. Britons are also prominent in international animal protection organisations that attempt to ban cruel sports and practices in which animals are mistreated.

Quarantine

The UK has traditionally had some of the toughest quarantine regulations in the world in order to guard against the importation of rabies and other animal diseases, and has been virtually free of rabies for over 60 years. All mammals, apart from those participating in the Pet Travel Scheme (PETS, see below) and some specific breeds of horses and livestock, must usually spend a period of six months in quarantine in an approved kennel to ensure that they're free of rabies and Newcastle disease (a highly contagious generalised viral disease of domestic poultry and wild birds). Quarantine regulations also apply to guide dogs for the blind and hearing dogs. Under EU law, pets from unlisted third countries are no longer required to enter quarantine provided they meet certain pre-entry requirements. Quarantine arrangements remain in place to deal with animals that do not meet EU entry requirements.

If you're coming to the UK for a short period only it may not be worth the trouble and expense of bringing your pet, and you may prefer to leave it with friends or relatives during your stay. Before deciding to import an animal check with the Department for Environment, Food and Rural Affairs (020-7238 6951 or 0845-933 5577, www.defra.gov.uk) for the latest regulations, application forms, and a list of approved quarantine kennels and catteries.

Warning

It's a criminal offence to attempt to smuggle an animal into the UK and it's usually discovered. Illegally imported animals are exported immediately or destroyed and the owners are prosecuted. Owners face a heavy fine and up to a year's imprisonment for deliberate offences.

Applications for the importation of dogs, cats and other mammals should be made at least eight weeks before the proposed date of importation. To obtain a licence to import your pet you must have a confirmed booking at an approved kennel and have enlisted the services of an authorised carrying agent (who transports your pet from the port to the quarantine kennels); pets must arrive at an approved UK port or airport (listed on the DEFRA website). Animals must be transported in approved containers, available from air transport companies and pet shops, and must be shipped within six months of the date specified by the licence.

You're permitted, and in fact encouraged, to visit your pet in quarantine, but you won't be able to take it out for exercise. There are different regulations for some creatures. Birds, for example, serve a shorter quarantine period than other animals, until it's established that there's no danger of psittacosis.

There is no dog registration or licence scheme in England, Wales or Scotland, but all dogs must be microchipped. In Northern Ireland, a dog licence must be obtained from your local district council office for a dog over six months old.

The PETS Travel Scheme

The PETS Travel Scheme was introduced in February 2000, and enables you to bring your dog or cat into the UK or re-enter the country with it and avoid quarantine, but only under stringently controlled conditions. Pet travel rules changed on 1st January 2012 when the UK brought its procedures into line with the EU. For information, see www.defra.gov.uk/wildlife-pets/pets/travel/pets/pet-owners.

Animals must be micro-chipped and have a 'passport' listing their vaccinations and other necessary veterinary treatments, have had an officially approved blood test no less than six months previously and have been issued with an official PETS certificate issued by a government-authorised vet. They can also only be imported from certain countries and on defined routes from those countries on specific flights, ferries or railways. Before your pet enters the UK it must be treated against ticks and tapeworm not less than 24 hours and not more than 48 hours before it's checked in with an approved transport company. Owners must also sign a declaration that their pet hasn't been outside of any of the countries participating in the scheme (listed below) during the past six months.

The list of countries the UK accepts pet passports from is growing, and it's essential to check the DEFRA website (www.gov.uk/take-pet-abroad/listed-and-unlisted-countries) to ensure that your country is covered by the scheme. Additional requirements apply to people travelling from certain countries, which vary depending on the country in question. Other regulations of a general nature pertaining to animal welfare while travelling also apply and are given in detail on the website.

For some domestic animals, e.g. horses (only certain breeds of which are kept in quarantine) an import licence and a veterinary examination are required. Dangerous animals (e.g. poisonous snakes, big cats and crocodiles) require a special import licence. You require a licence from your local council to keep a poisonous snake or other dangerous wild animal, which must be properly caged with an adequate exercise area, and must pose no risk to public health and safety.

There's no VAT or duty on animals brought into the UK as part of your 'personal belongings', although if you import an animal after your arrival, VAT and duty may need to be paid on its value.

It isn't mandatory to have your dog (or any pet) vaccinated against any disease in the UK, although most dog owners have dogs vaccinated against distemper, hepatitis, parvovirosis and leptospirosis. Cats can have vaccinations for diseases which include feline infectious enteritis, feline herpes virus, feline chlamydophilosis, feline leukaemia, feline calicivirus, feline panleucopenia and feline bordetellosis. They can also be vaccinated against rabies.

A list of vets can be obtained from the Royal College of Veterinary Surgeons (020-7222 2001, www.rcvs.org.uk) or the British Veterinary Association (020-7636 6541, www.bva.co.uk), which also publishes a series of booklets on pet care. If you cannot afford a vet's fees the People's Dispensary for Sick Animals (0800-731 2502, www.pdsa.org.uk) may provide free treatment. The RSPCA (030-1234 999, www.rspca.org.uk) is the main organisation for animal protection and welfare in the UK, and operates a number of animal clinics and welfare centres. Many Britons are also concerned about the welfare of wild animals and there's even a British Hedgehog Preservation Society (although they have yet to teach them how to cross roads safely!).

The work of the RSPCA is complemented by the Dogs Trust, formerly the National Canine Defence League (020-7837 0006, www.dogstrust.org.uk), a national charity devoted to the welfare of dogs that takes in lost, abandoned and abused dogs and turns them into healthy, well-adjusted pets. No healthy dog is ever destroyed by the Dogs Trust. There are over 40 animal shelters in the UK, including those run by the Blue Cross, the Cats Protection League, The Dogs Home (Battersea), the Dogs Trust, the RSPCA and Wood Green Animal Shelters.

After a series of savage dog attacks on children the British government introduced a ban on the ownership of certain breeds of fighting dogs. These include Pit Bull Terriers, Japanese Tosas, Dogo Argentinos and Fila Brazilieros, none of which may be imported or bred in the UK (males must be neutered), and all of which must be registered and muzzled in public. If the law is broken a dog can be destroyed, and if it attacks anyone you're liable to a fine (and your dog may also be destroyed). You can be heavily fined (in addition to paying compensation) if your dog kills or injures livestock and a farmer can legally shoot a dog that molests farm animals.

POLICE

The UK doesn't have a national police force but rather 45 regional police forces, each responsible for a county, region or a metropolitan area such as London. Northern Ireland is policed by the Police Service of N. Ireland. There are no special uniformed traffic or tourist police, all routine duties being performed by regular policemen and policewomen (assisted by 'special' constables).

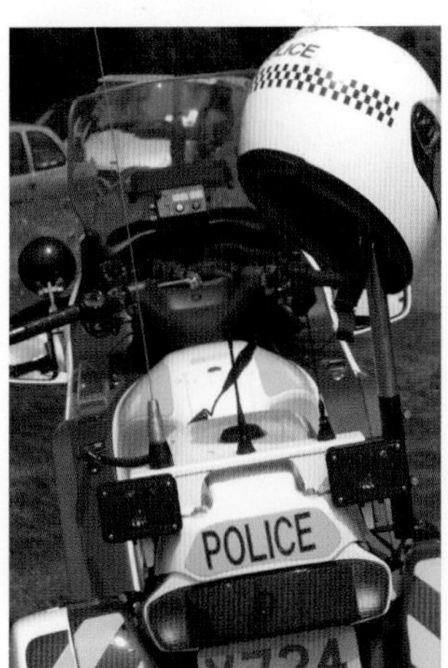

Police forces in England, Scotland and Wales are among the few in the world that don't carry firearms as a matter of course, although in recent years an increasing number of policemen have been armed for special services such as the prevention of terrorism and when dealing with armed suspects. This is a controversial issue, as a number of innocent people have been shot dead by police marksmen in recent years. Some police forces have also been issued with telescopic truncheons, pepper sprays and tasers, all of which have been responsible for a number of injuries and even deaths. The Police Service of Northern Ireland (PSNI) has always been armed.

The uniform worn by police forces is generally the same throughout the UK, and male bobbies (police officers) on the beat in England and Wales wear the famous British police helmet. Other police officers wear a flat cap with a chequered black and white band. Although Scotland has a different legal system, your rights regarding the police are roughly the same as in the rest of the UK. In addition to full-time police officers, each force has a part-time attachment of unpaid volunteer 'special' constables. Traffic wardens are responsible for traffic and parking, and come under the control of the local police force. There's also an auxiliary force of security wardens in some urban areas with fewer powers than police officers.

If you're seeking compensation against the police in England or Wales, you must usually seek redress in a county court, as the Independent Police Complaints Commission (IPCC – www.ipcc.gov.uk) cannot ensure that you'll receive compensation. In Scotland, complaints against the police involving criminal conduct are investigated by independent public prosecutors, while in Northern Ireland complaints involving death or serious injury are supervised by the Independent Commission for Police Complaints.

POPULATION

The estimated resident population of the UK was around 65,250,000 in autumn 2016 – an increase of some 2.5 million since 2010 and 5 million since 2005 – with a population density of 269 per km^2 (697 people per mi2). The population is forecast to exceed 75 million by 2050. The average age is around 40 and roughly a fifth of the population is under 16 and another fifth over 65 (for more information, see www.worldometers.info/world-population/uk-population).

England is the most populous part of the UK, with almost 55 million inhabitants and a density of 413 people per km^2, compared with 149 people per km^2 in Wales (pop. 3 million), 135 people per km^2 in Northern Ireland (pop. 1.9 million) and a density of 68 people per km^2 in Scotland, which has a population of around 5.4 million. Greater London has a (official) population – many people believe that it's much higher – of 8.6 million, with 5,285 people per km^2.

The central belt, which stretches across England from London to North Yorkshire, contains around half of the UK's population. Outside this area, there are a few high-density areas, including Bristol, the south coast and Tyne and Tees in England, southeast Wales and Clydeside in Scotland. Some 90 per cent of the UK's population live in urban areas, half of them in cities of over 500,000.

RELIGION

The UK has a tradition of religious tolerance, and everyone has total freedom of religion without hindrance by the state or community. The British, with a few notable exceptions, aren't particularly pious (church attendance has been declining for years), which perhaps explains their traditional tolerance towards the faiths of others. However, discrimination does raise its ugly head occasionally and Muslims and, more rarely, Jews, have been the targets of bigots in recent years. (England was notably anti-Semitic in the 12th century, but helped to atone for events by giving refuge to Jews

stained glass window, Canterbury Cathedral

escaping persecution in the late 19th and 20th centuries). The UK has few of the fire-eating, bible-thumping, Evangelists to be found in North America, and religious programmes on television are mainly confined to a few televised church services on Sunday, none of which make pleas for pots of money to pay for your salvation.

Most of the world's significant religious and philosophical movements have religious centres or meeting places in London and other major cities. Over 50 per cent of the British population theoretically belongs to the Church of England (or its counterparts), of which the Queen is the head; and the religious leader is the Archbishop of Canterbury, who's the 'Primate of all England' (the Archbishop of York is the 'Primate of England'). The Church in England was founded by St Augustine in AD597 and, following the 16th century Reformation, emerged as the established Church of England. Around 10 per cent of the population are Roman Catholics.

Other Christian groups or 'free churches' include various Presbyterian denominations, Congregational churches, Evangelicals, Methodists, Baptists, Pentecostals, United Reformed Church adherents and the Salvation Army, all of which admit men and women to the ministry. The Church of Scotland is Presbyterian and more puritanical than the Church of England. Scotland also has a substantial number of Roman Catholics. The Methodists have a strong following in Wales. In Northern Ireland, Protestants and Roman Catholics each make up around 40 per cent of the population.

The UK also has around 2.5 million Muslims, 600,000 Hindus (1.5 million unofficially) and 350,000 Sikhs, most originating from the Indian subcontinent, and around 300,000 Jews, the second-largest number of any European country. Other religions represented in the UK include the Baha'i Faith, Buddhism, Christian Science, Jehovah's Witnesses, Mormonism, the Quakers, Seventh-day Adventists, Sufis, Theosophists and Unitarians, to name but a few.

British churches include some of the oldest and most magnificent buildings in the world, particularly the great cathedrals, many dating from the 11th or 12th centuries. You don't need to be religious to enjoy the splendid architecture and grandeur of these buildings. Most cathedrals have gift shops, and many also have a café where profits go towards the cathedral's upkeep. Some cathedrals have introduced an entrance fee in recent years.

British state schools teach 'religious education' as part of the curriculum, although classes comprising more than simple bible study are segregated by denomination, and

TIME DIFFERENCE					
LONDON	CAPE TOWN	BOMBAY	TOKYO	LOS ANGELES	NEW YORK
Noon	2pm	5.30pm	9pm	4am	7am

parents can request that their children don't attend religious education classes.

TIME DIFFERENCE

The UK is on British Summer Time (BST) in summer and Greenwich Mean Time (GMT) in winter. The clocks go back at 1am on the last Sunday of October. The change to BST is made in the spring (usually at the end of March), when people put their clocks forward one hour. Time changes are announced in local newspapers and on radio and TV. The time is given on the BT 'speaking clock' service number (tel. 123), on TVs and computers.

When making international telephone calls or travelling long distance by air, check the local time difference, which can be obtained online from www.timeanddate.com. The time difference between London (when it's noon GMT, the time on which the BBC World Service operates) and some major international cities is shown below:

TIPPING

Whether you tip or not is a personal choice and may depend on whether you think you've received exceptional service or good value for money. Tipping is customary in restaurants (when service isn't included) and when using taxis, when a tip of around 10 to 15 per cent is normal. Most Britons are anti-tipping (but usually too timid not to leave a tip), and would like to see it abolished and replaced with a universal service charge.

The tipping of hotel staff (e.g. hotel chambermaids) and porters is more discretionary, although most people tip hotel and other porters at least £1 per suitcase, or around the same to a doorman who gets you a taxi (Visit Britain recommends a tip of 10 to 15 per cent for hotel staff when service isn't included in the price). Tipping in hotels depends whether you're staying at Claridges or some back street hovel. Tipping hairdressers (£1 or £2 or 10 per cent of the bill, depending on the service), cloakroom attendants and garage staff (who clean your car's windscreen, or check its oil or tyre pressures) is fairly common. It isn't usual to tip a bartender in a pub, although it's customary to tip in bars and hotels when drinks are served at a table.

Many restaurant bills have 'service not included' printed on them, which is an open invitation for you to leave a tip. Even when service is included in the bill, it doesn't mean that the percentage added for service goes to the staff, although 'service included' deters many people from leaving a tip. The service charge is usually discretionary and it's okay to have it removed from your bill and (if you wish) to tip a waiter in cash. Don't be shy about asking whether service is included, which should be shown on the menu and bill (see also page 237).

TOILETS

Although public toilets are usually free and are cleaner than many found on the continent, the general standard is poor. The most sanitary (even luxurious) toilets are found in hotels, restaurants and department stores, and are for customers only. Toilets in public offices, museums and galleries are also usually clean; railway stations, bus stations, airports, multi-storey car parks and petrol stations generally have reasonably clean toilets; while pub toilets vary from bad to excellent. Toilets provided by local councils are located in towns, parks, car parks and on beaches, and are generally among the worst. However, the financial squeeze on local authorities in recent years has resulted in the closure of many public toilets. There's a charge of 20p to use toilets at London's mainline railway stations and in some department stores (£1 at Harrods). There are also continental-style pay-per-use WCs in some cities. You can find toilets in the UK via the Great British Public Toilet Map (https://greatbritishpublictoiletmap.rca.ac.uk).

People in the UK don't use the American euphemisms of powder room, washroom or bathroom when referring to a toilet, which is also known colloquially as the loo (as well as by numerous other less polite names). WCs are fitted with a variety of flushing methods, including chains to pull, buttons to push (located on the WC or on the wall), knobs to pull and foot buttons to tread on. Some even flush automatically.

Toilets are fitted with a variety of hand-washing facilities (or none at all) which include wash basins with taps or knobs that you hold down to obtain water, which may be cold only. There may be a bar of soap, although soap is usually provided in liquid or foam form in a dispenser. Hand-drying facilities include disposable paper towels, roll linen towels and hot air dryers, which may operate manually via a button or automatically (and which always stop just before your hands are dry!).

An increasing number of department stores, large supermarkets, larger chemists (such as Boots), Mothercare stores, restaurants, pubs and public toilets for motorists provide nappy-changing facilities or facilities for nursing mothers (breastfeeding isn't usually performed in public). Many shopping centres have special toilets for the disabled, as do airports and major railway stations.

19. THE BRITISH

Who are the British? What are they like? Let's take a candid and totally prejudiced look at my compatriots, tongue firmly in cheek, and hope they forgive my flippancy or that they don't read this bit (which is why it's hidden away at the back of the book).

The typical Briton is introspective, patriotic, insular, xenophobic, small-minded, polite, insecure, arrogant, a compulsive gambler, humorous, reserved, conservative, reticent, hypocritical, a racist, boring, a royalist, condescending, depressed, a keen gardener, semi-literate, hard-working, unambitious, ironic, passionless, cosmopolitan, a whinger, hard-headed, liberal, a traditionalist, a couch potato, obsequious, a masochist, complacent, homely, pragmatic, cynical, decent, melancholic, unhealthy, a poor cook, pompous, eccentric, inebriated, proud, self-deprecating, tolerant, inhibited, a shopaholic, conceited, courageous, idiosyncratic, mean (a poor tipper), courteous, jingoistic, stuffy, generous, obese, well-mannered, pessimistic, disciplined, a habitual queuer, stoic, modest, gloomy, shy, serious, apathetic, honest, wimpish, fair, snobbish, friendly, quaint, decadent, civilised, dogmatic, scruffy, prejudiced, class conscious and a soccer hooligan.

If the above list contains a few contradictions, it's because there's no such thing as a typical Briton, and few people conform to the standard British stereotype (whatever that is). Apart from the multifarious differences in temperent between the people from different parts of England (particularly between those from the north and south), the population of the UK encompasses a disparate mixture of English, Scots, Welsh, Irish and assorted ethnic groups originating from throughout the British Commonwealth, other EU countries (including millions of Eastern Europeans in recent years), plus miscellaneous other foreigners from all corners of the globe who've chosen to make the UK their home (London is the most ethnically diverse city in the world).

One of the things which initially confuses foreigners living in the UK is its class system – a curious British affectation. Entry to the upper-class echelons is rooted in birthright, and ill-bred upstarts with pots of 'new' money (particularly foreigners with unpronounceable names) find they're unable to buy entry to the most exclusive clubs and homes of England, even when they're seriously rich. Many Britons are obsessed with class, and for some, maintaining or improving their position on the social ladder is a full-time occupation (the ultimate aim being to acquire a knighthood or peerage). The rest of us pretend we're a 'better' class than we actually are, with the exception of politicians, who are busy trying to live down their privileged past (which may include Eton, Oxbridge, etc.) in order to court popularity with the hoi polloi.

At the top of the heap, there's the upper class (the 'blue-bloods' or aristocracy), crowned by the royal family, followed at a respectable distance by the middle class (which is subdivided into upper middle class, middle middle class and lower middle class), the working class or lower class, and two relatively new (or re-invented) categories that are the legacy of the unbridled 'market' economy of the last few decades: the underclass and the beggar class. In the UK, people were traditionally officially classified according to their occupations, under classes A to E. (One 'class' which cuts across the class system is the 'ruling' class, which sets the political policy – the movers and shakers who control the government and business.) However, owing to the burgeoning middle class in the last few decades (we are apparently all middle class now), the government has introduced no fewer than 17 new classes (including a meritocratic super class of top professionals and managers earning zillions a year).

Class is, of course, no longer relevant in the UK, provided you attended public school and the 'right' university, speak with a posh accent and have oodles of inherited money.

The UK has been uncharitably described (with a hint of truth) as a society based on privilege, inherited wealth and contacts. Class is also what divides the bosses from the workers, and the class struggle is at the root of many industrial disputes. A blue-collar (manual) worker must never accept a position that elevates him to the ranks of the lower middle class (a white-collar job), otherwise his workmates will no longer speak to him and he'll be banned from the local working men's club. (As a consolation, he may be accepted as a member at the Conservative club). Similarly, middle-class management mustn't concede an inch to the workers and, most importantly, must never have direct discussions with them about anything, particularly pay rises or improved working conditions.

One thing that would probably cause a strike in any country is British food, particularly in most company canteens and schools, where everything is served with chips or ice-cream. Of course, British food isn't always as bad as it's painted by foreigners. (What can people who eat anything that crawls, jumps, swims or flies, possibly know about real food?). While it's true that British food is often bland, may look terrible and can make you sick, it's simply a matter of getting used to it. (What's wrong with a diet of brown sauce, chips, biscuits and tea, anyway?). Anyway, it's usually necessary to become acclimatised to the food in any foreign country…

The secret of dining in the UK is to drink a lot, as when you're drunk, most food tastes okay. The British even make their own wine; not just home-brewed stuff made from elderberries and dandelions, but commercially produced wine made from real grapes! Although in the past it hasn't exactly caused panic among continental wine producers, some of it's quite palatable (particularly the fizzy stuff) and is gaining serious international respect (some French champagne houses have even bought into British vineyards). However, despite the popular stereotype of inebriated

Britons, in gross terms they don't drink more per head than many other Europeans; it's just that when many people do drink, they drink to excess (binge drinking is a serious problem).

The British do, however, know how to make a good cuppa (tea) and by and large don't believe in polluting it with lemon or herbs (just milk and sugar). The recipe for any national disaster, whether it's a thrashing at cricket by the Aussies or a power cut during *Coronation Street*, is to make a 'nice cup of tea'. Tea is drunk at almost any time (some 200 million cups a day!), not just in the morning or 'afternoon tea'. Many Britons drink tea in the same quantities as other Europeans drink mineral water or wine.

Unfortunately, coffee is a different matter altogether and although the British have been drinking it since the 16th century (long before tea), most have yet to master the art of brewing a half-decent pot, which just goes to show that practice doesn't always make perfect. Many Britons still make 'coffee' using instant coffee, although in recent years coffeeholics have taken to making real coffee at home, although it's more likely to be with a gourmet coffee machine and coffee capsules (such as Nespresso) rather than grinding their own beans. The good news is that there are now thousands of proper coffee shops in the UK – including the omnipresent Costa Coffee, Starbucks and Caffè Nero chains – along with numerous independents.

You may sometimes get the impression that the British are an unfriendly lot as your neighbours won't always say hello and probably won't drop by or invite you to their home for a cup of tea. If you wish to start a conversation with your neighbour (or anyone), a remark such as "nice weather" usually elicits a response (particularly if it's raining cats and dogs). The weather is a hallowed topic and it's the duty of every upstanding citizen to make daily weather predictions due to the awful hash made of it by the meteorologists. The UK has rather a lot of weather, and there's often rain, gales, fog, snow and a heat wave in the same day, although it's always described as 'nice' or 'not very nice'. When it snows, everyone and everything is paralysed and people start predicting the end of civilisation as we know it.

The fact that no people anywhere have shown such a consistent desire to emigrate as the British may have more than a little to do with the climate.

It's a common misconception among foreigners that the British speak English. There are numerous accents and dialects in the UK, half of which are so thick that you could be forgiven for thinking that people are conversing in an ancient secret tongue. Some 25 per cent of inhabitants are immigrants who speak only Hindi, Bengali, Chinese, French, Gujarati, Arabic, Xhosa, Russian, Punjabi, Swahili, Urdu, Italian, Turkish, Spanish, Esperanto, Yiddish or Polish. The best English is spoken by tourists, i.e. most people in London, but unfortunately they don't remain in one place long enough to hold a conversation with anyone…

Many Britons are prejudiced against foreigners and the English are also prejudiced against people from other UK regions (northerners, southerners, the Irish, Scots, Welsh – you name it), Yanks, Europeans, Asians, Aussies and most other foreigners; and anyone who speaks with a different (i.e. lower, middle or upper class) accent. The British, in common with most other races, don't have a lot of time for foreigners, particularly rich tourists and foreigners who buy up all the best property, businesses and soccer clubs – who should all stay at home!

The British are masters of the understatement, and rarely rave about anything. If they're excited about something, they sometimes enthuse "that's nice" and, on the rare occasion when they're deliriously happy, they've been known to exclaim "I say, that's rather good". On the other hand, if something disastrous happens (such as their house burning down) it might be termed "a spot of bother". The end of the world will probably be pronounced "unfortunate" or, if there was something particularly good on TV that evening, it may be greeted as "a jolly bad show" (the ultimate tragedy). The true character of the British is, however, revealed when they're at play, particularly when they're engaged in sport.

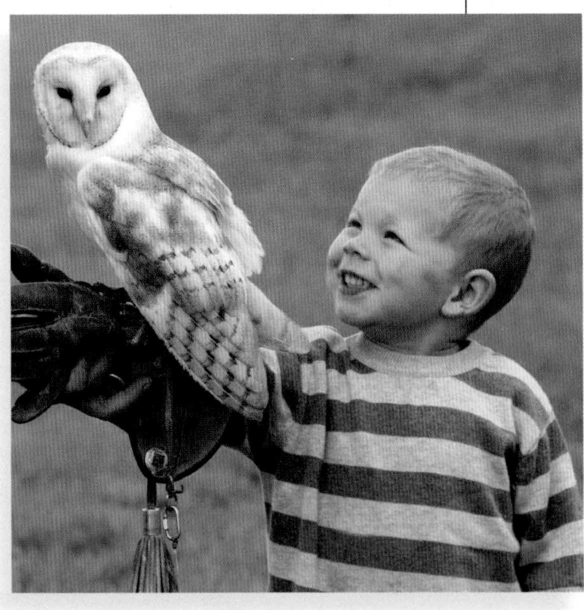

The British are sports mad, although most people confine their interest to watching or gambling rather than taking part. The British, or at least the English, are famous for their sense of fair play and playing by the rules – cheating is considered very bad form. Football (soccer) is the UK's national sport, and if we hadn't taught all the other nations to play we could even be world champions (like the Yanks who play among themselves and call it the 'World Series').

However, the real character and true sporting traditions of the English (other Brits have better things to do) are embodied in the game of cricket, a study of which provides a valuable insight into these strange islanders (and their attitude towards tea parties, religion, sex and foreigners). Foreigners may, at first, have a bit of difficulty understanding what cricket is all about (although it's far easier to understand than British politics), but after a few decades most get the hang of it (unlike British politics which remain a complete mystery). The first thing you must understand is that cricket is a game for gentlemen, embodying the great British traditions of fair play, honour and sportsmanship (except when played by Australians, who haven't the remotest notion of these things).

It's tempting to make comparisons between cricket and a minority sport played in the US, called baseball. (The nearest equivalent in the UK is rounders, a sissy game played by girls.) Imagine if you can, a baseball match that lasts five days with interminable breaks for breakfast, drinks, rain, streakers (naked runners), lunch, injuries, stray dogs, more rain, rest days, more drinks, tea, bad light, dinner, supper, and even more rain, and always ends in a draw (if not abandoned due to rain) – and you'll have a rough idea what it's all about. Despite the length of a cricket match, which varies from one to five days, it's an enthralling and thrilling sport. On the rare occasions when things get just a teensy bit boring, there's always something exciting to liven things up, such as a newspaper blowing across the pitch, a stray dog or pigeon on the field or, on a good day, a streaker.

The rules of cricket are a little complicated (Einstein's theory of relativity is much easier to understand), so I won't bore you by trying to explain them in detail, fascinating though they are. A cricket team consists of 11 players, and a 12th man who has the most important job of all – carrying the drinks tray during breaks in play. He's also sometimes called on to play when one of his teammates collapses from frostbite or is overcome by excitement. Like baseball, one team bats and the other team attempts to get them out (or committed to hospital) by hurling a ball at the batsman's head. The team in the field (not batting) stands around in set positions with peculiar names such as gulley, slips, short leg, square leg, long leg, peg leg, cover point, third man (they made a film about him), mid-off, mid-on and oddest of all – silly mid-off and silly mid-on (only someone who's a few pence short of a pound stands directly in front of a batsman as he's about to hit a very hard ball in your direction at 100mph).

> One of the problems with foreigners is that they have no concept of how gentlemen should behave, and fail to realise that the real purpose of sport is taking part and nothing at all to do with winning. Gallant losers are feted as heroes in the UK and heroic defeats against overwhelming odds are infinitely preferable to hollow victories.

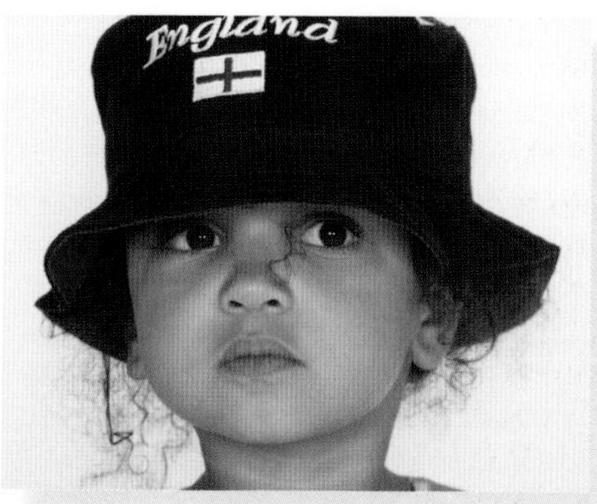

When the bowler strikes the wicket or the batsman with the ball, everyone shouts in unison "howzat" (very loudly, on the assumption that the umpire is asleep, hard of hearing, short-sighted or all three). Cricketers play in a white uniform (when not wearing coloured pyjamas), and the only colourful things about the game are the ball (usually red) and the language used by the batsman (blue) when he's hit by the ball or when the umpire gives him out leg before wicket (lbw) to a ball that didn't touch him, and in any case was a million miles away from the wicket. One of the unwritten rules of cricket is that the players (gentlemen) never argue with the umpire, no matter how short-sighted, biased and totally ignorant of the rules the twit is.

The Aussies (Australians), whom everyone knows have no respect for tradition (and couldn't give a XXXX for anything that doesn't emanate from a tinny or a barrel), have attempted to brighten up the game's image by dressing like clowns for one-day matches. One of the worst mistakes the English ever made was to teach foreigners how to play cricket (or any other sport), as the ungrateful blighters get a sadistic delight from rubbing their mentors' noses in the dirt (although the boot has been on the other foot in recent years – hooray!).

The British have a passion for queuing (lining up), and appear to outsiders to have endless patience – as you would expect from a nation that can endure a five-day cricket match. Queuing isn't always a necessity, but a herd instinct that compels people to huddle together (in winter it helps to keep warm), except of course when travelling by public transport, when the rules are somewhat different. On public transport, you must never sit next to anyone when an empty seat is available, and you must spread yourself and your belongings over two or three seats, and never move for anyone. You must avoid looking at your fellow passengers at all costs (in case a stranger smiles at you), usually achieved by staring fixedly at the back of a newspaper or out of the window.

There is, of course, not a word of truth in the rumour that British men are lousy lovers (or all gay), which is a scurrilous lie put about by sex-mad Latinos so that they can keep all the women for themselves. Slanderous foreign propagandists have calculated that the British make love an average of twice a month. To add insult to injury, they add that this is more often than we bathe (which is a damn insult, as the average Briton washes at least once a week).

Although perhaps not the most romantic of lovers (but much better than those unctuous Italians, who are all talk and no trousers, and have the lowest birth-rate in Europe), the British know what it's for and don't need a ruler to measure their manhood (neither do we all get our kicks flashing, mooning or being whipped by women in leather underwear). 'No Sex Please, We're British' is simply a challenge to women who've had their fill of Latinos with short fat hairy legs. Sex is definitely not simply a person's gender in the UK and most Britons take more than a hot-water bottle to bed with them.

British women are among the most emancipated in the world – not that the weaker sex (men) gave in graciously – and are allowed to vote and drive cars. Nevertheless, it's difficult, if not impossible, for women to claw their way to the top of most professions or into boardrooms, which remain bastions of male chauvinism. Of course, no self-respecting man would allow himself to be dominated by a mere woman, unless of course he's a wimp and she's a handbag-wielding, belligerent battler. If British (male) politicians learnt nothing else during the Thatcher years, it was the utter havoc a woman can wreak in the boardroom.

The main problem with the British economy (apart from the ineptitude of British politicians) is that many Britons lack ambition. They certainly want 'loadsamoney', but would rather do almost anything than work for it; contrary to the popularly held misconception that 'hard work never did anyone any harm', the British know only too well that it can prove fatal.

Most people prefer to try their luck at gambling (rather than work), and will bet on almost anything, including the national lottery (which was only introduced in the '90s, but the Brits took to it like a duck to orange sauce), football pools, horse and greyhound racing, bingo, casinos, names of royal babies or ships,

public appointments, election results and who the Prime Minister will sack next (or who will resign) – you name it and someone will make a book on it. If the British injected as much energy into work and business as they do into gambling, they might even be able to compete with German and Japanese productivity.

The UK's electoral system is, of course, unique (nobody would be daft enough to copy it), where elections are decided by the first horse (or ass) past the post. This means that the party in power rarely gets more than around 35 per cent of the total vote, and minority parties can poll 25 per cent of the vote and end up with only a handful of seats. Of course, nobody in the UK actually votes for a political party, particularly the one that wins the election (or at least nobody admits it). Most are registering a protest vote, voting for the party they hope will do the least damage, or voting strategically – trying to defeat the candidate they like least.

Despite their singular lack of success, the minority parties battle manfully on, and include such defenders of democracy as the Monster Raving Loony Party (the only British political party with an honest name). The low calibre of British politicians may have something to do with the fact that politicking is the only 'job' that doesn't require education, qualifications, training or brains.

Some people (usually foreigners) think that the British are out of step with their 'partners' in the European Union (we certainly are now after Brexit, but that's another matter…). Of course, as any Briton will tell you, the only reason we don't always see eye to eye with bloody foreigners (who make up the insignificant part of the EU) is that they refuse to listen to us and do as we tell them. (Whatever happened to the good old days when Johnny Foreigner knew his place?). It must be obvious to everyone that we know best; just look at our manufacturing industry, modern infrastructure, culinary traditions, public transport, roads, soccer and rugby teams, etc. – er, em, well having a successful economy and things that work isn't everything.

> However, not **everything** is depressing in Britain, and the quality of life is considered by many foreigners to be excellent and among the best in the world.

The notion that the UK doesn't always know best is ridiculous, and if there's to be a united Europe, those foreign bounders had better mend their ways. (We didn't fight two world wars so that Jerry and the Frogs – who we bailed out twice – could tell us what to do!). They can start by adopting British time, driving on the left, making English their national language, anglicising their ridiculous names and moving the EU headquarters and parliament to London – which every civilised person knows is the centre of the universe. Perhaps then we would all get on much better! If they don't agree, we can always fill in our end of the Channel Tunnel and refuse to answer the telephone. **And if that doesn't work we'll have a referendum and leave the bloody European Union!**

The secret of life in the UK is to maintain a sense of humour (and carry a big umbrella). Most Brits have a lively sense of humour and a keen sense of the ridiculous, which helps make life in the UK bearable. (The worst insult is to accuse someone of having no sense of humour). One of the things that endears the British most to foreigners is their ability to poke fun at themselves (the British don't take themselves too seriously) and everyone else, as typified in TV programmes such as *Monty Python* and *Dead Ringers;* the most popular magazine in the country is the satirical fortnightly *Private Eye*. Nothing escapes the barbs of the satirists: from the Pope to the Prime Minister, the President of the US to the Royal Family, everyone is lampooned with equal affection.

Enough of this flippancy – now for the serious bit! The UK has its fair share of problems, and is still failing in many vital areas, including public transport, health, education and manufacturing (apart from those industries we've sold to foreigners). However, we're world leaders in pageantry, binge drinking and general hooliganism. Major concerns include rising crime (particularly juvenile and white-collar crime), the uneven quality of state education, a flourishing drugs culture, the failing health service, inequality (the growing gulf between rich and poor), a looming pensions crisis, a spendthrift overpaid public sector, pollution, awful (and outrageously expensive) public transport, homelessness, overcrowded roads, urban blight and a burgeoning underclass. Apart from these trifling details, everything is perfect.

The worst crisis is among the UK's young working class males, who lack a sense of purpose and ambition, and among whom unemployment is rife. This is reflected in their suicide rate which has risen sharply in the last decade. Perhaps the most serious decline in British life is shown in the combined effects of loss of social cohesion and sense of community, and the breakdown of the family unit. Some 50 per cent of marriages end in divorce, and almost half of all births are to unmarried mothers – which has resulted in a high proportion of one-parent families.

Many working class families haven't seen any real increase in their salary or standard of living since the economic crisis in 2008, and the gap between the wealthy and those struggling to make ends meet has never been wider; this has been made more painful for the underclass by recent cuts in state support for the poorest members of society. This no doubt influenced many people to vote to leave the European Union, although there were many other issues not least uncontrolled EU immigration; lack of democratic accountability (i.e. widespread corruption) and sovereignty; an abhorrence of ever closer political union (despite opt-outs) and the creation of an EU super-state; British law and parliament being constantly overridden by EU law and the European Court of Justice; the high cost of EU membership (not just financially); and – not least – the general feeling that the EU is a failing organisation beyond reform.

> The UK is a caring society, highlighted by the abundance of charitable and voluntary organisations, unparalleled in most other countries, all of which do invaluable work (both nationally and internationally).

The British enjoy superb entertainment, leisure, sports and cultural facilities, which for their sheer variety and accessibility are among the best in the world (but increasingly expensive). The quality and huge choice of goods in the shops is excellent, and explains why many people travel from far and wide simply to shop in Britain. British television has no equal, national and local radio is excellent, and the country has an unrivalled choice of quality newspapers, magazines and literature. The UK remains a centre of scientific excellence, underlined by its number of Nobel prize-winners (second only to the USA). It's also one of the least corrupt and most civilised countries in the world.

The British have more freedom from government interference than the people of most countries, to do, say and act in any way they like, something most people take for granted. The UK is still a great enlightened power (if a little frayed at the edges), and a positive influence in the world, and London remains the centre of the English-speaking world. Whatever else it may be, life in the UK is spiritually, mentally and intellectually stimulating, and rarely dull. Although foreigners may complain about British food and weather, most feel they're privileged to live here and wouldn't dream of leaving (in fact they queue up on the other side of the channel to enter the country illegally).

Last, but certainly not least, there are the British people, who, although they can be infuriating at times, will charm and delight you with their sense of humour and idiosyncrasies. When your patience with the UK and the British is stretched to breaking point, simply decamp to the nearest pub and order a pint of bitter or a large gin and tonic: the UK looks a much nicer place through the bottom of a (rose-tinted) glass, and, with a bit of luck, you won't even notice that it's still raining.

Long Live Britain! God Save the Queen!

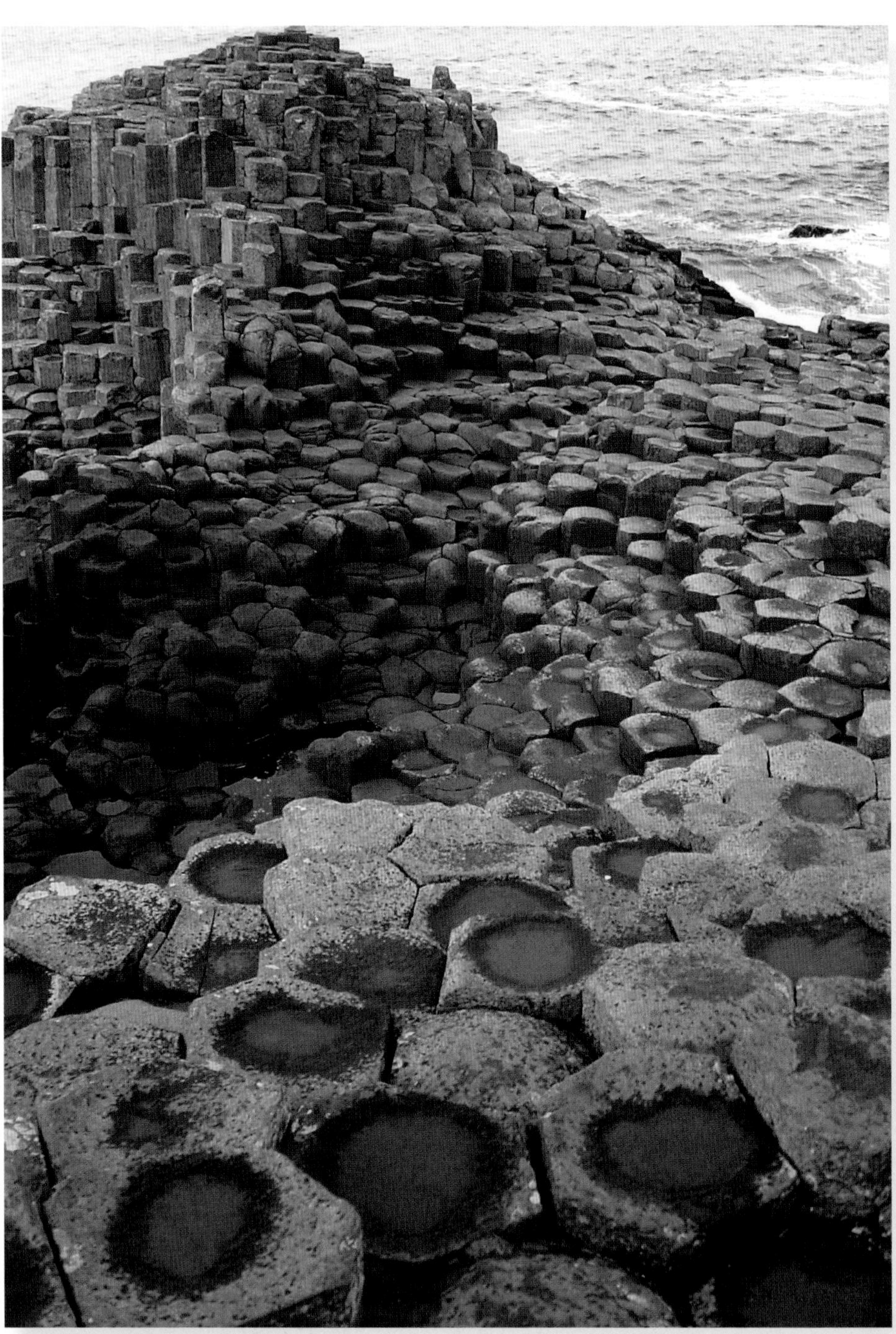
Giant's Causeway, County Antrim, NI

20. MOVING HOUSE OR LEAVING BRITAIN

When moving house or leaving the UK, there are many things to be considered and a 'million' people to be informed. The checklists contained in this chapter are designed to make the task easier and help prevent an ulcer or a nervous breakdown (provided, of course, you don't leave everything to the last minute). Only divorce or bereavement can cause more stress than moving house!

MOVING HOUSE

When moving house within the UK, the following items should be considered:

- If you live in rented accommodation, you must give your landlord notice (the period depends on your contract). If you don't give your landlord sufficient notice, you're required to pay the rent until the end of your contract or for the full notice period. This also applies if you've a separate contract for a garage or other rented property, e.g. a holiday home.
- Inform the following:
  - Your employer.
  - If you're moving to a new district or borough council area, you must inform your present council when you move, and re-register in your new council area after arrival. When moving to a new county or borough you may be entitled to a refund of a portion of your council tax.
  - If you're registered with the police (see page 69), you must inform them of your new address or re-register at the nearest police station in your new area.
  - Your electricity, gas and water companies.
  - Inform your telephone company, if you've a telephone.
  - Your insurance companies (for example health, car, home contents and private pension); banks, building societies, post office (e.g. savings account), stockbroker and other financial institutions; credit card and hire purchase companies; solicitor and accountant; and local businesses where you have accounts.
  - Your family doctor, dentist and other health practitioners. Health records should be transferred to your new doctor and dentist, if applicable.
  - Your children's (and your) schools. If applicable, arrange for schooling in your new area. Try to give a term's notice, and obtain a copy of any relevant school reports or records from your children's current schools.
  - All regular correspondents, subscriptions, social and sports clubs, professional and trade journals, and friends and relatives. Give or send them your new address and telephone number. Arrange to have your mail redirected by the post office (see **Change of Address** on page 92).
  - If you've a British driving licence or a British-registered car, inform the Vehicle License Registration Office (see page 154) as soon as possible after moving.

- Your local consulate or embassy, if you're registered with them (see page 70).

- Return any library books or anything borrowed.
- Arrange for a cleaning company and/or decorating company for rented accommodation, if necessary.
- If renting, contact your landlord or the letting agency to have your deposit returned (with interest, if applicable). He will need an opportunity to inspect the property for damage, cleanliness, etc.
- Cancel milk and newspaper deliveries.

> Arrange removal of your furniture and belongings by booking a removal company well in advance. If you've only a few items of furniture, you may prefer to move them yourself, in which case you may need to hire a van.

LEAVING BRITAIN

Before leaving the UK permanently or for an indefinite period, the following items should be considered in addition to those listed above under Moving House:

- Give notice to your employer, if applicable.
- Check that your own and your family's passports are valid.
- Check whether any special requirements (e.g. visas, permits or inoculations) are necessary for entry into your country of destination by contacting the local embassy or consulate in the UK. An exit permit or visa isn't required to leave the UK.
- Book a removal company well in advance. International removal companies usually provide a wealth of information and may also be able to advise you on matters concerning your relocation. Find out the exact procedure for shipping your belongings to your country of destination from the local embassy or consulate in the UK of the country to which you're moving (don't rely entirely on your shipping company). Special forms may need to be completed before arrival.
- You may qualify for a rebate on your tax and national insurance contributions (check with your local tax office). If you're leaving the UK permanently and are a member of a company pension scheme or have a personal pension plan, you should contact your company personnel office or pension company regarding your options.
- Arrange to sell anything you aren't taking with you (e.g. house, car and furniture), and to ship your belongings. If you've been living in the UK for less than a year, you're required to export all personal effects, including furniture and vehicles, that were imported tax and duty-free.
- If you've a British registered car which you're permanently exporting, you should complete a 'permanent export certificate' (available from the DVLA – www.gov.uk/contact-the-dvla), and register the vehicle in your new country of residence on arrival (as necessary).
- Depending on your destination, your pets may require special inoculations or may be required to go into quarantine for a period (see page 293).
- Contact your telephone and utility companies well in advance, particularly if you need to get a deposit reimbursed (see **Chapter 7**). You may be entitled to a refund on the unused part of your tv licence: see www.tvlicensing.co.uk/refund.
- Arrange health, travel and other insurance, as necessary (see **Chapter 13**).
- Depending on your destination, arrange health and dental check-ups for your family before leaving the UK. Obtain a copy of all health and dental records and a statement from your health insurance company stating your present level of cover.
- Terminate any British loan, lease or hire purchase contracts and pay all outstanding bills (allow plenty of time, as some companies may be slow to respond).

Eilean Donan Castle, Scotland

- Check whether you're entitled to a rebate on your road tax, car and other insurance. Obtain a letter from your British motor insurance company stating your number of years no-claims' discount.
- Sell your house, apartment or other property or arrange to let it through a friend or a letting agency (see **Chapter 5**). If you own more than one property in the UK you must pay capital gains tax on any profits from the sale of a second home above a certain amount (see page 216).
- Check whether you need an international driving licence or a translation of your British or foreign driving licence for your country of destination or any countries you pass through.
- Give your friends and business associates in the UK a temporary address and telephone number where you can be contacted abroad.
- If you'll be living abroad for an extended period you may wish to give someone 'power of attorney' over your financial affairs in the UK so that they can act for you in your absence. This can be for a fixed period or open-ended, and can be for a specific purpose only. You should, however, take legal advice before doing this.
- If you're travelling by air you should allow plenty of time to get to the airport, check-in your luggage and to clear security and immigration.

Have a safe journey!

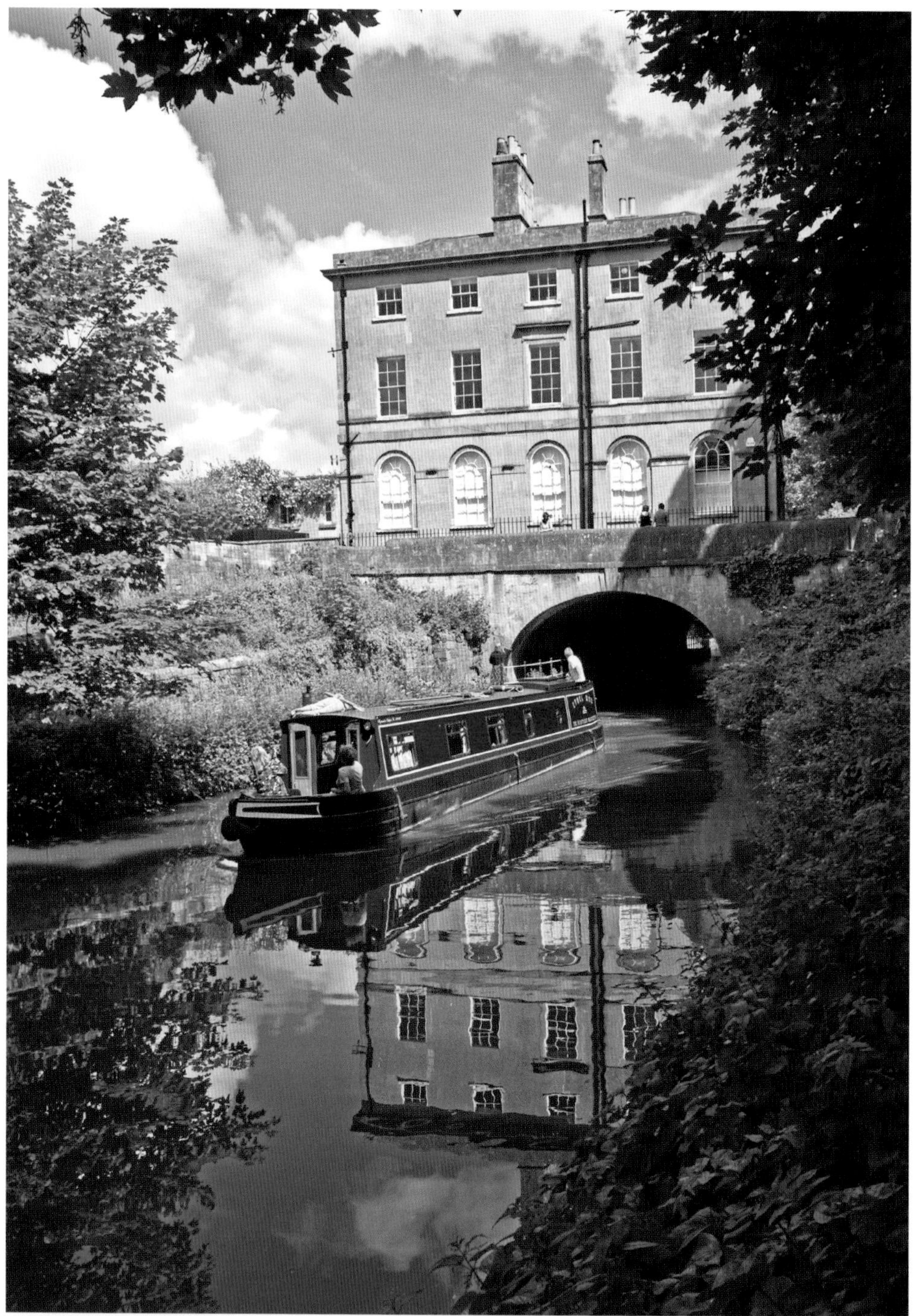

APPENDICES

APPENDIX A: USEFUL WEBSITES

he following list of websites (by subject) will be of interest to newcomers planning to live or work in Britain.

Business & Working

British Business (www.britishbusinesses.com). Online UK business directory.
Business Link (https://data.gov.uk/publisher/businesslink). Includes hot topics, latest news, plus e-commerce and e-business pages.
Business – Visit London (http://business.visitlondon.com). London's official convention bureau.
Jobcentre (www.jobseekers.direct.gov.uk). The government website for job seekers, with advice on job hunting, training, recruitment and benefits.
Linkedin (www.linkedin.com). A business and employment-oriented social networking service.
London Jobs (www.londonjobs.co.uk). One of London's best jobs websites.
Northern Ireland Business Info (www.nibusinessinfo.co.uk). Practical information for Northern Ireland business.
Scottish Enterprise (www.scottish-enterprise.com). Helping Scotland's businesses grow.
UK Visas (www.gov.uk/government/organisations/uk-visas-and-immigration). All you need to know about British visas.
Volunteering (www.volunteering.org.uk). A useful site for those looking for volunteering work, with helpful 'I want a volunteer' pages to help you find a job in London.
Welsh Business Directory (www.welshbusinessdirectory.com). Wales business to business directory.
Work Gateways (www.workgateways.com). Organises work for visitors on temporary working visas.

Culture

Black Presence (www.blackpresence.co.uk). The history and culture of black people in Britain.
British Empire (www.britishempire.co.uk). Timelines, maps, biographies, and articles on various aspects of British and imperial history, culture, technology and armed forces.
British Museum (www.thebritishmuseum.ac.uk). Houses a vast collection of world art and artefacts.

Project Britain (http://projectbritain.com). All about British life and culture by the pupils of Woodlands Junior School.
Culture Northern Ireland (www.culturenorthernireland.org)
Scottish Culture (www.scottishculture.org).
Victoria & Albert Museum (www.vam.ac.uk). The website of one of England's most celebrated museums, established in 1857.
Welsh Traditions (www.wales.com/about-wales/welsh-traditions).

Education

BBC Northern Ireland/Schools (www.bbc.co.uk/northernireland/schools).
BBC Schools (www.bbc.co.uk/schools). General information about UK schools.
BBC Scotland Learning (www.bbc.co.uk/scotland/learning).
BBC Wales Learning (www.bbc.co.uk/wales/learning).
British Council (www.britishcouncil.org). The UK's international organisation for educational opportunities and cultural relations.
Department for Children, Schools and Families (www.dfes.gov.uk). The DCSF is responsible for improving the focus on all aspects of policy affecting children and young people, as part of the Government's aim to deliver educational excellence.
Education UK (www.educationuk.org). Everything foreign students need to know about education in the UK (from the British Council).
English in Britain (www.englishinbritain.co.uk). Online database of over 1,600 British Council Accredited English language courses at over 300 schools.
Learn English (www.learnenglish.org.uk). Learn English online with the help of this free website from the British Council.
London Business School (www.london.edu). Website of the LBS, one of the leading business schools in the world.
Office for Standards in Education (www.ofsted.gov.uk). The government department responsible for inspecting and regulating education and schools in England.
Student Accommodation (www.accommodationforstudents.com). Search engine for students seeking accommodation in and around the UK's major cities.

Estate & Letting Agents

Countrywide (www.countrywide.co.uk). The UK's largest provider of estate agency and property related finance & professional services.
Estate Agent (www.estateagent.co.uk). Advertise your house for sale free.
Find a Property (www.findaproperty.com). Property for sale in London and surrounding counties; includes a list of London estate agencies;
Fish 4 Homes (www.fish4homes.co.uk). Selection of properties and directory of estate agents around the UK.
Foxtons (www.foxtons.co.uk). London's largest chain of estate and letting agents.

Hamptons International (www.hamptons.co.uk). Specialises in the top end of the property market, i.e. all of central London!
Home Pages (www.homepages.co.uk). Sell your home for £50.
Homes Online (www.homes-on-line.com). Useful information about buying, selling, home improvements and financing a property.
Houseweb (www.houseweb.co.uk). Independent property website that contains comprehensive advice and tips for homebuyers.
New-Homes (www.new-homes.co.uk). Comprehensive database of new home developments throughout the UK.
On The Market (www.onthemarket.com). The UK's latest nationwide property website.
Prime Location (www.primelocation.com). Consortium of estate agents advertising properties.
Property News (www.propertynews.com). Ireland's property finder.
Right Move (www.rightmove.co.uk). The UK's largest selection of new and resale homes.
S1 Homes (www.s1homes.com). Property in Scotland.
Smart New Homes (www.smartnewhomes.com). Search for new homes.
Zoopla (www.zoopla.co.uk). The UK's largest online property market resource.

Finance & Mortgages

Charcol (www.charcol.co.uk). Mortgage broker.
Money Extra (www.moneyextra.co.uk). Financial services, including the best mortgage deals.
Money Net (www.moneynet.co.uk). Financial services, including mortgage deals.
Money Quest (www.moneyquest.co.uk). Mortgage brokers.
Money Saving Expert (www.moneysavingexpert.com). Financial advice.
Money Supermarket (www.moneysupermarket.com). General finance, including mortgages.
This is Money (www.thisismoney.co.uk). Data and statistics on money matters, as well as useful finance guides.
Virgin Money (www.uk.virginmoney.com). The Virgin Group's financial services online.
What Mortgage (www.whatmortgage.co.uk). Mortgage information and comprehensive advice on buying a property.
Your Mortgage magazine (www.yourmortgage.co.uk). A wealth of information about mortgages and all aspects of buying and selling property.

Government

10 Downing Street (www.number-10.gov.uk). Official website of the British Prime Minister.
Directgov (www.direct.gov.uk). Portal to public service information from the UK Government, including directories, online services, and news and information of relevance to specific groups.
Government Gateway (www.gateway.gov.uk). Access to over 1,000 government websites. Government Gateway is a centralised registration service that enables you to sign up for online government services.
Government UK (www.gov.uk). The best place to find official government services and information.

National Health Service (www.nhsdirect.nhs.uk). The gateway to government health information, services and assistance.
National Statistics (www.statistics.gov.uk). The government agency that produces and disseminates social, health, economic, demographic, labour market and business statistics.
Northern Ireland Assembly (www.niassembly.gov.uk). Site of the Northern Ireland Assembly.
Northern Ireland Office (www.nio.gov.uk). UK government's NI office.
Scottish Government (www.scotland.gov.uk).
UK Government Guide (www.ukgovernmentguide.co.uk). An easy way to access local UK government websites.
UK Parliament (www.parliament.uk). Official UK parliament website.
UK Visas & Immigration (www.gov.uk/government/organisations/uk-visas-and-immigration). All you need to know about UK visas.
Wales Office (www.walesoffice.gov.uk). Office of the Secretary of State for Wales.
Webmesh (www.webmesh.co.uk/government.htm). Links to government departments.
Welsh Assembly Government (http://new.wales.gov.uk).

Media

BBC (www.bbc.co.uk). Excellent, comprehensive website from the British Broadcasting Corporation, one of Britain's great institutions.
BBC England (www.bbc.co.uk/england). Provides local news, sport, entertainment and debate for England.
BBC Northern Ireland (www.bbc.co.uk/northernireland).
BBC Scotland (www.bbc.co.uk/scotland).
BBC Wales (www.bbc.co.uk/wales).
British Papers (www.britishpapers.co.uk). Links to the websites of major British newspapers.
The Economist (www.economist.com). The UK's leading business, finance and world affairs magazine.
Loot (www.loot.com). Log on to buy and sell virtually anything under one roof.
Northern Ireland Media (www.nidex.com/media.htm).
Scottish Newspapers (www.world-newspapers.com/scotland.html).
This is England (www.thisengland.co.uk). The website of *This is England* magazine.
Time Out (www.timeout.com). Weekly entertainment guide for London and other UK cities.
Welsh Newspapers (www.world-newspapers.com/wales.htm).
What's On (www.whatsoninlondon.co.uk). Weekly entertainment guide.
Which? magazine (www.which.net). Monthly consumer magazine, available on subscription.

Miscellaneous

Advice Guide (www.adviceguide.org.uk). Established by the Citizens' Advice Bureau (CAB), with down-to-earth advice, including information about civil rights, benefits and the legal system.
BBC Weather (www.bbc.co.uk/weather). Provides UK and worldwide weather services and maps for temperature, wind, satellite, lighting, pressure and radar.

Britannia (www.britannia.com/history). The internet's most comprehensive information resource for the times, places, events and people of British history.
British Library (www.bl.uk). Search the BL catalogues, order items for research, view exhibitions, etc.
British Monarchy (www.royal.gov.uk). Official website of the British Monarchy.
Finder (www.finder.com/uk). The UK's first comparison site for shopping deals and internet TV products.
Football Association (www.thefa.com). The Official Website of the England Team, The FA Cup and football (soccer) at all levels in England.
Get A Map (www.getamap.co.uk). Free downloadable Ordnance Survey neighbourhood maps.
Medical Care (www.med4u.co.uk). The leading UK online medical service. Obtain health advice and a second opinion with ease.
Met Office (www.metoffice.gov.uk). Metrological office.
Multimap & Streetmap (www.multimap.com and www.streetmap.co.uk). Invaluable resources for finding your way around if you haven't got an *A-Z*, where you can find any street or postcode in London.
Ordnance Survey (www.ordnancesurvey.co.uk). Downloadable maps.
Premier League (www.premierleague.co.uk). Official website of England's top soccer league.
Rampant Scotland (www.rampantscotland.com). Comprehensive directory of Scottish websites.
Rated People (www.ratedpeople.com). Find a tradesman.
Scoot (www.scoot.co.uk). Find essential services for homeowners.
Sports Link (www.sportslink.co.uk). Lists sports and leisure facilities throughout the UK.
UK Online (www.ukonline.gov.uk). Comprehensive information about local services and neighbourhoods, including schools, health, housing and crime statistics.
UK Weather (uk.weather.com). Provides a ten-day summary forecast for cities, with maps for shorter periods ahead.

Moving Home

British Association of Removers (www.bar.co.uk). Association of removal companies offering a professional service, with a conciliation and arbitration service.
I am Moving (www.iammoving.com). Will inform companies on your behalf that you're moving.
The Move Channel (www.themovechannel.com). General property website containing everything you need to know about moving house.
Really Moving (www.reallymoving.com). Comprehensive information about property, including home-moving services and a property finder.

Professional Associations

Building Societies' Association (www.bsa.org.uk). Central representative body for building societies.
Council for Licensed Conveyancers (www.conveyancer.org.uk). Council for licensed conveyancers.

Council of Mortgage Lenders (www.cml.org.uk). Trade association for mortgage lenders.
Federation of Master Builders (www.fmb.org.uk). Includes a directory of members.
Land Registry (www1.landregistry.gov.uk). Practical information about registering land and land registry archives.
The Law Society (www.lawsociety.org.uk). Professional body for solicitors in England and Wales.
The Law Society of Scotland (www.lawscot.org.uk).
National Association of Estate Agents (www.naea.co.uk). The main organisation for estate agents.
Ombudsman for Estate Agents (www.oea.co.uk). Independent arbitration for property buyers with complaints about registered estate agents.

Property

Accommodation London (www.accommodationlondon.net). Help with finding a place to live in London, with text in English, French, Italian, Spanish and Swedish.
English Heritage (www.english-heritage.org.uk). The organisation responsible for protecting and promoting the historic environment, officially known as the Historic Buildings and Monuments Commission for England.
Environment Agency (www.environment-agency.gov.uk). Check the occurrence of flooding and other natural hazards in an area.
Home Check (www.homecheck.co.uk). Local information about the risks of flooding, landslip, pollution, radon gas, landfill, waste sites, etc. Also provides general information about neighbourhoods.
Hometrack (www.hometrack.co.uk). Online property reports.
Home Pages (www.homepages.co.uk). Comprehensive property database and information about buying and selling property.
Into London (www.intolondon.com). London's longest-running website for flat sharers.
Knowhere (www.knowhere.co.uk). An alternative look at over 2,000 UK towns.
My Village (www.myvillage.com). Community sites for London and 20 other cities.
Neighbourhood Statistics (http://neighbourhood.statistics.gov.uk). Contains a wide range of statistics for neighbourhoods in England and Wales.
Proviser (www.proviser.com). Local property prices and street maps for England and Wales.
Property Live (www.propertylive.co.uk). The National Association of Estate Agents' property website.
Property Snake (www.propertysnake.co.uk). See at a glance whether property prices are up or down in a particular area – and by how much.
Student Accommodation (www.accommodationforstudents.com). A search engine for students seeking accommodation in London and other UK cities.
Up My Street (www.upmystreet.co.uk). Information about neighbourhoods, including property prices, local services, schools, local government, etc.

Shopping & Services

Amazon (www.amazon.co.uk). The UK's largest online retailer.
British Shopping (www.british-shopping.com). UK online shopping directory.
Consumers' Association (www.which.net). The UK's consumer champion who publish the monthly *Which?* consumer magazine and others.
Ebay (www.ebay.co.uk). The UK's foremost auction site.
John Lewis (www.johnlewis.com). The website of Britain's favourite retailer.
London Rate (www.londonrate.com). Useful resource for Londoners containing a collection of service-industry contacts, which are rated and searchable with prices. Everything from babysitters to builders, computer experts to cleaners, and hairdressers to housekeepers.
Price Runner (www.pricerunner.co.uk). Compare the prices of a wide range of goods and services.
Shopping Net (www.shopping.net). The UK's most comprehensive shopping website, which allows you to search thousands of websites for products and services at the best prices.

Tourism

British Hotel Reservation Centre (www.bhrc.co.uk). Has been operating hotel booking desks at London airports and railway stations since 1971.
Discover Northern Ireland (www.dicovernorthernireland.com). Official site of the Northern Ireland Tourist Board.
English Heritage (www.english-heritage.org.uk). See Property above.
Enjoy England (www.enjoyengland.com). The website of the English Tourist Board.
Historic Scotland (www.historic-scotland.gov.uk). Official Scotland heritage site.
Itchy London (www.itchylondon.co.uk). Online version of the city guidebook, with reviews of bars, clubs and pubs and suggestions for places to go out.
London (www.londonby.com or www.londonnet.co.uk). Two of the most comprehensive London websites for both residents and visitors.
London Town (www.londontown.com). Comprehensive site featuring articles and reviews of restaurants, films and theatre shows, hotel and travel bookings and general information.
National Trust (www.nationaltrust.org.uk). The website of one of Britain's most beloved charitable institutions that looks after over 350 historic houses, gardens, industrial monuments and mills, all of which are open to the public.
Restaurants.co.uk (www.restaurants.co.uk). One of the UK's most comprehensive restaurant search portals.
Scotland (www.scotland.org). The official online gateway to Scotland.
The Scotland Channel (www.scotland.com). Comprehensive information for visitors to Scotland.
This is London (www.thisislondon.com). General information from the *Evening Standard* newspaper.
Toptable (www.toptable.co.uk). Online restaurant booking service, offering deals such as two-for-one offers and tables at hard-to-book London restaurants.
Trivago (www.trivago.com). The world's top hotel comparison website.
UK Travel (www.uktravel.com). Comprehensive UK travel information.

Visit Britain (www.visitbritain.com). The official site of the British Tourist Authority.
Visit England (www.visitengland.com). The official site of the English Tourist Board.
Visit Scotland (www.visitscotland.com). The official site of the Scottish Tourist Board.
Visit Wales (www.visitwales.com). The official site of the Welsh Tourist Board.
Welcome to London (www.welcometolondon.com). London's most widely read online visitor magazine.

Travel

A-Z (www.a-zmaps.co.uk). Publisher of the UK's best (and invaluable) street maps.
At UK (www.atuk.co.uk). The foremost UK travel search engine and directory.
British Airways (www.britishairways.com). Britain's national carrier.
Easyjet (www.easyjet.co.uk). Britain's best budget airline.
Multimap (www.multimap.co.uk). Invaluable resource for finding your way around if you haven't got an 'A–Z'.
National Express (www.nationalexpress.com). The UK's largest scheduled coach travel company.
National Rail (www.nationalrail.co.uk). For when you want to get out of London. Timetables, special offers and a journey planner for all the UK's railway services.
Public Transport Information (www.pti.org.uk). Covers all travel by rail, air, coach, bus, ferry, metro and tram within the UK (including the Channel Islands, Isle of Man and Northern Ireland), and between the UK and Ireland.
Rail (www.rail.co.uk). The best independent rail information, including timetables.
Ryanair (www.ryanair.com). Britain's (although Irish-owned) largest budget airline.
Streetmap (www.streetmap.co.uk). Another invaluable resource for finding your way around.
Translink (www.translink.co.uk). Travel in Northern Ireland.
Transport Scotland (www.transportscotland.gov.uk) The national transport agency for Scotland.
Transport for London (www.tfl.gov.uk). Everything you need to know about London's public transport systems.
Travel Britain Guide (www.travelbritain.com). Travel and Tourism Deals and Resources Pages for travel and entertainment resources in the UK.
Travel Line (www.traveline.org.uk). The UK's premier website for impartial information on planning a journey by bus, coach or train.
Travelling Cymru (www.traveline-cymru.org.uk). Travel in Wales.
Virgin Atlantic (www.virgin-atlantic.com). The website of Britain's best airline.

INDEX

A

B

C

D

E

F

G

H

I

L

M

N

O

P

Q/R

S

SKETCHBOOK SERIES

ISBN: 978-1-907339-37-0

Jim Watson

A celebration of one of the world's great cities, London Sketchbook is packed with over 200 evocative watercolour illustrations of the author's favourite landmarks and sights. The illustrations are accompanied by historical footnotes, maps, walks, quirky facts and a gazetteer.

Also in this series:

Cornwall Sketchbook (ISBN: 9781909282780, £10.95)
Cotswold Sketchbook (ISBN: 9781907339108, £9.95)
Devon Sketchbook (ISBN: 9781909282704, £10.95)
Lake District Sketchbook (ISBN: 9781909282605, £10.95)
Yorkshire Sketchbook (ISBN: 9781909282773, £10.95)

see www.survivalbooks.net

London's Secrets: Peaceful Places

ISBN: 978-1-907339-45-5, 256 pages, hardback, £11.95

David Hampshire

London is one of the world's most exciting cities, but it's also one of the noisiest; a bustling, chaotic, frenetic, over-crowded, manic metropolis of over 8 million people, where it can be difficult to find somewhere to grab a little peace and quiet. Nevertheless, if you know where to look London has a wealth of peaceful places: places to relax, chill out, contemplate, meditate, sit, reflect, browse, read, chat, nap, walk, think, study or even work (if you must) – where the city's volume is muted or even switched off completely.

London for Foodies, Gourmets & Gluttons

ISBN: 978-1-909282-76-6, 288 pages, hardback, £11.95

David Hampshire & Graeme Chesters

Much more than simply a directory of cafés, markets, restaurants and food shops, *London for Foodies, Gourmets & Gluttons* features many of the city's best artisan producers and purveyors, plus a wealth of classes where you can learn how to prepare and cook food like the experts, appreciate fine wines and brew coffee like a barista. And when you're too tired to cook or just want to treat yourself, we'll show you great places where you can enjoy everything from tea and cake to a tasty street snack; a pie and a pint to a glass of wine and tapas; and a quick working lunch to a full-blown gastronomic extravaganza.

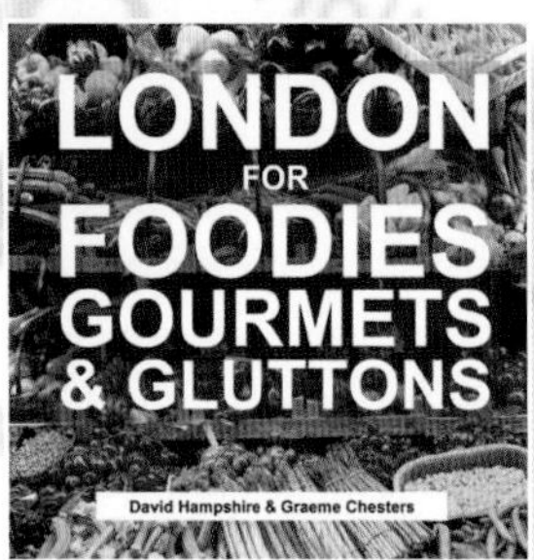

London's Cafés, Coffee Shops & Tearooms

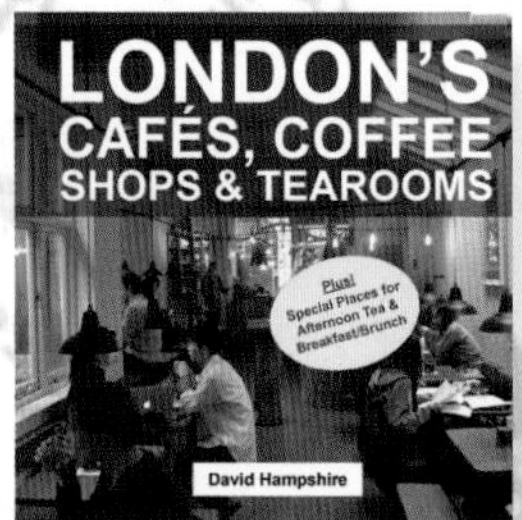

ISBN: 978-1-909282-80-3, 192 pages, £9.95

David Hampshire

This book is a celebration of London's flourishing independent cafés, coffee shops and tearooms – plus places serving afternoon tea and breakfast/brunch – all of which have enjoyed a renaissance in the last decade and done much to strengthen the city's position as one of the world's leading foodie destinations. With a copy of *London's Cafés, Coffee Shops & Tearooms* you'll never be lost for somewhere to enjoy a great cup of coffee or tea and some delicious food.

London's Best Shops & Markets

ISBN: 978-1-909282-81-0, 256 pages, hardback, £12.95

David Hampshire

The UK is a nation of diehard shoppers. Retail therapy is the country's favourite leisure activity – an all-consuming passion – and London is its beating heart. It's one of the world's most exciting shopping cities, packed with grand department stores, trend-setting boutiques, timeless traditional traders, edgy concept stores, absorbing antiques centres, eccentric novelty shops, exclusive purveyors of luxury goods, mouth-watering food emporiums, bustling markets and much more.

see www.survivalbooks.net

London's Best-Kept Secrets

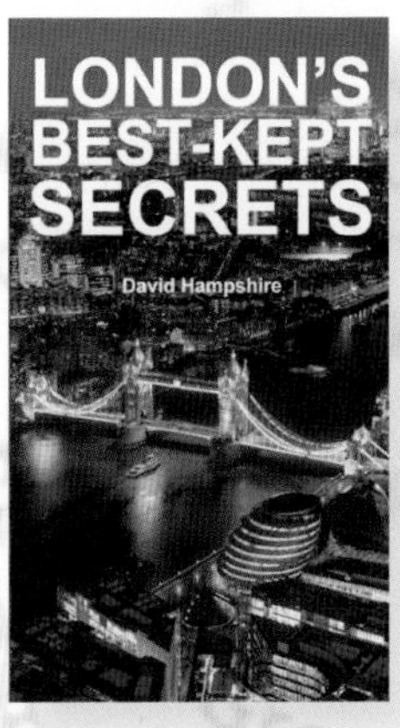

ISBN: 978-1-909282-74-2, 320 pages, £10.95

David Hampshire

London Best-Kept Secrets brings together our favourite places – the 'greatest hits' – from our London's Secrets series of books. We take you off the beaten tourist path to seek out the more unusual ('hidden') places that often fail to register on the radar of both visitors and residents alike. Nimbly sidestepping the chaos and queues of London's tourist-clogged attractions, we visit its quirkier, lesser-known, but no less fascinating, side. *London Best-Kept Secrets* takes in some of the city's loveliest hidden gardens and parks, absorbing and poignant museums, great art and architecture, beautiful ancient buildings, magnificent Victorian cemeteries, historic pubs, fascinating markets and much more.

London's Hidden Corners, Lanes & Squares

ISBN: 978-1-909282-69-8, 192 pages, £9.95

Graeme Chesters

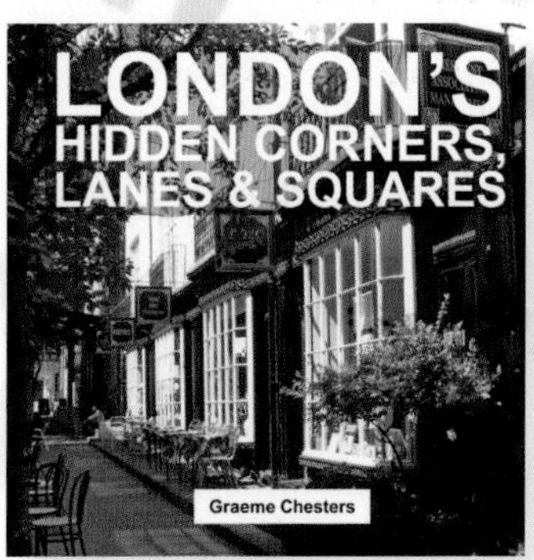

The inspiration for this book was the advice of writer and lexicographer Dr Samuel Johnson (1709-1784) – who was something of an expert on London – to his friend and biographer James Boswell on the occasion of his trip to London, to 'survey its innumerable little lanes and courts'. In the 21st century these are less numerous than in Dr Johnson's time, so we've expanded his brief to include alleys, squares and yards, along with a number of mews, roads, streets and gardens.

A Year in London: Two Things to Do Every Day of the Year

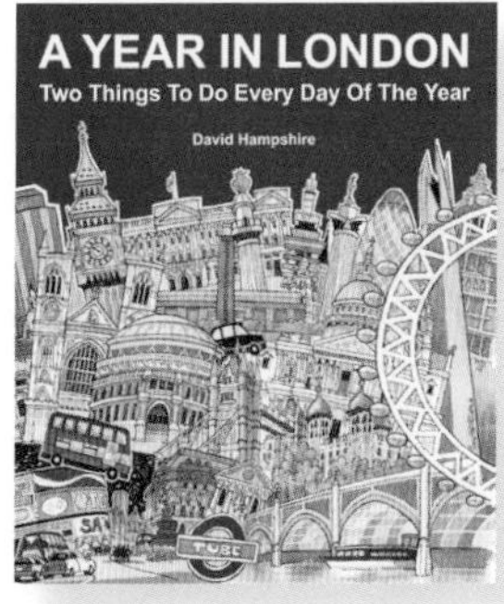

ISBN: 978-1-909282-68-1, 256 pages, £11.95

David Hampshire

London offers a wealth of things to do, from exuberant festivals and exciting sports events to a plethora of fascinating museums and stunning galleries, from luxury and oddball shops to first-class restaurants and historic pubs, beautiful parks and gardens to pulsating nightlife and clubs. Whatever your interests and tastes, you'll find an abundance of things to enjoy – with a copy of this book you'll never be at a loss for something to do in one of the world's greatest cities.

see www.londons-secrets.com

LONDON'S HIDDEN SECRETS

ISBN: 978-1-907339-40-0
£10.95, 320 pages
Graeme Chesters

A guide to London's hidden and lesser-known sights that aren't found in standard guidebooks. Step beyond the chaos, clichés and queues of London's tourist-clogged attractions to its quirkier side.

Discover its loveliest ancient buildings, secret gardens, strangest museums, most atmospheric pubs, cutting-edge art and design, and much more: some 140 destinations in all corners of the city.

LONDON'S HIDDEN SECRET'S VOL 2

ISBN: 978-1-907339-79-0
£10.95, 320 pages
Graeme Chesters & David Hampshire

Hot on the heels of London's Hidden Secrets comes another volume of the city's largely undiscovered sights, many of which we were unable to include in the original book. In fact, the more research we did the more treasures we found, until eventually a second volume was inevitable.

Written by two experienced London writers, LHS 2 is for both those who already know the metropolis and newcomers wishing to learn more about its hidden and unusual charms.

LONDON'S SECRET PLACES

ISBN: 978-1-907339-92-9
£10.95, 320 pages
Graeme Chesters & David Hampshire

London is one of the world's leading tourist destinations with a wealth of world-class attractions. These are covered in numerous excellent tourist guides and online, and need no introduction here. Not so well known are London's numerous smaller attractions, most of which are neglected by the throngs who descend upon the tourist-clogged major sights. What London's Secret Places does is seek out the city's lesser-known, but no less worthy, 'hidden' attractions.

LONDON'S SECRET WALKS

ISBN: 978-1-907339-51-6
£11.95, 320 pages
Graeme Chesters

London is a great city for walking – whether for pleasure, exercise or simply to get from A to B. Despite the city's extensive public transport system, walking is often the quickest and most enjoyable way to get around – at least in the centre – and it's also free and healthy!

Many attractions are off the beaten track, away from the major thoroughfares and public transport hubs. This favours walking as the best way to explore them, as does the fact that London is a visually interesting city with a wealth of stimulating sights in every 'nook and cranny'.

see www.londons-secrets.com

LONDON'S SECRETS: BIZARRE & CURIOUS

ISBN: 978-1-909282-58-2
£11.95, 320 pages
Graeme Chesters

London is a city with 2,000 years of history, during which it has accumulated a wealth of odd and strange sights. This book seeks out the city's most bizarre and curious attractions and tells the often fascinating story behind them, from the Highgate vampire to the arrest of a dead man, a legal brothel and a former Texas embassy to Roman bikini bottoms and poetic manhole covers, from London's hanging gardens to a restaurant where you dine in the dark. *Bizarre & Curious* is sure to keep you amused and fascinated for hours.

LONDON'S SECRETS: MUSEUMS & GALLERIES

ISBN: 978-1-907339-96-7
£10.95, 320 pages
Robbi Atilgan & David Hampshire

London is a treasure trove for museum fans and art lovers and one of the world's great art and cultural centres. The art scene is a lot like the city itself – diverse, vast, vibrant and in a constant state of flux – a cornucopia of traditional and cutting-edge, majestic and mundane, world-class and run-of-the-mill, bizarre and brilliant.

So, whether you're an art lover, culture vulture, history buff or just looking for something to entertain the family during the school holidays, you're bound to find inspiration in London.

LONDON'S SECRETS: PARKS & GARDENS

ISBN: 978-1-907339-95-0
£10.95, 320 pages
Robbi Atilgan & David Hampshire

London is one the world's greenest capital cities, with a wealth of places where you can relax and recharge your batteries. Britain is renowned for its parks and gardens, and nowhere has such beautiful and varied green spaces as London: magnificent royal parks, historic garden cemeteries, majestic ancient forests and woodlands, breathtaking formal country parks, expansive commons, charming small gardens, beautiful garden squares and enchanting 'secret' gardens.

LONDON'S SECRETS: PUBS & BARS

ISBN: 978-1-907339-93-6
£10.95, 320 pages
Graeme Chesters

British pubs and bars are world famous for their bonhomie, great atmosphere, good food and fine ales. Nowhere is this more so than in London, which has a plethora of watering holes of all shapes and sizes: classic historic boozers and trendy style bars; traditional riverside inns and luxurious cocktail bars; enticing wine bars and brew pubs; mouth-watering gastro pubs and brasseries; welcoming gay bars and raucous music venues. This book highlights over 250 of the best.

see www.londons-secrets.com

NOTES

NOTES

Living & Working
Series

see www.survivalbooks.net